CW00602522

The Digital Humanities and Islamic & Middle East Studies

The Digital Humanities and Islamic & Middle East Studies

Edited by
Elias Muhanna

DE GRUYTER

ISBN 978-3-11-037454-4
e-ISBN (PDF) 978-3-11-037651-7
e-ISBN (EPUB) 978-3-11-038727-8

Library of Congress Cataloging-in-Publication Data
A CIP catalog record for this book has been applied for at the Library of Congress.

Bibliographic information published by the Deutsche Nationalbibliothek
The Deutsche Nationalbibliothek lists this publication in the Deutsche Nationalbibliografie; detailed bibliographic data are available in the Internet at http://dnb.dnb.de.

Printing and binding: CPI books GmbH, Leck
♾ Printed on acid-free paper
Printed in Germany

www.degruyter.com

Table of Contents

Acknowledgments

The editor would like to thank the following individuals and institutions for their support of this volume. The Humanities Research and Teaching Fund at Brown University sponsored the 2013 conference at which many of these essays were first read, and Dean Kevin McLaughlin and Associate Dean Anne Windham have continued to support the research initiative that has grown out of it. I am especially grateful to Beshara Doumani, who has been a crucial advocate of this project from the outset, and to Barbara Oberkoetter, who has contributed essential logistical support and grace under pressure. Elli Mylonas and Maxim Romanov freely lent their expertise and advice, and Tony Watson introduced me to Alissa Jones Nelson, our editor at De Gruyter, who has shepherded this project along with care and professionalism.

Elias Muhanna

Islamic and Middle East Studies and the Digital Turn

It's early on a fall weekday morning in New England. I am trying to sneak in an hour of work before my family is awake and the morning is consumed by preparations for school. A knot presents itself in the text I am reading: an Arabic cosmographical compendium by the thirteenth-century Cairene bookseller, Jamāl al-Dīn al-Waṭwāṭ (d. 718/1318). In his discussion of the Egyptian mongoose (*nims*), al-Waṭwāṭ writes that the Bedouin Arabs knew this animal as the "*ẓaribān*" and would refer to it habitually in the form of a proverb: "The *ẓaribān* farted among them" (*fasā baynahum al-ẓaribān*), which was said of a group of people who fell out over some dispute and could not be reconciled.[1] The saying was derived from the animal's proverbial stench, which was so potent that it would make even a large herd of camels disperse.

The proverb is intriguing, and although my instinct tells me to press on and not waste the precious morning hour, it's too late. I've been seduced. Does the Egyptian mongoose really have a deterrent spray? Might al-Waṭwāṭ have mixed up the skunk and the mongoose? I consult a digital collection of Arabic dictionaries, and my suspicion is validated: the word *nims* means "ichneumon, Egyptian rat, ferret, weasel," while the *ẓaribān* apparently refers to some kind of polecat.[2] Some quick online scavenging tells me that the Egyptian mongoose (*Herpestes ichneumon*) and the polecat (a common name for various species belonging to the subfamily Mustelinae) are not related, but look similar. Perhaps, then, they were not readily distinguished in the thirteenth century, and al-Waṭwāṭ's text conflated the two species. If so, I wonder: Did this conflation take place upstream in one of his many sources, or was he responsible for it himself? Setting aside matters of zoological classification, one might also wonder how this proverb was remembered by the Arabic-Islamic intellectual tradition.

---

1 Muḥammad ibn Ibrāhīm ibn Yaḥyā al-Waṭwāṭ, *Manāhij al-fikar wa-mabāhij al-ʿibar*, eds. F. Sezgin and M. Amawi (Frankfurt am Main: Institute for the History of Arabic-Islamic Science, 1990), vol. 2, 70–71.

2 On the *nims*, see J.G. Hava, *al-Farāʾid al-durriyya* (Beirut: Dar al-Mashreq, 1982), 800. For the *ẓaribān*, see ibid., 445. According to the *Encyclopaedia of Islam, 2nd ed.*, the *ẓaribān* may denote either the ratel (*Mellivora capensis*, also known as the honey badger) or the zoril (*Ictonyx striatus*, also known as the striped polecat or African skunk); see *EI2*, "Ḳunfudh" and "Djazīrat al-ʿArab."

Did it retain currency in late medieval prose, or was it preserved for its curiosity value?

Not very long ago, answering these questions might have required a week of careful work in a research library, assuming one was familiar with al-Waṭwāṭ's sources and the cosmographical tradition in which he was writing. On this early morning at my kitchen table, I launch a search for the proverb in a digital repository of classical Arabic texts, *al-Maktaba l-Shāmila*, and brew a fresh pot of coffee while I wait for the program to finish combing through several thousand books, representing about a billion words of text.[3]

A few minutes later, the archive has spoken. The proverb appears in a couple dozen Arabic sources, and I spend some time looking through the citations. A search result in an earlier work confirms that al-Waṭwāṭ was following an established practice of connecting the *nims* with the *ẓaribān*.[4] This is not proof that the two terms referred to the same species, but we can at least be certain that al-Waṭwāṭ was not the first authority to claim that they did. Other citations answer the last question that had crossed my mind about the currency of the proverb. All of the medieval sources that *Shāmila* finds contain glosses of the proverb, explaining it to a reader who was probably unfamiliar with it. Like millions of logia associated with the culture and lore of the pre-Islamic Bedouin Arabs, the proverbial stench of the *nims-ẓaribān* seems to have been preserved largely for its antiquarian value.

Among scholars in the contemporary academy, the novelty of instantaneous searches across entire libraries of historical texts has, by now, worn off. The tens of thousands of volumes in *al-Maktaba l-Shāmila*'s collection are a tiny corpus in comparison to the 30 million books digitized by Google.[5] For graduate students across the humanities, such digital repositories, catalogues, and databases are becoming resources of first resort. This transformation in the technique and approach of scholarship prompts us to consider the lines of inquiry opened by these new resources, just as it asks the question of what methodological instincts and practices may be eroded by the rise of computational paradigms.

---

3 This repository of texts ("The Comprehensive Library") is published by Muʾassasat al-Maktaba l-Shāmila. Accessed April 27, 2015. http://www.shamela.ws.

4 Mufaḍḍal ibn Salama, *al-Fākhir* (Cairo: Wizārat al-Thaqāfa wa-l-Irshād al-Qawmī, al-Idāra l-ʿĀmma lil-Thaqāfa, 1960), 300.

5 The figure of 30 million books dates to April 2013 and has likely been exceeded. See Robert Darnton, "The National Digital Public Library is Launched!" *The New York Review of Books*, April 25, 2013, accessed April 24, 2015, http://www.nybooks.com/articles/archives/2013/apr/25/national-digital-public-library-launched.

I'd like to offer a few reflections on these questions and the corollaries they imply. At first glance, this book appears to be implanted within a familiar, 'pre-digital' mode of scholarship. Its chapters represent the expanded proceedings of a traditional academic conference.[6] There are no interactive graphs or simulators embedded into its pages, and no possibilities for annotation or post-publication markup, all features that are becoming increasingly common in scholarly publication. On the other hand, much of the work that follows draws upon terms, concepts, practices, and even languages that will be unfamiliar to most scholars in Islamic and Middle Eastern studies. As someone who frequently feels lost in the sea of acronyms and computational principles that grows larger each day, I have gone to some length to make this culture shock as painless as possible for the reader. My work as editor has been facilitated by the enthusiasm of the contributors for communicating the innovative nature of their scholarship to colleagues in their respective fields, and making their methodology as transparent as possible.

1. Varieties of Digital Scholarship

What are the digital humanities? This is a question that has attracted much debate.[7] Self-identified digital humanists include scholars building websites and databases; digitizing texts, images, and sounds; marking up ancient inscriptions and modern periodicals; sifting through court probate records; mapping transportation networks across the Roman Empire; tracking text reuse in the medieval Islamic world; and scraping metadata off YouTube and Spotify. This range of activities is as diverse as the humanities themselves, and for similar reasons: its practitioners come from different disciplines, use different methodologies, ask different questions, and constitute their research objects in different ways. What is common to them is a reliance upon computational practices and devices, but this criterion grows less significant as such practices and devices become ubiquitous within the academy.

My aim in this introduction is not to prosecute an argument about the precise scope of the digital humanities (DH). However, for readers with little exposure to the subject, a rough-and-ready description would seem to be useful. Let

6 Many of the articles in this volume originated as papers at a conference entitled "The Digital Humanities + Islamic & Middle East Studies," held at Brown University on October 24–25, 2013. For a program and webcast of the conference, visit http://islamichumanities.org.

7 A good introduction to the contours of this debate may be found in Matthew K. Gold, *Debates in the Digital Humanities* (Minneapolis: University of Minnesota Press, 2012).

me begin by proposing that most projects in this field involve some combination of three basic activities: *digitization*, *publication*, and *interpretation*. Digitization is the conversion of a document, image, sound, or signal into digital form, such that it may be processed by a computer. Many DH projects involve some sort of digitization component or depend upon previously digitized materials. Digitization is generally a means to an end: the purpose of creating a digital surrogate is usually to make it available to an audience through some form of publication—such as an online exhibit, a downloadable archive, an e-book, or a collection of digital images. In other cases, the objective of digitization is interpretation: the analysis of data using computational methods and tools.

The nexus between digitization and presentation may be the most populated territory in the field of DH. Across the world, museums, libraries, government agencies, and universities are using digital technologies to increase the accessibility of their collections of documents and artifacts, to make these collections available for different purposes, and to reach new audiences. In an essay for this volume, Dwight Reynolds reflects on the process of implementing such an initiative in the form of the *Sirat Bani Hilal Digital Archive*, a collection of field recordings, Arabic texts, and English translations of an oral epic poem. Approaching the problem from the perspective of research libraries and collections of rare book manuscripts, Dagmar Riedel discusses the challenges of sustainability and open access raised by these projects. While increased accessibility may be an uncontroversial desideratum in the humanities, the mechanisms for supporting it are still in flux and need to be considered carefully. Examining similar questions in the context of scholarly publishing, Chip Rossetti discusses the ways that the *Library of Arabic Literature* has bridged the divide between traditional edition-translations of classical texts and custom-built markup languages for digital publication.

Many projects involve all three of the abovementioned components. An example of this type of scholarship is the work of Maxim Romanov, whose essay "Toward Abstract Models for Islamic History" explores the rise and fall of various professional, tribal, and toponymic identifiers in medieval Islamic history, based upon the computational analysis of an enormous chronicle, Shams al-Dīn al-Dhahabī's (d. 748/1348) *Taʾrīkh al-Islām*. As textual repositories become larger, cleaner, and more interoperable, this type of "distant reading" is becoming ever more inviting.[8] It offers scholars a wide-angle lens to train on a galaxy of

8 On distant reading, see Franco Moretti, *Distant Reading* (London: Verso, 2013); ibid., *Graphs, Maps, Trees: Abstract Models for a Literary History* (London: Verso, 2005); Matt Jockers, *Macroanalysis: Digital Methods and Literary History* (Urbana: University of Illinois Press, 2013).

sources, finding patterns in a corpus of data too large to synthesize without the aid of computation.

However, digital scholarship need not be macroscopic. It may focus, instead, on a single object, as in the case of Alex Brey's analysis of an illuminated Quran manuscript using advanced imaging techniques. Much digital scholarship gravitates toward problems that are best explored in non-linear, non-narrative ways. In his article "Mapping Ottoman Damascus Through News Reports," Till Grallert discusses the use of Geographical Information Systems (GIS) to map the locations of specific incidents mentioned in Ottoman-era newspapers, demonstrating a very useful tool for analyzing the correlations between the representation of historical events and the spaces in which they occurred. Similarly, Joel Blecher describes a digital project on the transmitters of early Islamic law, conducted by several undergraduate students under his direction at Washington and Lee University, which produced several visualizations of the database that emerged from the project. Such projects—benefitting from social network analysis, dynamic imaging, and user interaction—represent a significant part of the DH world, occupying the shared space between digitization, publication, and interpretation.

2. Digital and Analogue Scholarship

As universities and foundations direct more resources to digital scholarship, the institutional impact of this new funding landscape is expressing itself in striking ways. On my own campus, library reference rooms are being renovated into digital studios, and tenure committees are developing protocols to accredit and recognize digital products. Elsewhere, one sees graduate students learning coding languages in anticipation of a job market that places a premium on such qualifications. No longer a quirky corner of the humanities, digital scholarship is becoming mainstream.

However, some mystery still surrounds this work, and much of it emanates from the question of how the digital humanities are different from the traditional humanities. Are digital humanists engaged in the same disciplinary enterprises as the traditional humanists in their departments, or does the introduction of quantification lead to a divergence in method, theory, and approach? What makes a project 'digital' in the first place? Does the occasional use of some visualization tool or online text repository make an otherwise 'analogue' project 'digital' in some way? Recognizing, again, the difficulty of speaking programmatically about such a diverse range of scholarship, I'd like to propose another working typology, which may be useful in characterizing the relationship between the digital and non-digital.

When one scans the ever-widening territory of DH, it would seem that most projects fall into one of three categories: (1) some use computational tools and digitized materials to facilitate traditional scholarly inquiries; (2) others begin with traditional inquiries but become qualitatively transformed in the course of their deployment of digital tools and methods; (3) finally, there are projects that use—and often develop—computational tools and datasets to ask entirely new questions from the outset, questions which are predicated on the use of digital technologies.

There may be some who claim that unless a scholar builds her own piece of software from scratch before using it in her work, she is not a bona fide digital humanist. I find this to be an unhelpful criterion and would argue that a more ecumenical typology such as the one proposed above is more useful in accounting for the variety of research being conducted under the banner of DH. If one accepts this as a starting point, it becomes clear that a great deal of DH work falls into the first category, which is fundamentally interested in using computation to perform certain interpretive tasks in the service of traditional humanistic scholarship. Interestingly, many of these kinds of projects were much more common in the humanities a generation or two ago than they are today. I am referring to activities like collecting one's research objects into sets, classifying and re-classifying them, parsing them along different categorical axes, creating indexes and concordances and catalogues, annotating and marking up texts, producing visual representations and structural diagrams, etc. As the subtitle to Ben Schmidt's digital history blog, *Sapping Attention*, puts it: digital humanities often amounts to "using tools from the 1990s to answer questions from the 1960s" on a given subject.[9] For many researchers, the introduction of computation has not affected the questions they are interested in exploring; it has merely given them another arrow in their methodological quiver.

In my own work, I have found the use of computational algorithms and digital corpora to be productive precisely in reconsidering certain well-worn questions in my field. Topics such as the molecularity of classical Arabic poetry and the rise of mannerism and its rhetorical functions are hardly new frontiers in the study of Arabic-Islamic civilization. However, the availability of text mining methods and enormous digital repositories offers us a way to reexamine and

---

9 The full subtitle of this useful blog, which covers nineteenth-century American history is: "Digital Humanities: Using tools from the 1990s to answer questions from the 1960s about 19th century America." http://sappingattention.blogspot.com.

test our assumptions, treating them as provisional. Similarly, in her essay for this volume, Nadia Yaqub describes how her work with a digital community of Palestinian refugees tested her own methodological assumptions about the "affective dimension" of history and the importance of social networking in maintaining an archive of communal memory. Projects that begin with fundamentally 'analogue' backgrounds and questions are often transformed as they take on board digital methods and modes of framing.

In some cases, scholars are building their own digital tools to develop projects that would be impractical or inconceivable without computation, at least within the atrophied timescale for humanities funding today. In their paper "'Find for Me!': Building a Context-Based Search Tool Using Python," José Haro Peralta and Peter Verkinderen describe the creation of a "context-based search tool" built in the scripting language Python, which is part of a larger project to reconstruct the economic history of the Islamic world during its first three centuries. Given the size of the corpus they are studying and the relative simplicity of the search functions offered by text repositories such as *al-Maktaba l-Shāmila*, the authors had to develop their own tool to take full advantage of the resources at their disposal. Even in this case, however, digital methods are being leveraged to address familiar historiographical problems.

3. Oracular Archives

My involvement in things digital stems from an experience I had while in graduate school, when I enrolled as an exchange scholar at Princeton to take a methodologies seminar taught by the historian Michael Cook in the Department of Near Eastern Studies. This was a famous seminar, a trial by fire, which virtually all graduate students in the department took before moving on to their dissertations. The structure of the course was quite simple. Each week, Professor Cook would hand us a set of four or five questions connected with a few short textual excerpts from this or that medieval Arabic work. The works ranged from historical chronicles to heresiographies to legal manuals, encompassing nearly every major genre of the Islamic intellectual tradition. Sometimes the title of the work and its author were not specified. The questions about the texts, phrased very innocently, seemed to be designed to commit the grad student who stuck with the seminar to at least twenty hours a week in the depths of Princeton's Firestone Library, poring over nineteenth-century editions of long-forgotten compendia by minor authors in remote locations of the medieval Islamic world, trying to identify the significance of an abstruse theological dispute or an inscription appearing on a millennium-old coin.

When I enrolled in the course in the fall of 2004, digital repositories of classical Arabic texts had only recently begun to appear online. My cohort and I made use of whatever sites we could find in order to solve the weekly puzzles, often eliciting a puzzled expression from our *shaykh*, who knew we had no business citing some of the texts we'd 'consulted' to answer the questions he had set. It was clear to all of us in those moments that the methodological foundations of our discipline were shifting. There was clearly something valuable to be gained by the use of these digital resources, but also something in danger of being lost, particularly if one relied too heavily upon a search-and-capture approach to the historical record.

Databases collapse time and space in dramatic ways. The trope that persists, hidden, through the centuries can now be traced effortlessly, as though one were fanning through an old manuscript and spotting the tunnels grooved into its pages by bookworms. Inhabiting this world of disembodied text is unlike the experience of working in any library, except perhaps the dystopic citadel described by Jorge Luis Borges in "The Library of Babel," an endless and interlocking labyrinth of identical corridors, staircases, and galleries. We know that the vistas the digital archive opens onto are impossibly wide, much more expansive than those of the scholar's bookshelf. We also know that it is uninterested in the hierarchies and search aids of library-based knowledge. Why, then, do its vistas often feel narrower, as though they were oriented inwards, toward the archive itself rather than the world beyond its walls?

As Travis Zadeh discusses in his wonderful meditation on the institutional history of Islamicate online repositories and the epistemological quandaries of working with them, there are profound and ironic uncertainties engendered by the digital archive. Some have to do with the question of what it excludes, and others with the authenticity of what it includes. Beyond these two sources of uncertainty, I would propose a third: the uncertainty spawned by the abundance or absence of evidence that the archive spills forth in response to our incessant queries. How to reconcile and contextualize these 'results' when they mass in their thousands, piled high by an oracular algorithm that traverses whole libraries of data in seconds? Conversely, what should we make of those moments when the digital archive stands silent? How to interpret the meaning of an empty search, a zero-signifier? Can a tree fall in the forest without its sound being recorded by the digital archive?

These are old questions. Human beings have produced archives of various shapes for thousands of years and developed a great array of tools to navigate and make sense of their contents. The sum total of what a single individual has read and learned constitutes a kind of personal archive, navigated through human memory, holistic systems of note-taking and wide-ranging reading, and the help of teachers and colleagues. The frailty of such analogue modes of 'querying' the archive may also be their strength, an inevitable smoothing of one's knowledge into a softer empiricism. The crystalline, hard-edged acuity of the digital archive affords a focus that is sometimes revelatory, but also, at times, blinding.

At the end of the day, what was once analogue-then-digital tends to become analogue again, as a result of our own interpretations and narratives. The archive may effortlessly track the digital scent of the mongoose, but it will not explain its significance; that is the task of the humanist. As scholars contemplate a universe of data, the pillars of traditional humanistic scholarship—historicization, comparativism, hermeneutics, and critique—are more important than ever.

Bibliography

Darnton, Robert. "The National Digital Public Library is Launched!" *New York Review of Books*, April 25, 2013. Accessed April 24, 2015. http://www.nybooks.com/articles/archives/2013/apr/25/national-digital-public-library-launched.

Gold, Matthew K. *Debates in the Digital Humanities.* Minneapolis: University of Minnesota Press, 2012.

Hava, J.G. *Al-Farāʾid al-durriyya.* Beirut: Dar al-Mashreq, 1982.

Ibn Salama, Mufaḍḍal. *Al-Fākhir.* Cairo: Wizārat al-Thaqāfa wa-l-Irshād al-Qawmī, al-Idāra l-ʿĀmma lil-Thaqāfa, 1960.

Jockers, Matthew Lee. *Macroanalysis: Digital Methods and Literary History.* Urbana: University of Illinois Press, 2013.

Al-Maktaba l-Shāmila. http://www.shamela.ws/

Moretti, Franco. *Distant Reading.* London: Verso, 2013.

Moretti, Franco. *Graphs, Maps, Trees: Abstract Models for a Literary History.* London: Verso, 2005.

Sapping Attention. http://sappingattention.blogspot.com/

Al-Waṭwāṭ, Muḥammad ibn Ibrāhīm ibn Yaḥyā. *Manāhij al-fikar wa-mabāhij al-ʿibar.* Ed. F. Sezgin and M. Amawi. Frankfurt am Main: Institute for the History of Arabic-Islamic Science, 1990.

Travis Zadeh

Uncertainty and the Archive

1. The Copyist, the Cataloguer, and the Prophet

al-ʿumru fāniyyun wa-l-khaṭṭu bāqiyyun – Life withers, but writing remains.

The master calligrapher Abū ʿAmr ʿUthmān al-Warrāq signed off with the above maxim as the final word to a Quranic codex that he had finished copying and gilding in his atelier in 466/1073–4 for a high-ranking religious official in the Ghaznavid court, in eastern Khurasan.[1] Given the magisterial artistry displayed in the folios, the Arabic expression *al-khaṭṭ bāqī* suggests not just writing, with the etymology of *khaṭṭ* rooted in the physical act of carving and engraving, but also the specific art of calligraphy. As for ʿUthmān's title, *warrāq*, it was often applied to copyists of Quranic codices and other religious material.[2] However, during this period the profession of *wirāqa* (and with it the title *warrāq*) could also connote a scribe, bookbinder, or bookseller.[3] Such enthusiasm for the written word is appropriate coming from the pen of a skilled *warrāq*—and also fitting for an age of reading and writing that was shaped so thoroughly by the technological transformation seen in the proliferation of paper, and with it the rise of book culture.[4]

Similar sentiments on the enduring power of the written word were recorded nearly a century earlier by another *warrāq*, the famed Imāmī Shiite bookseller of Baghdad, Ibn al-Nadīm (d. 380/990), in the opening chapter of his bio-bibliographic collection, *al-Fihrist* [The Catalogue]. His catalogue on "the books of

1 Mashhad, Astān-i Quds Raḍawī, MS 4316, at the end of *juzʾ* 30, cited in Aḥmad Gulchīn Maʿānī, "Shāhkārhā-yi hunarī-i shigift-i angīzī az qarn-i panjum hijrī wa-sar *gudhasht-i ḥayrat-āwar-i ān*," *Hunar wa-mardum* 157 (1354 Sh./1975), 56. This overlaps with the first half of the first Hippocratic aphorism, generally translated into Arabic as *al-ʿumru qaṣīrun wa-l-ṣināʿatu ṭawīlatun*. See Franz Rosenthal, "'Life is Short, the Art is Long': Arabic Commentaries on the First Hippocratic Aphorism," *Bulletin of the History of Medicine*, 40 no. 1 (1966), 226–45.

2 See Abū Saʿd ʿAbd al-Karīm al-Samʿānī (d. 562/1166), *al-Ansāb*, ed. Akram al-Būshī et al., 12 vols. (Cairo: Maktabat Ibn Taymiyya, 1976–84), 12:236, s.n. *warrāq*.

3 See Shawkat Toorawa, *Ibn Abī Ṭāhir Ṭayfūr and Arabic Writerly Culture: A Ninth-Century Bookman in Baghdad* (London: Routledge, 2005), 56–60.

4 See Jonathan Bloom, *Paper Before Print: The History and Impact of Paper in the Islamic World* (New Haven: Yale University Press, 2001), 47–56.

all the nations of Arabs and foreigners alike available in the Arabic language" opens with a comparative exposition on writing.[5] Here, in a flourish of worldliness that characterizes the encyclopedic range of the entire collection, Ibn al-Nadīm offers a description of all the different writing systems of the world known to him. In addition to Arabic, Syriac, Persian, Hebrew, and Greek, he includes accounts of the various scripts used in China, Sogdia, Sind, and the Sudan, along with the writing systems of the Turks, the Rus, the Franks, and the Armenians.

Ibn al-Nadīm makes clear that much of his material is derived directly from native informants; this is itself a testament to the power of Baghdad, the capital of the Abbasid Empire, to draw scholars, merchants, and travelers from around the world. Our bookseller even supplies samples written out in his own hand, which—given his penchant for accuracy and authenticity—undoubtedly reflected the scripts described.[6] Unfortunately, as the successive copyists ultimately responsible for the transmission of Ibn al-Nadīm's work evidently found this material largely unrecognizable, the samples preserved in the codicological record bear relatively little resemblance to the promised scripts enumerated, at least as they are known to us today.

Despite the hope that the written word can both convey and perdure, this problem of interference, of the signal and the noise in any transmission, ineluctably shapes the textual condition. As a measure of uncertainty, such entropy of information is, for positivist pursuits, undoubtedly a limiting force. These epistemic boundaries are conditions of communication itself, and as such, they have shaped the transition from the analogue technology of the written word to its digital form. To be sure, the materiality of the digital text in its binary expression raises a host of issues that are often quite distinct from those born of the preceding generations of the analogue corpus.[7] Yet, despite the obvious transformations in access, presentation, distribution, and scale, many of the basic problems occasioned by the textual condition carry over directly into the digital age.

For instance, in the modern academic fields of Middle Eastern and Islamic studies, however construed or configured, the acts of presentation, access, and curatorial selection are often implicated in larger divides that separate secular

5 Ibn al-Nadīm, *Kitāb al-Fihrist*, ed. Ayman Fu'ād Sayyid, 4 vols in 2 (London: Al-Furqan Islamic Heritage Foundation, 2009), "*hādhā fihrist kutub jamīʿ al-umam min al-ʿarab wa-l-ʿajam al-mawjūd minhā bi-lughat al-ʿarab*," 1:3.

6 Ibn al-Nadīm, *Fihrist*, 1:14–46.

7 For more on the question of materiality, see in the present volume Dagmar Riedel, "Of Making Many Copies There is No End: The Digitization of Manuscripts and Printed Books in Arabic Script," 73–79.

academic values of knowledge production, whether implicit or explicitly stated, from those oriented around religious, nationalist, or regional commitments. The historical structure of these competing values, which have found expression in numerous analogue forms, has continued to infuse the construction of Islamic knowledge in this age of information technology. Digitization is not a neutral process; rather, it is tied to what are often competing values, motivations, and commitments that shape the form of digital information and guide its consumption and reduplication. In this light, the present chapter seeks to trace the wider epistemic ramifications of the digital condition for the study of Islamic cultural and intellectual history.

The archival act of preservation is, in a basic sense, predicated upon the socially conditioned value invested in the material to be preserved. In certain contexts and under particular conditions, as ʿUthmān the *warrāq* rightly affirms, the materiality of the written word can indeed outstrip the inevitable decay of the human body. In this regard, the fact that ʿUthmān's artistry as a calligrapher is known to us offers a testament to this reality. Similarly, the survival of Ibn al-Nadīm's collection, not to mention the information contained within it, reflects this written power of dissemination.

Along these lines of preservation, Ibn al-Nadīm also includes, in his menagerie of writing systems, a specimen of the script said to have been developed by the Prophet Mani (d. c. 277 CE), the founder of a dualist religious movement that spread through the Roman and Sasanian empires, traveled across Egypt and North Africa, and penetrated Central Asia and China in late antiquity. According to Ibn al-Nadīm, just as Mani drew his religion from Zoroastrianism and Christianity, so too did he derive his script from Persian and Syriac. Here we learn that the followers of Mani wrote their gospels and their books of religious laws using the same script; and since the residents of Transoxiana and Samarqand used it to write their books of religion, it was called the script of religion (*qalam al-dīn*). These remarks fit into a larger discussion on Manichaean religious thought and doctrines that Ibn al-Nadīm developed in greater depth later in his bibliographic survey.[8]

Until the European archeological discoveries of autochthonous Manichaean writings along the Silk Road in the Turfan Basin during the course of the early

8 Ibn al-Nadīm, *Fihrist*, 1:40–41; cf. 2:378–405. On the Manichaean alphabet and its relation to the Aramaic and Mandean scripts, see Prods Oktor Skjærvø, "Aramaic Scripts for Iranian Languages," in *The World's Writing Systems*, ed. Peter Daniels and William Bright (Oxford: Oxford University Press, 1996), 519 (table 48.2), 530–3; also see Desmond Durkin-Meisterernst, "Manichean Script," *Encyclopædia Iranica*, online edition (New York, 1996–), available at www.iranicaonline.org/articles/manichean-script (accessed 27 May 2015).

twentieth century, the information available to modern scholars on Mani 'the Apostle of Light' and his religious movement was derived almost entirely from hostile sources. Although clearly not a neutral account, Ibn al-Nadīm's chapter on Manichaean beliefs and practices and his list of the Manichaean writings that were known to him in Arabic is one of the more exhaustive treatments of the topic. It demonstrates a thorough familiarity born of the influential presence of Manichaeans in the region and their role in the development of eastern gnosticism. This is further attested by another *warrāq* of Baghdad, Abū ʿĪsā Muḥammad b. Hārūn (fl. 250/865), who took a keen interest in and possessed detailed knowledge of Manichaean thought and the beliefs and practices of other dualist religious groups; indeed, Ibn al-Nadīm identifies Abū ʿĪsā as a self-professed Manichaean.[9] It is of note that Ibn al-Nadīm's material only became widely accessible after Gustav Flügel published his German monograph on Mani, which offered an edition, translation, and extensive commentary on Ibn al-Nadīm's chapter on Mani and his followers (1862).[10] Flügel most famously followed this study with an Arabic edition of and extensive commentary on the *Fihrist* (1871–2). Although imperfect (owing, in great measure, to the manuscripts then available to Flügel), the edition—produced in the readily transmitted capital of mechanical reproduction—made the reading list of the Baghdadi bookseller available to an audience the size of which had never been seen before.[11]

With regard to Manichaean religious thought, the irony, of course, is that we now know (through the fragmentary record that has been pieced together from Turfan and beyond) that Mani's followers envisioned their prophet above all

9 Ibn al-Nadīm, *Fihrist*, 2:405, cf. 1:600; David Thomas, *Early Muslim Polemic against Christianity. Abū ʿĪsā al-Warrāq's 'Against the Incarnation'* (Cambridge: Cambridge University Press, 2002), 25–9; cf. Sarah Stroumsa, *Freethinkers of Medieval Islam: Ibn al-Rawāndī, Abū Bakr al-Rāzī and Their Impact on Islamic Thought* (Leiden: Brill, 1999), 40–6. On Manichaean thought in early Islamic history more broadly, see Melhem Chokr, *Zandaqa et zindiqs in islam au second siècle de l'hégire* (Damascus: Institut Français de Damas, 1993), particularly 49–56; also Karim Douglas Crow, "The 'Five Limbs' of the Soul: A Manichaean Motif in Muslim Garb?" in *Reason and Inspiration in Islam: Theology, Philosophy and Mysticism in Muslim Thought. Essays in Honour of Hermann Landolt*, ed. Todd Lawson (London: I.B. Tauris, 2005): 19–33; cf. Cyril Glassé for a provocative (if overstated) reflection on the matter, "How We Know the Exact Year the Archegos Left Baghdad," in *New Light on Manichaeism: Papers from the Sixth International Congress on Manichaeism*, ed. Jason David BeDuhn (Leiden: Brill, 2009), 129–44.

10 Gustav Flügel, *Mani, seine lehre und seine schriften; ein beitrag zur geschichte des Manichäismus* (Leipzig: F.A. Brockhaus, 1862); see also Friedrich Spiegel, *Erânische Alterthumskunde*, 3 vols. (Leipzig: Von Wilhelm Engelmann, 1871–8), 2:195–232; and Konrad Kessler, *Mani. Forschungen über die manichäische Religion* (Berlin: Georg Reimer, 1889).

11 On the codicological record and the lacunae between the surviving manuscripts, see Sayyid's introduction to his edition, Ibn al-Nadīm, *Fihrist*, 1:66–80.

as an avid writer. Indeed, writing was how Manichaeans distinguished themselves from other religions, for their prophet directly wrote down the scriptures revealed to him. A particularly well-known folio fragment found in Turfan and written in Middle Persian preserves a homiletic account that enumerates ten reasons the Manichaean religion surpasses all previous religions. Among these reasons, Mani is said to have argued that "the religions of those of old were in one land and in one language, while my religion is of that kind that will manifest in every land and in all languages, and it will be taught in far-away lands."[12] Furthermore, the revelation (*abhumišn*) Mani received of the two principles (namely of light and darkness), his wisdom and knowledge, and his living scriptures (*nibēgān zīndagān*) all surpass those of previous religions. The folio takes us through the first four arguments for Manichaean primacy, then breaks off midway, at the fifth point, where the fragment ends.

However, unlike most of these textual lacunae, the remaining ten reasons for religious superiority fortuitously survive in a parallel tradition in the Coptic *Kephalaia*, which was discovered in Egypt during the first half of the twentieth century. This account also states that because Mani wrote his scriptures immediately, they were not subjected to the same kind of tampering, distortion, and alteration that befell the sacred writings of other religions, whose founders did not leave any documents behind, written in their own hands.[13] This same critique is stressed in the opening to the *Kephalaia*, which observes that neither Jesus, nor Zoroaster, nor the Buddha wrote their own scriptures, but rather their disciples after them were charged with writing down their teachings.[14] In a similar

---

12 Turfan Collection, Berlin M5794 I, "*yek, ku dēn ī ahēnagān pad yek šahr ud yek izwān būd; ēg dēn ī man ād ku pad harw šahr ud pad wisp izwān paydāg bawād; ud pad šahrān dūrān kēšīhād*," transcribed and transliterated in Mary Boyce, *A Reader in Manichaean Middle Persian and Parthian* (Leiden: E.J. Brill, 1975), 29–30, text a, l.1. On this folio and its relation to M5761, see Werner Sundermann, *Mitteliranische manichäische Texte kirchengeschichtlichen Inhalts* (*Berliner Turfantexte XI*) (Berlin: Akademie-Verlag, 1981), 131–2, §24.1.

13 *Kephalaia*, ch. 151, 370.16–375.15, translated by Iain Gardner in *Manichaean Texts from the Roman Empire*, ed. Iain Gardner and Samuel Nan-Chiang Lieu (Cambridge: Cambridge University Press, 2004), 265–8, §91; cf. Samuel Nan-Chiang Lieu's translation of the parallel Middle Persian passage, op. cit., 109. On the discoveries from Narmouthis (Madīnat Māḍī), Fayyum, a military colony from the Ptolemean period, see James Robinson, "The Fate of the Manichaean Codices of Medinet Madi 1929–1989," in *Studia Manichaica: II. Internationaler Kongress zum Manichäismus*, ed. Gernot Wießner and Hans-Joachim Klimkeit (Wiesbaden: O. Harrassowitz, 1992): 19–62; and Iain Gardner and Samuel Nan-Chiang Lieu, "From Narmouthis (Medinet Madi) to Kellis (Ismant el-Kharab): Manichaean Documents from Roman Egypt," *Journal of Roman Studies* 86 (1996), 148–54.

14 *Kephalaia*, ch. 1, 7.22–8.7, translated by Iain Gardner in *The Kephalaia of the Teacher: The Edited Coptic Manichaean Texts in Translation with Commentary* (Leiden: E.J. Brill, 1995), 13. Cf.

vein, Manichaean liturgical prayers preserved in Greek argue that Mani's religion of light reaches around the world, as his teachings have been translated into all languages (*πάσαις ἑρμήνευται φωναῖς*).[15]

Flying in the face of its fragmentary form, the surviving material stresses that writing not only ensures preservation for later generations, but also guards against corruption, contamination, and distortion. Furthermore, written translations are a sound means of transmission and dissemination. In a very basic sense, the modern discovery and decipherment of the Manichaean corpus is a testament to the power of the written word suggested in these texts. Over the course of the last century, the discoveries of Manichaean writing in such languages as Middle Persian, New Persian, Parthian, Sogdian, Bactrian, Old Turkish, Tokharian, Chinese, Coptic, and Greek bear witness to the catholicity of Mani's movement and to the durability of the written word. Yet this stands in stark contrast to the fate of Manichaean practice and institutions, which faced annihilation as a result of persecution and their absorption into other religions.[16] Contrary to the aspirations displayed in the disjointed corpus that remains, the technology of the written word was ultimately not sufficient to protect and preserve it as a living tradition. The Manichaean writings, including notably the *Living Gospel*, known in Middle Persian as the *Ewangelyōn zīndag*, survive in varying states of dispersion and fragmentation, largely through serendipity. As with everything that faces the perfidious passage of time, the written body, unless meticulously preserved—one might even say entombed or enshrined—is easily condemned to oblivion.

In this pastiche of the copyist, the cataloguer, and the prophet, I have sought to highlight that, even before moving from an analogue to a digital means of storage and diffusion, the promise of writing and publishing, of transmitting beyond the material limits of human existence, requires, foremost, a living community invested in preservation, retention, and reinscription. Such communal transmission is, in turn, profoundly implicated in values and norms, as it is also intimately contingent on the structures of power that govern access to the

---

Abū l-Rayḥān al-Bīrūnī (d. c. 442/1050), *Kitāb āthār al-bāqiya ʿan al-qurūn al-khāliya*, ed. C. Eduard Sachau (Leipzig: F.A. Brockhaus, 1878), 207.

15 Discussed in Fernando Bermejo-Rubio, "'I Worship and Glorify': Manichaean Liturgy and Piety in Kellis' Prayer of the Emanations," in *Practicing Gnosis: Ritual, Magic, Theurgy, and Liturgy in Nag Hammadi, Manichaean and other Ancient Literature. Essays in Honor of Birger A. Pearson*, ed. April De Conick et al. (Leiden: Brill, 2013), 259.

16 For the later continuation and absorption of Manichaean teachings and devotion in China, see Samuel Nan-Chiang Lieu, *Manichaeism in the Later Roman Empire and Medieval China*, 2d rev. ed. (Tübingen: J.C.B. Mohr, 1992), 263–304.

material capital needed for both writing and preserving. To this end, the endurance of the written word is very much a question of what one generation values sufficiently from the previous generation to preserve for the next. Systems of value—in ethical, aesthetic, religious terms, etc.—are, needless to say, subject to the particularities and demands of time and place, conditioned, as it were, by the vicissitudes of human history. As for the curatorial choice of selection, preservation, and transmission, such value systems—however unstated, implicit, or transparent—are ultimately intermediary forces, not neutral transmitters of information; they serve to encode, reinscribe, and amplify themselves in the very process of transmission.[17] This is obviously the case with canonicity in the formation of any given textual corpus of material. But it also proves true in the archival state that amasses and collects, seemingly in encyclopedic totality, from the quotidian bureaucratic records of institutions to the codicological remains of ancient peoples and foreign lands.

2. The Promise of the Digital Archive

Another *warrāq* sought to change everything—at least with regard to Arabic letters and the classical fields of Islamic writing. It all happened well after the rise of the printed book and the wane of manuscripts, after the guilds of copyists and calligraphers had ceased to provide printed material on any mass scale, after lithographs and moveable type, amid the stylized, calligraphic artistry of typesetters, embossers, and bookbinders who, nonetheless, cumulatively continued to invest the Arabic script with a certain numinous materiality.[18] The move from an analogue to a digital means of dissemination meant that the vast expanse of Arabic classical letters—volumes upon volumes—the encyclopedic weight of which would give pause to even the most hardened bibliophiles, could be collapsed into the easily transportable and—most importantly—searchable form of binary information.

---

17 For this use of mediation versus intermediation (here and below), see Bruno Latour, *Reassembling the Social: An Introduction to Actor-Network-Theory* (Oxford: Oxford University Press, 2005), 37–42.

18 There is a growing body of scholarship on the historical rise of print in Muslim book culture. For a general overview, see Geoffrey Roper, "The Printing Press and Change in the Arab World," in *Agent of Change: Print Culture Studies after Elizabeth L. Eisenstein*, ed. Eric Lindquist, Sabrina Alcorn Baron, and Eleanor Shevlin (Boston: University of Massachusetts Press, 2007), 250–67; see also Nile Green, "Journeymen, Middlemen: Travel, Transculture, and Technology in the Origins of Muslim Printing," *International Journal of Middle East Studies*, 41 no. 2 (2009): 203–24.

The digital library hosted under the name al-Warrāq (al-waraq.net) went online in 2000, with the stated aim of promoting Arabic and Islamic heritage globally through the power of information technology (*taknūlūjiyā l-maʿlūmāt*). The name, al-Warrāq, which evoked at once the papermaker, the copyist, and the bookseller, was now telegraphed through the modern medium of Internet communication and transposed from the physical to the virtual page. A subsidiary of al-Qarya al-ilaktrūniyya (The Electronic Village), a company based in the United Arab Emirates, al-Warrāq offered a potpourri of classical Arabic texts organized under broad categories: literature and poetry, Quranic and *ḥadīth* studies, jurisprudence, geography and travelogues, history, Islamic doctrine, mysticism, medicine, dream interpretation, genealogies, biographies, philosophy, and bibliographic studies. Here a digital text of Ibn al-Nadīm's *Fihrist* could be searched alongside the travelogues of Ibn Baṭṭūṭa (d. c. 779/1377) and Ibn Jubayr (d. 614/1217), the poetry of al-Mutanabbī (d. 354/965), the *Maqāmāt* of al-Ḥarīrī (d. 516/1112), the ancient tales of *Kalīla wa-Dimna*, al-Ṭabarī's (d. 310/923) multivolume history, and Ibn Saʿd's (d. 230/845) vast compendium of early religious scholars. It was as though a promethean power had been handed to humanity, or at least to those working in the fields of Arabic letters, who were now granted the ability to instantaneously retrieve detailed information from a vast and disparate corpus that stretched back over a millennium.[19]

Even before the rise of the Internet, the movement from analogue to digital, from physical print to binary encoded letters, already marked a transformation of the book. In the 1990s and early 2000s, several software companies, many based in the Gulf and Iran, began designing, distributing, and selling proprietary computer programs—stored on CDs, DVDs, and external hard drives—of text-searchable books selected from the various fields of classical Islamic learning. Programs such as the software designed by Turāth (heritage; aljamea.net) enabled full-text searches of a broad array of classical Islamic sources and, with increasing success, performed advanced procedures, such as field-restricted, proximity, and phrase searches, as well as Boolean queries.

---

19 In addition to my personal experience as an early user of al-Warrāq, this information on the website and its stated mission is drawn from: http://www.alwaraq.net/arabic_books_About.htm; http://www.electronicvillage.org; archives of the website captured through the Internet Archive Wayback Machine, http://web.archive.org/web; and a report by the technical administrator for al-Warrāq, Muʿtaṣim Zakkār, "Istiʿmāl taknūlūjīyā l-maʿlūmāt fī istikshāf wa-nashr al-turāth al-ʿarabī," presented at *al-Nadwa al-iqlīmiyya ḥawl "Tawẓīf taqniyāt al-maʿlūmāt wa-l-ittiṣālāt fī l-taʿlīm ʿan buʿd (maʿ al-tarkīz ʿalā l-muḥtawā l-ʿarabī ʿalā shabakat al-intarnat)"* July 15–17, 2003, published online: http://www.ituarabic.org/PreviousEvents/2003/E-Education/Doc8-alwaraq.doc.

The disciplines of religious learning were particularly well represented, with software dedicated to classical exegesis, jurisprudence, *ḥadīth*, etc. Programs focusing on belletristic, historical, and lexicographical material were also featured. In addition to designing software, which ran exclusively on Microsoft Windows operating systems, these companies contracted teams of typists to manually key in text from printed editions of books widely available in published form. The advertising invariably promoted the vast quantity of material—millions of pages, thousands of books!—now readily accessible in a compact digital form that could be navigated with the lightning speed of complex text searches.

Generally, references to the actual printed editions were not given. This made citation for scholarly purposes rather difficult, as it involved finding the corresponding material in its printed form. As for the digital texts themselves, it is of note that the modern editions of Arabic and Persian texts exhibit a wide range of variation in terms of accuracy and reliability. Certainly, the rigors of Lachmannian stemmatics can be felt across the modern field of classical Islamic learning, first promoted by Western Orientalists and then adopted by generations of non-European scholars working in classical Arabic and Persian material. Yet, as is well known, many of the modern editions of Islamic sources effectively follow the rather pragmatic practices of classical copyists, who might have had at their disposal only a single manuscript, and who in the course of their transmission may well have introduced a range of errors into the text. Yet, even when drawing on scholarly editions, such software almost universally excised the critical apparatus of marginal notes, and with it the rather important textual history of variants. But such limits—in terms of text selection, redaction, and citation—are admittedly quite minor when compared to the vast array of material that could now be indexed in a way that the technology of printed books could not possibly accommodate.

What made al-Warrāq so powerful was the transposition of these materials onto an online platform, which, rather than relying on particular system specifications, only required an Internet connection. Instead of purchasing physical software to install on a single computer, requiring operating systems and hardware that were subject to the industrial principle of planned obsolescence, users could now turn directly to a single website. After amassing a sizable following, the company that started al-Warrāq tried to monetize the website through a paywall. After all, they had invested significant capital in the digitization of the materials and the production and design of the site. The company, also a digital bookseller, produced and marketed software for Arabic books on CDs. Yet the genie was already out of the bottle, as it were, as many other websites, not motivated so much by the principle of profit as by religion, began to fill the void.

Many of these sites were formed specifically to serve as broad resources for Muslims, such as Nidāʾ al-īmān (The Call of Faith; al-eman.com), which promotes itself as a website for all Muslims (though clearly directed at Sunnis) and hosts a searchable collection of texts from traditional Islamic sources, in the fields of jurisprudence, exegesis, and *ḥadīth*. Similarly, Shabakat mishkāt al-islāmiyya (The Islamic Lamp Network; almeshkat.net), an avowedly Salafī website whose stated goal is to return to the Quran and the sunna according to the understanding of the forefathers of the community (*hadafunā al-ʿawda ilā l-kitāb wa-l-sunna bi-fahm salaf al-umma*), began hosting text files from a range of Sunni religious sources in Arabic that could be downloaded freely. This corpus drew widely from preexisting digitized texts, including al-Warrāq, and built on the power of crowd sourcing, allowing users to contribute material. One of the most extensive sites to emerge is al-Maktaba al-shāmila (The Complete Library; shamela.ws), based in Mecca, Saudi Arabia; it hosts thousands of titles that can be accessed online.

Notably, users can contribute material, download al-Shāmila as a standalone program, and build up a personal library of individual titles hosted on the website, which can also be utilized from mobile devices. All of these sites generally focus on Sunni religious sources, largely in the form of jurisprudence, *ḥadīth*, exegesis, and historical material. A telling contrast can be found in al-Tafsīr (altafsir.com), funded by the Jordanian royal family through the Royal Aal al-Bayt Institute for Islamic Thought. While this website's purview is solely Quranic exegesis, it showcases authorities and texts from an assortment of sectarian, juridical, and ethical frameworks. These commentaries are searchable, mostly in Arabic, though the site has made material available in English translation.

Similarly, the Maktabat Yaʿsūb al-Dīn (Library of the Leader of the Religion, i.e., ʿAlī b. Abī Ṭālib; yasoob.com) hosts a range of largely Arabic religious texts that, while clearly promoting Imāmī Shiite sources, also includes a broad sweep of classical Sunni materials. This site is run under the supervision of Imāmī religious authorities and is aimed at explicitly promoting a Shiite vision of Islamic orthodoxy. Many of these materials can also be found on the Iranian cultural and religious network run by the Muʾassasa-i farhangī wa-iṭṭilāʿ rasānī-i tibyān (The Tebyan Cultural and Informational Institute; tebyan.net), whose website serves as a multimedia platform for the promotion of Islamic and Persian cultural heritage; it is supported under the general auspices of the Sāzmān-i Tablīghāt-i Islāmī (The Organization for Islamic Propagation), a governmental agency of the Islamic Republic of Iran. As part of this emphasis on propagation, large portions of the Tebyan website are available in multiple languages. As for classical material, the site offers a spectrum of literary, historical, and religious sources in Persian and Arabic.

A driving force for the digitization of these particular Arabic and Persian materials has been the Markaz-i taḥqīqāt-i kāmpyūtarī-i ʿulūm-i islāmī (The Computer Research Center of Islamic Sciences; noorsoft.org), an Iranian information technology organization established in 1989 under the aegis of the Supreme Leader Ayatollah Khamenei. An early focus of the center has been text digitization, distributed in the form of the package of Nūr software programs (i.e., light, transliterated *noor*), covering an expansive corpus of Arabic and Persian works. In addition to the major authorities in the fields of Imāmī learning, from gnosis to jurisprudence, it has also included a significant body of materials in the fields of classical Persian literature. Such sweeping breadth is also reflected in their digitization of Arabic and Persian exegetical writing, which, while covering major Shiite sources, also includes a panoply of authorities from various sectarian and juridical professions. While the center continues to focus on software, a good deal of the resources they have developed are available online, represented notably in the Kitāb-khāna-i dījītāl-i nūr (Noor Digital Library; noorlib.ir), which hosts a searchable interface of Arabic and Persian books in a variety of fields. The Pāygāh-i majallāt-i takhaṣṣuṣī-i nūr (Noor Database of Journals, noormags.ir), a searchable portal for modern Persian journals, contains an impressive body of articles by modern Muslim scholars and writers. This website hosts searchable material in Arabic and Persian that spans such fields as literature, language, religion, history, and culture from the late nineteenth century up to the present. As a counterweight to the dominant Sunni presence online, often packaged through the prism of Salafī piety, such materials highlight the theological, juridical, and interpretive heterogeneity of Islamic intellectual history.

The Internet has readily served as a means of articulating and demarking communal identities; it has also empowered both state and non-state actors, from the very large to the rather small. Many sites are tailored to specific groups, as in the case of Anā Zaydī (I am a Zaydī; anazaidi.com), an avowedly Zaydī website run by the Study and Research Center of Imam ʿIzz al-Dīn b. al-Ḥasan, which hosts many Arabic Zaydī religious texts. Likewise, there are an increasing number of religious texts available from the Ibāḍī community, hosted, for instance, on the Istiqāma website (rectitude; istiqama.net), which has benefitted from the collective power of user contributions.

The materials discussed thus far have predominantly been in the form of digital text files. In contrast to the early years of digitization online, when it was often impossible to discern the original print basis for a given digital text, it is now common to find text files keyed to specific editions. Thus, while the search function of the Maktabat Yaʿsūb al-Dīn is not particularly sophisticated or useful, the texts hosted on the website almost always correspond to identified printed materials with page numbers and marginal notes. Many of these materials were originally digitized by Noor software developers who, with their close ties to seminary education in Iran, prided themselves on the accuracy of their digitized texts, which were generally drawn from published edited sources. Similarly, we find that texts posted on such Sunni sites as al-Mishkāt and al-Maktaba al-shāmila often agree with the page numbers of the printed books from which they were originally copied.

Yet, beyond searchable text files, a new wave of materials has been changing the shape of Islamic textual resources online: the dissemination of printed books scanned in the open standard of the Portable Document Format (PDF). An overwhelming number of the major sources in Arabic and Persian are freely available online as scanned PDFs of published books. Vast collections of scanned material can be downloaded through such file sharing platforms as BitTorrent, 4shared, and Archive.com. The prominence of these resources has been amplified through social media. This has also enabled a large user base, which produces and shares scanned materials. Likewise, platforms specifically designed for the exchange of information have facilitated the movement and circulation of PDF copies, from printed books to manuscripts, through links posted on such sites as the Alūka network (The Message; alukah.net) and the Multaqā ahl al-ḥadīth (The Forum of the People of Hadith; ahlalhdeeth.com). Entire websites are devoted to collecting and hosting scanned copies, from such aggregators as al-Maktaba al-waqfiyya (The Endowment Library; waqfeya.com), which has direct ties with the massive al-Maktaba al-shāmila, to comparatively smaller sites, such as the Jāmiʿ al-kutub al-muṣawwara (The Collector of Scanned Books; kt-b.com) and the Maktabat al-Iskandariyya (Library of Alexandria; bib-alex.com), which has posted links to books that were scanned as part of the digitization project of the Bibliotheca Alexandrina (bibalex.org). Again, many of these sites have a stated Sunni—and often a very explicit Salafī—perspective. However, as with text digitization, by no means have Sunnis cornered the market. A good deal of the Ibāḍī juridical corpus is available as scanned PDFs; similarly, many Zaydī sources are accessible in the same format. Likewise, a wide selection of Imāmī religious material is available in a variety of locations, such as the Maktabat narjis (The Library of the Narcissus; narjes-library.com). In addition, there has been an increasing presence of scanned copies of Persian books on such sites as Kitābnāk (Bookish; ketabnak.com), which enables users to download entire books, in contrast to the Noor Digital Library (referenced above), which allows only a limited number of pages to be downloaded in a given session.

Both the Noor Digital Library and the Noor Database of Journals have made scanned materials available for searches on their respective websites. This service differs from that of other websites, which offer scanned Arabic and Persian books for download from the Internet. The current technology for consumer-based optical character recognition (OCR) of the Arabic script is still in its infancy and has not been widely integrated into PDF viewers. Optical character recognition, which is widely available for Latin, Greek, Cyrillic, and Hebrew scripts, enables image files of text that has been scanned to be searched much like text files, and with increasing improvements in text recognition software these searches are often quite reliable, even throughout an entire database. The Noor collection, rather than relying on OCR technology, has actually keyed in the text to numerous books and mapped this information onto the corresponding pages of each individual scan, such that searches conducted are made in the separate text files that lie beneath the image files; thus the results retrieve both the scanned pages of the book in question and the underlying text. The main difference between text recognition and this particular search procedure is that optical character recognition allows for an automated digital process, which obviates the need to retype the entire source text. Although it currently has a limited quantity of materials, Google Books hosts an increasingly large number of scans of Arabic and Persian sources, many of which have been uploaded by individual users. As with other alphabets, Google has developed text recognition capability for the Arabic script and can search scans of Arabic and Persian printed material. With the exponential growth in information technology, it is not hard to predict that in the coming years such capability will be widely available at the level of individual users.

Even without the current capacity to search through this vast trove of scanned books, the rapid dissemination of material has radically shifted access to the archives. Extensive bookmarking of scanned files has enabled rapid searches of multivolume works without the physical labor of moving through stacks. Toggling back and forth between text files and scanned editions is one of the most obvious outgrowths of the current digital landscape. This is particularly well suited for the vast encyclopedism that characterizes much in the way of Arabic writing, with its tomes of jurisprudence, historical and encyclopedic literature, lexicography, poetry, philosophy, theology, and Quranic exegesis, not to mention the sprawling *ḥadīth* corpus with its concomitant biographical literature on transmitters, all of which span volumes. Much of this is now widely shared, stored, and searched with incredible speed, collapsing the vast archive of physical books into the reducible digital space of zeros and ones in a computing format that, following the predictions of Moore's Law, has logarithmically sped up processing power and increased storage capacity in ever-smaller configurations of circuits.

The advances in information technology have given a growing circle of readers access to materials that no single research library could physically possess.

The epistemic shifts occasioned by what has rightly been called an information revolution are indeed seismic and by all appearances long-lasting. The promise of the digital archive is, of course, the ability to harness an encyclopedic inclusivity that, in its global scope, is truly universal and that frees the physical capital from its corruptible physical form and from the institutions that historically served as gatekeepers of knowledge and, with it, power.

3. The Threat

In the early and rather heady days of it all, one could not help but feel a certain amount of ambivalence about the ill-gotten gains. Not about the problems of ownership, piracy, or labor, which would all come later, but rather about the actual search capacities that reduced books to configurations of information, to be scanned and quantified in a cycle of input and output that chewed through and spat out voluminous corpora. On list services, before graduate seminars, or at conference proceedings here and there, one could hear the lament for a bygone era. For in many ways, what we were losing was the cult of erudition that had sculpted the ideal of the academic who, over the course of a lifetime, mastered a body of knowledge through the painstaking labor of physically working through and taming this immense corpus. Now, with information so widely available (and thus cheap), it also became apparent that synthesis and analysis were ever more at a premium. Yet, with so much more information and so many new works to be reckoned with and included in the conversation, the very idea of synthesis at times has felt rather forced.

Every technology of writing demands its own mode of reading. The clay bullae with tokens of commercial transitions, the stone reliefs of emperors marking conquest and territory, multilingual cuneiform inscriptions by scribes, and the mystifying hieroglyphics of priests all depended on the economic mastery of tools and materials as well as the capital of literacy to telegraph and to decipher. The move from the clay tablet to the papyrus scroll and then the parchment codex necessitated very different physical means of storing and conveying. Each medium also predicates distinct points of entry. The archeological record reveals that these differing technologies of writing did not immediately replace each other, but rather existed side by side for centuries, just as writing today inhabits different spaces in varied forms, often for very different ends. The genius of the codex lay in its facilitation of movement across the entire body of the text, which could be accessed easily at multiple points and indexed or rubricated with cross-references. It not only occasioned new types of reading practices, but it also allowed for the production of writing in new forms and on distinct topics.

Paper (which required much less in the way of capital), in turn, could accommodate even more information with far less expense. So too, the invention and adoption of the printing press in turn drove down the cost of books and ultimately expanded the market of readers. Not only has the move from an analogue to a digital means of storage and conveyance transcended the physical limitations of the printed page, but it has also opened up new ways of reading. In this ever-expanding horizon of information, the questions that we can ask and the ways that we can reconfigure our corpus give off the sheen of unbounded possibility.

One consequence of the digital revolution of information has been a growing emphasis on quantity and, with it, quantification. With text now liberated from the physical limits of the book, it can be quickly transposed into data sets, mined for patterns and relations, subjected to tests of frequency, occurrence, and proximity—all sped up through the power of automation. What better way to confront the prodigious encyclopedism of Arabic letters, which could otherwise consume the labor of countless lives? Prolixity and volume are truly the hallmarks of this corpus: the *Musnad* collection of *ḥadīth* by the Baghdadi traditionist Aḥmad b. Ḥanbal (d. 241/855), as edited by Shuʿayb al-Arnāʾūṭ and others, consists of over 27,000 *ḥadīth* entries, in 45 volumes, not counting five volumes of indices; the biographical collection on early *ḥadīth* transmitters compiled by Abū l-Ḥajjāj al-Mizzī (d. 742/1341) spans 35 volumes in its modern published form, with over 8,000 biographical entries; the massive compilation of Imāmī sources by the Safavid traditionist Muḥammad Bāqir al-Majlisī (d. 1110/1698), in its printed edition, consists of 110 volumes. In the face of all this, the edition of the Arabic dictionary composed by the Indian lexicographer Murtaḍā Zabīdī (d. 1205/1791) in 20 volumes seems quite modest.

The digitization of this material has certainly opened up epistemic possibilities. With a host of novel analytical tools, from Boolean searching to XML tagging, texts can be read against the grain, in ways never intended or anticipated. Now patterns of text reuse, of copying across the corpus, come into sharp relief, from *ḥadīth* collections with their chains of transmitters to the immense body of historical and belletristic writing long known to have voraciously absorbed pre-existing sources, often without any direct citation. Knowledge networks can be more fully reconstituted in the monumental weight of biographical writings that have preserved such rich prosopographical details on the countless lives of religious authorities. Diachronic analysis of shifts in language and word usage can take on a breadth never seen before. The distribution of texts and titles can shed further light on reading patterns and structures of canonicity. This is not to mention the potential for social history along the lines first developed, in an analogue form, by Richard Buillet, who sought to track the history of Islamic conversion through onomastic shifts in biographical writings.[20]

Buillet's case is interesting, though, largely because criticism of his prosopographical analysis continues to emphasize the problem of extrapolation. Quantitative data mining has notable limitations, specifically for the corpus at hand. As for social history, the available Arabic and Persian biographical sources focus almost entirely upon a male, urban, religious elite. We must wonder to what extent this rather rarefied group reflects anything other than the routinized maintenance and production of juridical and theological authority. The biographical collections were not designed to function as a census documenting the kind of information on conversion that would be relevant to modern social historians. As much as we may wish to read these writings against the grain of their original design and divide the material into quantitative units for analysis, the primary sources at our disposal do not offer neutral accounts of history; rather, they are involved in a process of shaping reality even as they describe it.[21] This was true before the digitization of our texts, and it remains so now.

As with any form of quantitative statistical analysis, the question at hand is actually that of *data quality*: How reliable is the information at our disposal, and how well suited is it for answering the questions that we pose? Of course the library of Arabic and Persian letters as it emerged in the first five centuries of the Islamic era is anything but homogenous. At the most basic level, however, what unites the public record is the economic and social means necessary to produce and disseminate the written word. While there are notable exceptions in the early expanse of Islamic history, this power of production, as with other pre-modern civilizational complexes, largely excluded women and the unlettered. Furthermore, much of this legacy is united by particular and often competing construc-

20 See Richard Bulliet, "Conversion to Islam and the Emergence of a Muslim Society in Iran," in *Conversion to Islam*, ed. Nehemia Levtzion (New York: Holmes and Meier, 1979), 30–51; idem, *Conversion to Islam in the Medieval Period: An Essay in Quantitative History* (Cambridge, MA: Harvard University Press, 1979). For a digital continuation of this line of analysis, see also John Nawas, "A Profile of the *Mawālī ʿUlamāʾ*," in *Patronate and Patronage in Early and Classical Islam*, ed. Monique Bernards and John Nawas (Leiden: Brill, 2005), 454–80.

21 See Richard Frye, "Comparative Observations on Conversion to Islam in Iran and Central Asia," *Jerusalem Studies in Arabic and Islam* 4 (1984), 82; Jamsheed Choksy, "Zoroastrians in Muslim Iran: Selected Problems of Coexistence and Interaction during the Early Medieval Period," *Iranian Studies* 20 no. 1 (1987), 19; Michael Morony, "The Age of Conversions: A Reassessment," in *Conversion and Continuity: Indigenous Christian Communities in Islamic Lands, Eighth to Eighteenth Centuries*, ed. Michael Gervers and Ramzi Jibran Bikhazi (Toronto: Pontifical Institute of Mediaeval Studies, 1990), 135–50.

tions of religious authority, in theological, juridical, and pietistic terms. This is not to suggest that such stated or unstated ideological frameworks of inclusion and exclusion, which ultimately shape all forms of writing and power, in any way diminish the utility of these materials.

"Ulemalogy" is indeed a fine science, and the digital configuration of our sources today would appear to all but demand it.[22] But the memorialization of religious authority gives us rather narrow insight into the broad array of movements and forces governing social history. This is not to mention the very fragmentary nature of the archive at our disposal. If we were to piece together from the available biographical dictionaries the history of the city of Nishapur in eastern Iran, for instance, during the fourth/tenth and fifth/eleventh centuries from the available biographical dictionaries, the image would be one dominated by traditionalist Shāfiʿī jurists, Ashʿarī theologians, and Sufi saints writing almost entirely in Arabic. This is the picture we would have because the surviving *ṭabaqāt* literature on the region during this period was written almost entirely by Shāfiʿī authorities, who promoted Ashʿarī theology and Sufi piety. While women make an appearance, they would be largely missing, just as the Ḥanafī elite that long dominated the city and the populist Karrāmī movement that stretched throughout Khurasan would be quite diminished. Also overlooked would be the strong currents of Muʿtazila thought, not to mention the various Shiite groups known to have been active in the region. Furthermore, we would have little indication of the immense scope of Persian vernacularization that occurred at this very moment in eastern Iran and Transoxiana. While we can piece some of this together from materials not solely dedicated to memorializing the religious elite, we still know relatively little about the unlettered rural masses or the presence, influence, and status of non-Muslims in and beyond the urban centers of the region.

Digitization does not solve this problem, for it is a legacy of the fragmentary state of the archive. In this regard, it is important to recognize the limits of the sources at our disposal, not only in terms of the questions that can be asked of them, but also with regard to their palpable discontinuities. This incompleteness stands in contrast to the language of the information revolution, which is that of completeness, of unprecedented volume in a sea of ever-expanding points of data. The vast web of interconnected information that makes up the Internet gives off a glow of pulsating encyclopedic comprehensiveness, of a super-

---

22 For a nuanced critique of 'ulemalogy' for the production of social history, see Roy Mottahedeh, "Review of R.W. Bulliet, *The Patricians of Nishapur*," *Journal of the American Oriental Society* 95 no. 3 (1975), 495.

collective consciousness for all humanity. When confronted with the sheer immensity of it all, it is hard not to feel humbled and entranced. Much of the marketing of the digital libraries of Arabic and Persian letters explicitly promotes this illusion of complete and total universality, in the light (*nūr, tibyān*) that illuminates the past with electronic speed, in a library that encompasses everything (*shāmila*, *jāmiʿ*). As with the traditional publishing industry, it is also a marking of culture (*thaqāfa*, *farhang*) and heritage (*turāth*, *mīrāth*), which, like all normative enunciations of communal identity, is conditioned by curatorial acts of exclusion, of choosing what is worthy to be passed on and what is not.

This illusion of totality is the siren's song that conditions, as it pleases, not to venture far beyond the comfort of the same. Despite the marketing of expansion and boundless information, a good deal of the digital resources at our disposal suffers from this very problem of homophily—birds of a feather flock together. Many of these websites and sharing platforms are designed to reconstitute and enunciate particular forms of normativity. This is not unique to the digitization of information. Indeed, earlier patterns of physical publishing followed similar lines of articulating and demarcating communal boundaries. But the promise of totality telegraphed across the Internet stands in marked contrast to the often-arresting absence of heterogeneity that governs many of these digital materials. Indeed, the all-consuming reach of the encyclopedia can as readily include as it can cover over dissent or difference. What we have now is the fragmentation of resources that in great measure follows modern sectarian divisions and preoccupations.

With regard to the Sunni sources, much of the material posted online is governed by a modern Salafī emphasis on the direct and unmediated return to the Quran and the sunna. One might easily be left with the impression, after engaging with these sites, that the most pivotal figure for all of Islamic history was Ibn Taymiyya (d. 728/1328), with his particular strain of Ḥanbalī reform. Scholars of Salafī traditionalism today suffer an embarrassment of riches; many of the foundational sources of modern Sunni fundamentalism are easily culled from the Internet. The promotion of Arabic is also intimately connected to this phenomenon, as it follows in tandem with the Salafī emphasis on the essential Arabic nature of Islam.[23] This in turn fits into the development of new modes of reading without the intermediaries of religious authorities, in a hermeneutical turn that

23 See Travis Zadeh, "The *Fātiḥa* of Salmān al-Fārisī and the Modern Controversy over Translating the Qur'ān," in *The Meaning of the Word: Lexicology and Tafsir*, ed. Stephen Burge (Oxford: Oxford University Press, 2015), 378, 406–7.

has advanced both the primacy and transparency of Arabic, while textualizing religion as a closed scriptural body of law.[24] The Internet, in many ways, is ideally suited for such personalized modes of promoting the supremacy of the text. Similar observations can be developed with regard to the confluence of Shiʿism, Persian, and modern Iranian nationalism, although the Imāmī resources online are, as to be expected from the very intellectual history of Imāmī Shiʿism, much broader, more inclusive, and heterogeneous.

The conflation of Islam with a body of texts is a reifying process meant not only to affirm orthodoxy, but also to assert particular modes of reading. It also tends to ignore the material and visual cultural productions and social practices historically associated with Islamic devotion. Furthermore, this specific form of textualization often serves to isolate Islamic history as disconnected from the larger civilizational currents that included, notably, Jews, Christians, Zoroastrians, Manichaeans, and Buddhists, to name a few. Perhaps even more arresting, in historical terms, is the way in which the expanse of digitization has noticeably underrepresented what was long the core of Islamic religious authority, namely *taṣawwuf* and its structures of education, power, proselytization, shrine veneration, charitable works, and even militant piety. In the modern period, *taṣawwuf* has often been constituted by both Sunnis and Shiites alike as a separate, heterodox branch of Islam. Such presentations, needless to say, overlook the largely normative status of Sufi piety, as promoted by the religious elite across various regions for centuries.

Other significant portions of Islamic culture and thought are also almost entirely missing from much of this digital archive. The great flourishing of Persian and Arabic learning under the Mughals of the Indian subcontinent is woefully underrepresented, not to mention the textual legacies of other dynasties from the region. This is undoubtedly due in part to the fact that Persian, which for centuries was the official language of Indian Muslim states, has long ceased to be actively cultivated in South Asia. Without a living community invested in digital preservation, many of these materials remain only accessible through archives, which often are not fully catalogued.[25] The case is not as dire with Ottoman Turk-

24 See A. Kevin Reinhart, "Fundamentalism and the Transparency of the Arabic Qur'an," in *Rethinking Islamic Studies, From Orientalism to Cosmopolitanism*, ed. Carl Ernst and Richard Martin (Columbia: University of South Carolina Press, 2010), 98–101.

25 A notable exception is the Digital Library of India (dli.gov), which has scanned and hosts online published books in an array of languages, including Urdu, Persian, and Arabic; the site also includes numerous rare lithographs. The materials available here, however, represent a small fraction of the early modern printed corpus. Similarly, while the National Mission for Manuscripts sponsored by the government of India (http://namami.org) has digitized numerous

ish documents or Persian writing under the Safavids and the Qajars, precisely because Turkish and Persian remain profoundly linked to the modern national identities of Turkey and Iran. Nonetheless, in historical terms, the early modern digital resources pale in comparison to the vast trove of material that focuses on classical Islamic thought as construed largely through the prism of religion and overwhelmingly in Arabic. This stultifying reality serves as a kind of linguistic and historical essentialism that holds that true Islam is rooted in the classical Arabic of the past.

Many of the digital resources under consideration form part, in some fashion, of the modern articulation of religious authority. This is not the neutral mediation of information, nor does it really pretend to be. In very obvious ways, such religious commitments stand in opposition to the field of the digital humanities, which is predicated foremost on the secular constitution of knowledge and information centered on the very coded values of liberal education, independent thought, and freedom of expression. Here religion is largely subsumed into the realm of either history or anthropology and is not promoted in theological, doctrinal, or deontological terms. Needless to say, both frameworks are particular ideological formations governed by preexisting epistemic commitments, which are either largely transparent (and thus unstated and evidently non-existent) or presented as self-evident and thus irrefutable. This situation warrants attention, as the digital corpus of Arabic and Persian letters has been shaped by values and assumptions that overlap with the humanistic enterprise in certain instances, but also in very noticeable ways diverge and stand in contrast to it. Thus the rarefied group of scholars operating within the context of Western academic education easily enters into this digital web of Islamic letters with values, assumptions, commitments, and objectives that often run contrary to the stated goals of the resources themselves. While the same proves true for printed books, the stakes are arguably quite different in terms of scale and magnitude. This is particularly so in light of the imagined completeness that is the currency of the digital archive.

Indian manuscript archives, this material is not available or searchable online and currently can only be obtained with written permission from the relevant regional archives. Also noteworthy for Urdu PDFs and ebooks are: http://besturdubooks.wordpress.com and http://rekhta.org.

4. The Digital Condition

Much of the academic ambivalence directed at the digitalized corpus of Arabic and Persian texts initially focused on the quality and reliability of the resources and the problem of how to cite them. Part of this is shaped by the legacy of textual criticism, which was originally developed at the beginning of the nineteenth century for the critical editions of Greek and Latin classics. The basis of textual criticism is fundamentally taxonomic, predicated on a principle of prior simplicity whereby the proliferation of textual variants, naturally distributed in manuscripts and inherent in the very idiosyncratic nature of manuscript production, all descend from an original common source. A monogenetic origin from a single parent is also generally assumed. Both assumptions prove rather problematic for medieval Arabic and Persian book culture.[26]

This process of textual reconstruction privileges accuracy and authenticity above all, as it attempts to identify the closest codicological witness to the original authorial intention. In contrast, corruptions and contaminations inherent in the universal variation of manuscript culture are exposed and ferreted out as spurious to the authorial original. Based upon a genealogical sequence (*stemma*), a reconstruction of variants is sought. Such a process sets out a hierarchic structure between the various manuscripts (*phyla*, *genera*, etc.), as they proliferated from an invariably lost, authorial archetype. Generally, this method is designed to marginalize or cut away entirely the often rather complicated and messy reception history of a given text in favor of establishing an authentic original that can serve as a foundation for positive historical knowledge.[27]

Many modern printed editions of classical Arabic and Persian texts have followed similar methods; however, the ideal of the critical edition has had mixed results in the region. Yet, even prior to the problem of textual accuracy, there is often a good deal of textual uncertainty, as the piracy of editions is quite common. Books originally printed by one publishing house are often reprinted and repaginated by another with no attribution. With regard to the texts themselves, the authority of the critical apparatus is by no means unknown, but in-

---

26 See Jan Just Witkam, "Establishing the Stemma: Fact or Fiction?" in *Manuscripts of the Middle East* 3 (1988): 88–101.

27 See David Greetham, "Phylum-Tree-Rhizome," *Huntington Library Quarterly* 58 no. 1 (1995), 99–126; Adam Gacek, *Arabic Manuscripts: A Vademecum for Readers* (Leiden: Brill, 2009), 266–8, s.n. "Textual criticism and editing." These observations are elaborated in greater depth in Travis Zadeh, "Of Mummies, Poets, and Water Nymphs: Tracing the Codicological Limits of Ibn Khurradādhbih's Geography," in *Abbasid Studies IV*, ed. Monique Bernards (Exeter: Short Run Press, 2013), 18.

creasingly the editorial focus, at least for classical Arabic religious material, has been directed toward the production of chains of transmission (*takhrīj*) associated with each appearance of a *ḥadīth*; this is a form of erudition that, needless to say, is much less valuable in a digital field, where such material is easily accessed through the power of search operations.

At times, the choice of which manuscripts to use and collate for a given edition proves to be rather arbitrary. Even with published editions that sport variants in the form of marginal notes, it is often necessary, particularly when working closely on a given text, to check other manuscripts for variant material that has not been included. This is hardly much of a critique, given the vast range of manuscripts that an editor might confront when preparing an edition.[28] Furthermore, the values animating the ideal of the critical edition, while certainly admirable in the positivist recuperation of the past, are by no means universal. In very meaningful ways, the artifact of textual criticism is the product of the secularization of history, specifically the development of skeptical inquiry as a means of assaying authenticity in the face of changing attitudes toward the divine origin of scripture.[29] Despite this, digital forms of presentation, particularly with hyper-textual nodes of interconnection, suggest obvious possibilities for elucidating the kinds of archival problems of radical variance that so many of the classical sources of Arabic and Persian literature exhibit.[30]

Initially, the move from the analogue realm of physical books to the digitization of the corpus magnified many of these problems, particularly with the utter lack of transparency regarding which sources were used in preparing the digital editions and the problem of the reliability and accuracy of the digital texts themselves. The landscape has changed somewhat, with the increasing availability of digitized texts keyed to specific printed materials. Similarly, the move toward scanning and posting entire editions of printed books has obviated this problem

---

28 For an extreme case, see Abū ʿAlī l-Balʿamī's (d. 363/974) *Tārīkh-nāma*, which has been edited by Muḥammad Rawshan, who, needless to say, does not rely on the roughly 180 manuscripts of the text for his edition, *Tārīkh-nāma-i Ṭabarī*, 5 vols. (Tehran: Surūsh, 1995–9). Missing from his edition is a significant body of material, which may or may not be spurious. On this problem, see Elton Daniel, "Manuscripts and Editions of Balʿamī's *Tarjamah-i Tārīkh-i Ṭabarī*," *Journal of the Royal Asiatic Society of Great Britain and Ireland* 2 (1990): 282–321; Andrew Peacock, *Mediaeval Islamic Historiography and Political Legitimacy, Balʿamī's Tārīkhnāma* (London: Routledge, 2007), 52–4.

29 See Talal Asad, *Formations of the Secular: Christianity, Islam, Modernity* (Stanford, CA: Stanford University Press, 2003), 41–3.

30 See Dino Buzzetti and Jerome McGann, "Critical Editing in a Digital Horizon," in *Electronic Textual Editing*, ed. Lou Burnard, Katherine O'Brien O'Keeffe, and John Unsworth (New York: Modern Language Association, 2006), 67–70.

to some degree; yet with this comes what, by all appearances, is the large-scale piracy of printed materials that in many cases would run afoul of international copyright law. However, here again the values of private capital and commercialization that serve to advance the industrial primacy of content producers stand in opposition to the explicitly religious motivations of propagation that often animate the dissemination of these materials.

With scans of printed books, the problem of citation would appear to be whether or not the editions in question are reliable. Once more, there is a range of quality and selection. The shifting field of citational practice, however, speaks to a deeper set of issues. Foremost is the matter of permanence and diffusion. This problem can be seen in the scholarship of earlier generations. Anyone who tries to track down some of the printed sources cited by Theodor Nöldeke, Ignáz Goldziher, or Joseph Schacht quickly realizes that the editions widely available now are not the same as those cited by earlier generations of scholars. While the printed page gives off a patina of permanence, many of the printed books in our field are often rare or difficult to access. Digitization promises to put an end to the temporal impermanence of the printed world. Yet now, after living through more than twenty years of the digital revolution, we understand that the Internet is a process, not a product, and as such it too is ephemeral. Websites have to be continuously maintained, updated, secured; hyper-textual links must be checked for validity; standards and codes need to be rewritten; it is the plight of the constant gardener, weeding away the inevitable march of entropy. This says nothing of storage and the grids of energy—and thus capital—necessary to maintain it all. While there have emerged scholarly standards for referencing content on the Internet, addresses of webpages (i.e., URLs [uniform resource locators], DOIs [digital object identifiers, etc.]) are notoriously fickle and, in the very architecture of the web, mercurial. Everything exfoliates in a constant state of flux, which entices with the allure of the new, the majestic immensity of innovation and productivity, generally pegged to the cyclical market forces driving information technology and its consumption.

Then there is the practice of citation itself, which today remains the very hallmark of scholarly authority. The textual apparatus of notes and bibliographical references serves many purposes. Ostensibly, these conventions authenticate, inform, and expand, although they also easily divert, malign, and obfuscate.[31] At a comparative level, the diverse practices of textual citation share in common the physical limits of the codex, as well as the textual produc-

31 See Bruce Lincoln, *Theorizing Myth: Narrative, Ideology, and Scholarship* (Chicago: University of Chicago Press, 1999), 207–16, particularly 208–9.

tion of *auctoritas*. The book allows for and even demands specific forms of referencing. Citation has long provided a means for grounding arguments in the power of individual authorities as well as in the authority of particular scriptures. The concordance and the index are outgrowths of these referential practices. The footnote, as a visual form, also descends from the marginal gloss and the peripheral commentary, which in Arabic and Persian manuscript culture are rooted in such diverse practices as scriptural, juridical, theological, and belletristic exegesis. At the edge, the marginal note can easily lure the reader away from the centrality of the text, while also advancing it.

With regard to the field of Islamic studies, the convention of *isnād* citations—of listing the numerous chains of narrators of a particular account, which generally stretch back to a saying or action of the Prophet or Companion—represents one of the more complex citational models, which, while assuring readers of the original oral source, is itself a thoroughly textual practice.[32] It purveys an authority that is both scholarly, in the sense of demonstrating knowledge (*ʿilm*), and religious, as it is rooted in the canonical power of scripture. Yet, regardless of the form, the epistemic value of citation generally advances the primacy of both the original and the verifiable in the ability to trace down and reveal the source.

The Arabic concept of transmission, or *riwāya*, accentuates, in its oral and textual forms, the preeminence of the source. Etymologically, the word relates to drawing, bearing, or conveying water (i.e., *rawā l-māʾ*), as from a well. The metaphor follows that, as with both speaking and writing, water flows out, spreads, irrigates, floods, inundates, quenches, subsumes, purifies, dissolves, hides, and washes over; it can be bottled up and also let loose—this expanse is promised in classical Arabic's titular fascination with the maritime totality.[33] Though compendious, water, once cut from its source, is easily muddied, quickly absorbed, and when left unattended, it evaporates. The *rāwī*—the narrator, the storyteller, the transmitter, the thirst-quencher who draws water—is always a mediator between the source and its transmission, who, while pointing back to the site of the original *logos*, moves forward in a temporal process of conveyance. While such movement is polyvalent, it is also largely unidirectional, not return-

32 See Gregor Schoeler, *The Oral and Written in Early Islam*, ed. James E. Montgomery, trans. Uwe Vagelpohl (London: Routledge, 2006), 28–61.

33 See Ibn Manẓūr, *Lisān al-ʿArab*, 15 vols. (Beirut: Dār al-Ṣādir, s.d.), 14:346, s.v. "r-w-ā," second column; see also Ḥājjī Khalīfa, *Kashf al-ẓunūn ʿan asāmī al-kutub wa-l-funūn*, ed. Muḥammad Sharaf al-Dīn Yāltaqāyā and Rifʿat Bīlga al-Kilīsī, 2 vols. (Istanbul: Maṭābiʿ Wikālat al-Maʿārif al-Jalīla, 1941), 1:220, 223–7, s.v. *biḥār* and *baḥr*, see also variants *majmaʿ al-baḥrayn*, etc., 2:1599–1602.

ing to the source, but rather moving away from it. This is to say nothing of the intermediating forces in the transmission of meaning (*riwāyat al-maʿnā*), which invariably undermine the immutability of the word (*riwāyat al-lafẓ*). Citations today can often function in rather similar terms.

The professed values of modern scholarship predicate the accessibility of information in both its dispersal and its recovery. As a value system, the citation advances transparency, attribution, and ownership. However, it usually remains silent about process. Indeed, our references place relatively little emphasis on the means or methods of acquisition. So while we may lay bare the location from which an idea or reference was obtained, citations do not require any disclosure as to how or by what means. This point deserves mention, as there has been relatively little academic discussion or acknowledgment of the way the digital corpus of Arabic and Persian sources shapes the kinds of queries that we pose, the methods of analysis that we develop, or the means by which we may now retrieve information. Indeed, a scan through recent academic publications in the field can easily leave the impression that our digital corpus does not exist at all, or if it does, it is of relatively little consequence. The reluctance to directly cite or engage these particular resources, widely available online, is certainly understandable. While published in the modern sense of the word, many of these materials are ephemeral, uncritical, or lack any explicit provenance and, as such, do not carry the same authority as the printed page. Furthermore, they often serve as tools, like indexes and concordances, to access the printed source, not ends in and of themselves.

This is by no means a new phenomenon. Generally speaking, the towering European Orientalists of the nineteenth century have left us very little record of the native translators, interpreters, and educators who opened up for them the vast trove of oriental letters. By preferring the authority of immediacy to the filters of mediation, history, as the direct witness of the past, generally effaces the go-between, the translator, and the local informant. And then there is the issue of the actual economic conditions necessary for authorship. It may seem trivial, but ignoring the processes and the capital by which we acquire knowledge effaces the complex means by which knowledge is produced. In our case, it posits information as largely a passive and transparent body that can be accessed and entered at will, to be mined, quantified, and reconfigured. However, digitization has not just transposed our texts into binary code; it has also shaped who we are as readers, how we think, the questions we pose, the concerns we have, our conception of the archive, and our very idea of the past.

Ignoring all this is certainly expedient. Our archive is messy and contingent, the product and labor of others, often with radically different values. Furthermore, however remunerated, access to this material is still the result of asymmetrical structures of power.[34] Contrast this to the digital resources housed at the libraries of elite universities and colleges, with revenue streams that are protected behind subscriptions and paywalls. Our citations certainly are not designed to account for such inequities. Footnotes assure expansion, illumination, and the possibility of retrieval, yet they are also wedded to replicating an established transmission and construction of knowledge. The digitization of information invites radically distinct forms of referencing, mapping, and recalling sources and materials. Yet, for our purposes, such a transformation in standards and modes of authority must first acknowledge the very digital condition of our texts.

Any knowledge transformation, whether in interpreting, distributing, or producing, occasions both loss and gain, as new techniques and technologies displace old ones. To use a mercantile metaphor, the adaptation of alternative modes of production, for both intellectual and material capital, results in both surplus and deficit. The idealized discourse of digitization, in the boundless reconfigurations of data, emphasizes above all progress, advancement, productivity, and liberation; it frees information from the physical constraints of the material world. Loss, if discussed at all, is usually couched in terms of outdated and retrograde practices that have historically hindered us. There are passive forms of loss, as the mere byproduct of any transformative process, as well as more active means of forgetting that are cultivated and conditioned. The production of memory, of what is preserved and commemorated communally, is also a curatorial process of leaving out, of ignoring, and even of destroying.[35] As opposed to abundance, gain, and presence—the very features of memory—lack, loss, and absence are all in the business of forgetting, of effacing the past and, with it, knowledge.

At the most basic level, uncertainty is occasioned by a lack of information; that ours is a state of uncertainty is undoubtedly an irony in this information age. Yet there are many sources of uncertainty facing the dispersed, decentralized, and fragmentary archives of digital information. First is the problem of inclusion. We may wonder, "If it is not online, does it really exist?" The question today may sound shrill, hyperbolic, or even disproportionate. Surely, in terms of ontology, much of our lives are lived in spaces beyond the Internet. But this is not so much the stuff of being, but that of knowing. When digitized, the searing abundance of information so quickly eclipses its analogue ancestor, the

34 For further discussion of this problem of access, see Riedel, "Of Making Many Copies There is No End."

35 See Aleida Assmann, "Canon and Archive," in *Cultural Memory Studies: An International and Interdisciplinary Handbook*, ed. Astrid Erll and Ansgar Nünning (Berlin: Walter de Gruyter, 2008), 98–9.

physical written word, that the problems of both displacement and inclusion, in epistemic terms, are certainly quite real. The Internet not only gives off an impression of immediacy, but also bears the mark of completeness. As we rely increasingly on digital means of accessing the archive, the archive that is not digitized risks losing both prominence and presence. Despite this professed ethos of encyclopedic inclusion, there is good reason to remain, in some basic sense, unsettled about the totality of the archive.

Furthermore, despite the vast quantity, there is still the issue of quality—yet another source of uncertainty. Can we rely on the information? Can we trust it? Can it be authenticated? How accurately does it render the analogue source? This is as much a matter of transmission as it is a question of origin. As with any structure of transmission or communication, there are values, assumptions, and motivations invested in the process of digitization. Such commitments, in turn, run directly into the problem of transparency (or the lack thereof), which is often born out of the decentralizing forces of network distribution; just as there are many actors conveying and relying on the same material, so there are many motivations, both stated and unstated (and often conflicting), that animate its distribution.

The process-oriented structures of dispersion, replication, and transmission that underwrite the communal bonds of the Internet would appear to transcend the power structures of center and margin. Nonetheless, such decentralized networks do not portend egalitarian or nonhierarchical economies of exchange. Traveling along the ligaments binding together these disparate points of connectivity, information is easily reproduced, pirated, stored, shared, sold, or repackaged. Here, the question of both the source and its owner are quickly obscured, and this in turn implicates the citational practices of modern scholarship and may occasion even more doubt or suspicion.

At times, such uncertainties may feel intractable. But as impasses, they are also possibilities, as they are the very generative grounds for the further cultivation of knowledge. Indeed, as with any act of communication, the points of rupture and discontinuity that amplify the noise over the signal are precisely the moments where the efficacy of the system and the transparency of the set of values and assumptions undergirding it are the most vulnerable. Such fissures and incongruities are the spaces that most need to be mapped out, for ignoring them means the ideological bases and structural biases shaping the archive remain unexamined.

5. The Production of Territory

As for the problem of mapping, the geographical corpus of letters, at first glance, it would appear to be a particularly rich resource for surveying this digital territory. This is true primarily for two reasons: 1) the body of writing is relatively compact compared to other fields; 2) much of it is freely available online. This is the case for many of the classical Arabic sources; the Persian and then subsequent Turkish and Urdu ventures into the field, which are quite significant in their own right, are far less represented. In a very basic sense, this situation is a product of the focus on the early classical Arabic corpus by the Orientalists of the nineteenth and early twentieth centuries (in general) over later developments, particularly in the diverse fields of science, philosophy, and theology.

A good number of the Arabic geographical texts available to Western scholars were edited before the end of the nineteenth century. Among some of the major works first published according to modern standards of textual criticism were the compendium of Abū l-Fidā' (d. 732/1331) and the geographical dictionary of Yāqūt al-Rūmī (d. 626/1229). These editions emphasized the utility of geographical writing for the broader historical understanding of Islamic civilization. During this period, the most important figure in the promotion of classical Arabic geographical and historical texts was the towering Dutch Orientalist Michael Jan de Goeje (d. 1909), whose influence on the field is still felt today. Following the model for editing manuscripts of Greek and Latin classics, de Goeje published with E.J. Brill in Leiden the *Bibliotheca Geographorum Arabicorum* (1870–94), a multivolume set that consisted of critical editions of geographical texts along with notes and indices. The focus of the compendium spanned the administrative to the belletristic and covered Abbasid imperial productions as well as works produced for regional dynasts and other learned patrons. The collection opened up a colorful spectrum of early material and consisted of writings by Ibn Khurdādhbih (fl. 270/884), al-Ya'qūbī (fl. 278/891), Ibn al-Faqīh (fl. 289/902), Ibn al-Rusta (fl. 300/912), Qudāma b. Ja'far (d. 337/948), Abū Isḥāq al-Iṣṭakhrī (fl. 340/951), Abū l-Ḥasan al-Mas'ūdī (d. 345/956), and Abū 'Abdallāh al-Maqdisī (fl. 375/985).

More than half of these works have been re-edited, often following further codicological discoveries. De Goeje issued a second edition of Maqdisī's geography, drawing on new readings from additional codicological material (1906); Johannes Hendrik Kramers used further manuscripts for his edition of Ibn Ḥawqal's geography in two volumes, which notably improved the *editio princeps* (1938–40); Iṣṭakhrī's collection was re-edited by Muḥammad Jābir 'Abd al-'Āl al-Ḥīnī (1961); Muḥammad Ḥusayn al-Zubaydī edited the entire unicum of Qudāma b. Jaʿfar's administrative manual, of which the geographical portions were a mere selection (1981); similarly, the discovery of a new manuscript of Ibn al-Faqīh's geography allowed Yūsuf al-Hādī to expand our knowledge of the work significantly (1996). This pattern is also reflected in Ibn Khurdādhbih's travel book, *al-Masālik wa-l-mamālik* [Routes and Realms], for de Goeje, who had access to a new manuscript, entirely supplanted the original edition of the geography by Charles Barbier de Meynard (1865). This short sketch of publication history highlights the fact that editions of these texts have remained, in some basic sense, a work in progress.

Today, the entirety of the *Bibliotheca Geographorum Arabicorum* is available for download in the form of scanned PDFs on archive.org and on multiple other sites; most are also accessible and can be searched by optical character recognition on Google Books, though its search capacity for the Arabic script still leaves much to be desired. Despite this digital diffusion, or perhaps in the face of it, Brill has recently reprinted the entire series in the analogue form of published books (2013–4). Yet even before digital scanning, de Goeje's library had long circulated in editions of photo-offsets issued by the publishing house Dār al-Ṣādir in Beirut. These high-quality reprints maintained the exact publication information, typesetting, and pagination of the original editions. In the case of Ibn Khurdādhbih's *Masālik*, however, the Beirut edition omits the rather informative French translation of the work that accompanies de Goeje's volume. Unauthorized reprints are not uncommon in the book publishing industry of the region, which historically has not always followed the strictures of international copyright law. For instance, I have a printed copy of *Nuzhat al-mushtāq fī ikhtirāq al-āfāq* [Pleasant Journeys into Faraway Lands] by the great geographer Abū ʿAbdallāh al-Idrīsī (d. 560/1165), originally published by the Istituto Universitario Orientale di Napoli in conjunction with E.J. Brill in a series of fascicules edited by a team of scholars under the direction of Enrico Cerulli (1970–84). My copy, however, makes no mention of this, but rather states that the geography, in two volumes, was published in Cairo by the Maktabat al-Thaqāfa al-Dīniyya (1994). Nonetheless, the text, pagination, notes in the critical apparatus, and the copyright restriction (in English) at the end of both volumes of the Cairo edition all match the European original. In contrast, the text of Kramer's Ibn Ḥawqal, originally printed by E.J. Brill, was reissued by a Beirut publishing house, Dār Maktabat al-Ḥayāt (1992), without any reference to the original; it is now shorn of its critical apparatus of textual variants and entirely repaginated. The only direct evidence that this is a copy of Kramer's text is the inclusion of his meticulously designed maps. Needless to say, both of these pirated works, which lay equal claim to their respective publishing rights, are now freely available for download as scanned documents from multiple websites.

All of these early Arabic geographical texts, including many more, have been digitized as searchable text files. They are available from several of the main online aggregators, including most notably al-Maktaba al-shāmila, through software that can be installed on computers and mobile devices. This website, which houses, as its name suggests, a vast trove of digitized books, follows a growing trend in Arabic and Persian e-books, as it keys the pagination of the text to that of the printed source (i.e., *tarqīm al-kitāb muwāfiq li-l-maṭbūʿ*). In such cases, al-Shāmila offers publication information for the respective editions used as the basis for typing out the e-books and supplies brief biographical notices on the authors. They also note the date when the file was first uploaded to the website, the original editor (if available), and they specify whether or not the text in question corresponds to a printed edition. This move toward greater transparency fits into a larger shift aimed at replicating the physical state of the editions from which the text files are copied. This would appear to be a step toward qualitatively improving the reliability of the texts and thus enhancing their value as reference tools, for the accuracy of the material can be compared easily to the printed page. It has become easier to check the online text against printed originals, as many of the print editions used, in and beyond the narrow field of Arabic descriptive geography, are now widely available online in the form of scanned copies.

However, on closer inspection, there is a good deal of heterogeneity. An example is al-Maqdisī's *Aḥsan al-taqāsīm fī maʿrifat al-aqālīm* [The Best Divisions on Knowledge of the Climes], posted on al-Shāmila. In addition to the name of the author and the title, the bibliographical information notes that the text was uploaded in 2010 and gives a list of how many times it has been viewed. The page lists the publishers in the following order: E.J. Brill, Leiden; Dār al-Ṣādir, Beirut; and Maktabat Madbūlī, Cairo. The only date given is for the Cairo edition (1411/1991), which may well be a copy of a copy. The entry also observes that all of these editions correspond to the same pagination, which is the basis for the digitized text. No mention is made here of the editor, de Goeje, or the fact that the text is based upon the second updated edition of the work published by E.J. Brill in 1906 and not the first edition issued in 1877, the third volume of the *Bibliotheca Geographorum Arabicorum*. As for the text, it follows the exact pagination of the original edition and includes de Goeje's detailed critical apparatus in the form of footnotes, where all the work of recording the significant codicological variants appears. While de Goeje's notes in Latin have been jumbled in the course of laying out the text, the record of divergence is quite clear and follows the printed page of the Leiden edition. This is of note, as Maqdisī's geography has survived in two distinct recensions that exhibit significant variations.[36] Any detailed work with the geography has to reckon in some fashion with these distinct recensions.

But al-Shāmila is not the only site to host this particular text file; indeed, the same file can be found on the Iranian-based Kitāb-khāna-i dījītāl-i nūr (Noor). Interestingly, the text files from both sites appear to be identical, with the exception that the Noor text has done a much better job of rendering the Latin in the footnotes. It is uncertain who produced the original text, which for all intents and purposes is the same, a matter that complicates the question of attribution and citation. But as these are copies of copies of copies, the question of origin and source is quickly obscured.

Nonetheless, the Noor site encourages citation with two links to bibliographic information files, keyed to the formats for the software of BibTex and Endnote, respectively, which follow standard bibliographic conventions. Here the name of the publisher appears as Dār al-Ṣādir, but there is no reference to the fact that the Beirut version is a copy of de Goeje's second edition published in Leiden. Included in the bibliographical information is what would appear to be a stable URL, but as al-Shāmila also offers an address for citing the online version, it remains unclear which text should be referenced.[37] However, in addition to a cleaner rendering of the critical apparatus, the obvious advantage of the Noor interface is that, in this particular case, it allows readers to switch seamlessly between the text file, noted as the book (*kitāb*), and the copy of the printed edition, referred to as the image (*taṣwīr*); this, in turn, enables easy verification that the information on a given page from the text file corresponds exactly to the printed book. The extent to which this feature will continue to be meaningful remains to be seen in the face of the growing power of text recognition software. For instance, de Goeje's second edition of Maqdisī's geography is also available on Google Books, which allows users to search through the Arabic text, though at this point with rather limited capability.[38] Both Google Books and the Noor Library have overlaid digital watermarks on every page of their scanned copies, asserting digital ownership of the material.[39] For Google's purposes, the work falls under the category of the public domain and thus can be freely download-

36 See *Bibliotheca Geographorum Arabicorum*, ed. Michael Jan de Goeje, 8 vols. (Leiden: E.J. Brill, 1870–94), 4:6–8.
37 See http://www.noorlib.ir/View/fa/Book/BookView/Image/4351; http://www.shamela.ws/index.php/book/23696.
38 See http://books.google.com/books?id=uQ8YAAAAYAAJ.
39 All Noor Library scans bear the watermark of the Computer Research Center of Islamic Sciences; Google similarly watermarks the books it uploads.

ed; in contrast, Noor only allows sections of the text to be downloaded in a given time interval, although the edition is readily accessible in the form of scans made by other institutions.[40]

Contrast this situation of relative transparency with the text file of the geography available for download on al-Miskhāt; according to the website, this file was uploaded in the spring of 2004. This version gives no indication of the publication history, makes no attempt to collate the work to a printed edition, and does not even have page numbers. The detailed and very important codicological record is missing, as the footnotes have been entirely ignored in the process of digitization. Perhaps the only redeeming feature of the text is that it can be downloaded directly, in a fairly universal word processing DOC file format.

At first glance, this may not appear particularly noteworthy. Yet both the Shāmila and Noor sites, which grew independently from stand-alone software, have embedded each page of the text with HTML markup and JavaScript coding typical of the server-side scripting of current web-based applications. While these two designs most clearly replicate the form of the book, they also force readers to work through individual pages at a time, as the websites retrieve information from their respective servers. This may not appear to be a constraining factor, especially in light of the profound gains that can be obtained through the text search functions. Yet such formats restrict, to a noticeable degree, the ability of individual readers to mark up the text or tag data (e. g., for prosopographical, historical, or geographical information) using the standards developed, for instance, by the Text Encoding Initiative (tei-c.org), among others.

Instead of freeing information and readily enabling its reconfiguration, such server-client transmissions, filtered as they are through the medium of websites, channel readers into preexisting paradigms that are designed for and capable of only certain kinds of interaction. There is a tension here between proprietary frameworks that restrict, limit, and funnel and the free circulation of information that can be easily reconfigured, rearranged, adapted, transformed, and telegraphed. That said, much of the material can be readily obtained through basic scripting applications that enable users to download content off the servers

40 In addition to the Digital Library of India (http://dli.gov.in), see also the Digital Assets Repository (http://dar.biblaex.org), developed with the Bibliotheca Alexandrina, which hosts scans of both the Dār al-Ṣādir and the Maktabat Madbūlī copies of the Leiden edition; the Dār al-Ṣādir copy is categorized as in the public domain, and thus fully accessible; in contrast, the Maktabat Madbūlī edition is marked as under copyright and thus only available in a restricted view, which enables five percent of the book to be accessed online. However, many of the books scanned by the Bibliotheca Alexandrina have been hacked, as it were, and this copy is also freely available on other websites.

of entire websites. Rather, we must emphasize that, just as the physical book privileges and conditions certain modes of ownership and reading, so too digital publishing platforms advance particular sets of expectations that both expand and limit the means by which readers can enter into and manipulate the material at hand.

As for this digital archive of geographical literature, it is by no means uniform. While we have access to a searchable text of Maqdisī's geography that corresponds page for page and note for note to the printed edition, the same is certainly not true for the entire corpus. The case of Ibn Khurdādbhih's geography here is emblematic. The text version on al-Shāmila corresponds to the edition published by Dār al-Ṣādir in Beirut, which is, in turn, based on the Leiden edition published in 1889, which is the sixth volume in de Goeje's series of Arabic geographical literature. The same information is also supplied by the Noor Library, which likewise hosts a text and a scanned copy of the published work. The text is the same on both sites. While it corresponds page for page with the printed edition it has been completely stripped of the detailed notes that accompanied the original. For de Goeje's edition of Ibn Khurdādhbih's geography, this is deeply problematic; the only way to begin to grasp the significant variants between the surviving codicological witnesses is to engage thoroughly and painstakingly with the critical apparatus of the Latin footnotes.[41] It is also of note that de Goeje includes a supplement to his edition: the geographical selection from Qudāma b. Jaʿfar's secretarial manual. The bibliographical information on the websites makes no reference to this, and the reader who merely searches through the text of the file without due diligence could easily assume Qudāma's work is a continuation of Ibn Khurdādhbih's geography. Here, rather than mediation, we have intermediation, distortion, and erasure in the process of translation. While this can be checked against the printed text, such slippage must be constantly borne in mind in an archive increasingly filled with greater uncertainty.

In this age of digital reproduction, such caveats may help to navigate this ever-evolving territory populated by simulacra, illusions, and forgeries. What is missing here is a map to guide us through it all, one that indicates not so much how to get there, but what to expect along the way. For the geographical corpus, this is doubly so, as the colorful legacy of cartography (which is so wedded to the enterprise of descriptive geography) is largely absent from these digital sources. In part, this is a legacy of the editing process of geographical literature, a process that has overwhelmingly privileged the textual over the detailed, if bewildering, cartographic supplements. The vaulting advance of de Goeje's li-

---

41 For more on this particular text and its reception history, see Zadeh, "Of Mummies."

brary of Arabic geography left behind, in its sheer ambition, almost the entirety of this cartographic enterprise.[42] By the time Cerulli turned to Idrīsī's horizon-traversing adventures, Islamic cartography had been cut loose from its moorings in descriptive geography. This is a profound irony, for Idrīsī's descriptions of far-off regions are dependent on his project to plot the world in its entirety—clime by clime, region by region, sea by sea—through maps that are ingeniously connected to the space of the physical book.[43]

The digital horizon would appear to be well suited for new configurations of text and image and the interplay between the two. Despite the potential of digital media, relatively little has been done in the way of reintegrating maps or images back into their original texts. An early exception in the field of the digital humanities is the multimedia computer program of Idrīsī's cartographic enterprise (published in the year 2000), which was digitized on the basis of a beautifully executed manuscript housed in the Bibliothèque nationale de France (Ms arabe 2221).[44] The interactive program, developed under the direction of Annie Vernay-Nouri, allowed users to navigate Idrīsī's *mappa mundi*, as pieced together from his visual projections of the various regions of the world; the maps themselves were interactive—they could be magnified or minimized, rotated, searched, and scrolled through. Along the way, the toponymic layers of place names and geographic features were linked to descriptions drawn from Idrīsī's text in Arabic and in French translation. This sensory experience was heightened by Andalusian music that could be played in the background. The program sought to transport its users through the power of the multimedia presentation back to the past of medieval learning and sophistication. Yet today the CD is largely obsolete, as it was designed for computer operating systems that have been quickly outpaced in technology's steady parade of the faster, newer, and

42 Notable exceptions are Kramer's edition of Ibn Ḥawqal, *Kitāb Ṣūrat al-arḍ* (Leiden: E.J. Brill, 1938–9) and Muḥammad Jābir ʿAbd al-ʿĀl al-Ḥīnī's edition of Abū Iṣḥāq al-Iṣṭakhrī, *al-Masālik wa-l-mamālik* (Cairo: Dār al-Qalam, 1961), which include editions of the maps integral to both works.

43 This work of separating the cartographic tradition as a discrete field, for Idrīsī and others, had already been undertaken by Konrad Miller, *Mappae Arabicae: arabische Welt- und Länderkarten des 9.–13. Jahrhunderts in arabischer Urschrift*, 6 vols. (Stuttgart: Selbstverlag des Herausgebers, 1926–31).

44 *La géographie d'Idrisi: un atlas du monde au XIIe siècle*, under the supervision of Annie Vernay-Nouri, CD-ROM (Paris: Bibliothèque nationale de France, Montparnasse multimédia, 2000). Minimum system requirements: 8xCD-ROM drive (i.e., 1.2 Megabytes/sec), Macintosh PowerPC (OS 7.5.3 or higher), 120 MHz processor, 27 megabytes of Random-access memory (RAM), 800 x 600 monitor with millions of colors; or Personal Computer, Pentium 166 MHz processor (Windows 95 or higher), 32MB of RAM, 800 x 600 monitor with millions of colors.

better. The website of the Bibliothèque nationale hosts a much diminished version of the program, largely shorn of the functionality of the original software. This project offers an object lesson in obsolescence and the difficulties of long-term storage and presentation inherent in the digital medium.[45]

A more recent example of using the interactive potential to engage with text and images in the field of Islamic mapmaking is Emilie Savage-Smith and Yossef Rapoport's online edition and translation of the *Kitāb Gharāʾib al-funūn wa-mulaḥ al-ʿuyūn* [The Book of Curiosities of the Sciences and Marvels for the Eyes], published in 2007. The heart of the website is a manuscript that preserves an anonymous copy of a Fatimid cosmography composed around 410/1020, with sections devoted to astronomy, astrology, and geography.[46] The manuscript on which the website is based was acquired in 2002 by the Bodleian Library of Oxford University (MS Arab. c. 90) and consists of several diagrams, maps, and charts.[47] Visitors to the site can make their way through the text of the work and the accompanying illustrations with high-quality reproductions of the manuscript that are tagged, element by element, line by line, to the Arabic text edition and to an English translation and notes. The scholarly edition and translation are accessed through 'hover boxes'—a graphical control script that activates pop-up windows when users scroll over specific areas of the manuscript pages that have been tagged. In addition to an introduction to the project, the site includes an Arabic-English glossary with further onomastic and toponymic notes, bibliographic references, guidelines for teachers wishing to use the website for pedagogical purposes, and a search function. Savage-Smith and Rapoport followed the website with a physical book (Brill, 2014), which presents an updated edition and translation that draws on further manuscripts of the text. Their work reflects a broader trend of offering some form of online presentation that is coupled with the traditional format of a printed book.

With the growing emphasis on digital publishing, we should expect to see more of such presentations of manuscript culture in the future, in and beyond maps and codices. These endeavors, which are collaborative by nature, require

---

45 See the website that was originally developed for the exhibition at the Bibliothèque nationale de France, entitled: *al-Idrîsî, la Méditerranée au XIIe siècle* (13 October 2001 through 16 January 2002), http://classes.bnf.fr/idrisi.

46 *An Eleventh-Century Egyptian Guide to the Universe: The Book of Curiosities*, ed. Emilie Savage-Smith and Yossef Rapoport (Leiden: Brill, 2014), 32–3.

47 *The Book of Curiosities: A Critical Edition*, ed. Emilie Savage-Smith and Yossef Rapoport, online publication, http://www.bodley.ox.ac.uk/bookofcuriosities (March 2007). See also Jeremy John and Emilie Savage-Smith, "*The Book of Curiosities*: A Newly Discovered Series of Islamic Maps," *Imago Mundi* 55 no. 1 (2003): 7–24.

a good deal of institutional support, funding, and technological capacity. Both examples cited above are proprietary and closed; they allow for certain kinds of interaction and engagement. They are similar in the sense that, while both are hosted on distinct platforms, they have been designed as final products and thus risk varying degrees of ossification. This is not so much a critique as an observation about the limits inherent in the digital medium itself. Yet in very creative and engaging ways, such projects demonstrate the power of digital presentation for opening up and integrating text and image in new ways of imagining and returning to the constraints of the physical book.

These examples, however, are largely the exception that proves the rule. Generally, the resources that Muslim institutions have invested in the digitization of Islamic learning have overwhelmingly focused on textualization. In addition to cartography, this has also largely meant the effacement of the great traditions of illumination and figural arts, which are highly developed in Arabic, Persian, and Turkish book cultures. Such textual emphasis extends beyond just the legacy of Orientalist philology, with its own fetish for the text; rather, it forms part of a wider trend in Islamic reform concerning the nature and history of religious authority. In this regard, we must continue to recognize the very distinct sets of values animating the digital presentation of Islamic material produced in the frameworks of secular Western academic institutions versus those funded by governmental and religious organizations operating in the modern spheres of Islamic piety.

6. Monolingualism and the Self

Given the weight placed on explicitly religious sources, the digitization of the geographical corpus is noteworthy in its own right, particularly because this corpus developed, in great measure, out of the larger absorption of classical Greek and pre-Islamic Persian models of learning and science. In part, this presence in the digital field results from the fact that geography has been so thoroughly sacralized and explicitly transformed into an 'Islamic' science. Yet, in light of the wide sectarian propensities of the geographers, their inclusion in the digital corpus perhaps reflects more than anything their utility as pragmatic sources of information for classical Islamic history writ large.

Contrast this state of abundance with the almost complete absence of digital material from the massive Greco-Arabic translation movement, sponsored largely by the early Abbasid elite. Largely missing from this digital expanse in Arabic letters is the record of translations that span the entire range of classical learning and include works on agriculture, alchemy, algebra, astrology, astronomy, botany, geometry, literary theory, fables and romances, magic, mathematics, medicine, pharmacology, meteorology, military manuals, mineralogy, music, optics, philosophy, veterinary science, and zoology.[48] Many of these titles, which were often translated via Syriac intermediaries, can be found quickly in the searchable versions of Ibn al-Nadīm's *Fihrist*, which in its catholicity reaches far beyond the narrowly defined genres of our modern digital platforms. Yet the texts themselves are almost nowhere to be seen. It is true that not all of these translations survive, and of those that do, many remain only in manuscript form, unedited; yet the last century has seen a steady increase in the publication of Greco-Arabica, which is, for the most part, unaccounted for in the massive expanse of the digital corpus.[49] The digital field produced outside of Western scholarship has also largely overlooked classical Arabic and Persian writings from the diverse fields of scientific learning that developed and expanded beyond the legacy of the scholastic movement of late antiquity, though many of these works are available in modern editions.

In part, this situation is a result of the modern hollowing out of Islamic civilization, which generally excludes the 'foreign' sciences from the purview of religious authority and authenticity. As so much of this classical learning no longer proves 'valid', having withered under the glare of secular empiricism, its immediate relevance to the projects of modernist scientific discourses in Islamic reform is by no means apparent.[50] After all, the teleological and wrongheaded narrative of the Western *translatio imperii et studii*, which claims that the 'Arabs' preserved the learning of Greek antiquity only so that the West could then inherit it, is not particularly meaningful in the diverse contexts of Islamic modernity—other than perhaps to nostalgically bemoan the great achievements of the past. Yet ignoring the legacy of science and learning that extended both in and beyond the frameworks of classical religious education risks a further reification of Islamic knowledge as the sole domain of jurists, *ḥadīth* scholars, and exegetes,

---

48 This list is drawn from Dimitri Gutas, who supplies bibliographical references in *Greek Thought, Arabic Culture. The Graeco-Arabic Translation Movement in Baghdad and Early ʿAbbāsid Society (2nd–4th/8th–10th centuries)* (London: Routledge, 1998), 193–6, cf. 1–2.

49 A notable exception, produced within the framework of Western scholarship, can be seen in the database *Glossarium Græco-Arabicum* (telota.bbaw.de/glossga), which is currently a research unit of "Greek into Arabic – Philosophical Concepts and Linguistic Bridges" (http://www.greekintoarabic.eu). A growing body of materials is also hosted as "A Digital Corpus for Greco-Arabic Studies" (http://alpheios.net/content/grecoarabic), part of the Alpheios Project, an open source initiative.

50 See Behrooz Ghamari-Tabrizi, "Is Islamic Science Possible?" *Social Epistemology* 10 no. 2/3 (1996): 323–7.

who use such ancillary fields as grammar, rhetoric, history, and geography purely for utilitarian ends.

The introduction, absorption, and naturalization of classical scholarship, which helped to transform Arabic into a cosmopolitan language of power, was itself predicated on acts of translation.[51] This is to say nothing of the expansive history of vernacularization and, with it, ultimately the eastward spread of Islamic learning and piety, which drew from and also transcended the idiom of Arabic religious vocabulary. Yet so many of our digital platforms promote, in monogenetic singularity, the primacy of Arabic writing as the sole emblem of Islamic authenticity.

In this essay I have emphasized that the classical corpus consists of sources in both Arabic and Persian. The two bodies of writing are by no means equal in size or range of fields, nor in the historical or geographical areas covered. This is also true, though in very different ways and for quite distinct ends, of the digital corpus, which places comparatively less weight on source material written in Persian. Yet, with its emergence in the fourth century of the Islamic era, early New Persian writing came to occupy areas of learning once reserved exclusively for Arabic. This process of vernacularization was fundamentally an activity of translation, as written Persian moved from a language associated with non-Muslims to a language of learning, piety, and authority promoted by the Muslim elite. The rise of Persian also laid the groundwork for subsequent vernacular expansions in Turkish, Urdu, Malay, and a host of other languages. This history is the reason many Muslims around the world refer to prayer with the Persian word *namāz* rather than the Arabic *ṣalāt*, a simple example that could easily be multiplied.

Today, the vocabularies of Islam inhabit staggeringly diverse fields linguistically and culturally. To be sure, as the language of scripture and learning, Arabic plays a central and one might say even transcendental role, but contrary to the suggestion of some, it is by no means the sole badge of Muslim identity.[52] Rather, today's plurality of experiences and conditions gives the lie to the myth of ethnolinguistic singularity and homogeneity. Although many of our digital resources of classical Arabic might suggest the opposite, this was also true of the classical pe-

---

51 In addition to Gutas, *Greek Thought*, see Hayrettın Yücesoy, "Translation as Self-Consciousness: Ancient Sciences, Antediluvian Wisdom, and the ʿAbbāsid Translation Movement," *Journal of World History* 20 no. 4 (2009): 523–57; Abdelhamid I. Sabra, "The Appropriation and Subsequent Naturalization of Greek Science in Medieval Islam: A Preliminary Statement," *History of Science* 25 no. 3 (1987): 223–43.

52 Cf. Ibn Taymiyya, *Iqtiḍāʾ al-ṣirāṭ al-mustaqīm li-mukhālafat aṣḥāb al-jaḥīm*, ed. Nāṣir b. ʿAbd al-Karīm al-ʿAql, 2 vols. (Riyadh: Dār al-ʿĀṣima, 1998) 1:468–9; for further context, see also Reinhart, "Fundamentalism," 101–2.

riod. It is likewise why we do not talk about 'Arab' learning or 'Arab' science when we mean an ethnic designation, as the majority of intellectuals writing in Arabic were not ethnically Arabs—indeed, this is a great testament to the early hegemonic force of the language. As the historian Marshall Hodgson highlighted in his study of Islamic civilization, a good many of the thinkers and authorities writing in Arabic were not even Muslim. In fact, some might argue that the term 'Islamic science' at times obfuscates more than it illuminates.[53]

From the Balkans to South Asia, Persian was cultivated as a sophisticated language of high culture. The modern period, however, has been marked by an ever-shrinking sphere of Persian linguistic activity. Scholars and administrators working within the often-competing gunpowder states of the Ottoman, Safavid, and Mughal dynasties could communicate with each other through the medium of Persian, a language of the educated elite. Yet by the end of the twentieth century, the linguistic and cultural reach of Persian had drastically narrowed. In terms of intellectual activity, this shrinkage has come to signify an identification of Persian with the Shiʿi religious history of Iran during the last century, despite the fact that Imāmī Shiʿism only truly gained hold in Iran as a state religion relatively late, under the Safavid dynasty.

Persian continues to be spoken and written in a variety of regions, particularly in Afghanistan and Tajikistan. Yet Iran has been the leading force behind the promotion of scholarship on Persian history, literature, and culture; as a language, it is profoundly tied to Iranian nationalism.[54] This modern national identification of Persian with Iran—and increasingly, after the Iranian Revolution, with Imāmī Shiʿism—has in part reduced Persian to a national and sectarian identity. Against this backdrop, there is little reason to wonder why the digital material that circulates on Salafī websites, largely in the Gulf, has taken no interest in the Persian corpus at hand, despite the fact that the overwhelming majority of the classical writings in Persian were produced by Sunni authorities. This, of course, says nothing of the basic problem of linguistic competency necessary to extend beyond the singular domain of Arabic learning. The digitization of early New Persian writing has largely fallen within the purview of modern Iranian institutions, as noticeably evinced by the work of the Computer Research Center of Islamic Sciences, which is closely tied to the Iranian state and to semi-

53 Marshall Hodgson, *The Venture of Islam*, 3 vols. (Chicago: University of Chicago Press, 1974), 1:45–8.

54 See Mehrdad Kia, "Persian Nationalism and the Campaign for Language Purification," *Middle Eastern Studies* 34 no. 2 (1998): 9–36; Mohamad Tavakoli-Targhi, "Refashioning Iran: Language and Culture during the Constitutional Revolution," *Iranian Studies* 23 no. 1/4 (1990): 77–101.

nary education. While no less impressive, the selection is relatively narrow and reflects a particular set of commitments and paradigms on the place and significance of classical Persian literature in the context of modern Iran. This linguistic division has further fragmented the fields of knowledge along the lines of national and sectarian identities, boundaries produced in great measure by the diverse forces of modernity. Thus, rather than offering a counterpoint to the often-stultifying divisions of the modern age, this vast body of writing that covers distinct regions and languages is easily put to the service of reaffirming the historical permanency of these very divides.

Many of the religious authorities from the period, however, straddled multiple divisions and inhabited diverse spheres of learning and modes of being. Take, for instance, the famed Ashʿarī theologian, Shāfiʿī jurist, and *ḥadīth* transmitter Abū l-Manṣūr ʿAbd al-Qāhir al-Baghdādī (d. 429/1037) from the city of Nishapur, who is best known today for his work on heresiography. In his own day, he was renowned as a *dhū l-funūn*, a master of arts, including Arabic grammar, poetics, letters, mathematics, and geometry; according to the biographical record, he taught some seventeen different branches of learning (*darrasa fī sabʿata ʿashara nawʿan min al-ʿulūm*), in the context of madrasa education.[55] We know that a wide range of scientific and philosophical material was featured in madrasas of the period, which, in turn, built upon the classical heritage of Greek learning.[56] While ʿAbd al-Qāhir's theological works on heresiography and creed are easily accessible online, both as scanned PDFs and as digitized text files, the modern editions of his writings on mathematics and geometry are currently not available online.

This whittling down of religious authority also forms part of the fragmentation of Islamic intellectual and cultural history. This can be seen in the work of ʿAbd al-Qāhir's son-in-law, Abū l-Muẓaffar al-Isfarāʾīnī (d. 471/1079), also an Ashʿarī theologian and Shāfiʿī jurist. He too wrote an Arabic work of heresiography, which is easily obtained online. Yet, if we relied only upon online Arabic

---

55 See ʿAbd al-Ghāfir al-Fārisī (d. 529/1134), *Tārīkh Nīshābūr, al-ḥalqa al-ūlā min al-Muntakhab min al-siyāq*, ed. Muḥammad Kāẓim al-Maḥmūdī (Qom: Jamāʿat al-Mudarrisīn, 1403/1983), 545–6, §1190; Ibn ʿAsākir (d. 571/1176), *Tabyīn kadhib al-muftarī fī-mā nusiba ilā l-imām Abī l-Ḥasan al-Ashʿarī* (Damascus: Maṭbaʿat al-Tawfīq, 1347/1928–9), 253–4; ʿAbd al-Wahhāb al-Subkī (d. 771/1370), *Ṭabaqāt al-shāfiʿiyya al-kubrā*, ed. Maḥmūd Muḥammad al-Ṭanāḥī and ʿAbd al-Fattāḥ Muḥammad al-Ḥilw, 10 vols. (Cairo: ʿĪsā al-Bābī al-Ḥalabī, 1964–76), 5:136–48, §467. For more, on ʿAbd al-Qāhir in the context of Nishapuri education, see Zadeh, *The Vernacular Qur'an: Translation and the Rise of Persian Exegesis* (Oxford: Oxford University Press, 2012), 338–42.

56 See Sabra, "Appropriation," 233–5.

resources, we would have very little inkling that Isfarāʾīnī produced a multi-volume Persian translation and commentary of the Quran that for many years has been available in a partial edition and now, through the power of digitization, is searchable, though still incomplete, on the Noor Library website.[57] Many of the scholars from the period and the region were *dhawū l-lisānayn*, masters of both Arabic and Persian. This expression, emphasizing bilingualism, is repeated as an epithet for various authorities by the historian Abū l-Ḥasan Ibn Funduq al-Bayhaqī (d. 565/1169–70), who also wrote in both Arabic and Persian and took a strong interest in philosophy, science, and religious learning. His writings are also divided across the digital landscape, split between Arabic and Persian digital resources.

Part of the challenge is that of assemblage, of reconstituting and reuniting what has been broken into parts and cordoned off into separate pieces in this process of transmission. This still remains fundamentally an archival activity of scouring through documents, records, material traces, and physical remains, regardless of venue or form. Much of this body of writing, of representing and refashioning the world, has been documented through editions and photographs, though a good deal of it continues undisturbed, as it were, in the rough form of unedited manuscripts and uncatalogued objects. But even here, through the force of digitization, what was accessible only in physical libraries and museums is increasingly available in digital forms, often online. As for the codicological record, there is a growing (if unequal) number of digitized manuscripts. In this regard, while a good deal of the digital sources for Islamic intellectual and cultural history are fragmented along linguistic and sectarian divisions, the sheer number of resources opens up—for the diligent—new possibilities of collation, aggregation, and synthesis.

A noteworthy example is the case of Abū Naṣr al-Ḥaddādī (fl. 400/1010), a Ḥanafī religious authority from Samarqand trained in Arabic grammar, poetry, and the diverse fields of Quranic learning, whose full significance as an exegetical authority is only now coming to light. If we were to rely on the very meager Arabic biographical record, we would only know that he was an expert in variant readings of the Quran. In addition, we would have the Arabic primer by Ḥaddādī on Quranic grammar, lexicography, semantics, and rhetoric that Ṣafwān ʿAdnān Dāwūdī published in 1988 (based upon a single manuscript housed in the Ches-

57 Abū l-Muẓaffar Shāhfūr b. Ṭāhir al-Isfarāʾīnī, *Tāj al-tarājim fī tafsīr al-Qurʾān li-l-aʿājim*, ed. Najīb Māyil Harawī and ʿAlī Akbar Ilāhī Khurāsānī, partial edition, 3 vols. (Tehran: Shirkat-i Intishārāt-i ʿIlmī wa-Farhangī, 1375 Sh./1996). See http://www.noorlib.ir/View/fa/Book/BookView/Image/19966.

ter Beatty Library).[58] Today, references to other manuscripts of the work can be found easily through online searches, just as a PDF copy of Dāwūdī's edition is widely available.

Yet an important piece of information can also be uncovered by turning to Yazmlar (yazmlar.gov.tr), a Turkish website run under the auspices of the Ministry of Culture and Tourism. The website provides for purchase direct digital access to images of countless Arabic, Persian, and Turkish manuscripts held in various archives in Turkey and also catalogue references to many more. From this website we learn that the public library of Kastamonu in northern Anatolia houses two manuscripts on Quranic exegesis by Ḥaddādī. The cataloguing is not entirely accurate in this particular case (as it gives the impression that these are separate works), nor are the images of the manuscript directly accessible online. However, the library officials in Kastamonu are more than happy to supply, via email, digital copies of manuscripts upon written request and after the standard transfer of funds to purchase the images. As with many of these smaller archives, there is no published catalogue of the full manuscript holdings in the Kastamonu Library. In this specific instance, the Yazmlar website opens a window onto material that otherwise would be forgotten. It turns out that the two Kastamonu manuscripts are of the same Arabic Quranic commentary; one is the complete work in a single volume (MS 3659), the other is an acephalous first volume from a set of two or three volumes (MS 306). This concise commentary, entitled *al-Itqān fī l-maʿānī l-Qurʾān*, is otherwise unknown and completely absent from the modern scholarly discussion on Arabic exegesis of the period. As with his Arabic primer for the study of the Quran, Ḥaddādī took great interest in poetry, grammar, variant readings, law, theology, and basic questions of comprehension —all matters particularly well suited for madrasa education and instruction.

However, what makes all of this so intriguing is that Ḥaddādī is also remembered for a major commentary and paraphrase of the Quran in Persian. No mention of this is made in the surviving Arabic materials. However, references to Ḥaddādī's *Tafsīr-i munīr*, as it is generally known, are scattered throughout later Persian exegetical writing. At least two manuscripts from sections of his Persian commentary have survived. However, only one copy gives the name of the author and the title of the work: *Maʿānī kitāb Allāh taʿāla wa-tafsīrihi l-*

58 See Abū l-Naṣr al-Ḥaddādī, *al-Madkhal li-ʿilm tafsīr Kitāb Allāh taʿālā*, ed. Ṣafwān ʿAdnān Dāwūdī (Damascus: Dār al-Qalam, 1988). For a critique of Dāwūdī's ascription of the anonymous fragment in Chester Beatty MS 3883 (fols. 228b–44a), which he published as the *Muwaḍḍiḥ* of Ḥaddādī, see Muḥammad Ajmal Ayyūb al-Iṣlāḥī, "A-hādhā *Kitāb al-Muwaḍḍiḥ li-ʿilm al-Qurʾān* li'l-Ḥaddādī?" in *Buḥūth wa-maqālāt fī l-lugha wa-l-adab wa-taqwīm al-nuṣūṣ* (Beirut: Dār al-Gharb al-Islāmī, 2007), 359–69.

munīr [The Meanings of the Book of God Almighty and Its Splendid Commentary]. This particular manuscript, the eighth volume of the commentary, is now housed in the Topkapı Palace Museum of Istanbul (E.H. 209). The lavish use of gold, the rich color palette, the extensive rubrics, the varying scripts, and the magisterial artistry of the calligraphy and decoration all point to the courtly provenance of the manuscript and highlight its value as a precious object. The colophon states that the volume was copied and gilded by the master calligrapher Abū ʿAmr ʿUthmān al-Warrāq, whose telling faith in the lasting power of the written word I introduced at the beginning of this essay. The finispiece, in turn, explains that the work was commissioned on the orders of the Ghaznavid sultan, Ibrāhīm b. Masʿūd (r. 451–92/1059–99). This royal provenance speaks volumes to the question of reception. Foremost, it suggests that Ḥaddādī's Persian commentary bore a prestige that for many centuries has been largely forgotten.[59]

The Topkapı Palace has placed much of its catalogue online, though currently no citations of Ḥaddādī's commentary can be found there. Until the recent work on the manuscript by the Iranian scholar Muḥammad ʿImādī Ḥāʾirī, there were only scattered references to the Topkapı copy; these references did not, in their own right, fully appreciate its significance for the field of Persian exegesis.[60] In addition to Ḥāʾirī's printed color facsimile, published in a limited run, the manuscript (or rather digital images of it) can be viewed at the Topkapı Palace, by appointment.

While fragments of Ḥaddādī's Persian *Tafsīr-i munīr* have now been brought to light, his Arabic commentary and its relation to his work in Persian have not been examined. This is not so much a case of negligence as it is a problem of amassing such diverse and scattered points of information in what is, by its very nature, an incomplete process of reassembly. It turns out, upon close inspection, that these are two distinct works that share many features and areas of emphasis but diverge in important and noticeable ways. This is unlike the case of Isfarāʾīnī's Persian commentary, which is, for all intents and purposes, an unacknowledged translation of *al-Kashf wa-l-bayān ʿan tafsīr al-Qurʾān* [The Unveiling and Elucidation in Quranic Interpretation] by the famed exegete of

59 For more on this, see Alya Karame and Travis Zadeh, "The Art of Translation: An Early Persian Commentary of the Qur'an," *Journal of Abbasid Studies* 2 no. 2 (2015): 119–95.

60 See Muḥammad ʿImādī Ḥāʾirī, "Muqaddima," in *al-Mujallad al-thāmin min maʿānī kitāb Allāh taʿālā wa-tafsīruhu al-munīr*, ed. Muḥammad ʿImādī Ḥāʾirī, facsimile edition of EH 209 held in the Topkapı Sarayı Müzesi Kütüphane (Tehran: Kitābkhāna, Mūzih wa-Markaz-i Asnād-i Majlis-i Shūrā-yi Islāmī, 1390/2011) 9–41; idem, *Kuhantarīn nuskha-i mutarjam-i Qurʾān: taḥlīl-i matn, bar rasī-i dastniwisht, zībāyī-shināsī-i hunar-i qudsī* (Tehran: Mīrāth-i Maktūb, 1389/2010).

Nishapur, Abū Isḥāq al-Thaʿlabī (d. 427/1035).[61] Rather, Ḥaddādī—or perhaps students working after him and in his name—produced two distinct works of Quranic exegesis: one for an audience interested in the fine points of Arabic grammar, poetry, and lexicography, and another that focuses on the meaning of the Quran through the filter of Persian paraphrases, stories, and translations of Arabic exegetical authorities.

In this particular example, Internet resources take us only so far before we must venture into the analogue archive. Yet even here, manuscripts are often tendered through the filter of digital reproductions. Certainly this is a vast improvement over the splotchy and often blurry uncertainty of the microfilm reader. The digital reproduction has increasingly replaced access to the primary codicological witness—a growing archival practice across a variety of fields and disciplines. Promised here is the fidelity of a digital transparency that mediates and transmits and also frees, as it protects the original from further handling. Yet in any process of translation from one medium to the next, there is always some form of intermediation that changes both the object of study and the experience at hand. Beyond the finer points of codicology, of the paper and binding, of the physical history of the book, or of legibility and decipherment, the question of the digital manuscript remains that of the actual weight of the corpus, of the tome, of the materiality of the object, and the very charismatic trace of the past—this is all largely sacrificed in the process of digital conversion.

But, to be sure, much is gained by the speed of transmission and the amount of information that can be quickly recovered. And it is precisely this potential of reassembling that should be most pursued along the divergent digital horizons. For the likes of Ḥaddādī and many others, this means reconstituting a fragmented body of writing that survives in the detritus of past generations, spread unevenly across a vast trove of documents. Even when partially reconstituted and reconnected, the corpus shows competencies and networks that extend beyond the modern concerns and expectations that often shape our entrance into and understanding of the past. One of the great possibilities of the digital arena is its potential to highlight the multilingual, transregional, and truly global areas of interconnectivity. Our sources for the history of Islamic civilization are certainly all of this and much more.

61 See Zadeh, *Vernacular Qur'an*, 382–418.

7. The Alchemy of Uncertainty

As a process of retrieving and telegraphing information, the digital field is fundamentally the product of translation. We see this most obviously in the translation from the analogue to the digital: books are keyed and scanned, transposed into binary sequences of information that can be rearranged and reconnected in new and unseen ways. This transformative process, in the sleight of hand that transforms from the physical into the ephemeral and the disembodied, is, one might say, basically alchemical.

In contrast to the public canons of writing, alchemy represents the other largely obscured side of the written word. Ibn al-Nadīm begins his bibliographic encyclopedia with a section (*maqāla*) on writing and scripture, only to end it with a detailed account of alchemy, the last of the ten sections that make up the *Fihrist*. As with anyone devoted to the art of cataloguing, throughout his survey Ibn al-Nadīm pays keen attention to various organizational principles, and his choice to bookend the catalogue with writing and alchemy is quite telling.[62] The structure comes full circle, as the two sections treat the very global and even divine expanse of the written word and its diverse scripts—one outward and manifest, the other hidden and esoteric. Ibn al-Nadīm ends with Hermes, the sage from Babylon, transplanted to Egypt; the messenger god of the Greek pantheon, the god of writing known to the ancient Egyptians as Thoth, the clever intermediary, the scribe, and the weigher of dead souls, known to Ibn al-Nadīm as Ṭāṭ.[63] Alchemy's first line of inquiry takes us deep into the pyramids of Egypt, the monumental temples (*barābī*) widely believed to have been built by Hermes as storehouses for divinely revealed esoteric knowledge.[64] We read

---

62 On the organizational principles of the *Fihrist*, see Devin Stewart, "The Structure of the *Fihrist:* Ibn al-Nadim as Historian of Islamic Legal and Theological Schools," *International Journal of Middle East Studies* 39 no. 3 (2007): 369–87; Shawkat Toorawa, "Proximity, Resemblance, Sidebars and Clusters: Ibn al-Nadīm's Organizational Principles in *Fihrist* 3.3," *Oriens* 38 (2010): 217–47.

63 Ibn al-Nadīm, *Fihrist*, 2:441–2, 443. See Johann Fück, "The Arabic Literature on Alchemy According to an-Nadīm (A.D. 987). A Translation of the Tenth Discourse of *The Book of the Catalogue* (*al-Fihrist*) with Introduction and Commentary," *Ambix* 4 no. 3/4 (1951): 112, §9. See also Jacques Derrida, *Dissemination*, trans. Barbara Johnson (London: Athlone Press, 1981), 84–94.

64 Ibn al-Nadīm, *Fihrist*, 2:443–4. On the Hermetic connection to the pyramids, see Alexander Fodor, "The Origins of the Arabic Legends of the Pyramids," *Acta orientalia academiae scientiarum hungaricae* 23 no. 3 (1970): 335–63; Michael Cook, "Pharaonic History in Medieval Egypt," *Studia Islamica* 57 (1983): 67–103; Mark Fraser Pettigrew, "The Wonders of the Ancients: Arab-Islamic Representations of Ancient Egypt" (Ph.D. diss., University of California, Berkeley, 2004), 93–101; also more broadly, Garth Fowden, *The Egyptian Hermes: A Historical Approach to the*

that the pyramids were designed for practicing the art of alchemy, for housing undeciphered inscriptions and writings in Chaldean and Coptic.[65] Ibn al-Nadīm, the ever-diligent bookman, relates that he read in the very handwriting of the famed occultist Ibn Waḥshiyya (d. 318/930–1) a transcription of the scripts (*aqlām*) in which the books of alchemy, magic, and incantations were written. The *Fihrist* even promises to provide the keys to decipher these various alphabets, including the very one used to write the ancient sciences in the Egyptian temples. Unfortunately, these mysterious letters have been lost in the course of the manuscript transmission of the *Fihrist*. In any case, Ibn al-Nadīm tellingly notes that only a master (*ʿārif*) of the discipline can truly understand the meaning of such cyphers.[66]

According to Ibn al-Nadīm, the alchemical art first and foremost seeks to produce the transmutation of gold and silver from other nonprecious metals. Yet a careful reading of his catalogue of alchemical writings reveals that the science, described by the philosopher-physician Abū Bakr al-Rāzī (d. 313/925) as the very pinnacle of philosophy, is much more ambitious, for it attempts to explain the hidden, interconnected nature of creation itself through the transmutation of inorganic matter.[67] A central figure in Ibn al-Nadīm's account is Jābir b. Ḥayyān (d. c. 200/815), whose life and teachings are shrouded in mystery. Ibn al-Nadīm notes that many groups—including not only alchemists, Sufis, and philosophers, but also importantly the Shia—claimed him as one of their own. This affiliation, given Ibn al-Nadīm's background as an Imāmī Shiʿi, sheds light on his spirited defense of Jābir's corpus.[68] Much of the material associated with Jābir in the alchemical and natural sciences reflects the absorption and reinscription of learn-

Late Pagan Mind, 2d ed. (Princeton: Princeton University Press, 1993); Kevin van Bladel, *The Arabic Hermes, From Pagan Sage to Prophet of Science* (Oxford: Oxford University Press, 2009).

65 Ibn al-Nadīm, *Fihrist*, 2:445.

66 Ibn al-Nadīm, *Fihrist*, 2:460–1, 461 n. 2. See Fück, "Arabic Literature," 139–40 nn. 64–7. For an example of this field of cryptology, see the study on ancient scripts and hieroglyphs, *Shawq al-mustahām fī maʿrifat rumūz al-aqlām*, ascribed to Ibn Waḥshiyya, edition and partial translation, *Ancient Alphabets and Hieroglyphic Characters Explained*, ed. and trans. Joseph Hammer-Purgstall (London: W. Bulmer and Co., 1806). However, on the question of authorship, see Jaakko Hämeen-Anttila, *The Last Pagans of Iraq, Ibn Waḥshiyya and his Nabatean Agriculture* (Leiden: Brill, 2006) 21 n. 45, 43 n. 112.

67 See Jamal Elias, *Aisha's Cushion: Religious Art, Perception, and Practice in Islam* (Cambridge, MA: Harvard University Press, 2012), 175–88.

68 Ibn al-Nadīm, *Fihrist*, 2:450–1. Ibn al-Nadīm appears to be much more sanguine on the matter of alchemy than Fück would have us believe; see "Arabic Literature," 84, §3. On the Shiʿi reception of Jābirian cosmology, see Mohammad Ali Amir-Moezzi, *The Spirituality of Shiʿi Islam, Beliefs and Practices* (London: I.B. Tauris, 2011), 108–9 n. 14, 115–6 n. 36, 165–6 n. 64.

ing from classical antiquity in Arabic letters, which draws together Hellenistic philosophy and Hermeticism, Mesopotamian astrology, and Indic astronomic traditions. Ibn al-Nadīm concludes the section (and with it the entire catalogue) with an observation on the origins of the alchemic corpus, which he notes is as innumerable as it is transnational: some claim it originated in Egypt, others claim it comes from the Persians, from the Greeks, from India, or even from China.[69]

The very global character of the field suggested here reflects, above all, the status of alchemy, not as a fringe discipline, but as an authoritative branch of scientific learning pursued by people the world over. Like astronomy and astrology, which during this period were integrated into Islamic scientific discourse largely through the absorption of Neoplatonic thought, alchemy represents a system of learning very much preoccupied with understanding the deep and hidden interconnections that bind together the cosmos. Today, as with most branches of occult learning so actively cultivated and developed throughout Islamic history, the alchemical arts, the basis for modern chemistry itself, are in great measure absent from the digitized corpus of Arabic and Persian letters. The pursuit of occult knowledge, however, was not restricted to a particular sectarian group. There is much evidence that a broad spectrum of the religious elite not only circulated occult learning, but also sought to harness it.

In this regard, the example of Abū l-Faḍl Muḥammad al-Ṭabasī (d. 482/1089), who lived much of his life in Nishapur, is illuminating. Referred to by the honorific title the "pride of the imams," Ṭabasī was known to be a reliable *ḥadīth* transmitter and a pious ascetic who composed numerous works. He delivered lectures in the Niẓāmiyya Madrasa, established by the powerful Seljuk vizier Niẓām al-Mulk (d. 485/1092) in the city of Nishapur. His scholarly pursuits fit into the normative network of the region's Shāfiʿī jurists and Ashʿarī theologians, who professed an outward expression of Sufi piety. However, of the writings associated with Ṭabasī, the only work that appears to have been disseminated widely in manuscript form is his *al-Shāmil fī l-baḥr al-kāmil* [The Comprehensive Compendium of the Entire Sea], a treatise on subjugating various occult forces through talismans and incantations.

The collection of spells focuses particularly on commanding angels and *jinn*. The incantations also showcase an underworld of forces that can be harnessed for various ends, from the benevolent to the nefarious. Over the course of Ṭabasī's grimoire, the sum total of spells conjures an entire demonology through the power of subjugation. Despite the avowedly monotheistic supremacy of God,

69 Ibn al-Nadīm, *Fihrist*, 2:466.

affirmed repeatedly in the course of the work, the pantheon of powers showcased suggests a world that is certainly dualistic. It reflects deep currents in autochthonous Persian religious and philosophical traditions, expressed notably in the competing structures of Mazdaean and Manichaean dualism. In Ṭabasī's work we read how to perform incantations summoning the "Lady Queen" (*al-sayyida al-malika*), the daughter of the devil, or the Indian demon King Mahākal (i.e., from Sanskrit *mahākāla*, meaning 'great time', one of the epithets for the god Śiva, the Destroyer). Ṭabasī justifies the inclusion of this material by his choice of title, *al-Shāmil*, as his work is meant to be inclusive and all-encompassing.[70]

Needless to say, Ṭabasī's collection of spells does not feature on the website of al-Shāmila, whose name also purports to represent encyclopedic comprehensiveness. As with a good many of the Arabic and Persian writings on magic, alchemy, and astrology, Ṭabasī's book of spells has never even made it to print. Multiple copies of the work are known to exist: notably, a complete manuscript housed in the Staatsbibliothek of Berlin (MS Or. fol. 52) and a fragmentary version located in Princeton University (MS Islamic NS 160). As with other holdings, Berlin can quickly dispatch a digital copy of the manuscript of Ṭabasī's book of spells, or it can be freely downloaded directly from Princeton Library's website of Islamic manuscripts.

All of these sundry examples of exclusion and dispersion point to the intractable difficulties of the digital archive and the serendipitous potential for discovery and reassembly. The abundance is daunting and requires new types of reading. Today, for instance, thousands of manuscripts housed in various archives around Istanbul can be searched and examined through computer terminals in the Süleymaniyye Library. In minutes, reading patterns within Ottoman madrasa education can be brought into view, with a power of cataloguing and indexing that in a previous era would have taken significantly more labor. Readily purchased, these manuscripts can, in turn, be transmitted, duplicated, and shared with a speed unimagined in the age of mechanical reproduction.

Entire manuscript collections are now stored on servers, diligently kept offline, under lock and key, in a replication of the very structures of access and exclusion that historically formed the physical domain of the archive. And like all

---

70 For more on Ṭabasī, see Travis Zadeh, "Commanding Demons and Jinn: The Sorcerer in Early Islamic Thought," in *No Tapping around Philology: A Festschrift in Honor of Wheeler McIntosh Thackston Jr.'s 70th Birthday*, ed. Alireza Korangy and Daniel Sheffield (Wiesbaden: Harrassowitz Verlag, 2014), 144–50; idem, "Magic, Marvel, and Miracle in Early Islamic Thought," in *Cambridge History of Magic and Witchcraft in the West, from Antiquity to the Present*, ed. David Collins (Cambridge: Cambridge University Press, 2015), 251–5.

digital information, such proprietary archives readily await further dissemination, escaping the centripetal forces of centralization that belie the assurance of singular totality. Such quicksilver transmutations from the physical page to the digital replica are all but magical—making something into nothing into everything, nowhere and everywhere. The mercurial fluctuations of the digital condition are what make observing it, in all of its uncertainty, and fixing it in writing so vexing, and yet so promising. As with the kinetic energy of quarks and other subatomic particles that produce their own uncertainty at the very basis of physical matter, these digital sparks and points of confluence can be missing one moment, only to suddenly reappear unannounced, recharged, and transformed the next.

Bibliography

Amir-Moezzi, Mohammad Ali. *The Spirituality of Shiʿi Islam, Beliefs and Practices.* London: I.B. Tauris, 2011.

Asad, Talal. *Formations of the Secular: Christianity, Islam, Modernity.* Stanford, CA: Stanford University Press, 2003.

Asmussen, Jes. *Manichaean Literature: Representative Texts Chiefly from Middle Persian and Parthian Writings.* Delmar, NY: Scholars' Facsimiles and Reprints, 1975.

Assmann, Aleida. "Canon and Archive." In *Cultural Memory Studies: An International and Interdisciplinary Handbook*, ed. Astrid Erll and Ansgar Nünning, 97–107. Berlin: Walter de Gruyter, 2008.

al-Balʿamī, Abū ʿAlī Muḥammad b. Muḥammad. *Tārīkh-nāma-i Ṭabarī.* Ed. Muḥammad Rawshan. 5 vols. Tehran: Surūsh, 1995–99.

Bermejo-Rubio, Fernando. "'I Worship and Glorify': Manichaean Liturgy and Piety in Kellis' Prayer of the Emanations." In *Practicing Gnosis: Ritual, Magic, Theurgy, and Liturgy in Nag Hammadi, Manichaean and other Ancient Literature. Essays in Honor of Birger A. Pearson*, ed. April De Conick et al., 249–70. Leiden: Brill, 2013.

Bibliotheca Geographorum Arabicorum. Ed. Michael Jan de Goeje. 8 vols. Leiden: E.J. Brill, 1870–94.

al-Bīrūnī, Abū l-Rayḥān. *Kitāb āthār al-bāqiya ʿan al-qurūn al-khāliya.* Ed. C. Eduard Sachau. Leipzig: F.A. Brockhaus, 1878.

Bloom, Jonathan. *Paper Before Print: The History and Impact of Paper in the Islamic World.* New Haven: Yale University Press, 2001.

The Book of Curiosities. See *Kitāb Gharāʾib al-funūn.*

Boyce, Mary. *A Reader in Manichaean Middle Persian and Parthian.* Leiden: E.J. Brill, 1975.

Bulliet, Richard. "Conversion to Islam and the Emergence of a Muslim Society in Iran." In *Conversion to Islam*, ed. Nehemia Levtzion, 30–51. New York: Holmes and Meier, 1979.

—. *Conversion to Islam in the Medieval Period: An Essay in Quantitative History.* Cambridge, MA: Harvard University Press, 1979.

Buzzetti, Dino, and Jerome McGann. "Critical Editing in a Digital Horizon." In *Electronic Textual Editing*, ed. Lou Burnard, Katherine O'Brien O'Keeffe, and John Unsworth, 51–71. New York: Modern Language Association, 2006.

Chokr, Melhem. *Zandaqa et zindiqs en Islam au second siècle de l'hégire*. Damascus: L'Institut Français d'études arabes de Damas, 1993.

Choksy, Jamsheed. "Zoroastrians in Muslim Iran: Selected Problems of Coexistence and Interaction during the Early Medieval Period." *Iranian Studies* 20 no. 1 (1987): 17–30.

Cook, Michael. "Pharaonic History in Medieval Egypt." *Studia Islamica* 57 (1983): 67–103.

Crow, Karim Douglas. "The 'Five Limbs' of the Soul: A Manichaean Motif in Muslim Garb?" In *Reason and Inspiration in Islam: Theology, Philosophy and Mysticism in Muslim Thought. Essays in Honour of Hermann Landolt*, ed. Todd Lawson, 19–33. London: I.B. Tauris, 2005.

Daniel, Elton. "Manuscripts and Editions of Balʿamī's *Tarjamah-i Tārīkh-i Ṭabarī*." *Journal of the Royal Asiatic Society of Great Britain and Ireland* 2 (1990): 282–321.

Derrida, Jacques. *Dissemination*. Trans. Barbara Johnson. London: Athlone Press, 1981.

Durkin-Meisterernst, Desmond. "Manichean Script." *Encyclopædia Iranica*, online edition. New York, 1996–. Available at: http://www.iranicaonline.org/articles/manichean-script. Accessed 27 May 2015.

An Eleventh-Century Egyptian Guide to the Universe. See *Kitāb Gharāʾib al-funūn*.

Elias, Jamal. *Aisha's Cushion: Religious Art, Perception, and Practice in Islam*. Cambridge, MA: Harvard University Press, 2012.

al-Fārisī, Abū Ḥasan ʿAbd al-Ghāfir b. Ismāʿīl. *Tārīkh Nīshābūr, al-ḥalqa al-ūlā min al-Muntakhab min al-siyāq*. Ed. Muḥammad Kāẓim al-Maḥmūdī. Qom: Jamāʿat al-Mudarrisīn, 1403/1983.

Flügel, Gustav. *Mani, seine lehre und seine schriften; ein beitrag zur geschichte des Manichäismus*. Leipzig: F.A. Brockhaus, 1862.

Fodor, Alexander. "The Origins of the Arabic Legends of the Pyramids." *Acta orientalia academiae scientiarum hungaricae* 23 no. 3 (1970): 335–63.

Fowden, Garth. *The Egyptian Hermes: A Historical Approach to the Late Pagan Mind*. Princeton, NJ: Princeton University Press, 1993.

Frye, Richard. "Comparative Observations on Conversion to Islam in Iran and Central Asia." *Jerusalem Studies in Arabic and Islam* 4 (1984): 81–88.

Fück, Johann. "The Arabic Literature on Alchemy According to an-Nadīm (A.D. 987). A Translation of the Tenth Discourse of *The Book of the Catalogue* (*al-Fihrist*) with Introduction and Commentary." *Ambix* 4 no. 3/4 (1951): 81–144.

Gacek, Adam. *Arabic Manuscripts: A Vademecum for Readers*. Leiden: Brill, 2009.

Gardner, Iain. *The Kephalaia of the Teacher. The Edited Coptic Manichaean Texts in Translation with Commentary*. Leiden: E.J. Brill, 1995.

Gardner, Iain, and Samuel Nan-Chiang Lieu. "From Narmouthis (Medinet Madi) to Kellis (Ismant el-Kharab): Manichaean Documents from Roman Egypt." *Journal of Roman Studies* 86 (1996): 146–69.

—. eds. *Manichaean Texts from the Roman Empire*. Cambridge: Cambridge University Press, 2004.

Ghamari-Tabrizi, Behrooz. "Is Islamic Science Possible?" *Social Epistemology* 10 no. 2/3 (1996): 317–30.

Glassé, Cyril. "How We Know the Exact Year the Archegos Left Baghdad." In *New Light on Manichaeism: Papers from the Sixth International Congress on Manichaeism*, ed. Jason David BeDuhn, 129–44. Leiden: Brill, 2009.

Green, Nile. "Journeymen, Middlemen: Travel, Transculture, and Technology in the Origins of Muslim Printing." *International Journal of Middle East Studies* 41 no. 2 (2009): 203–24

Greetham, David. "Phylum-Tree-Rhizome." *Huntington Library Quarterly* 58 no. 1 (1995): 99–126.

Gutas, Dimitri. *Greek Thought, Arabic Culture. The Graeco-Arabic Translation Movement in Baghdad and Early ʿAbbāsid Society (2nd–4th/8th–10th centuries)*. London: Routledge, 1998.

al-Ḥaddādī, Abū l-Naṣr. *al-Madkhal li-ʿilm tafsīr Kitāb Allāh taʿālā*, ed. Ṣafwān ʿAdnān Dāwūdī. Damascus: Dār al-Qalam, 1988.

Ḥāʾirī, Muḥammad ʿImādī. *Kuhantarīn nuskha-i mutarjam-i Qurʾān: taḥlīl-i matn, bar rasī-i dastniwisht, zībāyī-shināsī-i hunar-i qudsī*. Tehran: Mīrāth-i Maktūb, 1389/2010.

—. "Muqaddima." In *al-Mujallad al-thāmin min maʿānī kitāb Allāh taʿālā wa-tafsīruhu al-munīr*, ed. Muḥammad ʿImādī Ḥāʾirī. Facsimile edition of EH 209 held in the Topkapı Sarayı Müzesi Kütüphane, 9–41. Tehran: Kitābkhāna, Mūzih wa-Markaz-i Asnād-i Majlis-i Shūrā-yi Islāmī, 1390/2011.

Ḥājjī Khalīfa, Muṣṭafā b. ʿAbdallāh. *Kashf al-ẓunūn ʿan asāmī al-kutub wa-l-funūn*, ed. Muḥammad Sharaf al-Dīn Yāltaqāyā and Rifʿat Bīlga al-Kilīsī. 2 vols. Istanbul: Maṭābiʿ Wikālat al-Maʿārif al-Jalīla, 1941.

Hämeen-Anttila, Jaakko. *The Last Pagans of Iraq: Ibn Waḥshiyya and His Nabatean Agriculture*. Leiden: Brill, 2006.

Harley, John Brian, and David Woodward, eds. *Cartography in the Traditional Islamic and South Asian Societies*. In *History of Cartography*. Chicago: University of Chicago Press, 1992.

Hodgson, Marshall. *The Venture of Islam*. 3 vols. Chicago: University of Chicago Press, 1974.

Ibn ʿAsākir. *Tabyīn kadhib al-muftarī fī-mā nusiba ilā l-imām Abī l-Ḥasan al-Ashʿarī*. Damascus: Maṭbaʿat al-Tawfīq, 1347/1928–29.

Ibn al-Faqīh. *Kitāb al-Buldān*. Ed. Yūsuf al-Hādī. Beirut: ʿĀlam al-Kutub, 1996.

Ibn Ḥawqal. *Kitāb Ṣūrat al-arḍ*. Ed. J. H. Kramers. 2 vols. Leiden: E.J. Brill, 1938–39.

Ibn Manẓūr. *Lisān al-ʿArab*. Beirut: Dār al-Ṣādir, n.d.

Ibn al-Nadīm. *Kitāb al-Fihrist*. Ed. Ayman Fuʾād Sayyid. 4 vols in 2. London: Al-Furqan Islamic Heritage Foundation, 2009.

Ibn Taymiyya. *Iqtiḍāʾ al-ṣirāṭ al-mustaqīm li-mukhālafat aṣḥāb al-jaḥīm*. Ed. Nāṣir b. ʿAbd al-Karīm al-ʿAql. 2 vols. Riyadh: Dār al-ʿĀṣima, 1998.

Ibn Waḥshiyya, ascribed. *Shawq al-mustahām fī maʿrifat rumūz al-aqlām = Ancient Alphabets and Hieroglyphic Characters Explained*. Ed. and partial trans. Joseph Hammer-Purgstall. London: W. Bulmer and Co., 1806.

al-Idrīsī, Abū ʿAbdallāh. *Opus geographicum = Nuzhat al-mushtāq fī ikhtirāq al-āfāq*. Ed. E. Cerulli et al. 9 fascicules. Naples and Rome: Istituto Universitario Orientale, 1970–84.

—. *La géographie d'Idrisi: un atlas du monde au XIIe siècle*. Ed. Annie Vernay-Nouri et al. CD-ROM. Paris: Bibliothèque nationale de France, Montparnasse multimédia, 2000.

al-Isfarāʾīnī, Shāhfūr b. Ṭāhir. *Tāj al-tarājim fī tafsīr al-Qurʾān li'l-aʿājim*. Ed. Najīb Māyil Harawī and ʿAlī Akbar Ilāhī Khurāsānī, partial edition. 3 vols. Tehran: Shirkat-i Intishārāt-i ʿIlmī wa-Farhangī, 1375 Sh./1996.

al-Iṣlāḥī, Muḥammad Ajmal Ayyūb. "A-hādhā *Kitāb al-muwaḍḍiḥ li-ʿilm al-Qurʾān* li'l-Ḥaddādī?" In *Buḥūth wa-maqālāt fī l-lugha wa-l-adab wa-taqwīm al-nuṣūṣ*, 359–69. Beirut: Dār al-Gharb al-Islāmī, 2007.
al-Iṣṭakhrī, Abū Isḥāq. *al-Masālik wa-l-mamālik*. Ed. Muḥammad Jābir ʿAbd al-ʿĀl al-Ḥīnī. Cairo: Dār al-Qalam, 1961.
John, Jeremy, and Emilie Savage-Smith. "*The Book of Curiosities*: A Newly Discovered Series of Islamic Maps." *Imago Mundi* 55 no. 1 (2003): 7–24.
Karame, Alya, and Travis Zadeh. "The Art of Translation: An Early Persian Commentary of the Qur'an." *Journal of Abbasid Studies* 2 no. 2 (2015): 119–95.
Kessler, Konrad. *Mani. Forschungen über die manichäische Religion*. Berlin: Georg Reimer, 1889.
Kia, Mehrdad. "Persian Nationalism and the Campaign for Language Purification." *Middle Eastern Studies* 34 no. 2 (1998): 9–36.
Kitāb Gharāʾib al-funūn wa-mulaḥ al-ʿuyūn = The Book of Curiosities: A Critical Edition. Ed. Emilie Savage-Smith and Yossef Rapoport, http://www.bodley.ox.ac.uk/bookofcuriosities (March 2007); *An Eleventh-Century Egyptian Guide to the Universe: The Book of Curiosities*. Ed. and trans. Emilie Savage-Smith and Yossef Rapoport. Leiden: Brill, 2014.
Latour, Bruno. *Reassembling the Social: An Introduction to Actor-Network-Theory*. Oxford: Oxford University Press, 2005.
Lieu, Samuel Nan-Chiang. *Manichaeism in the Later Roman Empire and Medieval China*. Second revised and expanded edition. Tübingen: J.C.B. Mohr, 1992.
Lincoln, Bruce. *Theorizing Myth: Narrative, Ideology, and Scholarship*. Chicago: University of Chicago Press, 1999.
Maʿānī, Aḥmad Gulchīn. "Shāhkārhā-yi hunarī-i shigift-i angīzī az qarn-i panjum hijrī wa-sar *gudhasht-i ḥayrat-āwar-i ān*." *Hunar wa-mardum* 157 (1354 Sh./1975): 45–65.
Miller, Konrad. *Mappae Arabicae: arabische Welt- und Länderkarten des 9.–13. Jahrhunderts in arabischer Urschrift*. 6 vols. Stuttgart: Selbstverlag des Herausgebers, 1926–31.
Morony, Michael. "The Age of Conversions: A Reassessment." In *Conversion and Continuity: Indigenous Christian Communities in Islamic Lands, Eighth to Eighteenth Centuries*, ed. Michael Gervers and Ramzi Jibran Bikhazi, 135–50. Toronto: Pontifical Institute of Mediaeval Studies, 1990.
Mottahedeh, Roy. "Review of R.W. Bulliet, *The Patricians of Nishapur*." *Journal of the American Oriental Society* 95 no. 3 (1975): 491–5.
Nawas, John. "A Profile of the *Mawālī ʿUlamāʾ*." In *Patronate and Patronage in Early and Classical Islam*, ed. Monique Bernards and John Nawas, 454–80. Leiden: Brill, 2005.
Peacock, Andrew. *Mediaeval Islamic Historiography and Political Legitimacy, Balʿamī's Tārīkhnāma*. London: Routledge, 2007.
Pettigrew, Mark Fraser. "The Wonders of the Ancients: Arab-Islamic Representations of Ancient Egypt." Ph.D. dissertation, University of California, Berkeley, 2004.
Qudāma b. Jaʿfar. *Kitāb al-kharāj wa-ṣināʿat al-kitāba*. Ed. Muḥammad Ḥusayn al-Zubaydī. Baghdad: Dār al-Rashīd, 1981.
Riedel, Dagmar A. "Of Making Many Copies There is No End: The Digitization of Manuscripts and Printed Books in Arabic Script." In *The Digital Humanities and Islamic & Middle East Studies*, ed. Elias Muhanna, 65–91. Berlin: De Gruyter, 2016.

Reinhart, A. Kevin. "Fundamentalism and the Transparency of the Arabic Qur'an." In *Rethinking Islamic Studies: From Orientalism to Cosmopolitanism*, ed. Carl Ernst and Richard Martin, 97–113. Columbia: University of South Carolina Press, 2010.
Robinson, James. "The Fate of the Manichaean Codices of Medinet Madi 1929–1989." In *Studia Manichaica: II. Internationaler Kongress zum Manichäismus*, ed. Gernot Wießner and Hans-Joachim Klimkeit, 19–62. Wiesbaden: O. Harrassowitz, 1992.
Roper, Geoffrey. "The Printing Press and Change in the Arab World." In *Agent of Change: Print Culture Studies after Elizabeth L. Eisenstein*, ed. Eric Lindquist, Sabrina Alcorn Baron, and Eleanor Shevlin, 250–67. Boston: University of Massachusetts Press, 2007.
Rosenthal, Franz. "'Life is Short, The Art is Long': Arabic Commentaries on the First Hippocratic Aphorism." *Bulletin of the History of Medicine* 40 no. 1 (1966): 226–45.
Sabra, Abdelhamid I. "The Appropriation and Subsequent Naturalization of Greek Science in Medieval Islam: A Preliminary Statement." *History of Science* 25 no. 3 (1987): 223–43.
al-Samʿānī, Abū Saʿd ʿAbd al-Karīm. *al-Ansāb*. Ed. Akram al-Būshī et al. 12 vols. Cairo: Maktabat Ibn Taymiyya, 1976–84.
Schoeler, Gregor. *The Oral and Written in Early Islam*. Ed. James E. Montgomery. Trans. Uwe Vagelpohl. London: Routledge, 2006.
Skjærvø, Prods Oktor. "Aramaic Scripts for Iranian Languages." In *The World's Writing Systems*, ed. Peter Daniels and William Bright, 515–35. Oxford: Oxford University Press, 1996.
Spiegel, Friedrich. *Erânische Alterthumskunde*. 3 vols. Leipzig: Von Wilhelm Engelmann, 1871–8.
Stewart, Devin. "The Structure of the *Fihrist:* Ibn al-Nadim as Historian of Islamic Legal and Theological Schools." *International Journal of Middle East Studies* 39 no. 3 (2007): 369–87.
Stroumsa, Sarah. *Freethinkers of Medieval Islam: Ibn al-Rawāndī, Abū Bakr al-Rāzī and Their Impact on Islamic Thought*. Leiden: Brill, 1999.
al-Subkī, ʿAbd al-Wahhāb b. ʿAlī. *Ṭabaqāt al-shāfiʿiyya al-kubrā*. Ed. Maḥmūd Muḥammad al-Ṭanāḥī and ʿAbd al-Fattāḥ Muḥammad al-Ḥilw. 10 vols. Cairo: ʿĪsā al-Bābī al-Ḥalabī, 1964–76.
Sundermann, Werner. *Mitteliranische manichäische Texte kirchengeschichtlichen Inhalts (Berliner Turfantexte XI)*. Berlin: Akademie-Verlag, 1981.
Tavakoli-Targhi, Mohamad. "Refashioning Iran: Language and Culture during the Constitutional Revolution." *Iranian Studies* 23 no. 1/4 (1990): 77–101.
Thomas, David. *Early Muslim Polemic against Christianity. Abū ʿĪsā al-Warrāq's 'Against the Incarnation.'* Cambridge: Cambridge University Press, 2002.
Toorawa, Shawkat. *Ibn Abī Ṭāhir Ṭayfūr and Arabic Writerly Culture: A Ninth-Century Bookman in Baghdad*. London: Routledge, 2005.
—. "Proximity, Resemblance, Sidebars and Clusters: Ibn al-Nadīm's Organizational Principles in *Fihrist* 3.3." *Oriens* 38 (2010): 217–47.
van Bladel, Kevin. *The Arabic Hermes, From Pagan Sage to Prophet of Science*. Oxford: Oxford University Press, 2009.
Witkam, Jan Just. "Establishing the Stemma: Fact or Fiction?" *Manuscripts of the Middle East* 3 (1988): 88–101.

Yücesoy, Hayrettın. "Translation as Self-Consciousness: Ancient Sciences, Antediluvian Wisdom, and the 'Abbāsid Translation Movement." *Journal of World History* 20 no. 4 (2009): 523–57.

Zadeh, Travis. "Commanding Demons and Jinn: The Sorcerer in Early Islamic Thought." In *No Tapping around Philology: A Festschrift in Honor of Wheeler McIntosh Thackston Jr.'s 70th Birthday*, ed. Alireza Korangy and Daniel Sheffield, 131–60. Wiesbaden: Harrassowitz Verlag, 2014.

—. "The *Fātiḥa* of Salmān al-Fārisī and the Modern Controversy over Translating the Qurʾān." In *The Meaning of the Word: Lexicology and Tafsir*, ed. Stephen Burge, 375–420. Oxford: Oxford University Press, 2015.

—. "Magic, Marvel, and Miracle in Early Islamic Thought." In *Cambridge History of Magic and Witchcraft in the West, from Antiquity to the Present*, ed. David Collins, 235–67. Cambridge: Cambridge University Press, 2015.

— "Of Mummies, Poets, and Water Nymphs: Tracing the Codicological Limits of Ibn Khurradādhbih's Geography." In *Abbasid Studies IV*, ed. Monique Bernards, 8–75. Exeter: Short Run Press, 2013.

—. *The Vernacular Qurʾan: Translation and the Rise of Persian Exegesis*. Oxford: Oxford University Press, 2012.

Zakkār, Muʿtaṣim. "Istiʿmāl taknūlūjīyā l-maʿlūmāt fī istikshāf wa-nashr al-turāth al-ʿarabī," *al-Taqrīr al-khatāmī al-Nadwa al-iqlīmiyya ḥawl "tawẓīf taqniyāt al-maʿlūmāt wa-l-ittiṣālāt fī l-taʿlīm ʿan buʿd (maʿ al-tarkīz ʿalā l-muḥtawā l-ʿarabī ʿalā shabakat al-intarnat* (July 15–17, 2003)." http://www.ituarabic.org/PreviousEvents/2003/E-Education/Doc8-alwaraq.doc

Dagmar Riedel

Of Making Many Copies There is No End: The Digitization of Manuscripts and Printed Books in Arabic Script[1]

> "The invisibility of the medium makes its use instrumental and decreases the fascination with technology."
>
> Marija Dalbello, "A Genealogy of Digital Humanities"

> "Ever since the fifteenth century those who have made facsimiles have been at pains to stress how close they are to their models. The claims of modern e-publishing are not new."
>
> David McKitterick, *Old Books, New Technologies*

The digitization of manuscripts and printed books occurs in a wide range of socio-economic and political contexts. In the following, I will use the distinction between "physical book" and "written text" to highlight the difference between the material artifact and its literary content. While a book's physicality is immediately experienced whenever we open a manuscript or printed book, the materiality of an e-book is primarily noticed whenever a reading device indicates that there is no storage space left for saving yet another digital file. The most common application of digitization remains the commercial and not-for-profit publication of written texts that were not "born-digital" as e-books. This application aims at facilitating access to literary content by creating a digital copy of a written text.[2]

A decade after the announcement of "Google Print" at the Frankfurt Book Fair and the launch of the "Google Books Library Project" in the US, electronic texts are no longer experienced as novel or strange,[3] even though many readers

---

1 This essay is a revised version of the paper "Manuscripts and Printed Books in Arabic Script in the Age of the e-Book: The Challenges of Digitization," presented on 23 October 2013 at the symposium on Digital Humanities and Islamic and Middle East Studies at Brown University. I am much indebted to Karin Hörner, Jane R. Siegel, and Elias Muhanna for their insightful comments on the essay's first version. All errors are mine.

2 With regard to the digitization of Arabic literature, the most recent project is NYU's Arabic Collections Online, which offers a digital library of public-domain Arabic-language content at: http://dlib.nyu.edu/aco/.

3 Wendy Hui Kyong Chun and Lisa Marie Rhody, "Working the Digital Humanities: Uncovering Shadows between the Dark and the Light," *differences: A Journal of Feminist Cultural Studies* 25 no. 1 (2014): "unless there is a core contingent of faculty who continue to distribute their work in typed manuscripts and consult print indexes of periodicals that I don't know about, everyone is already a digital humanist" (9); cf. Hubertus Kohle, *Digitale Bildwissenschaft* (Glückstadt: Verlag Werner Hülsbusch, 2013), 9.

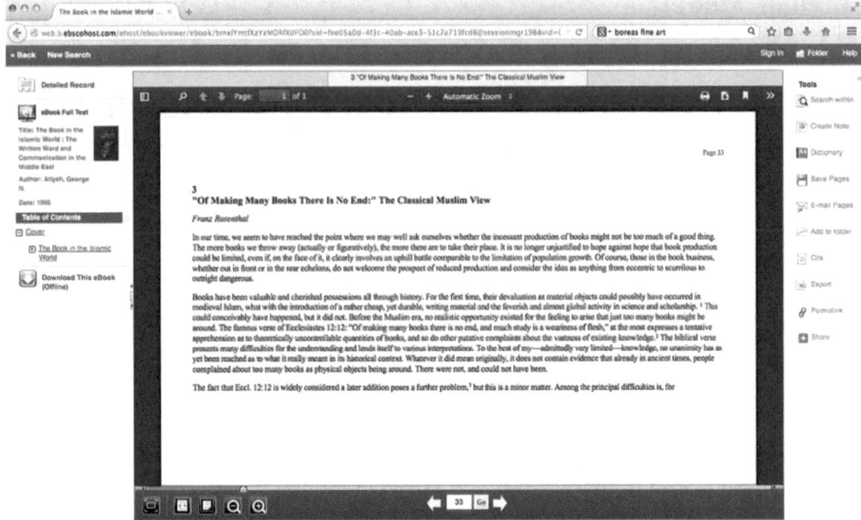

Page 33

3
"Of Making Many Books There Is No End:" The Classical Muslim View

Franz Rosenthal

In our time, we seem to have reached the point where we may well ask ourselves whether the incessant production of books might not be too much of a good thing. The more books we throw away (actually or figuratively), the more there are to take their place. It is no longer unjustified to hope against hope that book production could be limited, even if, on the face of it, it clearly involves an uphill battle comparable to the limitation of population growth. Of course, those in the book business, whether out in front or in the rear echelons, do not welcome the prospect of reduced production and consider the idea as anything from eccentric to scurrilous to outright dangerous.

Books have been valuable and cherished possessions all through history. For the first time, their devaluation as material objects could possibly have occurred in medieval Islam, what with the introduction of a rather cheap, yet durable, writing material and the feverish and almost global activity in science and scholarship. [1] This could conceivably have happened, but it did not. Before the Muslim era, no realistic opportunity existed for the feeling to arise that just too many books might be around. The famous verse of Ecclesiastes 12:12: "Of making many books there is no end, and much study is a weariness of flesh," at the most expresses a tentative apprehension as to theoretically uncontrollable quantities of books, and so do other putative complaints about the vastness of existing knowledge.[2] The biblical verse presents many difficulties for the understanding and lends itself to various interpretations. To the best of my—admittedly very limited—knowledge, no unanimity has as yet been reached as to what it really meant in its historical context. Whatever it did mean originally, it does not contain evidence that already in ancient times, people complained about too many books as physical objects being around. There were not, and could not have been.

The fact that Eccl. 12:12 is widely considered a later addition poses a further problem,[3] but this is a minor matter. Among the principal difficulties is, for

Figure 3.1. *The Book in the Islamic World*, ed. George Atiyeh (Washington: Library of Congress, 1995), 33. Viewed on EBSCOhost (screenshot, 21 January 2015).

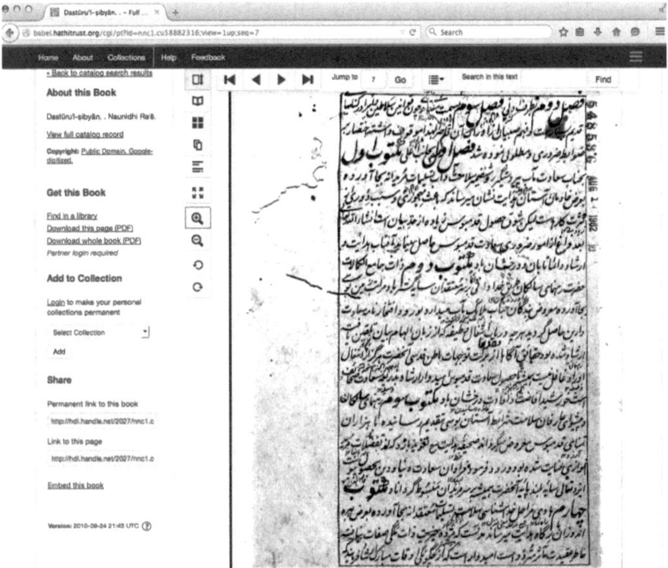

Figure 3.2. Naunidhi Raʾē, *Dastūr al-ṣibyān* ([Lucknow]: Maṭbaʿ-i Ḥasanī 1261/1845), 3. Persian lithographed pamphlet, paper, no measurements provided. From the library of Saʿīd Nafīsī (1895–1966). Rare Book and Manuscript Library of Columbia University, 892.84 N225. Viewed in the HathiTrust Digital Library (screenshot, 29 January 2015).

report that, if at all possible, they still prefer the tangibility of physical books for the reading of monographs.[4] But manuscripts and printed books are also digitized in order to create digital surrogates of physical books as material artifacts.

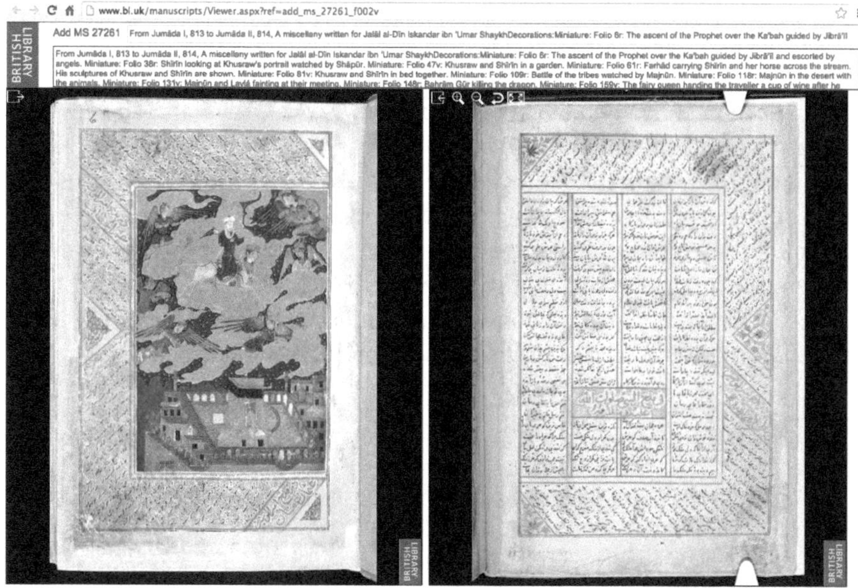

Figure 3.3. Miscellany of 23 literary works, fols. 6a and 6b. MS pers., paper, 18.4 x 12.7 cm. Compiled for Sulṭān Jalāl al-Dīn Iskandar b. ʿUmar Shaykh, a grandson of Timur and ruler of Fārs, between 813/1410 and 814/1411. British Library, Add MS 27261. Viewed in the British Library's collection of Digitised Manuscripts (screenshot, 21 January 2015).

These digital surrogates preserve not only the originals' literary content, but they also show, as far as possible in two-dimensional images, the originals' physical evidence and paratexts, both of which document the historical circumstances of the originals' manufacture, ownership, and use.[5] The different appli-

4 Roger C. Schonfield, "Stop the Presses: Is the Monograph Headed toward an E-only Future?" issue brief, Ithaka S+R, 10 December 2013, 5 n. 10, available at: http://sr.ithaka.org/sites/default/files/files/SR_BriefingPaper_Presses_120913.pdf

5 For the digitization of Islamic art, see for example the Yousef Jameel Projekt at the Museum für Islamische Kunst in Berlin, which is accompanied by a blog: http://jameel.hypotheses.org/; the digital surrogates are accessible via the database SMB-digital: http://www.smb-digital.de/eMuseumPlus. For a reflection on how the experience and understanding of three-dimensional mobile objects—that is, books—is changed, when they are accessed as a series of two-dimensional digital scans, see David McKitterick, *Old Books, New Technologies: The Representation,*

cations of digitization cannot be strictly separated from each other. For example, digitally published critical editions and facsimiles are instances of e-book production in the service of textual scholarship and preservation.[6] While the technology itself has become invisible with regard to the reading of written texts via e-books, the materiality of which is now studied by book historians,[7] digitization creates distance and marks discontinuity whenever the technology is employed to transform written texts and physical books into digital files in order to enable the application of computational research methods. For example, scholars need digitized manuscripts and printed books in order to employ digital paleography, text mining, or distance reading in their research.

A critical reflection on the digitization of manuscripts and printed books in Arabic script has to begin with the fact that neither book history nor the digital humanities (DH) are well-established subfields in Middle Eastern and Islamic studies.[8] The recent material turn in the humanities[9] has generated a growing interest in the cultural history of the manuscript book in Muslim societies,[10] and

Conservation and Transformation of Books since 1700 (Cambridge: Cambridge University Press, 2013), 1–26.

6 See, for example, Eva Mroczek, "Thinking Digitally about the Dead Sea Scrolls: Book History before and beyond the Book," *Book History* 14 (2011): 241–69.

7 See, for example, Alex Galey, "The Enkindling Reciter: E-Books in the Bibliographical Imagination," *Book History* 15 (2012): 211–47.

8 The 48th meeting of the Middle East Studies Association of North America (MESA), held from 22–25 November 2014 in Washington, DC, offers a representative case study. Ranjit Singh organized panel 009 on Social Media and the Arab Spring, while panel 016, organized by Sharon C. Smith and Sean E. Swanick, was dedicated to the politics of digitization, and panel 080, organized by Rebecca L. Stein, explored the digitization of analogue photographs vis à vis current practices in digital photography. With regard to book history, panel 123 offered John Curry's roundtable on the publishing of a new sourcebook of medieval Middle East history, and panel 216 was organized by Kathryn Schwartz under the auspices of the Society for the History of Authorship, Reading and Publishing (SHARP). Yet events such as a Wikipedia Write-In or a THATCamp (http://thatcamp.org) did not take place in conjunction with the meeting. Even though this was the first MESA conference with a dedicated twitter hashtag (#MESA2014DC), conference tweeting was largely limited to announcements.

9 For an early reflection on the current popularity of material history, see Leora Auslander, Amy Bentley, Leor Halevi, H. Otto Sibum, and Christopher Whitmore, "AHR Conversation: Historians and the Study of Material Culture," *American Historical Review* 114 no. 5 (2009): 1354–1404.

10 For representative studies of book cultures in pre-modern Muslim societies, see Antonella Ghersetti, ed., *The Book in Fact and Fiction in Pre-Modern Arabic Literature*, special issue, *Journal of Arabic and Islamic Studies* 12 (2012); Nelly Hanna, *In Praise of Books: A Cultural History of Cairo's Middle Class, Sixteenth to the Eighteenth Century* (Cairo: American University in Cairo Press, 2003); Konrad Hirschler, *The Written Word in the Medieval Arabic Lands: A Social and Cul-*

scholars of Middle Eastern and Islamic studies write influential blogs and maintain popular social media accounts on platforms such as Facebook and Twitter. The extent to which electronic word processing has impacted book production in the Middle East and North Africa can be gauged from the lavish appendices that have become a distinctive feature of academic books published, for example, in Egypt, Lebanon, and Iran. Considering the amazing power of relatively straightforward full-text search engines for text files, it is now customary to find in printed scholarly books, which presses often also issue as PDF files, computer-generated indices for personal names, tribal names, place names, Quran verses, first lines of classical poetry, and so forth. But the available public information about digitization projects for material in Arabic script tends to be praise that foregrounds the number of pages newly digitized.[11] The focus on countable, though not always comparable, units probably reflects the pressure of sponsors and grant-making agencies that need concrete outcomes in order to justify their funding decisions. The impact of digitization on the preservation of cultural heritage in Muslim societies[12] or its interaction with commercial publishing in Arabic script in Africa[13] and Eurasia remains to be studied. Nor has digitization been applied to research challenges, such as the paleography[14] of the Arabic script and the deciphering and analysis of illegible written texts.[15] In general, scholars in Middle Eastern and Islamic studies encounter digitization as an excellent tool

---

tural History of Reading Practices (Edinburgh: Edinburgh University Press, 2012); and Houari Touati, *L'armoire à sagesse: Bibliothèques et collections en Islam* (Paris: Aubier, 2003).

11 Typical recent examples include: Richard Davies, "Revealing Gulf History Online," *British Library: Living Knowledge Blog*, 2 December 2014, available at: http://britishlibrary.typepad.co.uk/living-knowledge/2014/12/revealing-gulf-history-online.html; and Ursula Sims-Williams, "15,000 Images of Persian Manuscripts Online," *British Library: Asian and African Studies Blog*, 27 January 2014, available at: http://britishlibrary.typepad.co.uk/asian-and-african/2014/01/15000-images-of-persian-manuscripts-online.html.

12 Marilyn Deegan and Simon Tanner, "Conversion of Primary Sources," in *A Companion to the Digital Humanities*, eds. Susan Schreibman, Ray Siemens, and John Unsworth (Malden, MA: Blackwell, 2004), 488–504.

13 Digitization is not mentioned by Elizabeth le Roux, "Book History in the African World," *Book History* 15 (2012): 248–300.

14 For medieval French paleography, see Marc H. Smith, "Numérisation et paléographie," *Le médiéviste et l'ordinateur* 40 (Fall 2001): 9–16; available at: http://lemo.irht.cnrs.fr/40/mo40-03.htm#P180_31761.

15 See, for example, these prominent examples in the field of classics: Melissa M. Terras, *Image to Interpretation: An Intelligent System to Aid Historians in Reading the Vindolanda Texts* (Oxford: Oxford University Press, 2006); Reviel Netz, William Noel, Nigel Wilson, and Natalie Tchernetska, eds., *The Archimedes Palimpsest* (2 vols., Cambridge: Walters Art Museum, 2011).

for facilitating access to literary content.[16] We are dismayed if our sources are not yet conveniently available as digital surrogates, as it is now *de rigeur* that our research monographs are published as printed hardcovers for tenure and promotion as well as in an electronic format with full-text search for ease of access and an affordable print-on-demand (POD) option for wider circulation.[17]

I find it striking that there seems to be no expectation that in Middle Eastern and Islamic studies we should get up close and personal with the challenges posed by digitization with regard to the field's research infrastructure. Even though our grasp of the current situation will determine how we interact with both the underlying digital technology[18] and the resulting digital surrogates in the future,[19] we do not debate among ourselves which books and texts should be digitized, how long-term accessibility to their digital surrogates can be maintained, and for whom.[20] In order to better understand why we have so far preferred the role of consumers of e-books, electronic texts, or digital surrogates, I will first explore the relationship between writing and digitization, and then examine that between digitization and DH. The essay will conclude with reflections on

---

16 Birte Kristiansen, "Digital Resources in Middle Eastern Studies," *Bibliotheca Orientalis* 71 nos. 3–4 (2014): cols. 388–400; and Ronald E. Kon, "Some Digital Resources for the Study of the Middle East," *Bibliotheca Orientalis* 71 nos. 3–4 (2014): cols. 400–403; the Netherlands Institute for the Near East has made this issue of *Bibliotheca Orientalis* available OA at: http://www.nino-leiden.nl.

17 Brill's MyBook program offers moderately priced Open-Access (OA) copies of all hardcover books available via BrillOnline to those who are affiliated with an institution that subscribes to BrillOnline.

18 For the current debate among digital humanists on the relationship between DH and the humanities, see, for example, Chun and Rhody, "Working the Digital Humanities," 1–25; Domenico Fiormonte, "Digital Humanities from a Global Perspective," *Laboratorio dell'ISPF* 11 (2014), DOI: 10.12862/ispf14L203; and Alan Liu, "What is the Meaning of the Digital Humanities to the Humanities?" *Proceedings of the Modern Language Association of America* 128 no. 2 (2013): 409–23.

19 For early reflections on the impact of digital surrogates and born-digital editions on the study of English literature, see Jerome McGann, *Radiant Textuality: Literature after the World Wide Web* (New York: Palgrave, 2001), 53–74. For an early exploration of the potential of digital reference works, see Alex Brymer Humphreys, "The Past, Present, and Future of Immersive and Extractive Ebooks," in *Digital Media: Transformations in Human Communication*, eds. Paul Messaris and Lee Humphreys (New York: Peter Lang, 2006), 159–72; a December 2004 version is available through the Social Science Research Network at: http://ssrn.com/abstract=1300567.

20 At the above-mentioned MESA panel on the politics of digitization, participants explored the curious lack of critical scholarly involvement with digitization projects; for a panel description and the abstracts, see https://mesana.org/mymesa/meeting_program_session.php?sid=e8557feb4e6e066a468dee5c17026fe8. I am grateful to Sean E. Swanick for sharing with me his paper on "The Politics of Digitization: Islamic Materials and Digital Divide."

how to improve our engagement with digital surrogates, as it seems that, for the time being, digitization will remain the dominant technology for the copying of written texts.

My starting point is the observation that Islamic traditions of the transmission of knowledge favor a textual pragmatism that privileges the written text over the physical book. Despite the intense reliance on writing and literacy in all pre-modern Muslim societies, the ideal form of communication remained the personal encounter among human beings.[21] From this perspective, the materiality of the physical book is secondary to the written word, which, in turn, is secondary to the spoken word.[22] It is one of the consequences of textual pragmatism that it separates the written text from the physical book in order to focus on literary content while deflecting attention away from the physical books and the nitty-gritty economics of their manufacture, distribution, and maintenance. Since scholarship in Middle Eastern and Islamic studies cannot but reflect the intellectual traditions of Islamic civilization, textual pragmatism continues to dominate the field's textual scholarship in the early twenty-first century. The Muslim Middle East is praised as "one of the most bookish of pre-modern cultures,"[23] and Islamic manuscripts are regarded as the most important resource for research on all aspects of Islamic civilization. The display of Islamic book culture in public exhibitions and the like is dominated by beautiful manuscripts from high-end workshops,[24] even though Muslim societies had thriving book markets for middle-brow audiences, and the arts of the Islamic book also flourished with regard to the commercial manufacture of cheap books, whether their content was religious or secular. Yet research on physical books

---

21 Franz Rosenthal, "'Of Making Books There is No End': The Classical Muslim View," in *The Book in the Islamic World: The Written Word and Communication in the Middle East*, ed. George N. Atiyeh (Washington, DC: Library of Congress, 1995)": "the never abandoned fiction [...] of the primacy of the spoken word" (35–36).

22 The understanding that books are surrogates of speech is not unique to Islamic civilization; see also Donald F. McKenzie, *Making Meaning: "Printers of the Mind" and Other Essays*, eds. Peter D. McDonald and Michael F. Suarez (Amherst: University of Massachusetts Press, 2002): "a phrase like 'the impact of print'—however carefully it is qualified—cannot help but imply a major displacement of writing as a form of record. In the same way, too great a preoccupation with writing and printing (as the technologies of literacy) may lead us to forget the superior virtues of speech. After all, we did not stop speaking when we learned to write, nor writing when we learned to print, nor reading, writing or printing when we entered the 'electronic age'." (238).

23 Walid A. Saleh, *The Formation of the Classical Tafsīr Tradition: The Qur'ān Commentary of al-Tha'labī (d. 427/1035)* (Leiden: Brill, 2004), 207.

24 The elite status of high-end manuscripts is nicely captured in the title of this exhibition catalog: Kjeld von Folsach, *For the Privileged Few: Islamic Miniature Painting from the David Collection*, Humlebæk, Denmark: Louisiana Museum of Modern Art, 2007.

as material artifacts is primarily conducted by Islamic art historians, and textual scholars occupy themselves with written texts in whatever format available.[25] Source criticism and the editing of texts in Arabic script continue to be practiced as the ahistorical evaluation of content[26] without any recourse to codicology, paleography, or bibliography,[27] which, consequently, are not integrated into university curricula.

Against this backdrop, I argue that the long intellectual tradition of textual pragmatism in Islamic civilization informs our current interaction with electronic texts and digital surrogates. In Middle Eastern and Islamic studies, digitization is primarily applied to improve access to literary content, as already mentioned, because the field is committed to textual pragmatism. On the one hand, we are comfortable with electronic texts and digital surrogates, since on a computer screen their literary content appears as immaterial, and they are therefore experienced as authentic copies of written texts.[28] However, the literary content's apparent immateriality veils the fact that authenticity is not an intrinsic characteristic of any digital file. Electronic texts and digital surrogates only seem authentic as long as the interference of computer technology, in particular the loss of information in different file formats, remains invisible to the readers who encounter them on their computer screens.[29] On the other hand, as scholars, we do not feel obliged to concern ourselves with the production of material

---

25 In editions prepared in Muslim societies, scholars distinguish between handwritten copy (Ar. *al-nuskhah al-khaṭṭiyyah*, Pers. *kitāb-i khaṭṭī*) and printed copy (Ar. *al-nuskhah al-maṭbūʿah*, Pers. *kitāb-i chābī*), but since both are copies (Ar. sing. *nuskhah*, Pers. *nuskhah*) of texts, they are comparable irrespective of the differences between writing by hand (Ar. *khaṭṭa*, Pers. *khaṭṭ kirdān*) and printing (Ar. *ṭabaʿa*, Pers. *chāb kirdān*).

26 For a discussion of how twentieth-century editors rely on common sense (Ar. *al-dhawq al-salīm*) without any recourse to critical bibliography and source criticism, see Jan Just Witkam, "The Son's Copy: Remarks on a Contemporary Manuscript of Ibn ʿAsākir's 'History of the City of Damascus'," in *Maqālāt wa-dirāsāt muhdāh ilā Doktor Ṣalāḥ al-Dīn al-Munajjid* (London: Furqan Foundation, 2002), 591–610. Witkam, however, describes "al-dhawq al-salīm" without offering an explanation for its acceptance as an editorial strategy.

27 See, for example, the description of eight manuscripts without any accompanying analysis of how these copies are related to each other and to the same Arabic text in Hasan Ansari and Sabine Schmidtke, "The Literary-Religious Tradition among 7th/13th Century Yemenī Zaydīs: The Formation of the Imām al-Mahdī li-Dīn Allāh Aḥmad b. al-Ḥusayn b. al-Qāsim (d. 656/1258)," *Journal of Islamic Manuscripts* 2 (2011): 178–80.

28 Siân Echard, *Printing the Middle Ages* (Philadelphia: University of Pennsylvania Press, 2008), 202.

29 David McKitterick, *Print, Manuscript and the Search for Order, 1450–1830* (Cambridge: Cambridge University Press, 2003), 18.

artifacts, since textual pragmatism focuses on written texts and not on physical books, whether they are manuscripts, printed books, or e-books.

1. Writing and Digitization

> "And further, by these, my son, be admonished: of making many books *there is no* end; and much study *is* a weariness of the flesh."
>
> Ecclesiastes 12:12

The title of this essay is a play on an article about medieval Muslim book culture by Franz Rosenthal (1914–2003).[30] Written in the early 1990s, after more than five decades of reading sources from late antiquity to the nineteenth century in a wide range of languages, Rosenthal uses this famous and much-debated verse from Ecclesiastes to illustrate an easily overlooked consequence of writing as a technology for the preservation of the spoken word: the unlimited reproducibility of the written word on whatever writing surface available makes it much harder to distinguish between new written texts and copies, or variations, of old written texts. Since books were—especially if seen from the vantage point of a rich western society in the early twenty-first century—a rare commodity in all pre-modern societies, the incentive to produce ever more copies of books was even greater. Rosenthal's insight is so startling because in general we rarely distinguish between a book as material artifact and its literary content. Consequently, the metonymy of using "book" for "text" is no longer recognizable as a rhetorical sleight of hand.

Approaching books as a reproducible commodity—comparable to luxury goods like Rolex watches and Tiffany jewelry, which circulate as expensive originals and in a variety of cheap spinoffs and outright fakes—allows us to take the long view, which, in turn, brings into focus the fact that digitization as a means of cost-efficient production of new copies of written texts does not constitute a rupture in the history of the book. The reproducibility of the physical book in order to preserve its literary content is integral to books, since no material artifact will last forever—whether it is kept as protected cultural heritage in a customized depository or stored as a digital file on multiple servers. Dedicated professionals have produced new copies of written texts for readers since the third millennium BCE, when Sumerian scribes preserved Mesopotamia's literate

30 Rosenthal, "'Of Making Books'," 36.

knowledge through the copying of cuneiform tablets.[31] In a microhistorical perspective, an examination of digitization as an isolated phenomenon will reveal its dramatic impact on the scale of book production during the last two decades. But in a macrohistorical perspective, the number of copies in which a text circulates among audiences has continually increased with each new technological invention: from scroll to codex, from papyrus to rag paper, from letterpress printing to lithography, from typewriter to personal computer. In each instance, the application of a new technology to commercial book production has also reflected economic pressures, since one of the drivers of technology adaptation is the goal of cost-efficient production to ensure continuing financial viability and commercial profitability.[32]

The 1980s rise of the "what you see is what you get" (WYSIWYG) systems for word processing and desktop publishing[33] has ensured that nowadays most readers distinguish a file with a digitized manuscript or rare printed book from a file with a new and unpublished piece of writing solely on the basis of their content, since text encoding and markup are only visible to those who know where to look for them. At the same time, editors expect that authors submit their manuscripts electronically as digital files, since the publishing industry has employed electronic word processing machines since the early 1960s.[34] The continued use of the anachronism "manuscript" for an author's unpublished work is noteworthy, since already in the twentieth century typescripts had, for the most part, replaced manuscripts in longhand.[35] The resilience of the concept of an "author's manuscript" in the digital age indicates that, in general, a book's literary content receives more attention than its materiality.[36] This reflexive,

---

31 Eleanor Robson, "The Clay Table Book in Sumer, Assyria, and Babylonia," in *A Companion to the History of the Book*, eds. Simon Eliot and Jonathan Rose (Malden, MA: Blackwell, 2007), 71.

32 Paul Luna, "Books and Bits: Texts and Technology 1970–2000," in *Companion to the History of the Book*, eds. Eliot and Rose: "changes in text composition were driven by economic imperatives, first to reduce the cost of turning an author's text into publishable data, and subsequently to extract maximum value from that data" (381).

33 Allen H. Renear, "Text Encoding," in *Companion to the Digital Humanities*, eds. Susan Schreibman et al., 229–30.

34 Luna, "Books and Bits," 383.

35 In the early 1990s, an author's handwriting was only discussed with regard to mathematical copy in *The Chicago Manual of Style* (14th ed., Chicago: University of Chicago Press, 1993), 438 para. 13.17.

36 As explicitly stated in *The Chicago Manual of Style* (16th ed., Chicago: University of Chicago Press, 2010): "The industry-wide goal for e-book versions of printed monographs has been one of approximation on screen the experience of reading the printed book. The discussion on the parts of a book—though it assumes electronic publication is an option for any scholarly book—

though nonetheless acquired focus on a book's written text makes it much harder to discern the different socio-economic circumstances of book production, which are documented by the material differences between manuscripts, printed books, and e-books.[37]

During the last decade, readers in industrialized societies have witnessed—courtesy of Google, Apple, and Amazon—the rise and naturalization of the e-book on hand-held devices—such as a smartphones, tablets, or Kindles—as well as on rather old-fashioned personal computers (see Figures 3.1, 3.2, and 3.3 above). At the same time, libraries in Europe and North America as well as in North Africa and the Middle East are continuing with large-scale digitization projects to fulfill their national mandates of providing citizens with Open Access (OA) to their cultural heritage. In Europe and North America, prominent examples of these efforts include the Online Gallery of the British Library (Figure 3.3),[38] Gallica at the Bibliothèque nationale de France,[39] or the recently opened Digital Public Library of America.[40] The Bibliothèque Nationale du Royaume du Maroc is working on making, within the next few years, all of its manuscripts and lithographs available via the Bibliothèque Numerique Marocaine.[41] This summer saw the long-awaited launch of the Arabic-English Qatar Digital Library,[42] which includes Arabic manuscripts. Iran maintains an online database of digitized manuscripts, which is named after the bibliographer Shaykh Āqā Buzurg Tihrānī (1293–1389/1876–1970).[43] All of the manuscripts in the Süleymaniye Library in Istanbul are now digitized, but these digital surrogates can only be ac-

therefore includes special considerations for electronic book formats only where these might differ from those for print." (4, para. 1.2).

37 McKenzie, *Making Meaning:* "the richness of evidence that all textual forms themselves contain and [...] the skilled labour that went into the choice of their materials, design, and execution. The signs that we read in the artefacts we keep tell us of lives lived by men and women who had identities just as distinct and valuable as our own. The point that I am making is fundamental to any history of the book which would seek to derive its primary evidence from original artefacts as products of distinctive contexts and yet also demonstrate their successive transformations in response to new needs." (271).

38 http://www.bl.uk/onlinegallery/virtualbooks/index.html.

39 http://gallica.bnf.fr/.

40 http://dp.la/.

41 http://bnm.bnrm.ma:86/Accueil.aspx; for a history of the digital depository and its work schedule, see "À propos de la Bibliothèque Numerique Marocaine," available at: http://bnm.bnrm.ma:86/apropos.aspx, accessed 3 December 2014.

42 http://www.qdl.qa/en.

43 Shaykh Āqā Buzurg Tihrānī: Bānk-i iṭṭilāʿāt-i nusakh-i khaṭṭī, available at: http://www.aghabozorg.ir/.

cessed on the computer terminals in its reading room.[44] The Bibliotheca Alexandrina in Egypt cooperates with the Internet Archive (IA) in order to create and maintain its Arabic Digital Assets Repository (DAR),[45] but rare printed books and manuscripts, as well as a collection of digital surrogates, are kept in the Manuscript Museum.[46] These national projects are complemented by international initiatives, which rely on digitization in order to preserve endangered collections of both manuscripts and printed books in Afghanistan,[47] Yemen,[48] West Africa,[49] and Iraq.[50] Manuscripts and printed books, though often only illuminated single leaves, are also included in all digitization projects at museums worldwide.[51]

The steadily increasing availability of digital surrogates and e-books veils the economic fact that each digitization project places a significant financial burden on an institutional budget. Since the interpretation of digital surrogates depends on the understanding of how two-dimensional images represent three-dimensional material artifacts,[52] digital surrogates cannot replace material artifacts, and best practice now requires that repositories maintain both the material artifacts and their digital surrogates. Consequently, digitization projects are not cost-neutral undertakings. Nor is the maintenance of digital surrogates and

---

44 Nir Shafir and Christopher Markiewicz, "Süleymaniye Library," *Hazine* (blog), 10 October 2013, available at: http://hazine.info/2013/10/10/suleymaniye-library/.

45 For an undated statement about the cooperation, see http://hazine.info/suleymaniye-library/, accessed 11 February 2015. The repository is under construction and currently only accessible via a beta version at: http://dar.bibalex.org/webpages/dar.jsf, accessed 11 February 2015.

46 Matḥaf al-makhṭūṭāt, http://manuscriptsmuseum.bibalex.org/.

47 Afghanistan Digital Library: http://afghanistandl.nyu.edu/; this project provides OA to all of its website statistics in real time: http://dl-pa.home.nyu.edu/adlstats/adl.

48 Yemeni Manuscript Digitization Initiative (YMDI): http://pudl.princeton.edu/collections/pudl0079; see also the project description by David Hollenberg at: http://ymdi.uoregon.edu/.

49 Federal Foreign Office, "Außenminister Steinmeier eröffnet internationales Strategietreffen zum Erhalt der Handschriften aus Timbuktu," press release, 17 June 2014, available at: http://www.auswaertiges-amt.de/DE/Infoservice/Presse/Meldungen/2014/140617-Strategietreffen_Kulturerhalt.html, accessed 2 December 2014.

50 Nikki Rajala, "HMML Makes Ancient Manuscripts Accessible to Scholars Worldwide," *The Visitor* 102 no. 23 (7 November 2014): 3, available at: http://visitor.stcdio.org/hmml-makes-ancient-manuscripts-accessible-scholars-worldwide/, accessed 2 December 2014.

51 A search of databases such as the Google Cultural Institute (https://www.google.com/culturalinstitute/home) and the Wikimedia Commons (http://commons.wikimedia.org/wiki/Main_Page) will reveal a wide range of digital images of manuscripts and printed books uploaded by public and private institutions as well as individual citizens worldwide.

52 For a description of this problem within the context of computational image analysis, see Kohle, *Digitale Bildwissenschaft*, 70–72.

e-books cheaper than the conventional storage of physical books.[53] The growth of an institution's digital resources, whether they are digital surrogates or e-books, usually involves difficult decisions about the deaccessioning and defunding of other holdings and services.[54] As regards the environmental impact of digitization, grant-making agencies such as the European Research Council (ERC) and the National Endowment for the Humanities (NEH) expect applicants to develop data management plans and dissemination strategies, but they do not yet require a discussion of their project's carbon footprint.[55]

Unfortunately, the complexity of digitization projects and electronic publishing is invisible to readers, as a few keystrokes on a keyboard are all that is needed to open the pages of an Islamic manuscript or a printed book on a computer screen.[56] This cognitive dissonance is reinforced by a mode of distant access that ideally requires no direct interaction with other human beings: we double-click on digital surrogates and e-books on our computer screens in the privacy of our homes and offices and no longer negotiate with librarians over how to use the material artifacts in library reading rooms. Consequently, it seems counterintuitive that the long-term use of digital surrogates and e-books will depend not only on the continuous upgrading of hardware and software, but also on the availability of human labor dedicated to the maintenance of efficient digital delivery systems.[57] That digitization projects rarely create permanent jobs is one of the

---

53 Several units of measurement—cataloguing record, title, and page—are provided in the assessment of the Islamic Heritage Project at Harvard University by Chapman, "The Harvard University Library Islamic Heritage Project," 19 and 27. Yet none of these can be related to the annual fee of managed storage and digital preservation services of $2.50 per gigabyte, which Harvard's Digital Repository charged between 2007 and 2009, when the digital surrogates were produced.

54 McKitterick, *Old Books:* "The costs of libraries in our own world, with all their complexities and challenges, are still only partially grasped." (3) Idem: "At every level, from school libraries to public libraries to university libraries to learned societies and to national libraries, books are being discarded and destroyed at an unprecedented rate." (212)

55 The curious silence about the environmental impact of digitization vis-à-vis print publications on paper could be considered an instance of "the vapid embrace of the digital," as discussed by Chun and Rhody, "Working the Digital Humanities," 3.

56 For a reflection on why humanists and digital humanists alike need to actively concern themselves with the accounting and budgeting modes of their institutions, in particular with regard to overhead calculations in grant administration, see Chun and Rhody, "Working the Digital Humanities," 10–12, 16, 19.

57 Deegan and Tanner, "Conversion of Primary Sources": "Understanding the capture processes for primary source materials is essential for humanists intending to engage in digital projects, even if they are never going to carry out conversion activities directly. Knowing the implications of the various decisions that have to be taken in any project is of vital importance for short- and

reasons why David McKitterick recently observed that "scanning programmes are built on weak foundations" and "too often show lamentable quality control."[58]

The high costs of digitization projects are mitigated by grant-making agencies that offer competitive funding opportunities for access to hidden collections and the preservation of endangered ones.[59] Since governments are underwriting digitization projects, they are also prestigious undertakings for private sponsors. From a fundraising perspective, digitization projects are attractive propositions for wealthy individuals, since digital surrogates can be made available as OA resources, which, thanks to their ethereal appearance on our computer screens, seem to have no tangible connection to contentious political debates on research funding and labor politics in the humanities.[60] Indeed, philanthropists and private foundations are indispensable supporters of the digitization of manuscripts in Arabic script, and, in general, privately funded projects are exposed to less public scrutiny. In contrast, taxpayer-funded projects are closely monitored in order to ensure that these projects fulfill their public mandates, and detailed information about their work is available in the public record. Still, protecting and championing the cultural heritage of a more or less exclusively defined community is often among the publicly stated goals of private sponsors. The Thesaurus Islamicus Foundation, which is the mother of The Islamic Manuscript Association (TIMA), runs the Dar al-Kutub Manuscript Project in Cairo, though an explicit digitization project is not publicly identified.[61] Other private sponsors are the Imam Zayd Cultural Foundation,[62] the Iran Heritage Foundation (IHF),[63] Yousef

long-term costs as well as for the long-term survivability of the materials to which time, care, and funds have been devoted." (502)

58 McKitterick, *Old Books*, 9.

59 The most prominent initiatives in the Anglo-American context are probably the Hidden Collections Program of the Council of Library and Information Resources (http://www.clir.org/hiddencollections) and the Endangered Archives Programme of the British Library (http://eap.bl.uk/). For the financial challenges small repositories face with regard to providing access to insufficiently cataloged holdings, see Sheila A. Bair and Susan M. B. Steuer, "Developing a Premondern Manuscript Application Profile Using Dublin Core," *Journal of Library Metadata* 13 no. 1 (2013): 2–3.

60 In western Europe and North America, the irrelevance of the humanities has received much political attention since the early 1980s. For an introduction to the 1980s debate in the US, see David Bromwich, *Politics by Other Means: Higher Education and Group Thinking* (New Haven: Yale University Press, 1992). For a glimpse of the current debate in the US, see Christopher Benfey, "How Bad Are the Colleges?" *New York Review of Books*, 23 October 2014: 14–18.

61 http://www.thesaurus-islamicus.org/.

62 www.izbacf.org/.

63 http://www.iranheritage.org/organisation.htm; the IHF's Persian Manuscript Digitization Project at the British Library is available at: http://www.iranheritage.org/BL_Project/.

Jameel,[64] and Prince Alwaleed Bin Talal.[65] They are funding several digitization projects in public and private collections in Europe and North America, thereby reclaiming manuscripts, as well as other material artifacts, as their respective cultural heritage. The degree to which the resulting digital surrogates are also intended as a means to the end of giving a boost to particular religious and political goals depends on the mission of the respective private sponsor.

2. Digitization and DH

> "Question: How many Digital Humanists does it take to change a lighbulb?
> Answer: Two. The first to change the lightbulb using the available, existing technology. The second to say 'You are not DH unless you make the lightbulb yourself.'"
> Melissa Terras' Blog, "How Many Digital Humanists Does it Take to Change a Lightbulb?", 8 April 2013

Digitization has an ambiguous status within DH: it is associated with access and electronic publishing and allows for the application of digital tools to datasets. The latter is a scholarly pursuit, whereas the former concerns communication and outreach. Digital humanists discuss the respective merits of digital and analogue methods of disseminating knowledge because computational methods of analysis often generate research data that cannot be meaningfully represented in print.[66] But digitization is primarily presented as a conversion tool that allows for the generation of hitherto unimaginable corpora of digitized written texts and images. This quantitative increase is adduced as the main argument whenever digital humanists describe digitization as a disruptive tool and champion its potential for the pursuit of a progressive research agenda.[67] At the same time, many DH studies are published as traditionally printed books on paper, and not of all

64 For an authorized official biography, see: http://jameelcentre.ashmolean.org/project/21.
65 For the Harvard University Library Islamic Heritage Project (http://ocp.hul.harvard.edu.ihp), see Stephen Chapman, "The Harvard University Library Islamic Heritage Project: Challenges in Managing Large-Scale Digitization of Islamic Manuscripts," *Journal of Islamic Manuscripts* 1 (2010): 18–30.
66 Susan Schreibman, Ray Siemens, and John Unsworth, "The Digital Humanities and Humanities Computing: An Introduction," in *Companion to the Digital Humanities*, eds. Susan Schreibman et al.: "The field also places great importance on the means of disseminating the results of these activities" (xxv); cf. Chun and Rhody, "Working the Digital Humanities," 9.
67 For quantitative methods in history, see Jo Guldi and Richard Armitage, *History Manifesto* (Cambridge: Cambridge University Press, 2014), 93, 153 n. 12; and 113, 159 n. 64. For the value of large data sets in art history, see Kohle, *Digitale Bildwissenschaft*, 9–11 and 76–95.

of these are complemented with an OA version on the Internet.[68] Digital humanists can rely on digitized sources and electronically publish their research without having to confront the economics of either digitization projects or electronic publishing, even though in every research infrastructure—whether local, national, transnational, or international—the financial resources for providing OA to sources, as well as research and references, are finite. [69] Since the limitation of the available resources for digitization seems to contradict our concrete experience of being surrounded by e-books and digital surrogates, there is not any debate about the obvious fact that we have neither the financial nor the human resources to digitize every manuscript, printed book, or document held in special collections right now.[70] As there is no recognition of our limited resources, there is also no debate about priorities and selection criteria, and we do not know how what is available as a digital surrogate is related to extant holdings in private and public repositories.

This situation partly reflects economic inequities in academia. Scholars with gainful employment at well-funded research institutions are shielded from exposure to the financial realities of both OA and restricted access to proprietary digital resources, such as bibliographies, encyclopedias, critical editions, databases of literary sources, and research publications. Whenever comprehensive library privileges are a crucial employment benefit, scholars can concentrate on their research and do not need to spend precious time getting hold of sources and scholarship.[71] Conversely, independent scholars and those working at institutions with limited resources[72] are so dependent on the generosity of others

---

68 Guldi and Armitage, *History Manifesto*, DOI: http://dx.doi.org/10.1017/9781139923880; and Kohle, *Digitale Bildwissenschaft*, DOI: http://archiv.ub.uni-heidelberg.de/artdok/volltexte/2013/2185.

69 For the failed Gutenberg-e dissertations project (1999–2003) of the American Historical Association and Columbia University Press, see http://www.gutenberg-e.org/aboutframe.html.

70 McKitterick, *Old Books:* "It is improbable that there will ever be a time when all the books that have ever been published, and that survive, will be available electronically" (9); cf. the parallel universe of an eternal library that houses all books of humankind in Jorge Luis Borges, "The Library of Babel," in *Collected Fictions*, trans. Andrew Hurley (London: Penguin, 1998), 112–18.

71 For a recent survey of the economic challenges in academic publishing, see Robert Darnton, "The World Digital Library Is Coming True," *New York Review of Books*, 22 May 2014: 8–11; and the subsequent exchange between Darnton and Robert A. Schneider, "Overpriced Scholarship," *New York Review of Books*, 6 November 2014: 56–57.

72 Not every college or university can afford its own OA repository of research publications; cf. Digital Access to Scholarship at Harvard (http://dash.harvard.edu/) and the Academic Commons of Columbia University (http://academiccommons.columbia.edu).

that they would rather not question how sources and scholarship are made available in OA.[73]

For scholars working in Europe and North America, economic inequities in academia determine their ability to conduct research, but economic inequities do not explain why engagement with DH varies so greatly between academic disciplines. In Middle Eastern and Islamic studies, there are very few scholars who have at least one foot firmly planted in computer science or electrical engineering and could thus be considered genuine digital humanists. Moreover, the digital divide in Muslim societies goes largely unnoticed,[74] even though the recent democratic protest movements in Iran, Tunisia, Egypt, and Turkey have ensured that the political impact of social media is now widely studied. Despite the harrowing news reporting about violence, poverty, and underdevelopment in Muslim societies, their perception is dominated by the actions of either westernized elites or Islamist terrorists. Both groups are committed Internet users, though primarily as consumers who are interacting with digital tools such as smart phones and computers. DH as an academic discipline has not yet taken root in most institutions of higher learning in the Middle East and North Africa.[75] Its integration into university curricula is facilitated via disciplines such as English studies, which has embraced DH since the 1990s, and prestigious institutions, such as the American University of Beirut (AUB), are now developing DH programs.[76]

Taken together, these observations indicate that Middle Eastern and Islamic studies is not a good match for DH. While our research questions respond to present-day concerns, our approaches still reflect the intellectual traditions of Islamic civilization. Computational methods of analysis are of little use to a field

---

73 Not all written texts and material artifacts whose digital surrogates are available OA on the Internet are also available for a free download. For example, those who are not associated with an institutional member of the HathiTrust Digital Library (http://www.hathitrust.org/) have limited access to its resources (Figure 3.2), though the University of Michigan offers the possibility of enhanced access via a "Friend Account;" see: http://www.hathitrust.org/help_digital_library#FriendAccount.

74 The ubiquity of cellphones veils the digital divide to some degree; see for example the description of how illiterate Cairenes rely on help in order to receive texts on cellphones in Peter Hessler, "Tales of the Trash: A Neighborhood Garbageman Explains Modern Egypt," *New Yorker*, 13 October 2014: 96–97.

75 The situation of DH in South Asia seems to reflect the importance of India's high-tech industry as well as the role of English, despite its colonial origins, as an indispensable lingua franca.

76 For AUB's first DH workshop, organized by the Department of English in 2013, see: http://www.aub.edu.lb/FAS/ENGLISH/Pages/DigitalHumanitiesatAUB.aspx; for Beirut's new DH Institute, see: https://dhibeirut.wordpress.com; and for the first THATCamp in the Middle East, see: http://beirut2015.thatcamp.org/.

that is committed to textual pragmatism, even if digital copies of written texts are experienced as a very convenient way of obtaining access to literary works. That this cognitive dissonance in Middle Eastern and Islamic studies is not particular to how we have adapted to the digital age is indicated by textbooks, such as Stephen Humphreys' widely used introduction to the study of Islamic history. Humphreys wrote his *vademecum* in the late 1980s for graduate students at North American universities.[77] Although an updated English edition was never published, a Turkish translation appeared in 2004.[78] The book begins with an analytical survey of the sources of Islamic history, and Humphreys opens the chapter with the observation that scholars of the Muslim Middle East "like to complain about the state of their sources, but in fact what they have is extraordinarily rich and varied."[79] Regrettably, Humphreys did not venture any explanation of why Islamic historians do not have a happy relationship with their sources, even though his introduction is a practitioner's guide to historical research about Muslim societies. The reader instead receives the sensible advice that the effective use of sources depends on asking good questions, which in turns demands knowing these sources. Nor did Humphreys pause to reflect on the question of why access to manuscripts in Arabic script was, and has remained, difficult and time-consuming.[80] The reader was merely warned that her research was likely to include work with manuscripts in Arabic script as a matter of necessity, since not all sources were available in printed versions.[81] Crucial to becoming and being a historian of Muslim societies was, therefore, the unconditional commitment to plodding through printed bibliographies and catalogues in order to hunt down manuscripts and rare printed books. Humphreys recommended the use of a personal computer with good citation software to get on top of the field's bibliographic challenges, but the indispensable reference works and bibliographies were printed books.[82]

In hindsight, it is stunning that Humphreys saw no need to include even a cautionary note that computer science would probably continue to change the methods of finding and accessing sources and scholarship. After all, in Europe

77 R. Stephen Humphreys, *Islamic History: A Framework for Inquiry* (Princeton: Princeton University Press, 1988, rev. ed.,1991); all references are to the 1991 edition.
78 *Islam tarih metodolojisi: Bir sosyal tarih uygulaması*, trans. Murtaza Bedir and Fuat Aydın (Istanbul: Litera, 2004); non vide.
79 Humphreys, *Islamic History*, 25.
80 Cf. the difficulties a field like DH has in embracing failure as a disciplinary value, as discussed by Chun and Rhody, "Working the Digital Humanities," 4–5, 15–16.
81 Humphreys, *Islamic History*, 32–40.
82 Humphreys, *Islamic History*, 7.

and North America, digital technology has directly impacted library and information science for about half a century. As already mentioned above, publishers started to experiment with computer-assisted composition and printing in the early 1960s.[83] The beginnings of OCLC/WorldCat as a computer-based cataloguing network in Ohio go back to the mid-1960s.[84] CD-ROMs, euphorically described as "the new papyrus," have been used for electronic publishing since the mid-1980s.[85] Since the late 1980s, students and faculty in North American research universities have been directly experiencing the impact of computer science on their research. Online library catalogues were available to search for books not available in their own institutions, while databases of digitized texts on CD-ROMs offered access to texts not available as manuscripts, printed books, or microfilms resp. microfiche. Against this backdrop, Humphreys' technological expectations with regard to the written sources of Islamic history were very modest indeed. He appreciated the Arab League's collection of photographed manuscripts[86] but dismissed microfilms as "no substitute for the real thing."[87]

Humphrey's hands-on attitude, however, reflects the peculiar situation of Middle Eastern and Islamic studies within the humanities in Europe and North America. The first characteristic of this situation is easy to miss, because it seems such a non-issue: size. Middle Eastern and Islamic studies as a field is not as large as history, but it is also not as small as Ancient Near Eastern studies. From the perspective of the second decade of the twenty-first century, it has become much easier to recognize how scale is crucial for the approaches taken by a particular field as a whole toward the adaptation of electronic research methods and independent online publishing. In small fields, the embrace of DH reflects in part the need to get the most out of very limited resources. As it is very difficult to sustain the publication of reference works, editions, and research monographs in small fields, there is no downside to effective data sharing across national borders and continents via OA. Even though research budgets have been steadily shrinking for more than a decade across the humanities as well as the sciences, large fields in the humanities still have more institutional resources and more researchers than smaller fields, and so for them it remains easier to hedge against the risk of failure that always accompanies change and innovation. The middling size of Middle Eastern and Islamic studies in Western academia

83 Luna, "Books and Bits," 383.

84 Charles Chadwyck-Healy, "The New Textual Technologies," in *Companion to the History of the Book*, eds. Eliot and Rose, 453.

85 Chadwyck-Healy, "New Textual Technologies," 458.

86 Humphreys, *Islamic History*, 27.

87 Humphreys, *Islamic History*, 36.

thus appears as one of the reasons why there are not yet tenure-track positions for digital humanists in Middle Eastern and Islamic studies departments, when there are already tenured digital humanists in departments with large faculties, such as English and history. The limited resources available for DH in Middle Eastern and Islamic studies are likely a contributing factor as to why projects for the digitization of manuscripts in Arabic script have not yet spawned a digital paleography of the Arabic script or the development of a proven optical character recognition (OCR) technology for languages written in Arabic script. On list services dedicated to Middle Eastern and Islamic studies, there are regularly requests for PDF files of Arabic or Persian texts with full-text search, and yet there are no debates about how full-text search is enabled. How often should a text be independently keyed in to achieve a modicum of accuracy, and which markup language should be used?[88] While some may argue that list services dedicated to Arabic literature, the medieval Middle East, or the sociology of Islam are the wrong places for such technical debates, digital paleography, OCR technology, and markup languages such as the Text Encoding Initiative (TEI) are popular themes in the DH community.

A second factor that is important for the successful integration of DH into a field's research program is its "scholarly infrastructure."[89] Humphreys, in a surprisingly emotional aside, considered it "a disgrace and a serious inconvenience" that bibliographers in Europe and North America never established "a regular, systematic survey of scholarly books and articles published in Arabic, Persian, Turkish and Urdu."[90] In fields such as the study of Greco-Roman antiquity or English literature, humanities computing provides scholars, who already have well-established standards and citation schemes for large research libraries of primary and secondary sources, with the tools for both access to sources and research about the sources. Unfortunately, such a scholarly infrastructure is not in place in Middle Eastern and Islamic studies, where textual criticism is shunned because it is identified with philology as the essence of Orientalist

88 Both the desideratum of a proven OCR technology for the Arabic script and the high labor costs for keying in and marking up a full text are obliquely mentioned by Chapman, "Harvard University Library Islamic Heritage Project," 26–27.

89 Greg Crane, "Classics and the Computer: An End of the History," in *Companion to the Digital Humanities*, eds. Schreibman et al., 46.

90 Humphreys, *Islamic History*, 7. That the situation did not significantly improve between the late 1980s and the 2000s is suggested by Andrew Rippin's observation of a "loose control over the reprinting of works by different publishers in many parts of the Arab world" ("Preface," in *The Blackwell Companion to the Qur'ān*, Blackwell Reference Online, 2008, DOI: 0.1002/9780470751428.fmatter).

scholarship.[91] Textual pragmatism, though, seems, at least in part, supported by the Saidian critique of and opposition to philology. Even though this line of reasoning rests on a false syllogism,[92] it explains our hands-off attitude regarding textual criticism. But it is not only an expression of our post-colonial rejection of philology that we remain silent about the textual condition of our written sources. The scholarly commitment to textual pragmatism unites an often quite factionalized discipline, since scholars working in Europe and North America can share this commitment with their colleagues in the Muslim societies of Eurasia and Africa. The still-indispensable bio-bibliographical reference works by Carl Brockelmann (1868–1956),[93] C. A. Storey (1888–1968),[94] and Fuat Sezgin (b. 1924)[95] provide systematic catalogues of the major works of Arabic and Persian literature, in which manuscripts and printed books are not separated from each other. Accordingly, any random sampling of Middle Eastern and Islamic studies dissertations accepted during the last two decades at US universities will yield odd bibliographical references for manuscripts, which indicates that research committees did not worry about different citation standards for manuscripts and printed books, respectively. In Muslim societies, there are many websites that offer free access—in a range of formats, though with a slight preference for downloadable PDF files—to various corpora of Arabic, Persian, Ottoman, or Urdu literatures.[96] Their number has been steadily increasing since the late 1990s. Routine references to these online libraries on list services show that they are widely used by scholars, even though many are rather collections of gray literature.[97] The texts are usually not accompanied by comprehensive cataloguing, and their legal status in terms of digital rights management (DRM) is treated as moot. [98] Their wide acceptance inside and outside academia illustrates

91 Edward W. Said, *Orientalism* (New York: Vintage, 1979): "Almost without exception, every Orientalist began his career as a philologist" (98).

92 The false syllogism equates textual criticism with philology, and philology with Orientalism.

93 *Geschichte der arabischen Litteratur: Grundwerk* (2 vols., 1st ed., Weimar: Felber, 1898–1902; 2nd ed., Leipzig: Amelang, 1901) and *Supplementband* (3 vols., Leiden: Brill, 1937–1942).

94 *Persian Literature: A Bio-Bibliographical Survey* (1/1-, London: Luzac, 1927–).

95 *Geschichte des arabischen Schrifttums* (1-, Leiden: Brill, 1967–).

96 For annotated lists of primary source material and web-based resources, see Kristiansen, "Digital Resources," cols. 396–400; and Kon, "Some Digital Resources," cols. 401–403.

97 For a reflection on the digital archives of Islamic literatures from a user's perspective, see Travis Zadeh's contribution to this volume.

98 See, for example, L.W.C. van Lit, "Full-Text Online Arabic Sources: A Preliminary List," *The Digital Orientalist* (blog), 16 January 2015, available at: http://digitalorientalist.com/2015/01/16/full-text-online-arabic-sources-a-preliminary-list/. Van Lit provides a list of six restrictions ac-

the efficiency of textual pragmatism in the digital age, since the adaptation of digitization to bookmaking is not hampered by theoretical concerns about the ontological differences between original and copy. In other words, the historicist awareness of the differences between material artifacts, their facsimiles, and their forgeries is as irrelevant as legal concerns about copyright law and best practices in DH. [99] As long as we remain committed to textual pragmatism, we will assume that literary works are preserved as stable written texts, so that it does not matter in which medium they are reproduced and can be read.[100]

3. Digitization and Access to the Cultural Heritage of Muslim Societies

> "Be explicit about your goals and your criteria, record your every doubt and misstep, and aspire to be remembered for the ignorance that was uniquely yours, rather than for the common sense you helped to construct."
> John Unsworth, "Documenting the Reinvention of Text: The Importance of Failure"

The good news is that the number of digitized manuscripts, typeset books, and lithographs in Arabic script is steadily increasing. The bad news is that the digitization of Islamic books is such a decentralized process that it is very difficult to determine whether a digital surrogate of a particular text is already available somewhere on the Internet, possibly even as an OA resource. In Muslim societies in Eurasia and Africa, the border between digital cultural heritage preservation and electronic publishing has been blurred, because digitization in the service of textual pragmatism reinforces indifference to the different historical and socio-economic contexts of textual production. At the moment, the blog AMIR, [101]

---

cording to which he compiled a list of 21 OA Internet depositories, but these restrictions do not extend to a depository's legal status (e.g., copyright) and the security of its website (e.g., virus infection). Also noteworthy is that van Lit's list excludes depositories of scanned images, as they presumably do not offer full-text search.

99 See David Hirsch's report about his 2012 workshop for Iraqi librarians in *TARII Newsletter* 8 no. 1 (2013): 22, available at: http://www.taarii.org/images/PDF/08-01.pdf.

100 Recent surveys of Middle East studies research do not include any consideration of how scholars obtain access to their literary sources: e.g., Uriel Simonsohn, "Conversion to Islam: A Case Study for the Use of Legal Sources," *History Compass* 11 no. 8 (2013): 647–62; Kevin W. Martin, "Middle East Historiography: Did We Miss the Cultural Turn?" *History Compass* 12 no. 2 (2014): 178–86.

101 *AMIR: Access to Mideast and Islamic Resources* (ISSN 2160–3049), http://amirmideast.blogspot.com/.

which was initiated by Peter Magierski and is modeled on Charles Jones' blog AWOL,[102] is the sole example of tracking digitized OA resources in Middle Eastern and Islamic studies. Scholars in other fields are usually surprised at this lack of coordination.[103] But this professional failure reflects the transnational framework of Middle Eastern and Islamic studies. Manuscripts in Arabic script are dispersed in private and public collections across the globe, and conversations about their digitization are conducted in emotionally charged contexts because of the political tensions between Europe and North America, on the one hand, and Muslim societies in Eurasia and Africa, on the other. We would therefore rather not admit that our field's textual pragmatism has not furthered bibliographic control over the manuscripts and printed books in Arabic script, even though in the current state of the cataloguing of Islamic books, it is impossible to determine with a modicum of reliability for any text in how many copies it has been preserved. We cannot match literary works with manuscripts or printed books, as there are neither inventories of known texts written in the languages of Muslim societies nor inventories of known copies. Against this backdrop, it is not surprising, though nonetheless regrettable, that painful decisions about the selection of Islamic books for digitization and their potential digital afterlife remain unacknowledged and are therefore not openly discussed. Instead, optimism about digitization prevails. We just need to get ahead of the technology, and those texts that are truly important, rare, or interesting will eventually be available as digital surrogates, even if not every book or document ever written can be digitized.

From my perspective, the most urgent desideratum is an open and honest debate about digitization among those who have a stake in Middle Eastern and Islamic studies. Since scholars inside and outside Muslim societies agree that written sources are crucial for our research, the question arises as to whether all of us bear at least some responsibility for their long-term preservation. If every society indeed has the government that it deserves, perhaps every academic field gets the sources as well as the accompanying reference works and catalogues that it deserves. But what would our scholarly obligation to contribute to the preservation of rare manuscripts and printed books in Arabic script for future generations look like? A modest first step in the move from being happy-go-lucky consumers of digital surrogates whenever they happen to be available to being

---

102 *AWOL: The Ancient World Online* (ISSN 2156–2253), http://ancientworldonline.blogspot.com/.

103 See in particular the exasperated post by Klaus Graf, "Adventskalender (Türlein XI): Islamische Handschriften online," *Archivalia* (blog), 11 December 2010, available at: http://archiv.twoday.net/stories/11445658/.

digital humanists would be the recognition that employing DH tools for humanities and social sciences research is different from digitizing material artifacts in order to facilitate access to their literary content.

Bibliography

The following list is limited to secondary sources, so that the names and URLs of websites, online databases, and DH projects are only given in the text and the accompanying footnotes. The URLs of subscription-based resources are not indicated, and access dates are only provided for sources such as press releases and newspaper articles.

Ansari, Hasan, and Sabine Schmidtke. "The Literary-Religious Tradition among 7th/13th Century Yemenī Zaydīs: The Formation of the Imām al-Mahdī li-Dīn Allāh Aḥmad b. al-Ḥusayn b. al-Qāsim (d. 656/1258)." *Journal of Islamic Manuscripts* 2 (2011): 165–222.

Auslander, Leora, Amy Bentley, Leor Halevi, H. Otto Sibum, and Christopher Whitmore. "AHR Conversation: Historians and the Study of Material Culture." *American Historical Review* 114 no. 5 (2009): 1354–1404.

Bair, Sheila A., and Susan M. B. Steuer. "Developing a Premondern Manuscript Application Profile Using Dublin Core." *Journal of Library Metadata* 13 no. 1 (2013): 1–16.

Christopher Benfey, "How Bad Are the Colleges?" *New York Review of Books*, 23 October 2014: 14–18.

Blair, Ann. *Too Much to Know: Managing Scholarly Information before the Modern Age*. New Haven: Yale University Press, 2010.

Borges, Jorge Luis. *Collected Fictions*. Trans. Andrew Hurley. London: Penguin, 1998.

Bromwich, Daivd. *Politics by Other Means: Higher Education and Group Thinking*. New Haven: Yale University Press, 1992.

Bynum, Caroline Walker. "Why Paradox? The Contradictions of My Life as a Scholar." *Catholic Historical Review* 98 no. 3 (July 2012): 433–55.

Chadwyck-Healy, Charles. "The New Textual Technologies." In *A Companion to the History of the Book*, eds. Simon Eliot and Jonathan Rose, 450–63. Malden, MA: Blackwell, 2007.

Chapman, Stephen. "The Harvard University Library Islamic Heritage Project: Challenges in Managing Large-Scale Digitization of Islamic Manuscripts." *Journal of Islamic Manuscripts* 1 (2010): 18–30.

The Chicago Manual of Style. Chicago: University of Chicago Press. 14th ed., 1993; 16th ed., 2010.

Chun, Wendy Hui Kyong, and Lisa Marie Rhody. "Working the Digital Humanities: Uncovering Shadows between the Dark and the Light." *differences: A Journal of Feminist Cultural Studies* 25 no. 1 (2014): 1–25.

Crane, Greg. "Classics and the Computer: An End of the History." In *A Companion to the Digital Humanities*, eds. Susan Schreibman, Ray Siemens, and John Unsworth, 46–55. Malden,MA: Blackwell, 2004.

Dalbello, Marija. "A Genealogy of Digital Humanities." *Journal of Documentation* 67 no. 3 (2011): 480–506.

Darnton, Robert. "The World Digital Library Is Coming True." *New York Review of Books*, 22 May 2014: 8–11.

Darnton, Robert, and Robert A. Schneider. "Overpriced Scholarship: An Exchange." *New York Review of Books*, 6 November 2014: 56–57.

Davies, Richard. "Revealing Gulf History Online." *British Library: Living Knowledge Blog*, 2 December 2014. Available at: http://britishlibrary.typepad.co.uk/living-knowledge/2014/12/revealing-gulf-history-online.html. Accessed 15 September 2015.

Deegan, Marilyn, and Simon Tanner. "Conversion of Primary Sources." In *A Companion to the Digital Humanities*, eds. Susan Schreibman, Ray Siemens, and John Unsworth, 488–504. Malden, MA: Blackwell, 2004.

Echard, Siân. *Printing the Middle Ages*. Philadelphia: University of Pennsylvania Press, 2008.

Federal Foreign Office. "Außenminister Steinmeier eröffnet internationales Strategietreffen zum Erhalt der Handschriften aus Timbuktu." Press release, 17 June 2014. Accessed 2 December 2014. Available at: http://www.auswaertiges-amt.de/DE/Infoservice/Presse/Meldungen/2014/140617-Strategietreffen_Kulturerhalt.html

Fiormonte, Domenico. "Digital Humanities from a Global Perspective." *Laboratorio dell'ISPF* 11 (2014). DOI: 10.12862/ispf14 L203.

Folsach, Kjeld von. *For the Privileged Few: Islamic Miniature Painting from the David Collection*. Humlebæk: Louisiana Museum of Modern Art, 2007.

Galey, Alex. "The Enkindling Reciter: E-Books in the Bibliographical Imagination." *Book History* 15 (2012): 211–47.

Ghersetti, Antonella, ed. *The Book in Fact and Fiction in Pre-Modern Arabic Literature*. Special issue, *Journal of Arabic and Islamic Studies* 12 (2012).

Guldi, Jo, and David Armitage. *The History Manifesto*. Cambridge: Cambridge University Press, 2014. DOI: http://dx.doi.org/10.1017/9781139923880.

Hanna, Nelly. *In Praise of Books: A Cultural History of Cairo's Middle Class, Sixteenth to the Eighteenth Century*. Cairo: American University in Cairo Press, 2003.

Hessler, Peter. "Tales of the Trash: A Neighborhood Garbageman Explains Modern Egypt." *New Yorker*, 13 October 2014: 90–99.

Hirschler, Konrad. *The Written Word in the Medieval Arabic Lands: A Social and Cultural History of Reading Practices*. Edinburgh: Edinburgh University Press, 2012.

Humphreys, Alex Brymer. "The Past, Present, and Future of Immersive and Extractive Ebooks." In *Digital Media: Transformations in Human Communication*, eds. Paul Messaris and Lee Humphreys, 159–172. New York: Peter Lang, 2006. A December 2004 version is available through the Social Science Research Network at: http://ssrn.com/abstract=1300567.

Humphreys, R. Stephen. *Islamic History: A Framework for Inquiry*. Princeton: Princeton University Press, 1988. Rev. ed. 1991.

—. *İslam tarih metodolojisi: Bir sosyal tarih uygulaması*. Trans. Murtaza Bedir and Fuat Aydın. Istanbul: Litera, 2004.

Kohle, Hubertus. *Digitale Bildwissenschaft*. Glückstadt: Verlag Werner Hülsbusch, 2013. DOI: http://archiv.ub.uni-heidelberg.de/artdok/volltexte/2013/2185.

Kon, Ronald E. "Some Digital Resources for the Study of the Middle East." *Bibliotheca Orientalis* 71 nos. 3–4 (2014): cols. 400–403. This issue of the journal is available OA on the website of the Netherlands Institute for the Near East at: www.nino-leiden.nl.

Kristiansen, Birte. "Digital Resources in Middle Eastern Studies." *Bibliotheca Orientalis* 71 nos. 3–4 (2014): cols. 388–400. This issue of the journal is available OA on the website of the Netherlands Institute for the Near East at: www.nino-leiden.nl.

Le Roux, Elizabeth. "Book History in the African World." *Book History* 15 (2012): 248–300.

Liu, Alan. "What is the Meaning of the Digital Humanities to the Humanities?" *Proceedings of the Modern Language Association of America* 128 no. 2 (2013): 409–23.

Luna, Paul. "Books and Bits: Texts and Technology 1970–2000." In *A Companion to the History of the Book*, eds. Simon Eliot and Jonathan Rose, 381–94. Malden, MA: Blackwell, 2007.

Martin, Kevin W. "Middle East Historiography: Did We Miss the Cultural Turn?" *History Compass* 12 no. 2 (2014): 178–86.

McGann, Jerome. *Radiant Textuality: Literature after the World Wide Web.* New York: Palgrave, 2001.

McKenzie, Donald F. *Making Meaning: "Printers of the Mind" and Other Essays.* Eds. Peter D. McDonald and Michael F. Suarez. Amherst: University of Massachusetts Press, 2002.

McKitterick, David. *Print, Manuscript and the Search for Order, 1450–1830.* Cambridge: Cambridge University Press, 2003.

—. *Old Books, New Technologies: The Representation, Conservation and Transformation of Books since 1700.* Cambridge: Cambridge University Press, 2013.

Mroczek, Eva. "Thinking Digitally about the Dead Sea Scrolls: Book History before and beyond the Book." *Book History* 14 (2011): 241–69.

Rajala, Nikki. "HMML Makes Ancient Manuscripts Accessible to Scholars Worldwide." *The Visitor* 102 no. 23 (7 November 2014): 3. Available at: http://visitor.stcdio.org/hmml-makes-ancient-manuscripts-accessible-scholars-worldwide/. Accessed December 2, 2014.

Renear, Allen H. "Text Encoding." In *A Companion to the Digital Humanities*, eds. Susan Schreibman, Ray Siemens, and John Unsworth, 218–39. Malden, MA: Blackwell, 2004.

Rippin, Andrew. "Preface." In: *The Blackwell Companion to the Qurʾān*, ed. A. Rippin. Blackwell Reference Online, 2008, DOI: 10.1002/9780470751428.fmatter.

Robson, Eleanor. "The Clay Table Book in Sumer, Assyria, and Babylonia." In *A Companion to the History of the Book*, eds. Simon Eliot and Jonathan Rose, 67–83. Malden, MA: Blackwell, 2007.

Rosenthal, Franz. "'Of Making Books There is No End': The Classical Muslim View." In *The Book in the Islamic World: The Written Word and Communication in the Middle East*, ed. George N. Atiyeh, 33–56. Washington, DC: Library of Congress, 1995.

Said, Edward W. *Orientalism.* New York: Vintage, 1979.

Saleh, Walid A. *The Formation of the Classical Tafsīr Tradition: The Qurʾān Commentary of al-Thaʿlabī.* Leiden: Brill, 2004.

Schonfield, Roger C. "Stop the Presses: Is the Monograph Headed toward an E-only Future?" Issue brief, Ithaka S+R, 10 December 2013. Available at: http://sr.ithaka.org/sites/de fault/files/files/SR_BriefingPaper_Presses_120913.pdf

Schreibman, Susan, Ray Siemens, and John Unsworth. "The Digital Humanities and Humanities Computing: An Introduction." In *A Companion to the Digital Humanities*, eds. Susan Schreibman, Ray Siemens, and John Unsworth, xxiii–xxvii. Malden, MA: Blackwell, 2004.

Simonsohn, Uriel. "Conversion to Islam: A Case Study for the Use of Legal Sources." *History Compass* 11 no. 8 (2013): 647–62.

Sims-Williams, Ursula. "15,000 Images of Persian Manuscripts Online." *British Library Asian and African Studies Blog*, 27 January 2014. Available at: http://britishlibrary.typepad.co.uk/asian-and-african/2014/01/15000-images-of-persian--manuscripts-online.html.

Touati, Houari. *L'armoire à sagesse: Bibliothèques et collections en Islam.* Paris: Aubier, 2003.

Unsworth, John. "Documenting the Reinvention of Text: The Importance of Failure." *Journal of Electronic Publishing* 3 no. 2 (1997). Available at: http://dx.doi.org/10.3998/3336451.0003.201

Witkam, Jan Just. "Establishing the Stemma: Fact or Fiction." *Manuscripts of the Middle East* 3 (1988): 88–101.

—. "The Son's Copy: Remarks on a Contemporary Manuscript of Ibn ʿAsākir's 'History of the City of Damascus'." In *Maqālāt wa-dirāsāt muhdāh ilā Doktor Ṣalāḥ al-Dīn al-Munajjid*, 591–610. London: Furqan Foundation, 2002.

Chip Rossetti

Al-Kindi on the Kindle: The Library of Arabic Literature and the Challenges of Publishing Bilingual Arabic-English Books

Recent innovations in electronic publishing offer enormous possibilities for the field of Middle East and Islamic studies, and in particular for the dissemination and searchability of Arabic texts. The growing number of academic institutions and libraries that have scanned their manuscript collections and are making them available online has been a great boon to scholars. My own work as managing editor for the Library of Arabic Literature (LAL) book series has introduced me to some of the digital possibilities for Arabic texts as well as the technological challenges that face a bilingual book series in particular.[1] The experience of the series, which publishes pre-modern Arabic texts in facing-page bilingual editions, may serve as a useful guide for similar scholarly projects aimed at publishing and/or translating texts in Middle Eastern languages.

Before turning to a discussion of some of our digital challenges, I provide below a brief overview of the Library of Arabic Literature series. The LAL is supported by a grant from the New York University Abu Dhabi Institute and is published by New York University Press. The originator and general editor of the series is Professor Philip Kennedy of NYU's Middle Eastern and Islamic Studies Department. As general editor, Kennedy heads an eight-member editorial board, which consists of scholars of pre-modern Arabic and Islamic studies from American and European universities. The role of the board is to consider proposals from would-be editor-translators, shepherd individual projects through to completion, and approve manuscripts for publication. The chronological scope of the series covers Arabic texts from the pre-Islamic period down to the *nahḍa* era, the nineteenth-century period of literary and cultural revival and reform sometimes referred to as the Arab Renaissance'. The thematic scope is wide as well, including such broadly diverse texts as the *Risāla* of al-Shāfiʿī, a foundational work of Islamic jurisprudence; the 1855 proto-novel *al-Sāq ʿalā al-sāq*, by pioneering journalist Aḥmad Fāris al-Shidyāq; and the *Risālat al-Ghufrān*, by the blind Syrian poet Abū l-ʿAlāʾ al-Maʿarrī.

1 The Library of Arabic Literature website, accessed January 10, 2015, available at: http://www.libraryofarabicliterature.org/. I should confess that the title of this article is a bit of a red herring, since we have not yet signed up a text by al-Kindi for the series. But the consonance was hard to resist.

The series aims for a broad range of genres, including poetry, poetics, biography, travel and geographical literature, theology, law, and *adab*, broadly defined. If nothing else, our experiences over the last few years have reiterated the centrality of collaboration in producing good translations. Every text in the series is assigned a project editor—an LAL editorial board member who acts as a sounding-board and advisor to the editor-translator, ensuring that she is adhering to series style and producing a quality edition and what we term a "modern, lucid English translation." A final manuscript must also meet the approval of its project editor before it can be accepted for publication.

Early in the series, the editors and I realized that if we were simply going to reprint entire contemporary edited Arabic texts, we would need to work out licensing agreements with Arabic-language publishing houses. Given the complexities and limitations involved in acquiring permissions from third parties, we came to the conclusion that we would have to ask our translators to produce their own Arabic editions. Thus, from early on, we stopped thinking of this as simply a "translation series," but rather as a series producing "edition-translations." We also adopted the term "editor-translators" to better reflect the role of the scholars who produce the books. In part because of the need to balance the facing-page layout, we decided not to require critical editions with a full *apparatus criticus* on the Arabic page. Instead, we ask editor-translators to produce "authoritative" editions, by which we mean that they consult original manuscripts as well as previous published editions in order to establish the LAL edition.

Our requirement that scholars get hold of original manuscripts and produce their own edition is a daunting one and has had the practical effect of limiting the number of scholars who are willing to undertake it. But if editing these pre-modern texts is challenging, translating them into contemporary English accessible to both scholars and non-experts is harder still; as we've learned, the pool of potential editor-translators for pre-modern Arabic texts is quite limited. A further obstacle is the fact that—as is well known among academic translators—tenure committees often look askance at translations, in spite of the intellectual heavy lifting involved in editing and translating a pre-modern Arabic text, and in spite of the level of scholarship required to establish an edition and provide a substantial introductory essay and detailed explanatory endnotes.

New York University Press brought to this project some experience with dual-language books in the form of the Clay Sanskrit Library, a similar series of pre-modern texts published with Romanized Sanskrit and English on facing pages.[2]

---

2 Jinaratna, *The Epitome of Queen Lilávati, Volume One*, ed. and trans. R.C.C. Fynes (New York:

Both the Library of Arabic Literature and the Clay Sanskrit Library are part of a recent trend of new facing-page series published by university presses, notably Harvard and Princeton. The antecedent to these new series is the Loeb Classical Library published by Harvard University Press; since 1912, the Loeb has published over 500 volumes of Greek and Latin literature in facing-page editions, and it continues to publish more texts as well as new translations of previously published texts for which the first English translation now seems out of date.[3] Harvard University Press has started a number of similar Loeb-style series: it now has the *I Tatti Renaissance Library*, the *Dumbarton Oaks Medieval Library*, and the *Murty Classical Library of India*, which is scheduled to publish its first books early in 2015).[4] Similarly, Princeton University Press publishes a bilingual poetry series titled *Facing Pages*, while in 2009 the University of Washington Press launched the *Classics of Chinese Thought* series.[5] Unfortunately, very few of the series listed above are available in electronic form, which means that LAL did not have many models to follow for our own digital formats.

The central element of LAL's digital production is its use of single-source XML files. XML (shorthand for eXtensible Markup Language) is a standard established by the World Wide Web consortium that provides rules for digitally encoding documents. XML has the advantage of being independent of any one hardware or software system, making it maximally applicable to any current or future iterations of a text. A document is said to be 'well-formed' when it obeys the syntax of XML: for example, XML elements that begin with an open tag, such as **<heading>**, to indicate that following words are part of a chapter

---

New York University Press, JJC Foundation, 2005), 9. Historically, Sanskrit has not had its own writing system but has been written in a variety of regional scripts. Thus, for the Clay series to print the texts without resorting to Roman transliteration, they would have had to use multiple scripts to accommodate the broad geographical and historical range of the texts they published. Alternatively, they would have had to transliterate all the texts into a writing system such as Devanagari, now commonly used for Sanskrit. Additionally, its editors envisioned their books as learning tools for beginning students of Sanskrit and thus decided to avoid the complexities of the spelling-changes associated with *sandhi* and the difficulties of scripts that do not mark separations between letters.

3 "History of the Loeb Classical Library," Harvard University Press, accessed January 11, 2015, available at: http://www.hup.harvard.edu/features/loeb/history.html.

4 "Murty Classical Library of India," Harvard University Press, accessed January 11, 2015, available at: http://www.hup.harvard.edu/collection.php?cpk=2015.

5 "Announcing a New Series: Classical Chinese Thought," University of Washington Press website, accessed January 11, 2015, available at: http://www.washington.edu/uwpress/books/series/ChineseThought.pdf.

heading must also have a corresponding closing tag, always marked by a slash (**</heading>**).

XML is best thought of as a metalanguage that in turn provides rules for defining a specific 'markup language' (informally referred to as a 'tag set', a markup language is in fact a formally defined file known as a DTD or schema) that a programmer or publisher applies to a text. Like many other projects coming from the humanities, LAL's markup language is a version of the guidelines set by the Text Encoding Initiative (TEI), an international consortium that maintains standards for electronically identifying and tagging elements of texts in digital format. First published in 1994 and regularly updated, TEI's guidelines ensure that these digitized elements are standardized across texts.[6] As a result, they are now commonly adopted by institutions, libraries, and publishers working in the humanities and social sciences for digitally encoding texts. The TEI's website explains succinctly the relationship between XML (the metalanguage) and TEI itself (the markup language): "A markup language must specify how markup is to be distinguished from text, what markup is allowed, what markup is required, and what the markup means. XML provides the means for doing the first three; documentation such as these Guidelines is required for the last." The coding added to a text in XML is descriptive rather than procedural; that is, a tag on a word describes a feature of that word, rather than indicating how or whether it should be treated differently on output. To take one example, TEI guidelines include a 'Foreign Word or Expression' tag to indicate that a particular word or phrase is in a non-English language. Likewise, it also includes a code to indicate that a series of words is a title (whether article, journal, monograph, series, or unpublished item). Thus, the following phrase in the translator's final text:

> ...al-Iṣfahānī, author of the *Book of Songs* (*Kitāb al-Aghānī*)...

is marked up in the XML file as follows:

> ...al-Iṣfahānī, author of the <title level="m" corresp="#kitabalaghani">Book of Songs</title> (<title level="m" xml:lang="ara-Latn" xml:id="kitabalaghani">Kitāb al-Aghānī</title>)...

Note, however, that the XML tag does not indicate how the titles are to be treated, such as by placing them in italics, or putting them in a different font, or simply leaving them unmarked. Instead, it provides semantic information about the

6 "3 Elements Available in All TEI Documents," Text Encoding Initiative website, accessed January 11, 2015, available at: http://www.tei-c.org/release/doc/tei-p5-doc/en/html/CO.html.

titles using a system of 'attributes': that they are monographs (**level="m"**), that the title of the second monograph, "Kitāb al-Aghānī," is in Romanized Arabic (**xml:lang="ara-Latn"**), and that "Book of Songs" is a translation of it (the **corresp** and **xml:id** attributes.) Decisions on formatting are thus made only when the XML is used to generate a particular output for the text, whether a page proof for a print book, a website, or an e-book.

As it happens, I was fortunate to be able to hire for the Library of Arabic Literature the same digital production manager who had designed the customized XML tags and scripting for the Clay Sanskrit Library series. Like the Clay series before it, the Library of Arabic Literature uses an XML-first workflow. In an XML-first workflow, an author's manuscript is tagged in XML right after it is delivered to the publisher; all further work on the manuscript—from copyediting to the generation of pages using desktop publishing software such as InDesign or TeX—is based on an underlying XML source. While some academic publishers now use an XML-first workflow for their books, other presses will add basic XML tagging to a book only after it has been copyedited, typeset, and proofread: that is, the structural electronic tags indicating chapter and paragraph breaks, headings, titles, and quotations, are inserted into an XML file created from the print-ready file. The XML-first workflow allows us to add not only broad structural tags, but to insert in-line semantic tags as well, such as glosses, titles, foreign words, verse, publication information, inline quotations, date ranges, and others.

During the set-up phase, the digital production manager, with my input, specified the full range of customized tags and elements that the Library of Arabic Literature series would need, including modifications to the generic tags outlined by the TEI guidelines. For example, since poetry appears so frequently in pre-modern Arabic texts, the digital production manager defined an extension of TEI's **<seg>** (for "segment") element—which is intended to represent any segmentation of the text below the block level—as a **<hemistich>** tag to designate a partial line of verse within the text. Other elements that are prominent in Arabic texts, such as Quranic quotations, are tagged as well, although with a customized 'Quranic Material' tag that we have added to the fairly generic set of tags defined in the TEI guidelines. The TEI guidelines, which are intended to be as flexible as possible, provide a system by which extensions such as these can be made fully compliant with the principles of TEI and even allow the user to generate corresponding documentation and schemas.

For individual texts, the bulk of the structural and semantic tagging is done by the digital production manager before the XML file is turned over to the copyeditor. Our copyeditors view the XML files using XMLMind software, which provides a user-friendly editing environment and allows them to view both Arabic and English texts onscreen at the same time. In general, our copyeditors tend to leave the Arabic text alone, since it is the product of the collation and comparison of manuscripts and earlier editions to which the copyeditor does not have access. Although the bulk of the XML tagging is done 'in-house', as it were, before being sent out for copyediting, the XMLMind application is also highly customizable, allowing our digital production manager to write a 'skin' specifically for our project, which allows our copyeditors to add or amend the existing tagging without a detailed understanding of how XML functions.

In general, the XML-first workflow required something of a learning curve for our freelancers. However, our small but growing band of copyeditors has quickly adapted to the requirements of XML tagging and to the quirks of generating copyeditor's queries in an XMLMind framework.

The print editions are generated from the XML using InDesign, customized to include scripts that ensure that the two facing texts remain parallel when laid out. For the printed typeface, we selected a traditional-looking 'calligraphic' font known as DecoType Naskh, designed by Dutch typographer Thomas Milo. As part of a software package known as Tasmeem, DecoType Naskh has the flexibility to allow for the stacking of Arabic letters and offers tools for text-shaping and spacing. Our ability to keep both texts aligned on the printed page depends not only on Tasmeem's flexibility, but on the numbered sections that simplify the layout. Early in the life of the series, as our first texts were being translated, the series editorial board made it a rule that editor-translators should divide their texts into short sections, generally from one to three paragraphs in length, and number the equivalent sections in both Arabic and English using an identical numbering system of their choosing, on the theory that the person best capable of making logical divisions in the text was the person who had translated it. The division of the text into short numbered sections allows the digital production manager to ensure that neither the Arabic nor the English side gets too far out of sync with the other when typeset.

The concept of a facing page series is premised on a print format, and thus converting our books to digital editions required some careful thinking. Since e-reader screens aren't ideally suited for double-column display, a parallel text alignment makes less sense on an iPad or Kindle. In fact, many other facing-page series published by university presses have not been made available as individual e-books. The Loeb Classical Library, for example, was digitized for the first time in 2014 and is now available as an electronic corpus on a subscription basis to both institutions and individuals.[7] With over 520 backlist titles to draw on, a corpus format made sense for the Loeb, and now that its texts are digitized, it may eventually decide to make e-books available for individual purchase as well.

For the Library of Arabic Literature, our foray into digital publishing has encountered some of the same obstacles that have limited the widespread use of e-books in the Arab world. Until recently, constraints both technical and practical —including publishers' concerns about piracy and the limited penetration of credit cards into the Arab consumer market—have hindered the widespread electronic publication of texts. As a result, Arabic-language e-books have been slow to catch on among the wider reading public. A major technical hurdle was crossed only in the last few years, with the introduction of the EPUB3 in late 2011. EPUB is the free and open standard for reflowable content and serves as the format for almost all electronic books (the major exception being Amazon's proprietary e-book format for its Kindle devices). Unlike previous EPUB versions, EPUB3 fully supports a right-to-left text-flow, which has lowered the barrier for electronic publishing in Arabic. Although sales numbers in the region are hard to come by, anecdotal evidence suggests that e-book readership in the Arab world is growing.[8] In 2014, the decision by one of the largest mobile phone companies in the Middle East to create an Arabic e-book app and store prompted a wave of publishers to offer their books in electronic format to be read on mobile phones rather than on dedicated e-readers.[9] Likewise, the introduction of numerous other apps specifically designed for Arabic e-books since 2014 also points to a growing audience of readers of e-books.[10] The Arabic e-book market, however, is still in its very early stages.

Using the same XML source from which we produce our print editions, we now create EPUB files for all of our new books. The EPUB format can accommodate texts in both directions and allows the Arabic text to be reflowed and re-

7 "The Digital Loeb Classical Library," Harvard University Press Website, accessed January 11, 2015, available at: http://www.hup.harvard.edu/features/loeb/digital.html.

8 "'An E-Book Frenzy': Talking with Mahmoud Aboulfotouh about the New World of Arabic Digital Publishing," last modified May 16, 2014, accessed January 11, 2015, available at: http://arablit.wordpress.com/2014/05/16/an-e-book-frenzy-talking-with-mahmoud-aboulfotouh-about-the-new-world-of-arabic-digital-publishing/.

9 "Fūdāfūn tuṭliq awwal maktaba ilīktrūniyya li-l-kutub al-ʿarabiyya,"*al-Ahrām al-Raqmī*, last modified February 12, 2014, accessed January 11, 2015, available at: http://www.ahramdigital.org.eg/Community.aspx?Serial=1536165.

10 "Five Must-Have Arabic E-book Readers," Arabnet, last modified January 27, 2014, accessed January 10, 2015, available at: http://news.arabnet.me/article-arabic-e-book-readers/.

sized, just as the English is. The MOBI format—used exclusively by Kindles—has proved more challenging, but we have found workarounds for it.

Our first challenge for both EPUBs and MOBI files was deciding how to display the two languages in relation to each other. One straightforward possibility was to treat them as separate sections within an e-book, such that a reader could elect to read only the English chapters and ignore the Arabic. While attractive, that format seemed to defeat the idea of the series, namely that it should give both languages equal visibility and prominence. As a result, since texts in both languages were already conveniently divided into numbered sections, we opted to alternate chunks of text as the reader scrolls down (i.e., section 1.1 in English, followed by 1.1 in Arabic, 1.2 in English, 1.2 in Arabic, etc.) Thus, a reader who could read only the English would at least be confronted with the Arabic text as she scrolled between English sections. On screen, the Arabic text is rendered in the same DecoType Naskh typeface, but using an older, True Type version. Unlike the version used to produce the print books, the True Type version has only basic character shapes and lacks the ligature and variant engine of the print version's Tasmeem interface.

Creating MOBI files for the Kindle, however, posed a different challenge, since Kindle devices cannot handle right-to-left directionality on their screens. The only real option was to treat the Arabic sections as image files rather than as text that automatically reflows its lines when the text size is increased or decreased or when the e-reader is turned sideways. Inevitably, this produces a large file size, since Kindles (and particularly the later models such as Kindle Fire) require a 300 DPI resolution in order to display properly. However, beyond the issue of large file sizes, the inevitable clunkiness of static Arabic text on the Kindle gave us pause for several months. However, despite the technological limitations of Kindle devices, our overriding concern was to make the books available on as many platforms as possible, so we now use the existing script that generates EPUB files and modify it so that it produces line-by-line image references for the Arabic text in a MOBI version for Kindle devices.

As I mentioned above, the Library of Arabic Literature sees translation as a collaborative enterprise, in which the involvement of two or more scholars invariably leads to an improved translation. At our semi-annual meetings, for example, the Library of Arabic Literature board participates in group translation workshops, often bringing in a few other scholars—including non-Arabists—as we make our way through a particularly challenging text. In that regard, our collaborative approach to editing and translating pre-modern Arabic texts shares much in common with the digital humanities as a whole, where crowdsourcing and team-based projects take precedence over solo-authored works. Neither translation nor the digital humanities adheres to the old-fashioned model of scholarship, in which a solitary scholar researches and produces a finished monograph in isolation. For me and for the series editors, the first years of the series have presented a steep learning curve on a number of digital issues.

The advantage of a well-formed XML source for the production of our books is that it ensures that our files will not be made obsolete by future publishing formats. For any format—existing or futue—a script can be written to provide instructions on how to treat each XML element. Ayas properly tagged as Quranic material, for example, can be instructed to print in a different color for a deluxe print edition or to link to an audio clip of a Quranic reciter for an enhanced electronic version. LAL is now working with a separate scholarly digitization project that has agreed to lemmatize our Arabic texts in XML. As a result, individual Arabic words will be marked with a tag indicating their root letters and perhaps a link to an Arabic lexicon. At the moment, those tags have no place in our print or individual e-book editions, but that kind of 'deep tagging' will be of significant value if and when LAL ever decides to produce a fully searchable electronic corpus.

For a born-digital series such as the Library of Arabic Literature, much of the promise of a single-source XML workflow lies in its manipulability and platform-independence; we are not restricted to particular formats or treatments, even if print books, individual e-books, and a searchable database seem like the only logical formats now. Our XML has already made it easy to produce English-only paperback editions via a script that strips away the Arabic from the underlying XML; for the same reason, it would likewise be a straightforward matter to generate Arabic-only print editions as well for the Arabic-speaking market.[11]

For similar scholarly bilingual initiatives, a well-formed XML can ensure that their data can merge smoothly with other corpora. Depending on the aims of a particular project, the XML format can help turn a set of texts into a language-learning tool, for example by lemmatizing individual words in a text, making it available on the web, and linking it to an online dictionary, so that hovering over a word opens a text box with the dictionary definition. Depending on the level of tagging added, XML can allow detailed, context-specific searches (such as searching across a diwan for verse tagged as *ṭawīl* or *rajaz*) across a variety of formats, or it can allow an end-user to manipulate the text as he prefers (such as by selecting and displaying onscreen all the verse that appears in an al-Jāḥiẓ text.) These are only a few of the many possibilities that a deeply-tagged

11 In the case of the Library of Arabic Literature, the metalanguage of our books is English, so an Arabic-only publication would likely require translating the editor-translator's introduction, note on the text, and backmatter.

XML system can offer scholarly digitization initiatives, and LAL itself is only now beginning to look ahead to the kinds of features and functionality we would like to see in a future electronic corpus. From the beginning, the editors of the Library of Arabic Literature have hoped that these edition-translations would have a transformative effect on the fields of Arabic and Middle Eastern studies. What we are only now coming to realize is how much the widening horizons of digital scholarship may end up having a transformative effect on the nature and scope of the series itself.

Bibliography

Books

Jinaratna. *The Epitome of Queen Lilávati, Volume One*. Ed. and trans. R.C.C. Fynes. New York: New York University Press, JJC Foundation, 2005.

Websites

Al-Ahram al-Raqmi. "Fūdāfūn tuṭliq awwal maktaba ilīktrūniyya li-l-kutub al-ʿarabiyya." Last modified February 12, 2014. Accessed January 11, 2015. Available at: http://www.ahramdigital.org.eg/Community.aspx?Serial=1536165.

Arabic Literature in English. " 'An E-Book Frenzy': Talking with Mahmoud Aboulfotouh about the New World of Arabic Digital Publishing." Last modified May 16, 2014. Accessed January 11, 2015. Available at: http://arablit.wordpress.com/2014/05/16/an-e-book-frenzy-talking-with-mahmoud-aboulfotouh-about-the-new-world-of-arabic-digital-publishing/.

Arabnet. "Five Must-Have Arabic E-book Readers." Last modified January 27, 2014. Accessed January 10, 2015. Available at: http://news.arabnet.me/article-arabic-e-book-readers/.

Clay Sanskrit Library. Accessed January 11, 2015. Available at: http://www.claysanskritlibrary.org/.

Harvard University Press. "The Digital Loeb Classical Library." Accessed January 11, 2015. Available at: http://www.hup.harvard.edu/features/loeb/digital.html.

Harvard University Press. "History of the Loeb Classical Library." Accessed January 11, 2015. Available at: http://www.hup.harvard.edu/features/loeb/history.html.

Harvard University Press. "Murty Classical Library of India." Accessed January 11, 2015. Available at: http://www.hup.harvard.edu/collection.php?cpk=2015.

Library of Arabic Literature. Accessed January 10, 2015. Available at: http://www.libraryofarabicliterature.org/.

Text Encoding Initiative. "3. Elements Available in All TEI Documents." Accessed January 11, 2015. Available at: http://www.tei-c.org/release/doc/tei-p5-doc/en/html/CO.html.

University of Washington Press. "Announcing a New Series: Classical Chinese Thought." Accessed January 11, 2015. Available at: http://www.washington.edu/uwpress/books/series/ChineseThought.pdf.

Nadia Yaqub

Working with Grassroots Digital Humanities Projects: The Case of the Tall al-Zaʿtar Facebook Groups

As universities discover new and exciting ways to harness digital technology for scholarship in the humanities, it is useful to pause and reflect on how other groups may also be engaging with the digital tools at their disposal for their own purposes. Such projects may overlap with those carried out by scholars, but because they bring different agendas to their practice and because their access to resources may be limited, they differ in significant ways. Scholars may dismiss them because of what they perceive as a lack of rigor. Conversely, they may rely on them as first-step research tools to identify key individuals or texts to facilitate their own projects without considering all the implications of such practices. I propose instead that they be read as grassroots digital archives that may offer individuals and institutions new perspectives on the possibilities, limitations, and complexities of the digital humanities, especially in relation to narrating or recuperating non-elite knowledge and perspectives.

My own engagement with the concept of grassroots digital humanities arose out of a plan to create a database documentary about the Tall al-Zaʿtar refugee camp in Lebanon, its destruction in 1976, and the social and cultural work that Palestinians engaged in after the fall of the camp to address the resulting trauma, material loss, and social fragmentation. My interest began with a remarkable institution, the orphanage *Bayt Aṭfāl al-Ṣumūd* (the Home for Steadfast Children) that was created by the PLO in the immediate aftermath of the siege and destruction of the camp to house children orphaned by the violence. A filmmaker who had worked with the PLO in Beirut in the late 1970s and early 1980s had film footage and photographs that were to form the starting point for the project. I planned to use these images to facilitate oral histories with children and caregivers who had participated in the orphanage. The oral histories would trace networks backward in time into the Palestinian refugee camp of Tall al-Zaʿtar and forward to the communities and institutions with which participants continue to engage today, more than three decades after the orphanage was destroyed during the Israeli invasion of Beirut in 1982. The project was to be restorative not just of the history of the orphanage itself, but also of the work of the General Union of Palestinian Women, one of the key sectoral organizations that implemented important Palestinian social programs in the 1970s and early 1980s, but one that has left relatively few traces in the literature documenting the social work of the PLO during this period.[1]

In the fall of 2012, in the context of that research, I learned of two Facebook groups that had been recently created by survivors of Tall al-Zaʿtar and their descendants: *Mukhayyam al-ṣumūd al-usṭūrī Tall al-Zaʿtar* (Tall al-Zaʿtar, The Camp of Legendary Steadfastness, hereafter *Mukhayyam*) and *Rābiṭat ahālī mukhayyam Tall al-Zaʿtar* (The Association of the People of Tall al-Zaʿtar Refugee Camp, hereafter *Rābiṭa*). As I began to monitor the groups, I was struck by how much group members' impulses to archive and map the past overlapped with mine, even as their primary goal—that of sustaining a community bound by a common past— diverged from my own. What were the implications, then, of my project for these groups and the people who created and sustained them? The groups were clearly an invaluable resource for my own research, offering ready access to images, anecdotes, names, and other useful information. What ethical issues were raised by my use of these groups as sources to create another publicly available digital representation of their history? How might my own project coexist with theirs? Would my work be useful to these group members? How did the existence of these groups affect the rationale for my own project? Do new questions surrounding citational practices arise from the potential intersection of their project and mine?

In this chapter, I will argue that understanding social media activities like the Tall al-Zaʿtar Facebook groups as grassroots digital archives created out of particular social and political contexts to serve particular local needs can open up an ethical and useful way for scholars to engage with such projects. Such an engagement would recognize the implications of context on their structure and content and remain sensitive to how community needs might necessitate practices and foci that differ significantly from those that usually frame scholarly archival or digital humanities projects. It would be sensitive to the primary importance assigned to the social aspects of the site—that is, how building and sustaining networks might be as important, if not more important, than the verifiability or completeness of material posted to the site. The demands of networking certainly overlap with those of the scholar who strives for complete, accurate, and verifiable information, but they are not always perfectly consonant with them. Information or images that shame a site member or her affiliates, or that contradict or complicate an accepted and valued narrative of events, may never be posted to the Facebook group pages, or if they do arise, they

---

1 Jihān Ḥilū, *al-Marʾa l-Filasṭīniyya: al-muqāwama wa-l-taghayyurāt al-ijtimāʿiyya* (al-Bīrah: Markaz al-Marʾa l- Filasṭīniyya lil-Abḥāth wa-l-Tawthīq, 2009).

may be buried or marginalized in the flood of postings and comments that sustain the accepted narrative, even as group members strive to accumulate as many different details and images as they can.

Relatedly, a sensitive engagement would recognize that such projects are bound by social conventions that both limit and structure the content of the group pages. Mention of life-changing events (births, weddings, graduations, deaths, etc.) necessitates formulaic expressions of congratulation and mourning that may appear to clutter the pages for those who want to use them as sources for information. A researcher may need to wade through 60 or more such comments while searching for nuggets of new information buried among them. Most importantly, a sensitive engagement with such projects must be aware that accuracy has an affective dimension. That is, the social and contextual nature of the sites (and the suppressing of particular information or counternarratives and the proliferation of ritual discourse that that might entail) are not necessarily impediments to a fuller understanding of these communities and their pasts; they can actually contribute to that understanding and to the significance of events to group members. This is particularly true for posts that engage with the past—with life in Tall al-Zaʿtar before its destruction, the siege of the camp, and the reconstitution of a Tall al-Zaʿtar community in Damour after its fall. These posts are often not just about what happened when and to whom, but also about reviving or sustaining certain feelings of collectivity and agency that existed in the community before 1982 for mobilization in the 2010s, a time that has been characterized primarily by social disintegration, economic precarity, and political impotency for Palestinians in Lebanon. They may also revive feelings of nostalgic loss and trauma, which, painful though they may be, also serve a social function in reinforcing communal ties for communities in Lebanon and elsewhere.

Finally, designers of digital humanities projects, particularly those emerging from the Western academy, must be cognizant of the power structures to which their scholarship contributes. Scholars must continually bear in mind that they cannot produce knowledge that is outside such structures. What implications might there be to taking information that resides in the memories of survivors and their networks (including Facebook groups) for incorporation into a scholarly project? While such work may at first glance seem to be purely recuperative (knowledge is 'saved' from oblivion, codified, and preserved in an archive for use by future generations, including future generations of survivors), one might ask what the broader implications of this process are. Should a DH scholar 'preserve' the social side of the Tall al-Zaʿtar narrative, given its contextual and emergent nature? 'Scrubbing' the story of Tall al-Zaʿtar of its contemporary social side almost certainly necessitates complicating the received narrative. Otherwise the project becomes merely a repetition of what is already known. What agendas might lie under such a drive to complicate the narrative of sacrifice and bravery that already exists? How might research on the sites alter the sites themselves? I cannot definitely answer all of these complex questions in this short chapter. What I will do is to describe in more depth the Facebook groups themselves and how reading them as grassroots digital archives might facilitate a productive and respectful scholarly engagement with them.

1. The History of Tall al-Zaʿtar

The Tall al-Zaʿtar refugee camp was founded in 1950 to the northeast of Beirut to house refugees of the 1948 war (the Nakba) who were expelled from Palestine to Lebanon. It grew quickly as Palestinian refugees from the south of Lebanon (as well as impoverished Lebanese) moved to the capital in search of work. In 1972, its population was approximately 17,000, of whom 13,000 were Palestinian.[2] By that time, the camp was a dense warren of unpaved streets, cement homes with zinc roofs, and open drains. It was among the largest camps in Beirut, the poorest, and had a reputation for being highly politicized. Families were large, and the population overall was very young. Roughly one-third of children aged 6–14 did not attend school, and healthcare was grossly inadequate. The poverty of refugee life in Lebanon in general was exacerbated by political tension and harassment that intensified throughout the 1960s. Lebanon's security police became more aggressive in their monitoring of camp life, and the mobility of refugees outside the camps was often constrained. When in 1969 Lebanon and the PLO signed the Cairo Agreement, which gave the PLO authority over the refugee camps in Lebanon and the right to wage armed struggle against Israel from within them, refugees were eager to participate in the nationalist project. As a woman from another camp, who was a schoolgirl at the time, told Rosemary Sayigh: "I was waiting for someone to make a revolution, and, thank God it came, and I can share it."[3]

The events leading to the fall of Tall al-Zaʿtar in 1976 were one of the major atrocities of the Lebanese Civil War. A coalition of right-wing Lebanese militias held the camp under complete siege for 53 days. No food or medical supplies were allowed in, and dead and wounded were not allowed out, except within

2 Hānī Mundus, *al-ʿAmal wa-l-ʿummāl fī l-mukhayyam al-filasṭīnī* (Beirut: Palestine Liberation Organization Research Center, 1974).

3 Rosemary Sayigh, *Palestinians: From Peasants to Revolutionaries: A People's History* (London: Zed Press 1979), 136.

the context of negotiated evacuations of the wounded near the end of the siege. The siege was finally lifted when camp residents surrendered after the last water faucet within the camp ran dry. Although there are no accurate statistics, at least 3,000 died during the siege itself and in the massacre that occurred as residents left the camp after their surrender on August 12, 1976. Survivors of Tall al-Zaʿtar resettled in camps throughout Lebanon; many moved to the abandoned village of Damour, where a Tall al-Zaʿtar community was reconstituted. Some moved to the Sabra and Shatila area, where they fell victim to another atrocity, the 1982 massacre of Sabra and Shatila. Damour was also destroyed in 1982, and its residents moved again.[4] Today Tall al-Zaʿtar survivors and descendants in Lebanon live mainly in the Shatila and Mar Elias camps of Beirut, the Beqaa Valley, and Badawi camp in North Lebanon.

The work of incorporating Tall al-Zaʿtar into a Palestinian narrative of the violence and sacrifice deemed necessary for national liberation began even before the siege had ended. No journalists or photographers were allowed into the camps, so images of the siege from within the camp were not disseminated. However, writings in Palestinian and sympathetic Lebanese publications referenced the bravery and sacrifice of the camp's residents as well as their steadfastness and resistance. Once the siege ended, the fall of the camp was quickly incorporated into Palestinian history. Yearly commemorative marches were held in Lebanon until the departure of the PLO from Lebanon in 1982–3. Within the first year of the siege, at least seven books were published about the siege, including three personal memoirs. Both the General Union of Palestinian Women and the Democratic Front for the Liberation of Palestine (DFLP) collected and published oral histories with survivors within weeks of the fall of the camp. The DFLP also published cable communications between the Palestinian leadership in West Beirut and military leaders within the camp. Tall al-Zaʿtar was also incorporated into Palestinian visual iconography through paintings and posters and inspired significant works of poetry, music, and fiction by, among others, Mahmoud Darwish, Muzaffar al-Nawab, Mustafa Kurd, Ahmad Fouad Negm, Sheikh Imam, and Liyana Badr. Among the outpouring of texts were at least seven Palestinian and Arab films created between 1976 and 1980 about the siege and fall of the camp. However, within a few years, Tall al-Zaʿtar was overshadowed by other events: the 1982 invasion of Lebanon, the massacre of Sabra and Shatila, the first intifada, Oslo, and so on.

4 Abdulrahim, Dima. "From Lebanon to West Berlin: The Ethnography of the Tall al-Zaʿtar Refugee Camp" (Ph.D. diss., University of Exeter, Exeter, UK, 1990).

The fall of the camp and ongoing violence in Lebanon accelerated a process already in place—that of Palestinian emigration out of Lebanon.[5] Because of its special status before the fall of the Berlin Wall, Berlin was a convenient entry point for asylum seekers trying to reach Western Europe. Thousands of Palestinians left Lebanon in the late 1970s and early 1980s. Later, another wave of immigrants settled in Norway and Sweden.[6] These communities maintained ties with family members in Lebanon and with each other. It is unclear how many survivors and descendants of Tall al-Zaʿtar live in Western Europe today. Estimates put the 1982 number of asylum seekers from Lebanon in West Berlin at 15,000 (45,000 for West Germany as a whole), of which Palestinians formed the largest group.[7]

The Tall al-Zaʿtar Facebook Groups

In *Heroes and Martyrs of Palestine*, Laleh Khalili speculates about the reasons for the disappearance of Tall al-Zaʿtar from Palestinian national discourses and practices of commemoration. Among the factors she lists are the utter destruction of the camp and the complete (and frequently multiple) dispersals of its survivors. In other words, the break in the geographically defined community was an important factor in the erasure of Tall al-Zaʿtar from the palimpsests of massacres and battles that Palestinians continue to commemorate.[8] Khalili conducted her field research in 2002, two years before the launch of Facebook and Myspace that heralded the beginning of the era of social media. She could not have imagined that in 2012, survivors of Tall al-Zaʿtar and their descendants would use this technology to launch a grassroots archival and commemorative project. Berlin residents launched the *Mukhayyam* Facebook group following a commemorative event held on September 1, 2012. A month later, the *Rābiṭa* Facebook group was started by survivors and descendants in Lebanon.[9]

Rhetorically, the Facebook groups perform a variety of acts: they network far-flung members, allowing a space for the phatic communication (that is, dis-

5 Of course, emigration was not an option for most refugees. Legal and economic hurdles to mobility of Palestinian refugees were and continue to be daunting.

6 Abdulrahim, *From Lebanon to West Berlin.*

7 Ibid.

8 Laleh Khalili, *Heroes and Martyrs of Palestine : The Politics of National Commemoration.* (Cambridge: Cambridge University Press, 2007), 178.

9 *Rābiṭa* itself was founded as an offline organization in June 2012 but did not launch its Facebook group until later.

course that functions solely or primarily to open up and sustain channels of communication) that maintains community or political networks.[10] Relatedly, they invite a familial gaze, creating affiliations "through various relational, cultural, and institutional processes—such as 'looking' and photography"[11] and constructing viewers as family members.[12] They are a site for commemoration, most conspicuously of the siege and fall of Tall al-Zaʿtar and its martyrs, but also for other events in Palestinian history. They are a site for documentation of current events relating to its members (e.g., their personal milestones, such as weddings and deaths as well as community gatherings) and for the collection of documents, photographs, and memoirs about life in Tall al-Zaʿtar before its destruction and about the siege and its aftermath. They are partly pedagogical —younger members ask questions of those who knew the camp personally— and so may play a role in the construction of postmemories of life in the camp and its fall.[13] Like museums, they serve as sites of display; images and documents are offered up (some are recycled through the site periodically) as fragments of history and culture for the edification and pleasure of site visitors. A significant percentage of the postings (perhaps the majority) consist of photographs of Tall al-Zaʿtar martyrs, survivors, and descendants, which elicit long trails of formulaic greetings, good wishes, condolences, or congratulations.

As digital archives, the Facebook groups serve as sites to elicit, store, and organize a range of materials. Group members use Facebook to remap both the geography of the destroyed camp and networks of affiliation. On both sites, formal mapping initiatives have been announced along with open calls to group members to report on the location of their family home and identify their neighbors. Informally, group members might crowdsource memories about particular aspects of camps life, such as the games children used to play, who had televisions, and how individuals wrangled opportunities to watch at shops and neighbors' or relatives' homes. Members discuss who was in each class at the camp's schools. Old photographs of the camp are valued both as memory aids (they may elicit threads in which one member's comments

---

10 Miriam Aouragh, *Palestine Online: Transnationalism, the Internet and the Construction of Identity* (London: I.B. Taurus, 2012); Vincent Miller, "New Media, Networking, and Phatic Culture," *Convergence* 14 (2008): 387–400.

11 Marianne Hirsch, *Family Frames: Photography, Narrative, and Postmemory* (Cambridge, MA Harvard University Press, 1997), 10.

12 Marianne Hirsch, "The Generation of Postmemory," *Poetics Today* 29 (2008): 113.

13 Marianne Hirsch and Leo Spitzer, "We would never have come without you: Generations of Nostalgia," in *Contested Pasts: the Politics of Memory* eds. Katharine Hodgkin and Susannah Radstone, 79–96 (London: Routledge, 2003).

jog the memory of others) and for their capacity to evoke feelings of nostalgia that in turn create a sense of collective belonging. Images and anecdotes about life in Damour after the siege of the camp play a similar role, although the memories may arouse slightly different emotions. Life in Tall al-Zaʿtar, known affectionately as *ʿāṣimat al-fuqarāʾ* or "the capital of the poor," before the siege is remembered as a difficult but beautiful time when people worked together to survive poverty and discrimination, but did so under conditions of dignity. For survivors, there are echoes in these memories of those of an earlier generation who remember life before the Nakba. Like the Nakba, the fall of Tall al-Zaʿtar is the traumatic rupture around which a collective identity is structured; an understanding of pre-rupture life as fundamentally different from both the time of trauma and the present is necessary to the Tall al-Zaʿtar narrative. In this regard, the Facebook groups play an important role as a digital archive not just of images and information, but also of the nostalgia that shapes viewers' reception of them.

The groups also archive memories, documents, and images of the final siege and fall of the camp. The narrative of that siege, the violence that accompanied it, and the heroic steadfastness with which residents of Tall al-Zaʿtar withstood it were for the most part narratively fixed in the outpouring of commemorative work that took place immediately after the siege. Group members rely heavily on this material as sources for their postings about the siege.[14] Such postings may appear at any time, but are particularly prevalent on anniversaries of significant events in the camp's history, such as the 1975 bus massacre or the siege and fall of the camp itself.[15] On *Mukhayyam*, the 53 days of the siege are marked with daily postings of quotes from newspapers and memoirs, often recounting what had happened on that particular day. The postings elicit a flood of painful memories and emotions from site members. This time is also frequently evoked with the posting of martyrs' photos, which can happen at any time of the year. Martyrs' photos are often accompanied by information of their role in the siege itself or elicit such information in comments from viewers.

The affective power of postings about the siege and fall of the camp dwarf those of almost any other type of post, since it is the fall of the camp that defines

---

14 Nadia Yaqub, "The Afterlives of Violent Images: Reading Photographs from the Tall al-Zaʿtar Refugee Camp on Facebook," *Middle East Journal of Culture and Communication*, 8:2–3 (2015): 327–354.

15 The bus massacre, recognized as the start of the Lebanese Civil War, occurred on April 13, 1975. Christian militiamen fired upon a busload of Palestinians traveling to Tall al-Zaʿtar, killing 28 and wounding 19 passengers.

the current dispersed community as a community.[16] Posts about the siege elicit feelings of revenge, determination ("We will survive despite hardships because we will win in the end"), encouragement ("We are a people of determination and pride"), and pain ("Good morning to the deep wound" and "Tall al-Zaʿtar is a wound residing in the heart. It is a painful memory buried deeply in our hearts and memories"). Many responses are formulaic, similar to expressions of mourning that members post under images of martyrs and expressions of congratulations that follow happier images.

Members of the Tall al-Zaʿtar Facebook groups also archive memories of the Palestinian resistance movement (roughly 1968–1982) more generally, although in a less complete or organized fashion than for events and memories related directly to Tall al-Zaʿtar. Memories of iconic battles and incidents of heroism and martyrdom—such as the battle of Karamah, withstanding the Israeli invasion of 1982, or the massacre of Sabra and Shatila—also appear frequently. Group members draw on their archive of memories of Tall al-Zaʿtar in times of hardship for other Palestinian communities today, such as the 2014 war in Gaza, the recent strife in Jerusalem, and the siege of the Yarmouk camp in Syria, which, of course, shares particular resonances with the siege of Tall al-Zaʿtar. Postings about these events and others (e.g., the rise of the Islamic State in Iraq and Syria) can appear without reference to the fall of Tall al-Zaʿtar, but it is common for members to draw on their own or their family's history with trauma to understand these events as consonant with the Palestinian experience generally. Such postings become sites for the performance of identity through comments. Through the repetition of appropriate expressions in response to such posts, a member's identity as a survivor or descendant of Tall al-Zaʿtar is performed and sustained. When this happens in conjunction with posts about iconic events from a Palestinian national past or current attacks on Palestinian communities, Tall al-Zaʿtar survivors and descendants are also constituted as Palestinian.

---

16 One exception to this is postings about current events related to Palestinians, many of which resonate with survivors' experiences in Beirut; these include the ongoing siege of Yarmouk camp in Damascus, which is reminiscent of the siege of Tall al-Zaʿtar (particularly since Hafez al-Asad, father of Bashar, played a role in the earlier siege); Israel's war on Gaza, because of the horrific scale of the violence; and the recent violence in Jerusalem and closure of al-Aqsa Mosque, because of its religious as well as its political implications.

2. Grassroots Digital Archives

There is much to discuss about these Facebook groups as social media sites, of course. For participants themselves, the social character of Facebook is of paramount importance. Members find pleasure in communicating across distances and building new connections with each other. Crowdsourcing has been an important resource for amassing images, anecdotes, and other historical information, a technique that is greatly facilitated by the social characteristics of Facebook. The social character is also invaluable to the present work of *Rābiṭa*, which exists as an offline, unofficial NGO in Lebanon working on behalf of community members. In the spring of 2014, for instance, *Rābiṭa* held elections for its officers. Members announced their candidacy through Facebook. Community members as far away as Australia asked how they might participate in the elections. At one point, *Rābiṭa* officers turned to their Facebook group to encourage more women to run for office, and election results were promptly announced on the group page. Much of these activities could have been performed through conventional media, but the social aspect of the page—the way in which it facilitates two-way communication—was also exploited. Individuals responded to postings by organizers, publicly raising questions that could be addressed immediately to everyone and communicating their support through relevant expressions of approval and congratulation. The offline *Rābiṭa* has also used the group to regularly report on its meetings and activities. Community members use it to make semi-public announcements about births, marriages, and deaths.

Using Facebook for digital archiving introduces its own precarity, of course. Not only is it cumbersome as a platform and severely limited structurally, but as a 'free' commercial product owned by its investors, it is constantly vulnerable to the whims of commercialism. Content, layout, and accessibility features can be changed at any time. The content of a Facebook page is 'owned' by Facebook, and researchers are required by its Terms of Use to obtain permission from the company before harvesting or mining data. The site is also subject to censorship by Facebook (e.g., one can imagine any Palestinian, Arab, or Muslim site being particularly vulnerable to specious charges of anti-Semitism or terrorism). The digital divide (particularly acute for Palestinians in Lebanon) is also a potential vulnerability. Facebook, then, is a digital platform for those without alternatives. What is significant, I would argue, is not what Facebook makes possible for Palestinian refugees, but rather the cultural work that Palestinians have managed to do with the clumsy digital tools at their disposal. Nonetheless, the importance of the social aspect of the sites mandates the use of an accessible, well-known platform like Facebook. In May 2014 I spoke with Youssef Iraki, a survivor who had served as one of the camp's two doctors during the siege and who is an active member of both groups today. I asked Iraki why the groups did not use a a different platform (e. g., Wordpress) that would have freed them from these commercial constraints. "Facebook is where the people are," he told me when explaining why this community has chosen to use this particular platform for its work.

However, if one considers these groups as a form of grassroots digital archiving, different implications (e. g., about knowledge preservation, dissemination, and production among marginalized groups) come to the fore. The idea of an archive resonates with the intentions of some of the founders of both these groups and others.[17] Such a conceptualization may have implications for the creation of collective identities that have the potential to be meaningful (slim though that may be) for the disenfranchised in Lebanon. There is also a good reason to think in terms of an archive here with regard to Palestinian history. Khalili outlines the systematic destruction of Palestinian archives, both personal and public, across history, beginning before 1948 and extending to the present day, which have been accompanied by problems of both shortsightedness and intra-Arab and intra-Palestinian politics that have also had a deleterious effect on the collecting and maintenance of information and documentation about controversial events in Palestinian history.[18] In other words, collected records of the Palestinian experience at all levels have been vulnerable. At the national level, Palestinians have faced concerted efforts—primarily on the part of Israel, but also others—to appropriate, prevent, or destroy any archives that they create for themselves. At the local and individual level, there has at times been a reluctance to gather and preserve narratives and information that threaten the nation-

---

17 Another Facebook group founded in the fall of 2013 by survivors of another destroyed camp, Nabaṭiyya refugee camp in South Lebanon, which was destroyed by Israel in 1974, makes this point clear in its name: Mawsūʿat Mukhayyam al-Nabaṭiyya (The Encyclopedia of Nabaṭiyya Camp). The group is much smaller, with just over 10% of the membership of *Rābita*, and appears to have a much more limited goal of preserving information about the camp from oblivion. Questions posed to site members often display the listing and categorical organization of information that defines the encyclopedia as a genre; members have been asked to name shops and their owners and school teachers, for instance. One posting lists all the prominent visitors to the camp (Lebanese, Palestinian, and UNRWA leaders). Many postings consist of photos and short biographical texts that also resemble entries in an encyclopedia or biographical dictionary. Old images are harvested from other online sources—almost always incompletely identified (e. g., "from Facebook" or "from a site for old photographs"). They are identified by their connection to Nabaṭiyya camp when posted.

18 Khalili, *Heroes and Martyrs*, 62–3.

al narrative or that may compromise the safety of family members.[19] Both national and local/individual archives have been vulnerable to the vicissitudes of violent history. While there is no denying this history of loss, a number of scholars, such as Diana Allan and Nick Denes, have argued that there has been too much of an emphasis on what Palestinians have lost and not enough on what they have made.[20]

Creating archives despite a history of loss is fundamentally agential. It is a declarative act of announcing one's presence over time. In the case of the Tall al-Zaʿtar Facebook groups, that declaration concerns not just individuals subject to the vicissitudes of history but also membership in a collective (in this case bound by a shared geography, although that geography is in the past) who share an experience with trauma (the siege and destruction of the camp) and/or its aftermath (dispersal). Moreover, creating an archive is an expression of hope for the future. Saving and organizing information and images is inherently forward-looking, even if future plans or imaginings remain tentative or inchoate. Archives are also partial. They consist of what survives and are always defined as much by what does not make it in (either through curatorial choices or happenstance). For instance, the Tall al-Zaʿtar pages are gendered and nationalist in predictable ways.[21] Thinking of these groups as archives encourages a healthy awareness of their framing and the voices and perspectives that do not appear

---

19 See, for instance, Abdelsalam Shehadeh's film about photography in Gaza, *To My Father*, 2008.

20 See, for instance, Diana Allen, "From Archive to Art Film: A Palestinian Aesthetics of Memory Reviewed," in *Visual Productions of Knowledge: Towards a Different Middle East*, eds. Hanan Sabea and Mark R. Westmoreland (Cairo: American University of Cairo Press, 2012), 145–166; and Nick Denes, "Between Form and Function: Experimentation in the Early Works of the Palestine Film Unit, 1968–1974," *Middle East Journal of Culture and Communication* 7 (2014): 220.

21 The story of Tall al-Zaʿtar itself reinforces accepted gender roles in which men engage in armed struggle and women cook, fetch water, and care for children and the wounded. While the sites include narratives and images of *zahrāt* (that is, young women and girls who participated in paramilitary training) and occasionally of women fighters, they do not include posts that challenge the patriarchal structures of Palestinian society. A case in point is the recent obituary for Umm N. on *Rābiṭa*. Umm N. is described as ukht al-rijāl (the sister of men), the mother of five martyrs, as having carried arms like men during the siege of Tall al-Zaʿtar, and having urged men to fight. Her active participation in armed struggle is rendered as compatible with the supporting roles (raising children—and in particular raising fighters and bolstering the bravery of men). The nationalist aspect of the Facebook groups is evident in a range of posts, including commemorations of events from Palestinian history (the Nakba, the massacre of Sabra and Shatila) and engagement with current events (e.g., the recent Israeli war on Gaza). Posts are often decorated with nationalist images (e.g., flags or the colors of the flag, *kuffiyyas*, house keys, and al-Aqsa mosque).

within them. At the same time, an archive has institutional characteristics. It follows an organizational logic, maintains degrees of accessibility, and helps shape the past for future generations. As such, a certain amount of power inheres in it. While the organizational logic of the Tall al-Zaʿtar Facebook groups may be intuitive rather than planned—arising as it does out of the posting and commenting patterns of its members—it is not random. There are clear norms that group members are expected to follow (e.g., the airing of political differences is often discouraged), and the social tensions that may exist within the community of survivors and descendants (e.g., surrounding family affiliation or class differences) is not visible on the sites.[22]

One must be mindful, however, of Beshara Doumani's observation, quoted by Rosemary Sayigh, about Palestinian archive fever: "The more remote that freedom, justice, repatriation, and self-determination seem to be, the greater the desire to preserve and record for posterity not only what was then but what is now."[23] One must be just as cautious about overestimating the potential of grassroots projects like the Tall al-Zaʿtar Facebook groups as one is about underestimating them.

Bibliography

Abdulrahim, Dima. "From Lebanon to West Berlin: the Ethnography of the Tal al-Zaʿtar Refugee Camp." Ph.D. dissertation, University of Exeter, Exeter, UK, 1990.

Allen, Diana. "From Archive to Art Film: A Palestinian Aesthetics of Memory Reviewed." In *Visual Productions of Knowledge: Towards a Different Middle East*, eds. Hanan Sabea and Mark R. Westmoreland, 145–166. Cairo: American University of Cairo Press, 2012.

Aouragh, Miriam. *Palestine Online: Transnatonalism, the Internet and the Construction of Identity.* London: I.B. Taurus, 2012.

Denes, Nick. "Between Form and Function: Experimentation in the Early Works of the Palestine Film Unit, 1968–1974." *Middle East Journal of Culture and Communication* 7 (2014): 219–41

Ḥilū, Jihān. *Al-Marʾa l-Filasṭīniyya: al-muqāwama wa-l-taghayyurāt al-ijtimāʿiyya.* Al-Bīra: Markaz al-Marʾa l-Filasṭīniyya lil-Abḥāth wa-l-Tawthīq, 2009.

Hirsch, Marianne. *Family Frames: Photography, Narrative, and Postmemory.* Cambridge, MA: Harvard University Press, 1997.

—. "The Generation of Postmemory." *Poetics Today* 29 (2008): 103–28.

22 See Abdulrahim, *From Lebanon to West Berlin.*

23 Rosemary Sayigh, "Oral History, Colonialist Dispossession, and the State: the Palestinian Case," *Settler Colonial Studies* (2014): 199.

Hirsch, Marianne, and Leo Spitzer. "'We would never have come without you': Generations of Nostalgia." In *Contested Pasts: the Politics of Memory*, eds. Katharine Hodgkin and Susannah Radstone, 79–96. London: Routledge, 2003.

Khalili, Laleh. *Heroes and Martyrs of Palestine: The Politics of National Commemoration.* Cambridge: Cambridge University Press, 2007.

Miller, Vincent. "New Media, Networking, and Phatic Culture." *Convergence* 14 (2008): 387–400.

Mundus, Hānī. *Al-ʿAmal wa-l-ʿummāl fī l-mukhayyam al-Filasṭīnī.* Beirut: Palestine Liberation Organization Research Center, 1974.

Sayigh, Rosemary. *Palestinians: From Peasants to Revolutionaries: A People's History.* London: Zed Press, 1979.

—. "Oral History, Colonialist Dispossession, and the State: the Palestinian Case." *Settler Colonial Studies* (2014): 193–204.

Yaqub, Nadia. "The Afterlives of Violent Images: Reading Photographs from the Tall al-Zaʻtar Refugee Camp on Facebook." Middle East Journal of Culture and Communication 8:2–3 (2015): 327–354.

Maxim Romanov

Toward Abstract Models for Islamic History

> "Remember that all models are wrong; the practical question is how wrong do they have to be to not be useful."[1]
>
> George E. P. Box

1. Why Models?[2]

The advent of the digital humanities has brought the notion of 'big data' into the purview of humanistic inquiry. Humanists now have access to huge corpora that open research possibilities that were unthinkable a decade or two ago. However, working with corpora requires a rather different approach that is more characteristic of the sciences than the humanities. In particular, one has to be transparent and explicit with regard to how data are extracted and how they are analyzed. Text-mining techniques rely on explicit algorithms for data extraction and analysis because this helps keep track of errors, correct them, and, ultimately, improve results.[3] Analytical procedures for studying extracted data rest on explicit algorithms for the same reason. As a way of constructing algorithms, modeling is part and parcel of developing complex computational procedures.

Working with big data also requires another kind of modeling. Opting for the breadth of data, we have to give up the richness of details. Close reading—to which humanists are most accustomed—becomes impossible.[4] Working with

1 George E. P. Box, *Response Surfaces, Mixtures, and Ridge Analyses* (2nd ed.; Hoboken, N.J: John Wiley, 2007), 63.

2 All data, graphs and cartograms used in the article were produced by the author. The data were extracted from the electronic text of a medieval Arabic biographical collection available online in open access. Graphs and cartograms are based on the extracted data and produced with R, a free software environment for statistical computing and graphics.

3 For more details, see chapter one in Maxim G. Romanov, "Computational Reading of Arabic Biographical Collections with Special Reference to Preaching (661–1300 CE)" (Ph.D. diss., University of Michigan, 2013).

4 While most humanists remain skeptical with regard to working with big data, the number of studies that show that close reading alone is not enough keeps on growing. They emphasize that case studies based on close reading do not allow for extrapolations, and that humanists are prone to putting too much effort into studying objects that are unique and for this reason are least likely to represent larger trends. The most vivid examples can be found in the field of literary history; see, e.g., Franco Moretti, *Graphs, Maps, Trees: Abstract Models for Literary History* (London: Verso, 2007); Franco Moretti, *Distant Reading* (1st ed.; London: Verso, 2013); Matthew

big data one cannot maintain the nuanced complexity of details that is the hallmark of close reading. Instead of relying on complex textual evidence and reading between the lines, one has to work with relatively simple textual markers—essentially, words or simple phrases—that are treated as indicators of large trends. Yet it is through such analysis that we can look into long-term and large-scale processes that are beyond the scope of close reading.

The literary historian Franco Moretti dubbed such an approach "distant reading," explaining "distance" not as an obstacle, but *a specific form of knowledge.*[5] By emphasizing fewer elements and their interconnections, we can begin to distinguish shapes, relations, and structures. Most importantly, we can trace small changes over long periods of time. Modeling is an important part of this approach. With models, we simplify reality down to a limited number of factors[6] through the analysis of which we can hope to gain insights into complex historical processes.[7] This simplification is the reason why, as the statistician George E.P. Box put it, "all models are false." However, models are valuable and powerful tools that improve our understanding of the world. Unlike theories, models are experimental and driven by data. Good models offer invaluable glimpses into the subjects of our inquiry.[8] With them, we can explore, explain, and project. Through them, we catch a glimpse of a bigger picture. That is why some models are useful.

L. Jockers, *Macroanalysis: Digital Methods and Literary History,* (1st ed.; Chicago: University of Illinois Press, 2013).

5 See Moretti, *Graphs, Maps, Trees,* 4.

6 For example, Ian Morris uses the size of the largest urban center as an indicator of the social development of the region to which it belongs; see Morris, *The Measure of Civilization: How Social Development Decides the Fate of Nations* (Princeton, NJ: Princeton University Press, 2013). Richard Bulliet uses onomastic data as the indicator of conversion; see Bulliet, *Conversion to Islam in the Medieval Period: An Essay in Quantitative History* (Cambridge, MA: Harvard University Press, 1979).

7 For valuable examples of modeling 'big data', see Moretti, *Graphs, Maps, Trees*; Ian Morris, *Why the West Rules–for Now: The Patterns of History, and What They Reveal about the Future* (New York: Farrar, Straus and Giroux, 2010). See also http://orbis.stanford.edu/ for a geographical model of the Roman world, developed by Walter Scheidel and Elijah Meeks. In the field of Islamic studies, see *Bulliet, Conversion to Islam in the Medieval Period.*

8 Bulliet's model of conversion is a great example of this. The very fact that this study is still criticized more than three decades after its publication shows that a solid model cannot be discarded through a critique of where it fails, if otherwise it still remains plausible and coherent. For the most recent critique, see David J. Wasserstein, "Where Have All the Converts Gone? Difficulties in the Study of Conversion to Islam in Al-Andalus," *Al-Qanṭara* 33 no. 2 (February 11, 2013): 325–42, DOI:10.3989/alqantara.2011.005.

What follows is an attempt to model Islamic élites based on the data from al-Dhahabī's (d. 748 AH/1348 CE) *Ta'rīkh al-islām*[9] in order to explore major social transformations that the Muslim community underwent in the course of almost seven centuries of its history. The main types of data used in the model are dates, toponyms,[10] linguistic formulae (or wording patterns), synsets (lists of words that point to a specific concept or entity),[11] and, most importantly, "descriptive names" (sing. *nisba*).

A detailed discussion of the main assumptions underlying these types of data as well as a discussion of more general issues relevant to the study of Arabic biographical collections can be found elsewhere.[12] It is most important, however, to say a few words here about our assumptions regarding "descriptive names," which are considered by some scholars to be the most valuable kind of data that literary sources offer to the social historian of the Islamic world, while others dispute this as highly problematic. The major problem with *nisba*s is that it is not always clear what they stand for. For example, if an individual is described in a biographical collection as a *ṣaffār*, does this actually mean that he was involved in "coppersmithing"? When our subject is just one particular individual, it is not so difficult to establish the more or less exact meaning of this descriptive name by cross-examining biographies of this individual in other biographical collections. This is particularly easy now, when dozens of electronic texts of biographical collections are just few mouse-clicks away.

However, such an approach becomes problematic when this rather time-consuming procedure has to be repeated for dozens of individuals. The approach becomes particularly difficult if our goal is to study some biographical collection in its entirety, since Arabic biographical collections often contain thousands of biographies, and most biographies offer multiple descriptive names for the same individual. After a certain threshold, it becomes utterly impossible to apply this approach. Our source, *Ta'rīkh al-islām*, is well beyond this threshold. In the analysis that follows, we will deal with the dataset of almost 70,000 *nisba*s

9 An electronic text of this source has been used in this study. The text is based on and collated with al-Dhahabī, *Ta'rīkh al-islām wa-wafayāt al-mashāhīr wa-al-a'lām* (ed. ʿUmar Tadmurī; 2nd ed.; 52 vols.; Bayrūt: Dār al-Kitāb al-ʿArabī, 1990).

10 Both toponyms proper and toponymic *nisba*s linked with relevant toponyms. Toponymic data is crucial for our understanding of the social geography of the classical Islamic world. For my modeling of the geography of the Islamic world based on the data from *Ta'rīkh al-islām*, see Romanov, "Computational Reading," 35–37, 41–42, 87–113.

11 As hierarchically organized word lists, synsets are here used for the grouping of toponymic and onomastics data into categories of higher level.

12 Romanov, "Computational Reading," 28–51.

(with about 700 unique ones) that represent about 26,000 individuals over the period of 41–700 AH/661–1301 CE. Working with such a dataset one cannot possibly know the exact meaning of each and every *nisba*. At the same time, we do not have any solid foundation to argue that descriptive names are to be treated in a particular manner or to be discarded altogether. Yet such a dataset is too valuable a tool to ignore simply because we are not entirely sure what all these data mean. This is where modeling offers an optimal solution: we must begin with assumptions and be transparent about them. Thus, in what follows, descriptive names will be treated according to their most common acceptations, if only because this is the most logical starting point.[13]

2. The Source: al-Dhahabī's *Taʾrīkh al-Islām*

The *Taʾrīkh al-islām* is the largest Arabic biographical collection, including over 30,000 biographies and covering almost seven centuries of Islamic history. The current dataset includes information on slightly over 29,000 individuals (the first three volumes of *Taʾrīkh al-islām* are structured differently from the rest of the collection and cannot be studied with the same computational method). Figure 6.1 shows a graph of the chronological distribution of the biographies in this data set. Biographies are grouped into 20 lunar year periods (quantities of biographies for each period are shown along the x-axis). The graph is transformed into a curve that smooths out the noise of data, emphasizing larger trends (see the line labeled *Smoothed Biographical Curve*). Finally, the main curve is the *Adjusted Biographical Curve*, which is shifted 30 years back in time to reflect "the years of floruit" of the biographees from *Taʾrīkh al-islām*.

The curve can be split into several periods, each beginning at a point that marks a noticeable diversion of the curve. The number of biographies grows quite rapidly until c. 160 AH/778 CE, when it begins to slow. During c. 270–470 AH/884–1078 CE there is a steady decline. After c. 470 AH/1078 CE the curve starts recovering, reaching its highest point around c. 570 AH/1175 CE, after which it keeps growing but slows its pace by the end of the period—with the second peak being somewhere after 700 AH/1301 CE. For convenience, many of the graphs that follow will include the scaled-down cumulative curve and color-coded periods.

13 For a detailed discussion, see ibid., 43–46.

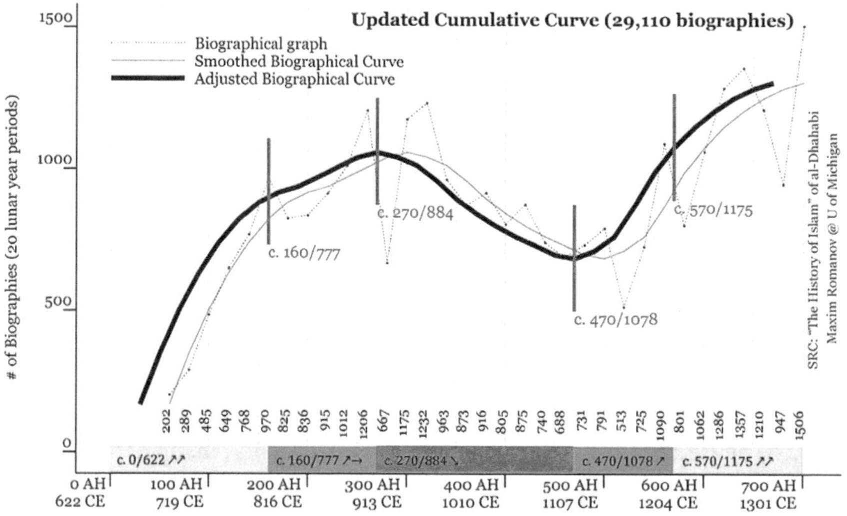

Figure 6.1. Cumulative Biographical Curve. The row of numbers shows the quantities of biographies per 20 lunar year periods, beginning with 41–60 AH/662–681 CE and up to 680–700 AH/1282–1301 CE.

3. Modeling Society

The individuals whose lives are described in biographical collections were not ordinary people. In most cases, they were noteworthy members of their communities, and almost every biographical note contains some information on a sphere of life to which its protagonist contributed—and "descriptive names," at least at this point, are the most manageable indicator of their place in society.

Major studies that use "descriptive names" for analytical purposes split them into categories. Cohen's classic study concentrates primarily on "secular occupations" during the first four centuries of Islamic history. [14] He offered a major division of occupational *nisba*s (textiles, foods, ornaments/perfumes, paper/books, leather/metals/wood/clay, miscellaneous trades, general merchants, bankers/middlemen) and supplied an extensive appendix with explanations for about 400 *nisba*s and relevant linguistic formulae. Unfortunately, the *nisba*s

---

14 See, Hayyim J. Cohen, "The Economic Background and the Secular Occupations of Muslim Jurisprudents and Traditionists in the Classical Period of Islam: (Until the Middle of the Eleventh Century)," *Journal of the Economic and Social History of the Orient* 13 (1970): 16–61.

in Cohen's appendix are not explicitly categorized and—since any categorization involves pushing the boundaries, especially in instances that stubbornly resist classification—the exact scheme remains somewhat unclear.

Petry's scheme is built on biographical data from Mamlūk Egypt (656–923 AH/1258–1517 CE). Petry divided his subjects into six major, often overlapping occupational groups: executive and military professions, bureaucratic (secretarial-financial) professions, legal professions, artisan and commercial professions, scholarly and educational professions, and religious functionaries. Although an explicit classification is not given in the "Glossary of Occupational Terms," numerous tables provide enough information to form a rather clear idea about the specifics of each category in Petry's classification scheme.[15]

Shatzmiller approached this issue from the much wider perspective of labor in general. Her scheme covers a much wider variety of occupational names and splits the entire society into three major sectors—extractive, manufacturing, services—with each sector having its overlapping subcategories. Shatzmiller offers an explicit categorization of each and every descriptive name.[16]

As is the case with any scheme, all three examples are designed to serve specific purposes. Although immensely helpful, none of them are suitable for the purposes of broader analysis: unlike the above-mentioned schemes, the scheme needed here must take into account *all* meaningful descriptors, not only those that can be classified as "occupations." In other words, it must consider anything that would allow discerning all potentially identifiable groups, so that their evolution could be traced. Some of these descriptors do not pose significant problems, while others are so complex that even presenting them as ideal types might be highly problematic.

The list of "descriptive names" from *Taʾrīkh al-islām* is based on frequencies, and for the moment I will consider only *nisba*s that are used to qualify at least ten individuals (slightly over 700 unique *nisba*s, with their total running up to almost 70,000 instances). My list of descriptive names overlaps only partially with those of Cohen, Petry, and Shatzmiller. Figure 6.2 shows how the categories of "descriptive names" from *Taʾrīkh al-islām* are interconnected from the individual's perspective.

The innermost layer of categories includes **trib**al, **topo**nymic, **ethn**ic and **phys**ical descriptions. These are descriptors over which individuals have the least control—in the sense that no one chooses into which **trib**e to be born,

15 Carl F. Petry, *The Civilian Elite of Cairo in the Later Middle Ages* (Princeton, NJ: Princeton University Press, 1981). For the "Glossary, " see pp. 390–402.
16 Maya Shatzmiller, *Labour in the Medieval Islamic World* (Leiden: E.J. Brill, 1994). For extensive lists of names/occupations, see pp. 101–168, 410–424.

Figure 6.2. Interconnectedness of Descriptive Names from the Individual's Perspective. Shifting circles and dashed lines denote the intricate interconnectedness of the three layers of name categories.

where to be born, what **ethn**ic group to belong to, and what **phys**ical peculiarities to have or suffer from. To a certain degree, these descriptions are also acquirable—in the early period, being a Muslim meant being affiliated with an Arab **trib**e; individuals were constantly moving around the Islamic world, changing their **topo**nymic affiliations; **phys**ical peculiarities could have resulted from life experience. However, these are only probable—and thus secondary—cases that would usually be piled up on top of primary, 'by-birth' descriptions. The first three categories—**trib**al, **topo**nymic, **ethn**ic—also tend to overlap.

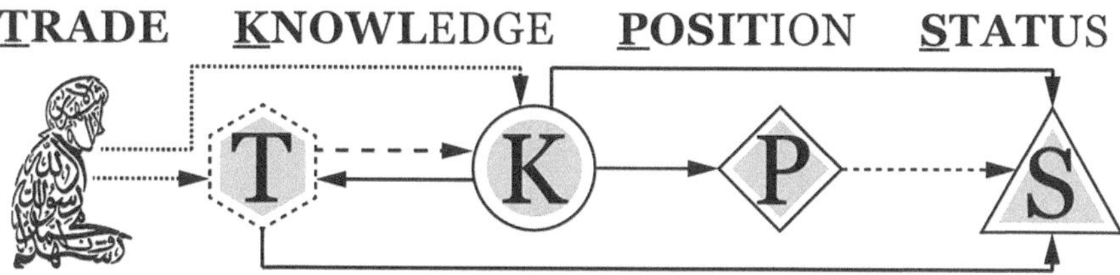

Figure 6.3. Hierarchical Connections of the Middle Layer.

The middle layer groups "descriptive names" in terms of acquirable qualities —**trade**, **knowl**edge, **posit**ion and **statu**s. These are not categories that rest on the same level, and their connections are better represented in a hierarchical manner (Figure 6.3). The main gateways to élites were **trade**s (or "secular occupations") and **know**ledge[s]. However, practicing some **trade** alone was almost never enough: biographical collections rarely—if ever—include individuals who were involved exclusively in some specific "secular occupation." In order to climb up the social ladder, a practitioner of any **trade** had to start converting his economic capital into social capital—this was most commonly done through acquiring religious **knowl**edge. **Knowl**edge—as specialized training in a specific area that would set an individual apart from the masses—opened ways for acquiring **posit**ions and **status**[es]; it could also allow one to practice **trade** on a new level, thus improving the individual's **statu**s.

The outermost layer represents the major sectors to which a person could belong in pre-modern Islamic society: **relig**ious, **admin**istrative, **milit**ary, and **'civil**ian'. The term civilian is problematic and is used here essentially as a negative blanket category that encompasses everything that does not clearly belong to the first three sectors. Descriptive names often cross boundaries among these categories, and most individuals do not clearly belong to one specific sector, but rather balance among them.

Figure 6.4. Interconnectedness of Descriptive Names from the Social Perspective.
Shifting circles and dashed lines denote the intricate interconnectedness of the three layers of name categories.

For our purposes, it will be more efficient to invert this scheme so that "descriptive names" are presented from the social perspective (Figure 6.4). Now, each category contributes to the composition of Islamic society, and every "descriptive name" can be seen as a social role. These roles are likely to receive a centripetal charge from individuals who attempt to expand their influence on society at large; how close they get to the center—i.e., how much social influence they can exercise—would depend on the success of particular individuals and/or historical circumstances that might be favorable to particular groups. Social influence here is understood broadly as a pressure that forces someone to do something that s/he otherwise would not have done; at this point, I do not make a distinction between physical threats and social pressures. Clearly, the sword of an *amīr* ("military commander") and the word of a *shaykh* ("religious authority") are different in their nature, but both may have equally serious societal consequences.

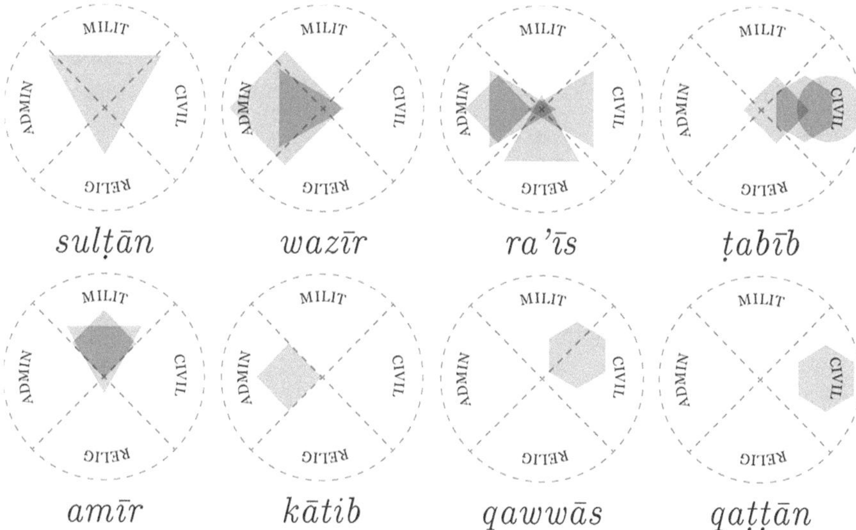

Figure 6.5. *Nisba* Classification Examples (a).

Figures 6.5 and 6.6 should provide a visual clue as to how these overlapping categories are used in the classification scheme. In Figure 6.5 : *amīr* ("governor, commander") and *sulṭān* ("sultan") both belong to the **milit**ary sector of society. *Amīr* can be seen primarily as a **posit**ion—in the sense that there is somebody above who granted this **posit**ion to a given individual; arguably, this **posit**ion provides one with a relatively high **statu**s. *Sulṭān* is the apex of the **milit**ary hierarchy and thus is primarily seen as **statu**s with significant influence over all other sectors. *Kātib* ("scribe") and *wazīr* ("vizier, prime minister") belong to the **admin**istrative sector, where the former is a **posit**ion with potential for social influence, while the latter is the apex of the **admin**istrative hierarchy, which gives one significant resources to influence society at large—hence, it is also **status**.[17] Somewhat equivalent to *amīr, ra'īs* ("chief, director") is a denomination of high **status** in either the **civil**ian, the **relig**ious, or the **admin**istrative sector (also **posit**ion in the latter). *Ṭabīb* ("physician") stands for special training—**knowl**edge—within the **civil**ian sector, which is also likely to fall into the categories of **trade** and **posit**ion, especially after hospitals (sing. *[bī]māristān*) become a constant element in the Muslim cityscape.[18] *Qaṭṭān* ("producer or seller of cotton") and *qawwās* ("bow-maker") are both secular occupations—**trade**s—and thus belong to the **civil**ian sector, although the latter—if bows are produced for war-making purposes—may cross into the **milit**ary one.

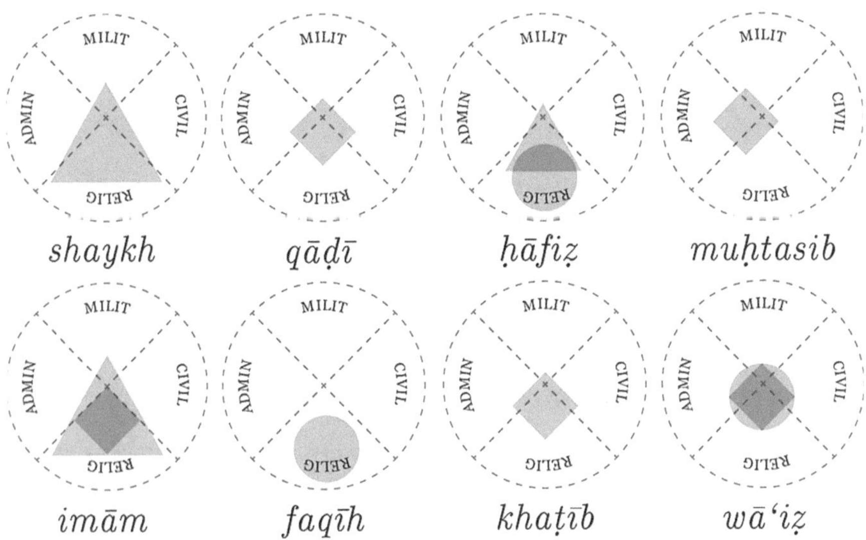

Figure 6.6. *Nisba* Classification Examples (b).

17 Some *wazīr*s rivaled their 'employers' in influence. The most prominent examples are the Barmakid family, who served the 'Abbāsid caliphs, and Niẓām al-mulk, who served Mālikshāh, the Great Saljuq *sulṭān*.

18 There are 322 physicians in the *'Uyūn al-anbā' fī ṭabaqāt al-aṭibbā'* of Ibn Abī Uṣaybi'a (d. 668 AH/1270 CE), and quite a few physicians are Jews and Christians, judging by their names. al-Dhahabī's count of physicians is about 200, which can be considered a very thorough coverage, since Ibn Abī Uṣaybi'a's book is devoted exclusively to the physicians (and, as often happens, tends to overstretch the definition of the group), while al-Dhahabī's book is a general history.

In Figure 6.6: *shaykh* (literally "elder") and *imām* ("leader") are the markers of the highest **relig**ious **statu**s, although in the later period *imām* also refers to a **relig**ious **posit**ion of "prayer leader" that was only marginally influential in social terms. *Faqīh* refers to the **knowl**edge of Islamic law, whereas social influence is exerted primarily through other roles, such as *qāḍī* ("judge"), which is always a **posit**ion—or *muftī* ("jurisconsult"), which turns into a **posit**ion in the later period (not graphed). *Ḥāfiẓ* denotes **knowl**edge of prophetic tradition and high achievement (**statu**s) within this area of **relig**ious expertise. *Muḥtasib* ("market inspector") is an **admin**istrative **posit**ion with strong **relig**ious underpinnings. Last on the list are *khaṭīb* ("Friday preacher") and *wāʿiẓ* ("public preacher"). Both belong to the **relig**ious sector, but while the former is always a **posit**ion, the latter refers to a specific field of religious **knowl**edge that tends to become a **posit**ion only during the later period.

Individuals in the Islamic biographical dictionaries usually wear many turbans and are qualified with more than one "descriptive name." Using the same method, each individual can be represented as a unique constellation of **trade**s, **knowl**edge[s], **posit**ions, and **statu**s[es] that are fitted into the diagram of the four major sectors. Pushing this approach even further, we may try to evaluate how the composition of Islamic élites—and, possibly, society at large—changed over time, although conventional graphs may be more efficient for this task.

4. Looking into Major Sectors

Introducing the categories of sectors—**milit**ary, **admin**istrative, **relig**ious, and **civil**ian—I hope to use them as markers of change within the composition of Islamic élites. Society would remain healthier when more social groups were represented in the élites, since a more diverse population would be participating in the [re]negotiation of the rules of the game. This is what the share and the diversity of the civilian sector—with a number of trades, crafts, and knowledge[s]—is meant to represent.

Figure 6.7 shows the cumulative curves of all four sectors. Although this is still a work in progress and the algorithms for determining the administrative and military sectors still need adjustment, the curves do agree with the major trends that we expect to be confirmed by quantitative analysis.

The religious sector keeps on growing throughout the period. Occasional fluctuations notwithstanding, it hits the 60 percent mark by the end of the period. One would expect this number to be higher, but a significant number of individuals participated in the transmission of knowledge without specializing in

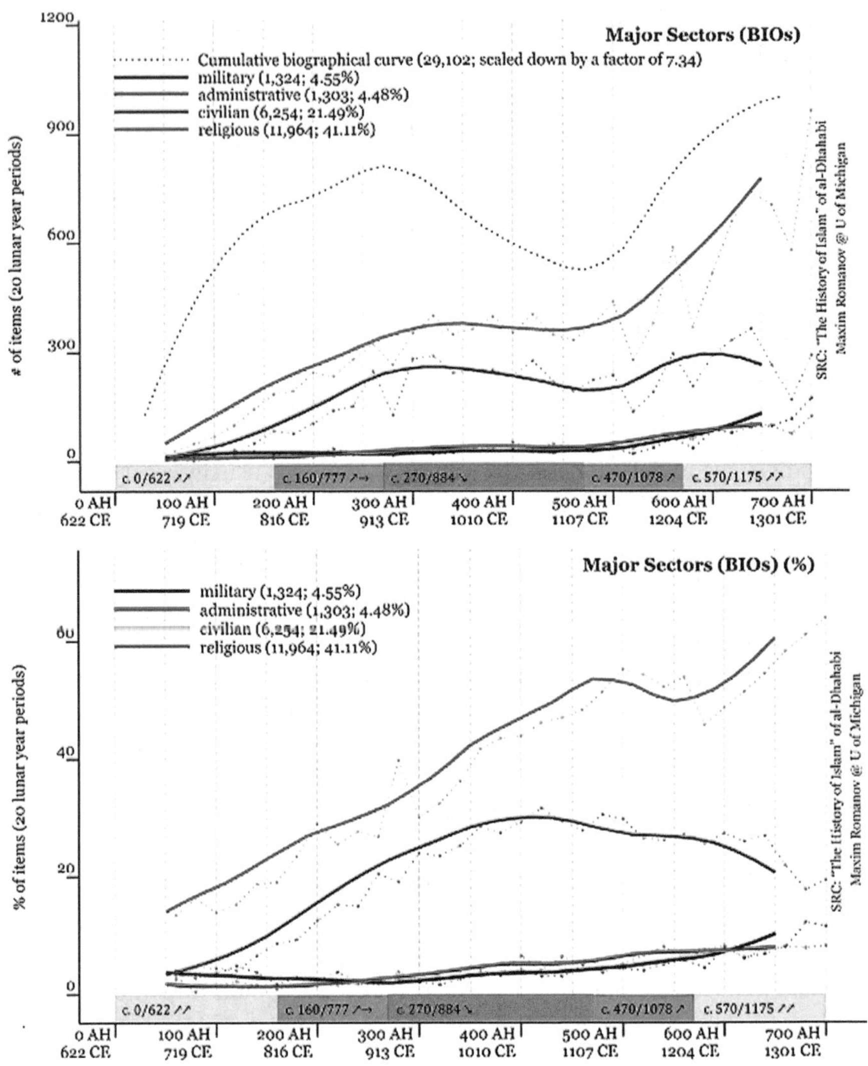

Figure 6.7. Major Sectors of Islamic Society (as represented in the *Taʾrīkh al-islām*)

specific fields of religious learning and thus did not earn relevant *nisbas*. This, of course, may result from irregularities in naming practices or the lack of verbal patterns in my synsets.[19]

19 For instance, the person is identified as a "jurist" if he is mentioned as a *faqīh* (or some other

The civilian sector is at its highest between 300–400 AH/913–1010 CE, when it reaches a 30 percent share. By the end of the period, it goes down to 20 percent. The number of individuals involved in trades and crafts is about 24–25 percent at its highest point around 400 AH/1010 CE and goes down to 13–14 percent by the end of the period.

The administrative and military sectors are not as significant in terms of numbers, but the representatives of these sectors are in better positions to make the most immediate and most striking impact on society at large. Both sectors keep growing, although while the growth of the administrative sector is constant, albeit rather slow, the growth of the military sector is quite remarkable, especially after 500 AH/1107 CE. Overall, the share of the military sector could have reached ten percent during the later periods, which is very significant considering that at some earlier periods, this sector is lacking altogether. The administrative sector may have hit the mark of about eight percent during the later periods.

5. Major Social Transformations

5.1 De-tribalization

De-tribalization is one of the most striking processes that the onomastic data allows us to discover. Islamic society starts as a tribal society, with up to 85 percent of individuals in the earliest periods qualified through tribal affiliations. As the Islamic community grows and spreads over the Middle East and North Africa, the number of individuals with tribal identities rapidly goes down (Figure 6.8), and by about 350 AH/962 CE only 20–25 percent of the individuals in the *Taʾrīkh al-islām* have tribal affiliations. From this point on—perhaps even earlier—tribal affiliations persevere in different capacities: some as dynastic (most prominently, the *nisba* al-Umawī that spikes again after 350 AH/962 CE in Andalusia), but in most cases as status markers.

Such *nisba*s as al-Anṣārī (Figure 6.9) and al-Qurashī (Figure 6.10) make quite a noticeable comeback. The numbers of al-Anṣārīs (this *nisba* is particularly frequent in Andalusia as well) begin to grow quite rapidly after 350 AH/962 CE, and the number of al-Qurashīs practically skyrockets right after 500 AH/1107 CE.

nominal descriptor pertaining to the field of Islamic law); however, at this point my approach does not take into account such instances as *tafaqqaha ʿalá fulān bn fulān*, "he studied [Islamic] jurisprudence under so-and-so." This more extensive approach will be implemented in the future.

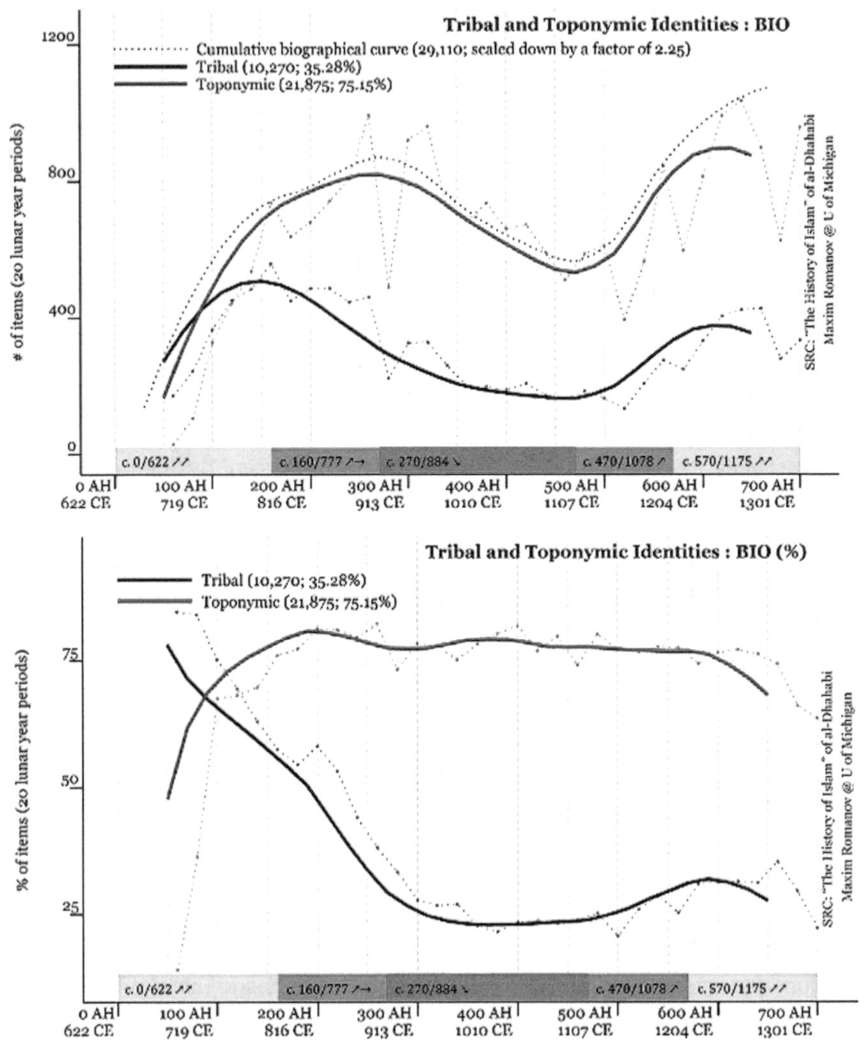

Figure 6.8. Individuals with Tribal and Toponymic *Nisba*s in the *Taʾrīkh al-islām*.

However, even though their absolute numbers are much higher in the later periods, their percentages never reach their early peaks: the highest peak of al-Anṣārīs in the earliest periods is 18.32 percent, while the highest one in the later periods is only 6.53 percent; with al-Qurashīs, these numbers are 8.42 percent and 3.31 percent, respectively. Some other tribal *nisba*s are re-claimed as well, but the overall number of individuals with names that associate them with Arab tribes remains rather low, only briefly going above the 30 percent mark.

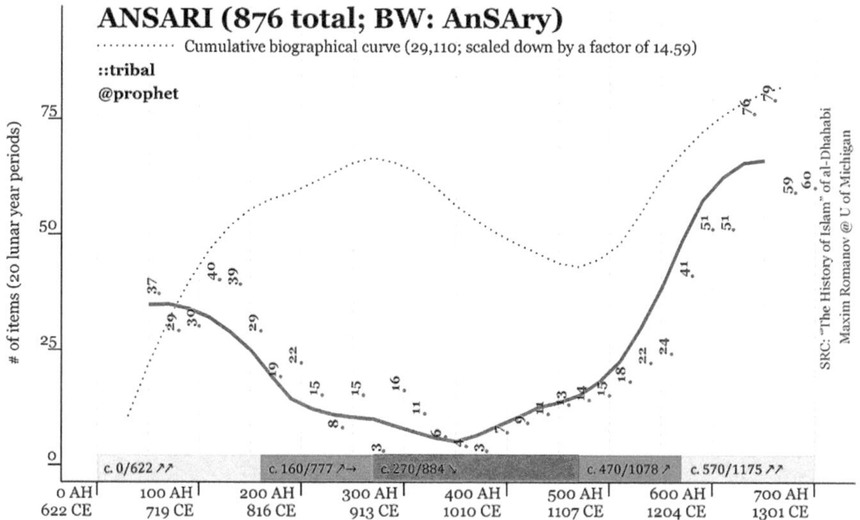

Figure 6.9. Individuals with *nisba* al-Anṣārī in the *Taʾrīkh al-islām*. Although al-Anṣār, "The Helpers [of the Prophet]," are not exactly a tribe, this group, being a product of the tribal society of Arabia, in many ways functioned as such.

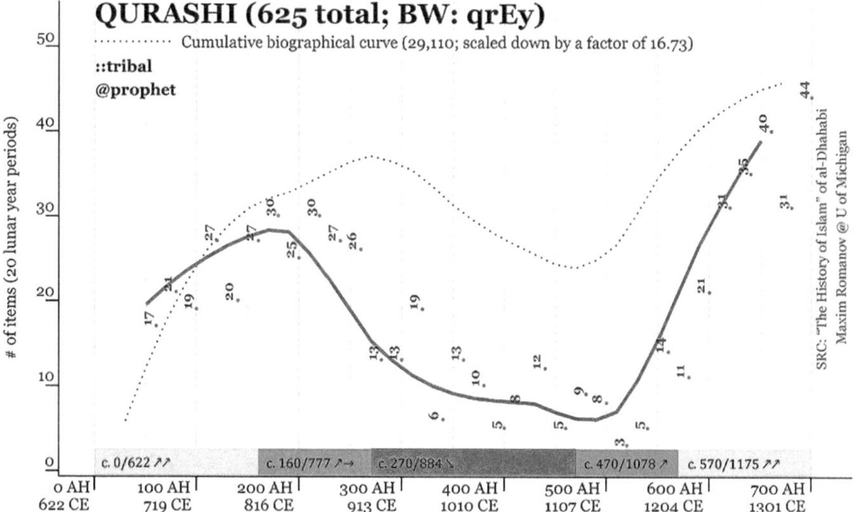

Figure 6.10. Individuals with *nisba* al-Qurashī in the *Taʾrīkh al-islām*.

Most tribal *nisba*s display rather distinctive orientations toward the East or the West of the Islamic world. 'Late bloomers' are most often oriented toward the West (Figure 6.11). For example, such *nisba*s as al-Qaysī (208) and al-Lakhmī (183) feature most prominently in Andalusia (84 al-Qaysīs and 83 al-Lakhmīs); al-Tujībī (127)—in Andalusia (57) and Egypt (46); al-Makhzumī (182)—in Egypt (33);[20] al-Saʿdī (191)—in Egypt (50) and Syria (25). But again, the percentages of 'late bloomers' never reach those of the earlier periods.

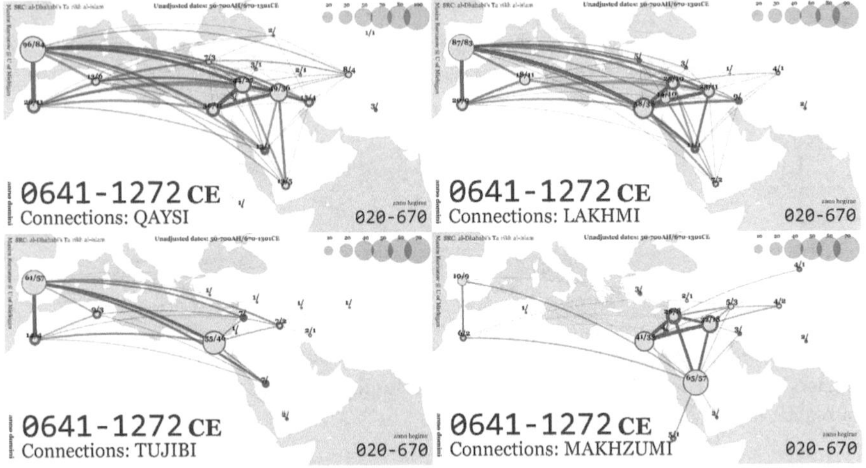

Figure 6.11. Western Orientation of Some Tribal 'Late bloomers'.
NB: Each map has its own scale.

The change in tribal identities can also be seen through the numbers of unique tribal *nisba*s per period (Figure 6.12). In general, they display a similar trend. At its highest, the number of unique tribal *nisba*s fluctuates at around 115 during the period 100–200 AH/719–816 CE. It drops to about 60 by 500 AH/1107 CE and then grows back to about 80—most likely through the re-appropriation of old tribal *nisba*s that are now used as status markers as well as through the introduction of Turkic and Kurdish tribal identities—but by the end of the main period, this number goes down to the 60–70 range.

20 The first major peak of the *nisba* al-Makhzūmī is around 150 AH/768 CE, and geographically it peaks largely in the Central Arabian Cluster (65 al-Makhzūmīs).

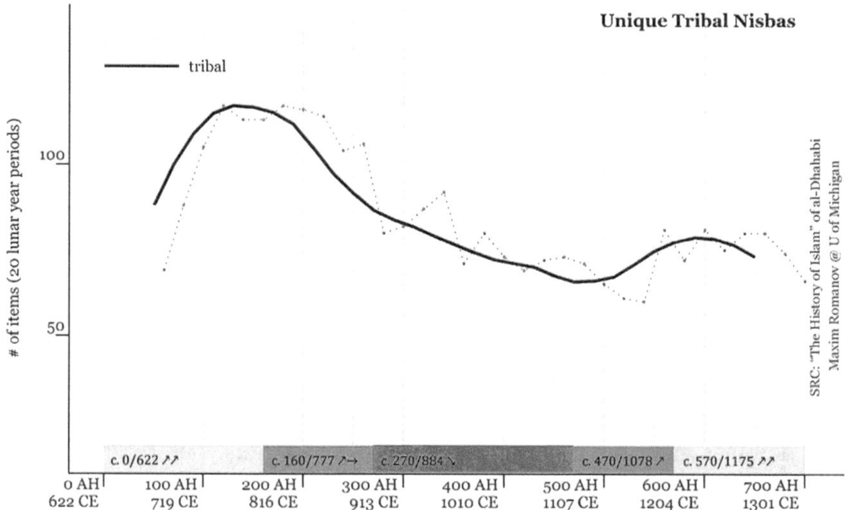

Figure 6.12. Unique tribal *nisbas* in the *Ta'*rīkh al-islām.

5.2 Militarization

Onomastic data from *Ta'rīkh al-islām* allows us to take a closer look at the process characterized by Hodgson as "perhaps the most distinctive feature of the Middle Islamic periods."[21] The absolute numbers on Figure 6.13 (left) show that the military sector of élites begins to grow rapidly after 500 AH/1107 CE—the numbers of *amīrs* included in the *Ta'rīkh al-islām* are staggering.[22] Geographically, this spike of militarization is clearly visible in Iraq, the Jazīra, and Egypt, but in Syria more than anywhere.

The relative numbers in Figure 6.13 (right) allow for a more detailed glimpse into how the military were treated by the learned class, who composed biographical collections that became the sources of al-Dhahabī's "History." And the percentages tell a somewhat different story. Interestingly, the turning points of the

---

21 Marshall G. S. Hodgson, *The Venture of Islam: Conscience and History in a World Civilization. Vol. 2. The Expansion of Islam in the Middle Periods* (Chicago: University of Chicago Press, 1974), 64.

22 Unfortunately, at the moment my algorithms are not tuned well enough to trace all individuals who belonged to the military sector. The *nisba* "*al-amīr*" should serve well as an indicator: it is the most frequent "descriptive name" within the military sector, and it is the easiest to trace computationally.

military curve coincide with those of the cumulative biographical curve. The military curve, however, has three clearly visible sections or periods. The first section, the early period up until 270 AH/884 CE, shows the decline of the military in Islamic society. This process of de-militarization went on hand-in-hand with de-tribalization, during which the diversity of the Islamic community grew, the ethos changed, and swords and horses were exchanged for pens and donkeys. The year 270 AH/884 CE marks the first peak of the cumulative biographical curve: the highest percentage of the learned and the lowest percentage of the military in the *Ta'rīkh al-islām*.

During the middle period of 270–570 AH/884–1175 CE, when the cumulative biographical curve takes a dive and then, after 470 AH/1078 CE, begins to recover, the share of the military in *Ta'rīkh al-islām* grows slowly. This can be marked as the beginning of the (re)militarization of Islamic élites. Unlike in the early period, however, now the *amīr*s are not Arab[ian] warriors, but Turkic military commanders.

After 570 AH/1175 CE—when the cumulative curve recovers and continues growing further—the percentage of military commanders in the élites begins to grow as rapidly as their absolute numbers. This third period shows a successful integration of the military into the élites, and their numbers strongly suggest that religious scholars take even minor commanders seriously.

Military commanders do a lot to make a place for themselves in the dense social space of Islamic society: as their biographies show, they build *madrasa*s, hospitals (*[bī]māristān*), and establish other *waqf* institutions. More and more often, they participate in the transmission of knowledge, which scholars report.

The military—the *amīr*s themselves and members of their families[23]—are not the only ones building *madrasa*s, and, judging by the frequencies of their mentions, their establishments are not the most prominent. However, they compensate for this in numbers: there are significantly more endowments established by the military than by members of other groups.[24] Figure 6.14 shows the curves of

23 Most prominently, women from their households. See, for example, R. Stephen Humphreys, "Women as Patrons of Religious Architecture in Ayyubid Damascus," *Muqarnas* 11 (January 1, 1994): 35–54, DOI:10.2307/1523208.

24 See, for example, al-Dhahabī, *Ta'rīkh al-islām*: v.28, 311–312; v.29, 68–76; v.37, 57–58; v.37, 185–186; v.38, 157–158; v.39, 370–387; v.41, 161–164; v.42, 407; v.44, 220; v.45, 119; v.45, 164; v.45, 311–313; v.45, 359; v.45, 402–406; v.46, 87–88; v.46, 289; v.46, 431–432; v.47, 165; v.47, 308; v.49, 192; v.50, 264; v.51, 196–197; v.51, 369–370; v.52, 368; v.52, 409–411. On military patronage, see also R. Stephen Humphreys, "Politics and Architectural Patronage in Ayyubid Damascus," in *The Islamic World from Classical to Modern Times: Essays in Honor of Bernard Lewis*, ed. Clifford Edmund Bosworth (Princeton, NJ: Darwin Press, 1989), 151–74.

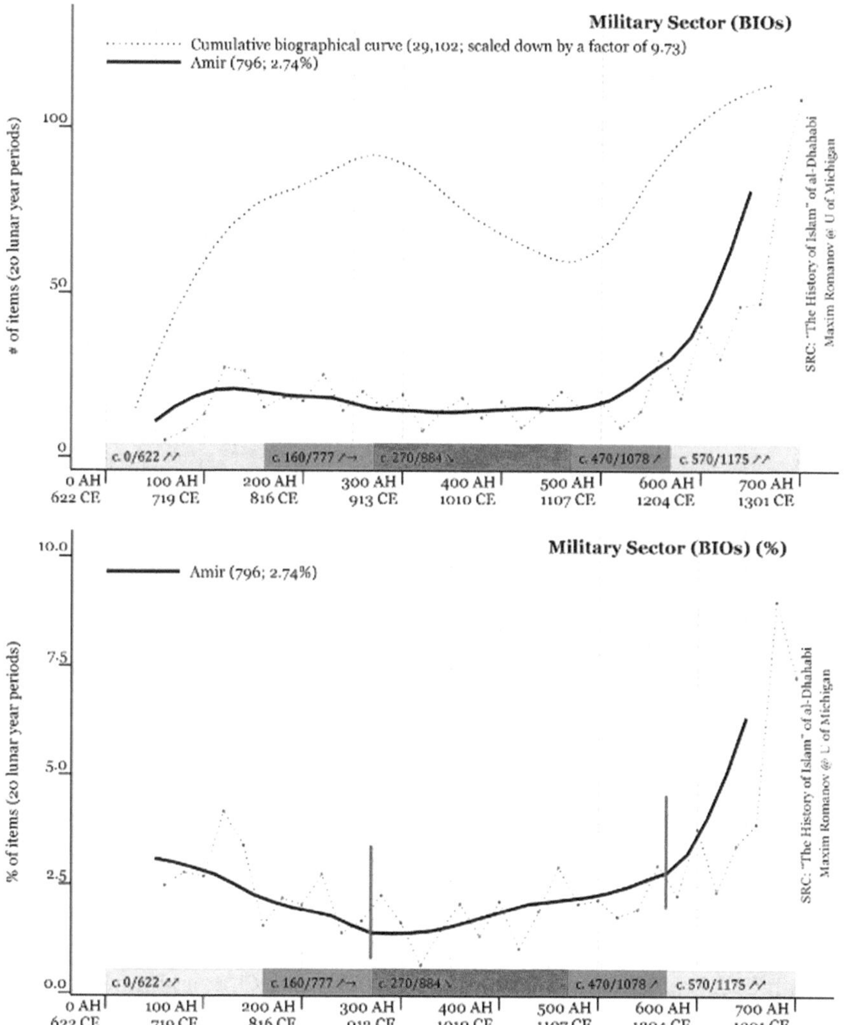

Figure 6.13. The Military Sector in the *Taʾrīkh al-islām*.

the most frequently mentioned *madrasa*s in the *Taʾrīkh al-islām*. The vizieral al-Niẓāmiyyas and the caliphal al-Mustanṣiriyya feature more prominently. However, the curves strongly suggest that their prime time is over, while 'military' *madrasa*s—al-Ẓāhiriyya, al-Amīniyya, al-Nāṣiriyya, al-Nūriyya, al-ʿĀdiliyya, al-Qaymariyya, and others—are on the rise.

The "Fulān al-dīn" honorifics, which in the earlier periods were reserved for religious scholars, become very common among the military, while the old pat-

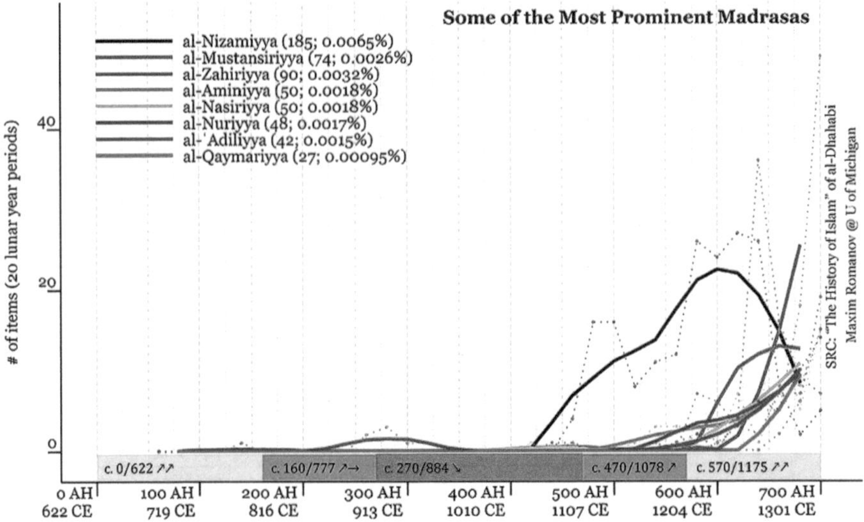

Figure 6.14. Mentions of Most Prominent Madrasas.

tern of "Fulān al-dawla" practically disappears (see Figure 6.15).[25] It is not entirely clear whether these names are given to the military by religious scholars or whether they are self-claimed (most likely both), but the fact that the military are listed under these honorifics in biographical collections implies that, at the very least, religious scholars endorsed them.

Frequencies of such words as *khalīfa/amīr al-muʾminīn*, *sulṭān*, and *amīr* in biographies show that the fourth/tenth century was a the period (Figure 6.16) when scholarly attention started shifting from caliphs to *sulṭān*s and *amīr*s, who were gaining more power and more social presence. This shift in frequencies also neatly marks the end of the period which Hodgson characterized as the High Caliphal Period (in his chronology, c. 692–945 CE)[26] and the beginning

25 Somehow, the "Fulān al-dīn" names still have a strong steel aftertaste. The most common first components of the "Fulān al-dawla" pattern are: Sayf al-dawla, "Sword of the Dynasty;" Nāṣir..., "Helper...;" Naṣr, "Victory;" Muʿizz, "Strengthener;" ʿIzz, "Strength;" ʿAḍud, "Support;" Tāj, "Crown;" Bahāʾ, "Splendor;" Ḥusām, "Cutting Edge." The most first components of the "Fulān al-dīn" pattern are: Sayf al-dīn, "Sword of Religion;" ʿIzz..., "Strength...;" Jamāl..., "Beauty...;" Badr..., "Full Moon...;" Shams..., "Sun...;" Ṣalāḥ..., "Goodness...;" Ḥusām..., "Cutting Edge..., " Quṭb..., "Pole...;" ʿAlam..., "Banner...".

26 There is also a late peak that corresponds to the temporal restoration of the independence of the ʿAbbāsid caliphate during the second half of the sixth/twelfth century, but it is equally short-lived.

of the Earlier Middle Islamic Period (in his chronology, c. 945–1258 CE): the era of *sulṭāns* and *amīrs*.

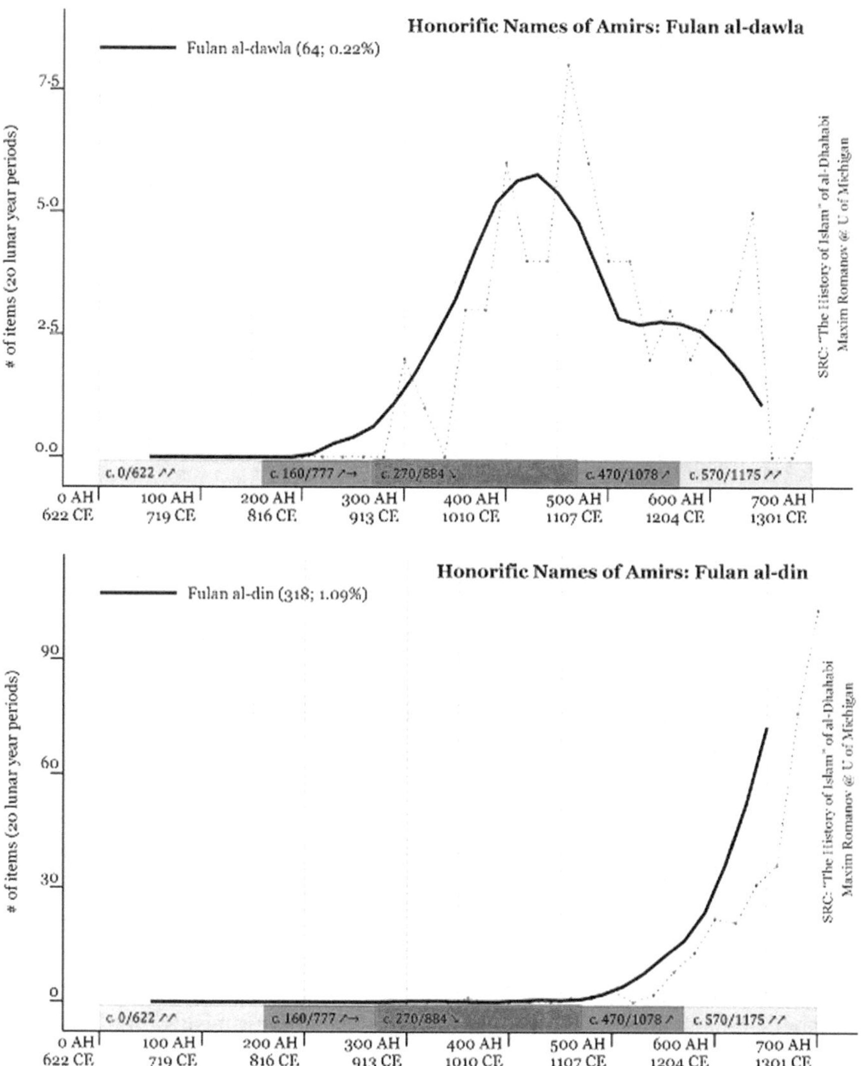

Figure 6.15. Patterns of Military Honorific Names: Fulān al-dawla, the most common pattern in the middle period, gets replaced by Fulān al-dīn pattern in the later period.

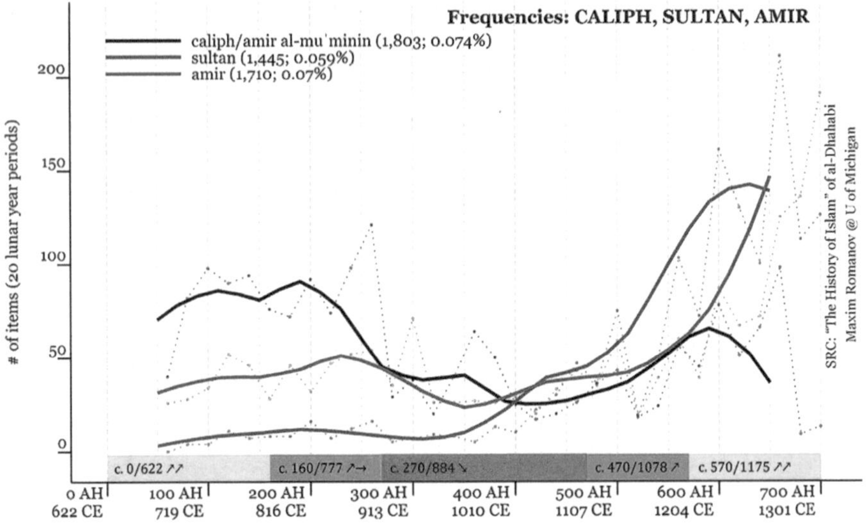

Figure 6.16. Frequencies of *khalīfa amīr al-muʾminīn, sulṭān, amīr.*

5.3 De-civilianization

As was noted above, the share of the civilian sector noticeably decreases after 400 AH/1010 CE. The diversity of crafts and trades within the civilian sector (Figure 6.17) reaches its highest point around 300 AH/913 CE, when 85 different trades and crafts are represented.[27] After 300 AH/913 CE the diversity goes down, getting to the 60s range by the end of the period.

Looking more closely into trades and crafts, it can be pointed out that several sectors are clearly distinguishable:[28] textiles (1, 495), foods (799), metalwork (331), "chemistry" (349),[29] clothes (306), finances (278), paper/books (253), brokerage (231), jewelry (218), and sundry services (170).

All sectors peak sometime between 300 AH/913 CE and 500 AH/1107 CE, but after that they show steady decline—even in those rare cases when absolute numbers remain quite significant, their percentages unmistakably go down.

---

27 I should remind the reader that only *nisbas* that are used to describe at least ten individuals are considered in this analysis.

28 Largely following Shatzmiller's classification; see *Shatzmiller, Labour in the Medieval Islamic World.* These sectors often overlap.

29 Trades that involve dealing with any complex compounds: al-ʿAṭṭār, "druggist, perfumer;" al-Ṣaydalānī, "apothecary, druggist;" al-Ṣābūnī, "soap maker/seller," etc.

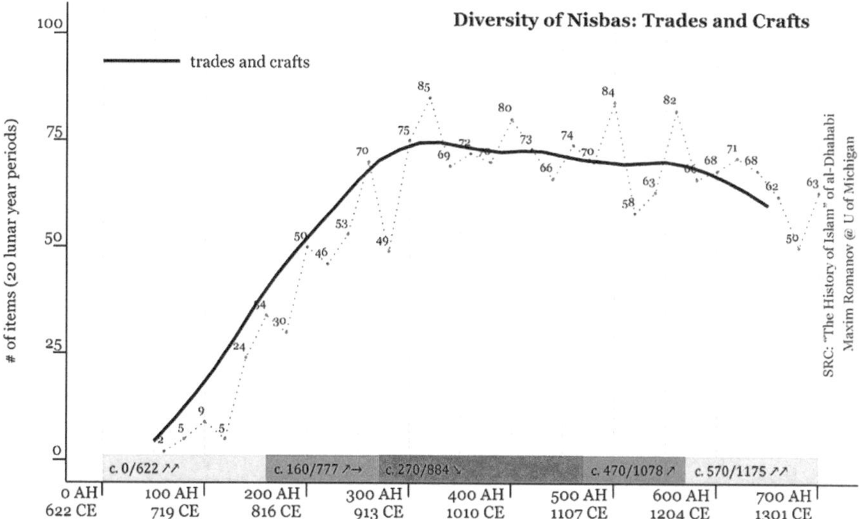

Figure 6.17. Diversity of Trades and Crafts: Numbers of unique *nisbas* referring to trades in crafts by 20 lunar year periods.

Practically all individual *nisbas* show the same trend. Merchants (sing. *tājir*, 294; Figure 6.19) constitute the only group that shows a different trend, and their numbers actually grow by the end of the period. This is, however, only because this is a blanket category that encompasses all the above listed 'industries' without emphasizing any specific one in particular. Figure 6.18 shows the cumulative trend of involvement of religious scholars in crafts and trades. The curve based on absolute numbers (*left*) shows that numbers of scholars—who were either directly involved in specific crafts and trades or came from families that made their fortune in those areas—remained rather high until 600 AH/1204 CE; relative numbers (*right*) show that the steady downward trend in this sector begins as early as 440 AH/1049 CE—about three decades before the cumulative biographical curve (470 AH/1078 CE) starts recovering.

By the end of the period, the emphasis on identities shifts, and while "secular occupations" are still not uncommon among the learned,[30] they are definitely no longer the main focus of biographers, who instead pay more attention to positions and family connections (see the section on professionalization below).

30 The decline does not appear as staggering as, for example, Cohen's study argued; see Cohen, "The Economic Background and the Secular Occupations of Muslim Jurisprudents and Traditionists in the Classical Period of Islam: (Until the Middle of the Eleventh Century)."

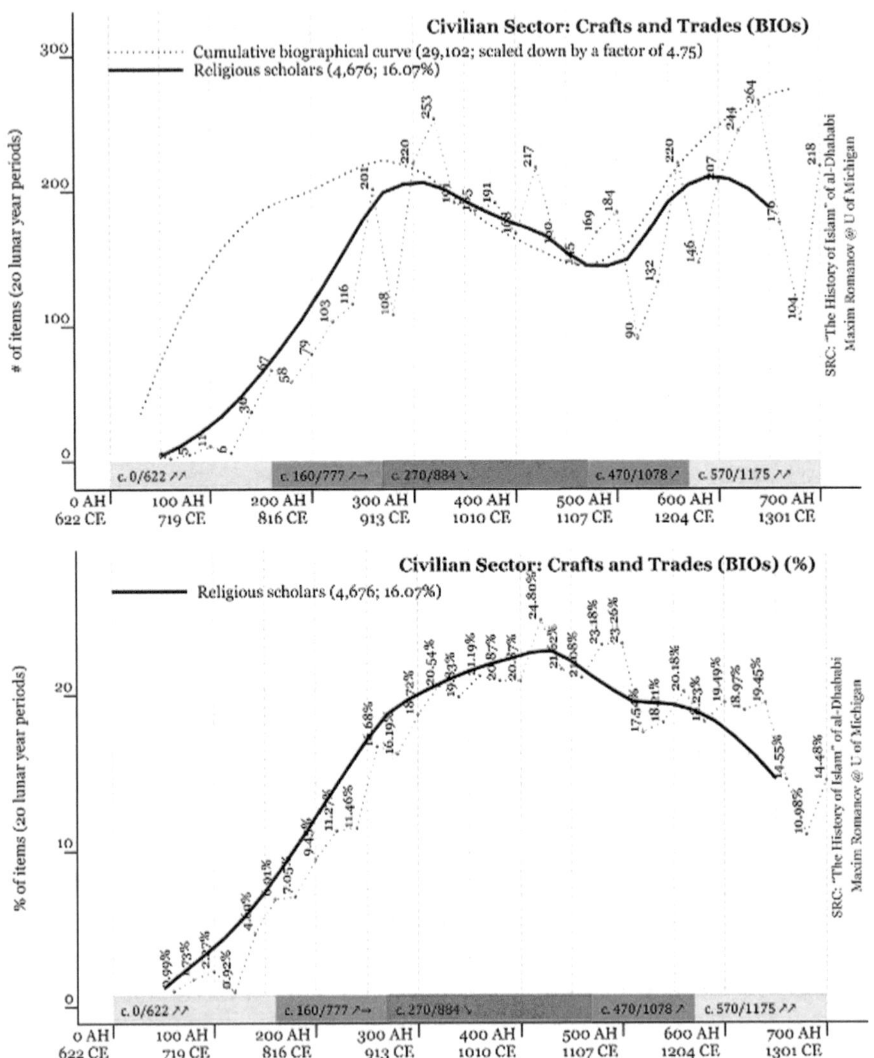

Figure 6.18. The Growth and Decline of Crafts and Trades.

The geographical distribution of these professions is most puzzling. Essentially, all 'industries' display the same pattern: the larger the region, the larger the presence of individuals involved in specific 'industries'. Iraq always comes first, followed by Iran (representation by sectors varies slightly, but northeastern Iran usually has highest numbers), then Syria and Egypt. Such a geographical distribution of 'industries' suggests that occupational *nisba*s were also used as necessary specifiers to distinguish among individuals in large communities.[31] This issue might be resolved by adding local biographical collections to the corpus and experimenting with data grouping until some distinctive patterns can be discerned. Data from non-literary sources will be crucial for advancing this inquiry, which requires undivided attention.

Whether this decline of the civilian sector is a result of the actual withdrawal of the learned from trades and crafts or the loss of awareness of this part of their identity, the general effect on the development of the religious sector would still be the same: the loss of connections with the broader population. It is not that religious scholars stopped maintaining connections with the populace at large, but they gradually turned into a self-reproducing class whose members were primarily concerned about their own group interests.

5.4 Professionalization and Institutionalization

The professionalization and institutionalization of the learned class are another two processes that take place during the period covered in the *Taʾrīkh al-islām*. These processes have been discussed at length in academic literature,[32] although in most cases the emphasis is on institutionalization.[33]

---

31 Very similar to what Bulliet argued regarding toponymic *nisbas*: "For example Karkh, a popular quarter of Baghdad, appears in the nisba al-Karkhī when representation from Iraq is high. When the proportion is smaller, the name of the major city itself is a common nisba. In the example given, a later resident of Karkh would appear as al-Baghdadī. Finally, when the proportion is very low, the nisba will frequently be derived from the entire province, that is, al-Baghdadī becomes al-ʿIrāqī." See Bulliet, *Conversion to Islam in the Medieval Period*, 12.

32 The most important studies are: George Makdisi, *The Rise of the Colleges: Institutions of Learning in Islam and the West* (Edinburgh: Edinburgh University Press, 1981); Jonathan P. Berkey, *The Transmission of Knowledge in Medieval Cairo: A Social History of Islamic Education* (Princeton, NJ: Princeton University Press, 1992); Michael Chamberlain, *Knowledge and Social Practice in Medieval Damascus, 1190–1350* (Cambridge/New York: Cambridge University Press, 1994). To a large extent, Berkey's and Chamberlain's studies are responses to Makdisi's "over-institutionalization."

33 It seems that Gilbert is the only one to use this term in her study of the learned of Medieval Damascus; see Joan E. Gilbert, "Institutionalization of Muslim Scholarship and Professionalization of the ʿUlamāʾ in Medieval Damascus," *Studia Islamica* 52 (January 1, 1980): 105–34, DOI:10.2307/1595364. However, in her study this term appears to blend into institutionalization, and both become practically indistinguishable. Other scholars mention professionalization almost exclusively with reference to Gilbert's work. See, for example, Chamberlain, *Knowledge and Social Practice in Medieval Damascus, 1190–1350*, 70; Daphna Ephrat, *A Learned Society*

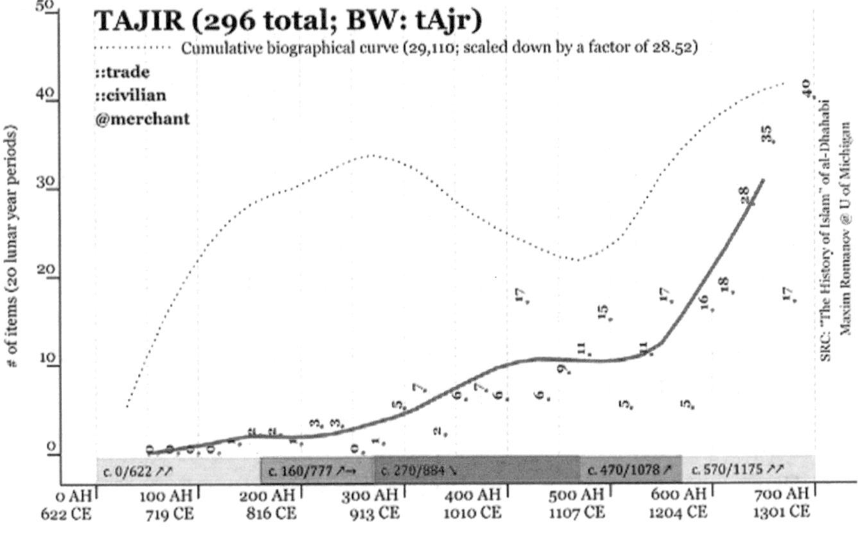

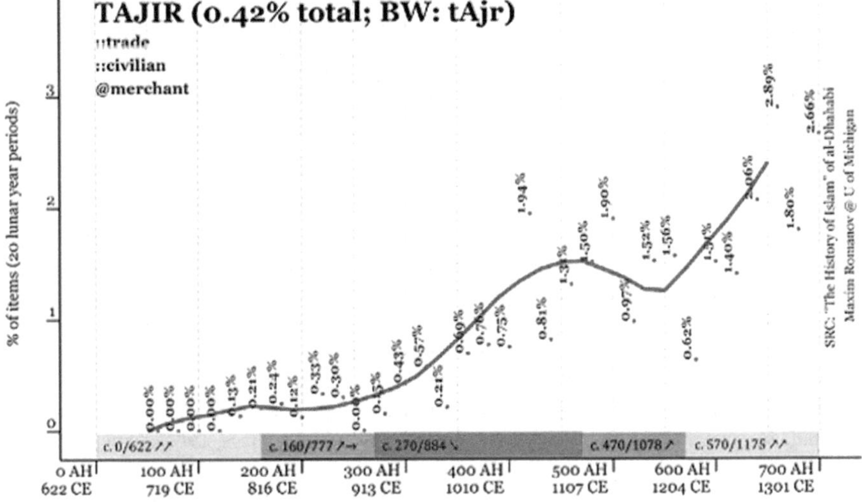

Figure 6.19. The Growth of Merchants.

Here 'professionalization' is understood as the growth of complexity of religious learning that leads to its branching into specific disciplines, mastering

in a Period of Transition: The Sunni 'Ulama' of Eleventh Century Baghdad (Albany: State University of New York Press, 2000), 104, 179.

which would eventually require full-time commitment. Professionalization implies the development of a community of specialists who maintain qualifying standards and ensure demarcation from the non-qualified; ideally, mechanisms of monetary and status compensation for professional services should also develop during this process.

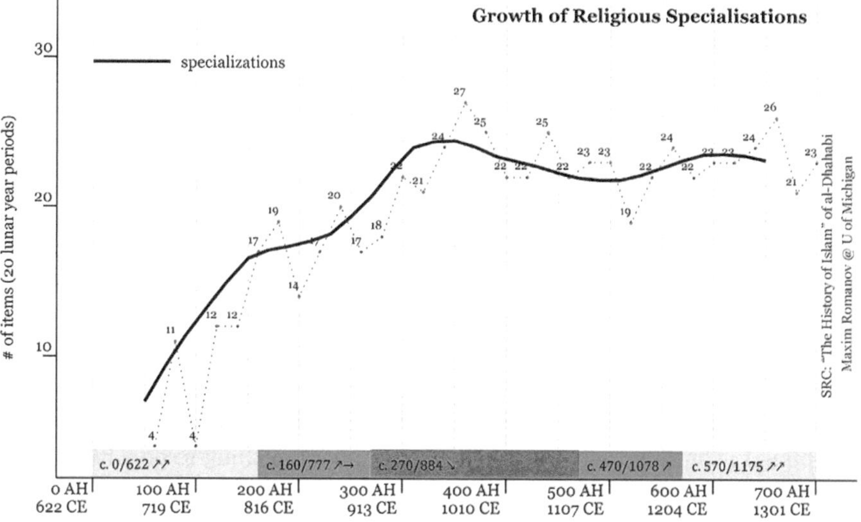

Figure 6.20. Growth of Religious Specializations: Numbers of unique *nisbas* referring to religious specializations by 20 lunar year periods.

If we agree on recognizing the process of the branching of the religious learning into specific disciplines as an indicator of professionalization, we may look at the growth of religious specializations as indicated through "descriptive names." Figure 6.20 shows that the process of branching reaches its highest point during 300–350 AH/913–962 CE, after which the number of specializations remains on the same level and fluctuates only slightly.

Although completely devoid of both buzzwords, Melchert's study is perhaps the most valuable insight into the process of professionalization.[34] In his book on the formation of the Sunnī legal schools (*madhhab*), Melchert offered three major criteria: the recognition of the chief scholar (*raʾīs*), commentaries (*taʿliqa*) on the summaries of legal teachings (*mukhtaṣar*) as a proof of one's qualification, and a

34 Christopher Melchert, *The Formation of the Sunni Schools of Law, 9th-10th Centuries C.E.* (Leiden/New York: Brill, 1997).

more or less regulated process of transmission of legal knowledge, through which the achievement of required qualification is ensured. Chronologically, Melchert placed this process for the Shāfiʿīs, Ḥanbalīs, and Ḥanafīs in Baghdad of the late ninth–early tenth centuries.[35] Keeping in mind this coincidence of Melchert's close reading of legal *ṭabaqāt* and my distant reading of *Taʾrīkh al-islām*, we may—at least tentatively—consider 300 AH/913 CE to be a turning point in the process of professionalization.

Data from the *Taʾrīkh al-islām* shows that the professionalization of religious knowledge (around 300 AH/913 CE) is not directly related to scholars' abandoning their gainful occupations in the civilian sectors, as this process will start only around 430 AH/1039 CE. However, professionalization failed to bring about one very important thing, namely more paid positions for the learned. This must have forced men of learning into difficult positions where they had to maintain a delicate but uncomfortable balance between keeping up with higher standards of religious learning and earning a living. The financial difficulties that professionalization imposed on the life of a scholar may have become quite a discouraging factor for the young who were considering career paths. Keeping in mind that the decline of the main curve begins c. 270 AH/884 CE—i.e., roughly around the time when the number of religious specializations reaches its highest point—it is tempting to consider that professionalization has something to do with this decline. After all, a full-time commitment to study religious sciences leaves one no time to earn a living through gainful occupations in the civilian sector. Charging money for teaching religious subjects was considered illicit, and there are hardly any indications that the number of positions for religious specialists grew to compensate for this unfortunate development. To succeed in such conditions, one had to be either extremely resolute or come from a wealthy family in order to afford the career of a scholar. And since both of these situations are in limited availability in any society, this could explain the decline in numbers of biographies.

The introduction and spread of *waqf* institutions is considered a turning point in the institutionalization of the learned. The salaried positions of these institutions offered a solution to the complication of professionalization. Frequencies of references to *waqf* institutions in biographies (Figure 6.21) show that they —most importantly the *madrasas*—become a noteworthy detail of biographies

35 Melchert explains the failure of the Mālikīs by their being too closely linked to the caliphal patronage, and when the caliphs were eclipsed, so were the Mālikīs. See ibid., 176.

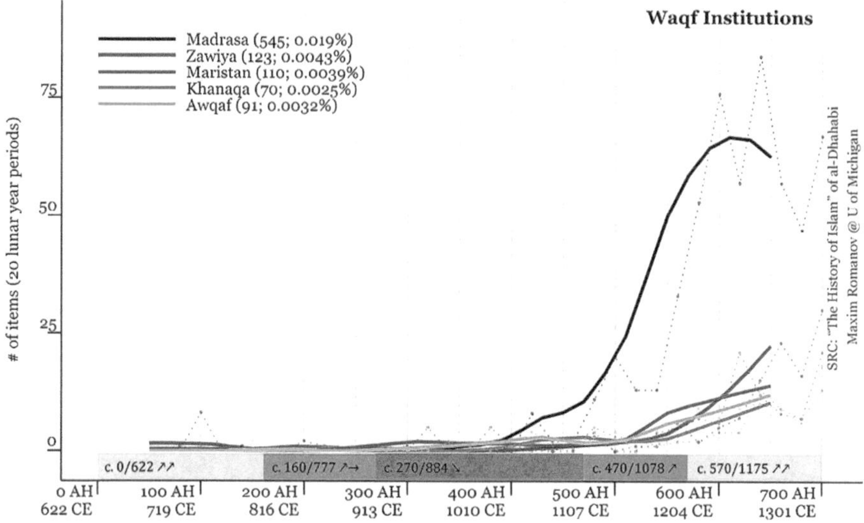

Figure 6.21. References to *Waqf* Institutions in Biographies.

soon after 400 AH/1010 CE, about 100 lunar years after the turning point in professionalization, and a very important one after 500 AH/1107 CE.[36]

However, by offering salaried positions, the *waqf* institutions also reconfigured the structure of the learned class, which in the long run had a very negative effect. In his study of medieval Damascus,[37] Chamberlain convincingly argued that salaried positions (*manāṣib*) became one of the major objects of contention among the learned, who were now concerned about winning and holding as many of these positions as possible. One of their strategies was to ensure that the positions stayed within a family—household—which led to the formation of dynasties of religious scholars and, in the long run, the transformation of the religious class into a rather closed social stratum, to which the word 'clergy' became more and more applicable as time went on.

As the data from the *Taʾrīkh al-islām* indicate (Figure 6.22), the role of family connections unmistakably increases after 400 AH/1010 CE. The tribal nature of early Islamic society explains the high frequency of references to close relatives in the early periods. However, references to parents are most frequent—largely to

36 The decline of the frequency of the word *madrasa* should not be interpreted as a decline of this institution, but rather as a change in the form of reference in general: most *madrasa*s are referred to by their "al-Fulāniyya" names (see Figure 6.14 above).

37 *Chamberlain, Knowledge and Social Practice in Medieval Damascus, 1190–1350.*

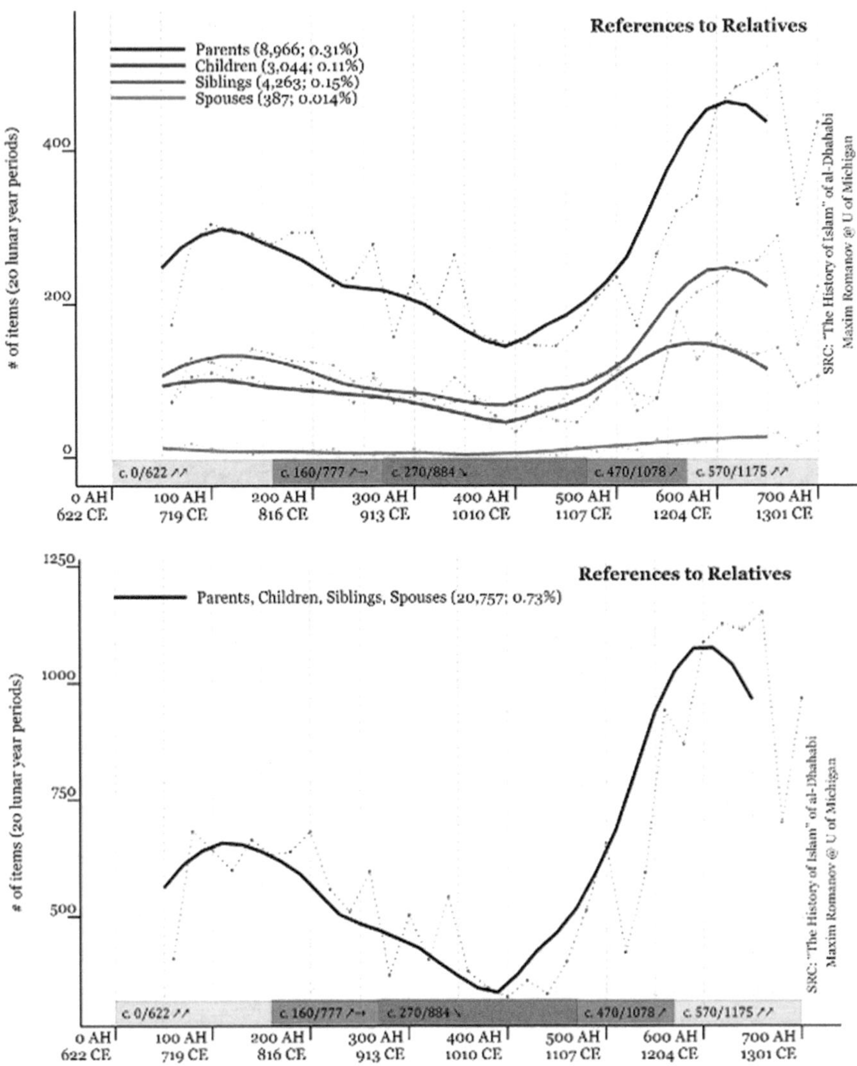

Figure 6.22. References to Relatives. The graph on the left shows the major categories of relatives, while the one on the right shows the same data combined into one graph.

fathers,[38] which is understandable, considering the importance of lineage through the male line within tribal society. But again, the curve of references

38 The most common references are the forms of *abū* ("father"). Since this word is also the es-

goes down steadily between 120 AH/739 CE and 380/991 CE, mirroring the curve of tribal identities that also goes down, while the number of biographies keeps on growing.

After 380 AH/991 CE, references to family members practically skyrocket and even increase in pace slightly around 500 AH/1107 CE. Unlike in the early period, references to most members of the immediate family become very common: parents (the word "parent" [*wālid[a]*] becomes particularly common), siblings (brothers and sisters—*akhū*, *ukht*), children (sons and daughters—*ibnu-hu*, *bintu-hu*, etc.), and, to a lesser extent, spouses (husbands and wives—*zawj[a]*). The same trend can be seen in the references to uncles, aunts, grandparents, and grandchildren. These shifts—not just the growth of frequencies, but also the growth of varieties of familial references—may be interpreted as a shift of scholarly attention from the lineage to the household.

If we accept these rates of frequencies as an indicator of the formation of households, then it appears that scholarly households begin growing earlier than *waqf* institutions. The growth of scholarly families thus may have been caused by professionalization and then boosted by institutionalization.

6. Concluding Remarks

Many of these social transformations have been discussed in the academic literature, and one may say that the present analysis shows only what "we already know," to use the most common dismissal of the digital humanities.[39] However, the exploratory model presented here offers a methodologically different *data-driven* perspective on the Islamic élites over the course of almost seven hundred years. With this model, we were able to identify and trace a number of major processes that took place over this long period: how Islamic society, which started as tribal entity, stopped being such by the beginning of the tenth century CE; how the role of the military commanders increased from the twelfth century on; how the diversity of social backgrounds of religious scholars gradually declined, and they turned into a rather isolated group. One should also keep in mind that our field is making its first steps into the digital realm, and this piece is a show-

sential part of *kunya*, an extremely common patronymic element of the Arab/Muslim name, only its forms with pronominal suffixes—such as *abū-hu* ("his father")—are considered. The same principle is applied to other ambiguous family terms.

39 My digital study of preaching tells a story that disagrees with the previous scholarship on this topic. See chapter three in *Romanov, Computational Reading of Arabic Biographical Collections.*

case and an invitation to work with explicitly described models that can be discussed, compared, modified, and applied to new sources. With models, we can stop futile discussions about the meaning and reliability of certain data and start exploring Islamic history experimentally. By developing and testing multiple complex models, we can eventually arrive at a better understanding of both our sources and the processes they describe. With models, we can compare multiple sources and evaluate entire genres. Right now, when scholars of Islam are entering the domain of digital humanities, there is a dire need for transparency in our methods—and modeling appears to be the most optimal option—especially if we venture to study the entire digital corpus of classical Arabic sources, which at the moment may have already exceeded 800 million words.

Bibliography

al-Dhahabī. *Taʾrīkh al-islām wa-wafayāt al-mashāhīr wa-al-aʿlām*. Edited by ʿUmar Tadmurī. 2nd edition. 52 vols. Bayrūt: Dār al-Kitāb al-ʿArabī, 1990.

Berkey, Jonathan P. *The Transmission of Knowledge in Medieval Cairo: A Social History of Islamic Education*. Princeton, NJ: Princeton University Press, 1992.

Bulliet, Richard W. *Conversion to Islam in the Medieval Period: An Essay in Quantitative History*. Cambridge, MA: Harvard University Press, 1979.

Chamberlain, Michael. *Knowledge and Social Practice in Medieval Damascus, 1190–1350*. Cambridge/New York: Cambridge University Press, 1994.

Cohen, Hayyim J. "The Economic Background and the Secular Occupations of Muslim Jurisprudents and Traditionists in the Classical Period of Islam: (Until the Middle of the Eleventh Century)." *Journal of the Economic and Social History of the Orient* 13 (1970): 16–61.

Ephrat, Daphna. *A Learned Society in a Period of Transition: The Sunni ʿUlamaʾ of Eleventh Century Baghdad*. Albany: State University of New York Press, 2000.

Gilbert, Joan E. "Institutionalization of Muslim Scholarship and Professionalization of the ʿUlamāʾ in Medieval Damascus." *Studia Islamica* 52 (January 1, 1980): 105–34. DOI:10.2307/1595364.

Hodgson, Marshall G. S. *The Venture of Islam: Conscience and History in a World Civilization. Vol. 2. The Expansion of Islam in the Middle Periods*. 3 vols. Chicago: University of Chicago Press, 1974.

Humphreys, R. Stephen. "Politics and Architectural Patronage in Ayyubid Damascus." In *The Islamic World from Classical to Modern Times: Essays in Honor of Bernard Lewis*, ed. Clifford Edmund Bosworth, 151–74. Princeton, NJ: Darwin Press, 1989.

—. "Women as Patrons of Religious Architecture in Ayyubid Damascus." *Muqarnas* 11 (January 1, 1994): 35–54.

Jockers, Matthew L. *Macroanalysis: Digital Methods and Literary History*. 1st edition. Chicago: University of Illinois Press, 2013.

Makdisi, George. *The Rise of the Colleges: Institutions of Learning in Islam and the West*. Edinburgh: Edinburgh University Press, 1981.

Melchert, Christopher. *The Formation of the Sunni Schools of Law, 9th-10th Centuries C.E.* Leiden/New York: Brill, 1997.
Moretti, Franco. *Distant Reading*. 1st edition. London: Verso, 2013.
—. *Graphs, Maps, Trees: Abstract Models for Literary History.* London: Verso, 2007.
Morris, Ian. *The Measure of Civilization: How Social Development Decides the Fate of Nations.* Princeton, NJ: Princeton University Press, 2013.
—. *Why the West Rules–for Now: The Patterns of History, and What They Reveal about the Future.* New York: Farrar, Straus and Giroux, 2010.
Petry, Carl F. *The Civilian Elite of Cairo in the Later Middle Ages.* Princeton, NJ: Princeton University Press, 1981.
Romanov, Maxim G. "Computational Reading of Arabic Biographical Collections with Special Reference to Preaching (661–1300 CE)." Ph.D. dissertation, University of Michigan, 2013.
Shatzmiller, Maya. *Labour in the Medieval Islamic World.* Leiden: E.J. Brill, 1994.
Wasserstein, David J. "Where Have All the Converts Gone? Difficulties in the Study of Conversion to Islam in Al-Andalus." *Al-Qanṭara* 33 no. 2 (February 11, 2013): 325–42.

Alex Brey

Quantifying the Quran

In the University of Pennsylvania Museum of Archaeology and Anthropology there is a complete manuscript of the Quran, shelfmark NEP-27, dated to 559/1164 by a colophon.[1] This places its production just after the death of the Sultan Ahmed Sanjar in 1157 CE, a period when the empire of the Great Seljuqs was splintering into smaller successor states. Copied in Hamadan by a scribe named Maḥmūd ibn al-Ḥusayn al-Kirmānī, the manuscript (or *muṣḥaf*, as manuscripts of the Quran are known) somehow eventually ended up in Egypt. There it was donated as a religious endowment (*waqf*) to the al-Azhar mosque in Cairo by Amīr Aḥmad Jāwīsh, who died in 1786. The manuscript, now disbound, was purchased by the museum in 1919 from Dmitri Andalaft, an antiquities dealer in Cairo.

This manuscript was the subject of an intensive study conducted by students in a graduate seminar taught by Renata Holod and Yael Rice in the spring of 2012 at the University of Pennsylvania. Students from the fields of history of art and Near Eastern languages and cultures worked together to systematically analyze the manuscript.[2] Topics of investigation included the palaeography, interlinear Arabic commentary, corrections, paper, colophon, frontispiece, verse markers, and *sūra* headings of the manuscript. In this article, I will present a very brief overview of the project before turning to two topics in more depth: the use of digital image enhancement and quantitative analytical approaches. While the conclusions that were reached using these techniques could also have been revealed by non-digital means, I will argue that these two approaches still provide unique insights—in the first case by illustrating the unseen, and in the second by revealing latent factors in the production of the manuscript that are not directly observable.

---

1 For an early overview of the manuscript's art historical importance, see Richard Ettinghausen, "A Signed and Dated Seljuq Qur'an," *Bulletin of the American Institute for Persian Art and Archaeology* IV (1935): 92–102.

2 I would like to acknowledge the valuable contributions made by all of my fellow students in the seminar: Elliot Brooks, Michael Falcetano, Quintana Heathman, V.K. Inman, Emily Neumeier, Raha Rafii, Elias Saba, and Agnieszka Szymanska. While I will not address every topic that they analyzed, this paper would not exist without the many conversations that we had together over the course the past two years. Their studies will be forthcoming in an edited digital publication about the manuscript. I would also like to thank conservators Julie Ream and Nina Owczarek, as well as Mitch Fraas, who oversaw the digitization of NEP-27 at the Schoenberg Center for Electronic Text and Image.

1. The State of the Manuscript

The analysis of NEP-27 began with a physical examination of each folio, followed by the creation of a database in which any repairs, corrections, or other unusual features were noted. This was complemented by a thorough conservation report on the manuscript, produced by paper conservator Julie Ream as part of her preliminary stabilization of the manuscript. The chemical compositions of several key pigments were analyzed using portable X-Ray Fluorescence Spectrometry conducted under the aegis of Nina Owczarek, Assistant Conservator at the University of Pennsylvania Museum of Archaeology and Anthropology.[3] Due to the use of a metal-based ink, many of the pages had been damaged by corrosion and were unstable. Forty one of the folios are undergoing further conservation at the time of writing. The manuscript was digitized and made available on the Penn Libraries website, known as Penn in Hand (Figure 7.1). This digitization allowed us to conduct most of the research without handling the fragile physical object.

2. Digital Imaging

I now want to delve a little deeper into the topic of digital imaging as it was used to clarify part of the manuscript. Folio 2 (Figure 7.2) at first appears to be an ordinary enough page. On the recto we find a decorated frontispiece that contains the number of verses in the various readings of the Quran. On the verso is the text of the first chapter, *Sūrat al-Fātiḥa*. However, more careful examination of the page reveals that this initial appearance is deceiving. The margins of the page, like several others in the manuscript, have been completely replaced with a different type of paper, and the decorative gold border around *Sūrat al-Fātiḥa* actually appears to sit on a different piece of paper than the text of the *sūra*. The list of the Quranic verse counts begins with the word “and” (*wa*). It would be grammatically incorrect and peculiar for a formal text to begin with this connector, which suggests that there should be some content preceding it. Above and below the first *sūra*, where we would expect to find the standard content of a *sūra* heading, instead we find another enumeration of the number of words and letters in the Quran. This too appears incomplete.

3 X-ray Fluorescence Spectrometry employs X-rays to produce a semi-quantitative spectrum of the elements present in a substance, in this case the pigments used in the production of the manuscript.

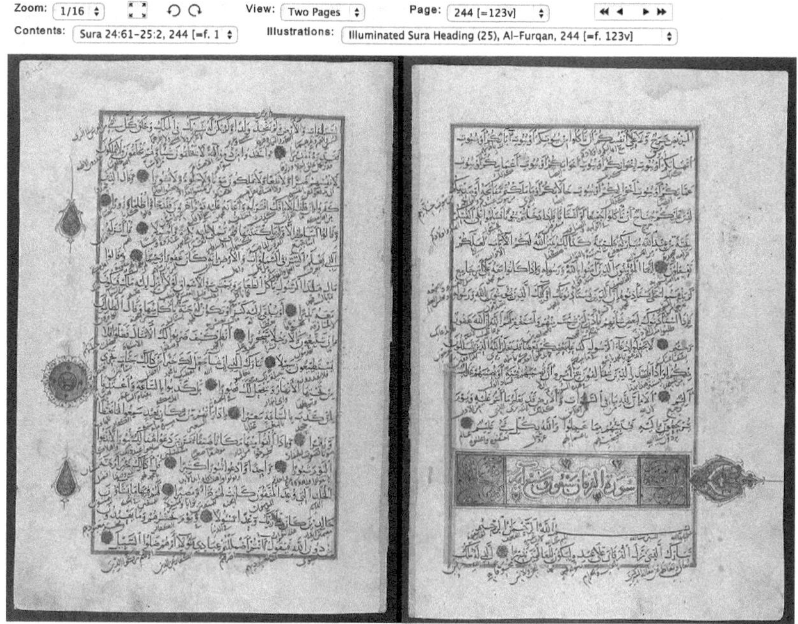

Figure 7.1. Penn in Hand: NEP-27. Staff from the University of Pennsylvania Kislak Center for Special Collections, Rare Books, and Manuscripts collaborated with faculty and students in the seminar to produce navigation menus customized to the textual and visual content of the manuscript (located at the top of this screenshot). Website and digital images created by the Penn Libraries (2012).

It is possible to clarify the construction of this collage with a consumer-grade digital camera by taking multiple photos of the folio in transmitted light at different exposures and combining these into a single, high dynamic range (HDR) image using widely available photo editing software in order to reveal a broader range of luminosity than a camera can capture in a single exposure. The HDR image of the folio reveals that the decoration of the border continues underneath the text of the first *sūra*, but it is badly damaged at its center (Figure 7.3). What now serves as the border of the first *sūra* must have originally been a fully decorated carpet-page that was later repurposed. While the decoration of the frontispiece is visible through the paper with the text of the *sūra*, this does not appear to have decoration on the reverse.

Taking all of these observations into consideration, it is possible to reconstruct the opening of the manuscript as a double frontispiece. This probably consisted of four consecutive carpet pages, with a mirror page of the current frontis-

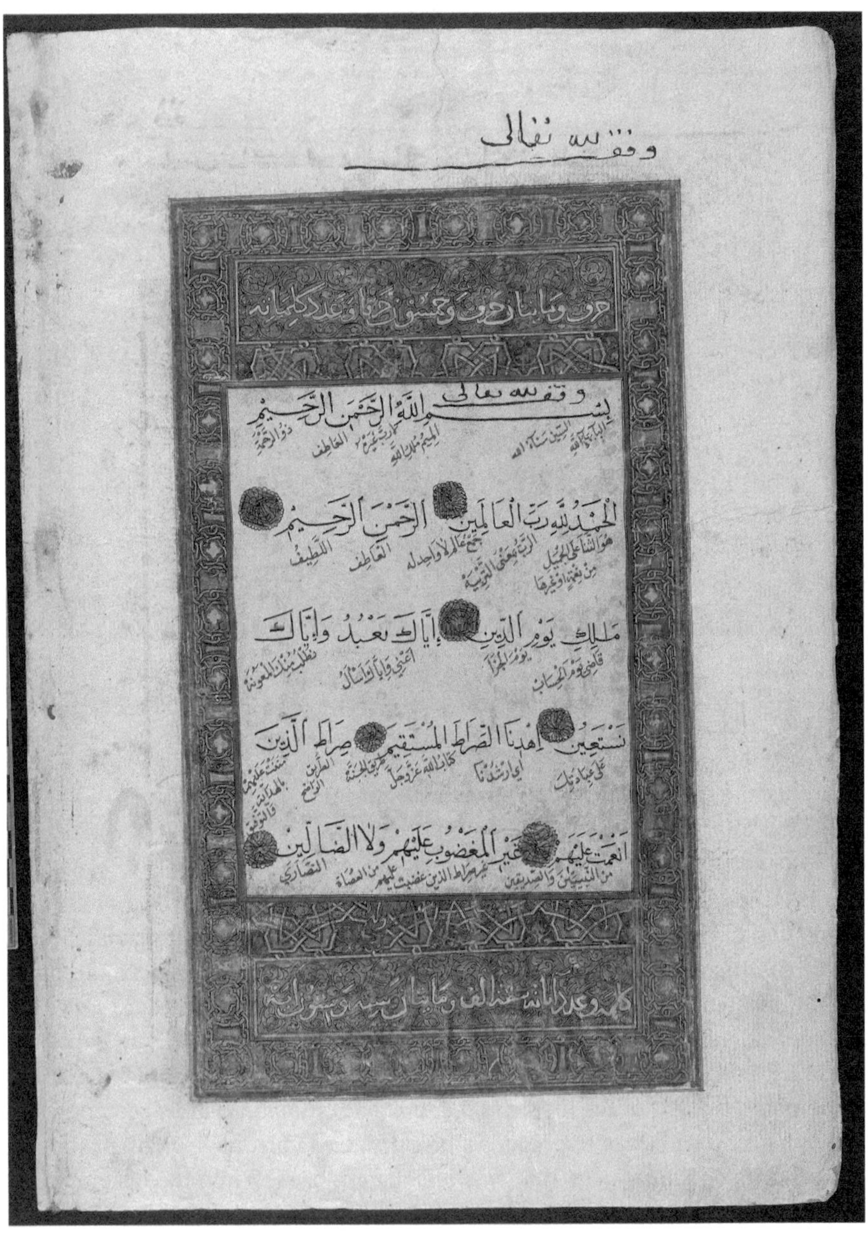

Figure 7.2. Sūrat al-Fātiḥa. Folio 2 verso, Manuscript of the Quran. Maḥmūd ibn al-Ḥusayn al-Kirmānī, 559/1164, Hamadan, Iran, with later alterations. Ink and gold on paper, 42 × 30 cm, University of Pennsylvania Museum of Archaeology and Anthropology, NEP-27. Digital images created by the Penn Libraries (2012).

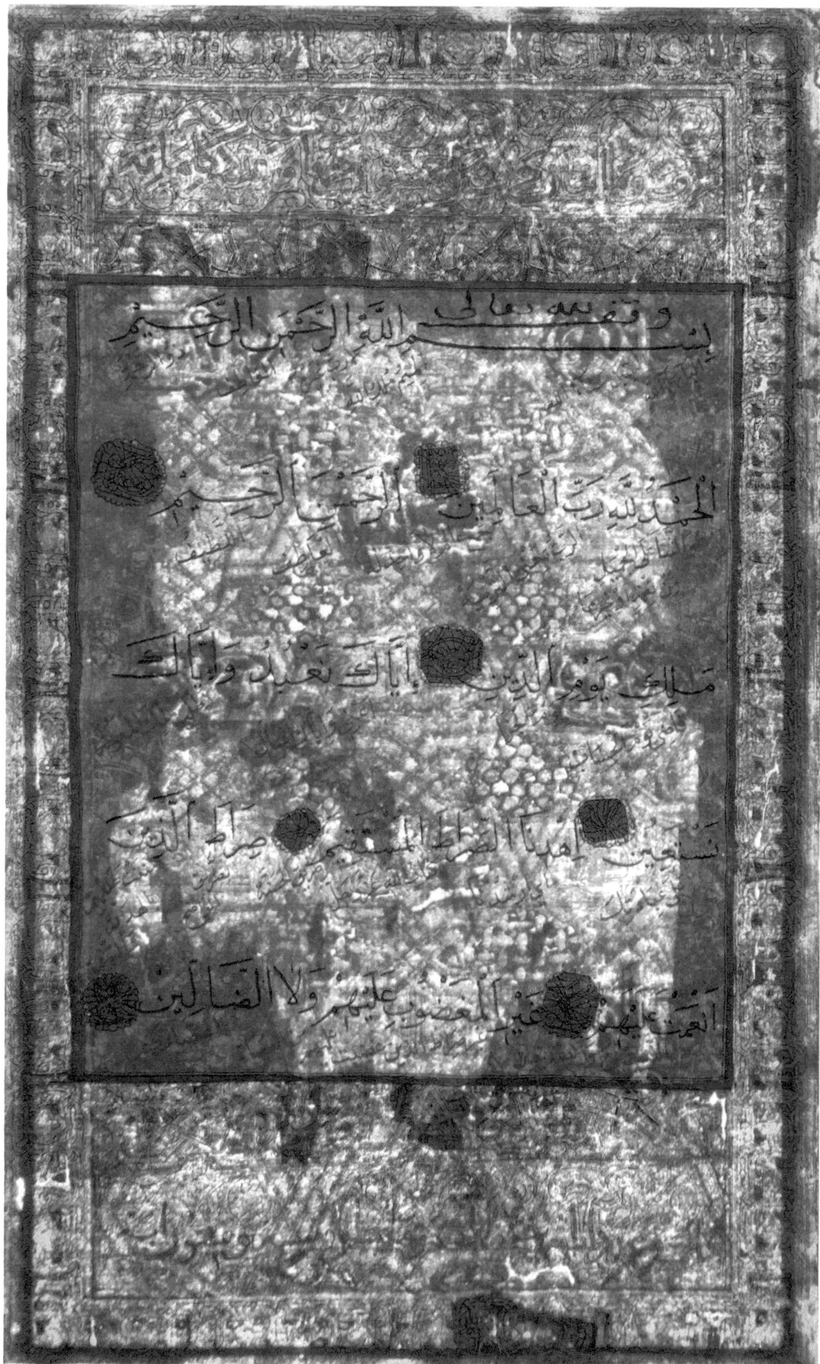

بسم الله الرحمن الرحيم
الحمد لله رب العالمين الرحمن الرحيم
ملك يوم الدين إياك نعبد وإياك
نستعين اهدنا الصراط المستقيم صراط الذين
أنعمت عليهم غير المغضوب عليهم ولا الضالين

Figure 7.3. High Dynamic Range Image of Folio 2 verso. A high dynamic range image of the text block of folio 2v in transmitted light reveals the hidden, damaged center of the folio.

piece and another matching page for the current carpet border of *Sūrat al-Fātiḥa*. At some point, the second page was lost, and the first and third pages were combined to make the composite page as it now exists (Figure 7.4). This reconstruction, although based on the visible evidence, is only hypothetical. While it would explain the absence of decoration on the reverse of the current frontispiece, it does not completely resolve either of the textual discrepancies I have noted. It is possible that the current frontispiece actually formed the second page of NEP-27, and it is instead the first page which was damaged or lost. Without dismantling the current composite page, it is difficult to be more certain.

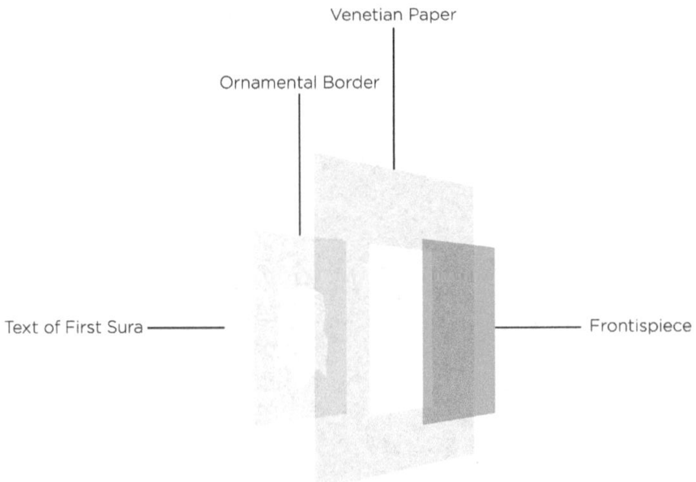

Figure 7.4. The Construction of Folio 2. Four distinct pieces of paper have been glued together to produce folio 2.

In its original form, the double frontispiece of the manuscript would have impressed readers with its abundance of costly materials and fine ornamentation, and it shifts how we should think of the workshop that produced it and the person who commissioned or purchased it. Understanding how and why the opening of the manuscript was altered to produce the current composite folio also allows us to better understand the goals of the person who conducted the most extensive refurbishment of the manuscript, probably Aḥmad Jāwīsh (d. 1786) or someone at al-Azhar on the occasion of its donation. HDR imaging provides a clearer view into the physical construction of the composite folio, which in turn prompts different questions about why the manuscript was altered, when, where, and by whom.

The ability to perceive and illustrate elements of the manuscript that are otherwise difficult to see and image is not a recent innovation. Techniques like multispectral and hyperspectral imaging, which capture wavelengths of light that are not visible to the human eye, were largely confined to the planning of conservation efforts and special cases like palimpsests, but the last few years have seen these techniques become increasingly affordable.[4] As these techniques become more widely available, and other low-cost imaging techniques like high dynamic range photography and reflectance transformation imaging (also known as polynomial texture mapping, which calculates the angle and intensity of reflection for every pixel in an image) are developed, it will become increasingly affordable to investigate how manuscripts were produced, altered, and used. The HDR photography of NEP-27 placed a special focus on a late moment in the manuscript's use, perhaps when it was donated as a *waqf*, and suggests how, as researchers grapple with the discoveries about the production and use of objects that these techniques provide, they are also prompted to explore previously unremarked facets of human engagements with material culture.

3. Quantitative Approaches

I now want to turn to the use of a quantitative approach to explore several aspects of NEP-27, both to locate it within a broader context of medieval Quran manuscripts and to analyze its decoration. This quantitative approach may sit uneasily within the academic discipline of art history, with its emphasis on qualitative analyses and historical context, but the manuscript of NEP-27 itself reveals that quantification played an important role in how users of the manuscript engaged with it. The double frontispiece that prefaces the *muṣḥaf* is a kind of premodern infographic, in which the number of verses in the various readings of the Quran as well the verses, words, and letters of this particular manuscript are enumerated. Each *sūra* heading provides the number of verses in the following *sūra*. Finally, the manuscript concludes with three pages appended at a later date, probably when it was given to al-Azhar in the eighteenth century (Figure 7.5). These too list the number of *sūras*, verses, words, and letters in the Quran, but go beyond the preface to tally the number of times each letter appears in the sacred text as well as providing tabulations of other minutiae.

4 See, for example, Michael Toth's work on the Archimedes Palimpsest (http://archimedespalimpsest.net/ and http://archimedespalimpsest.org/) and the Syriac Galen Palimpsest (http://digitalgalen.net/).

The overall impression that these quantifications give is that tables and infographics, like the Arabic gloss of NEP-27 or commentaries long enough to fill their own manuscripts, provided one important way of experiencing and coming to know the Quran. A numerical approach to the sacred text was considered useful not only at the moment when NEP-27 was produced, but also at other important moments later in the history of the manuscript. Perhaps it is time art historians considered the utility of quantitative approaches for understanding manuscripts of the Islamic world more broadly.

The quantitative approaches that I employed are primarily oriented towards discerning correlation, which is at the heart of statistical analysis.[5] Some basic quantifiable aspects of luxury *muṣḥafs*—including page dimensions and the number of lines per page—gathered from auction, museum, and archival catalogues provide a sense of how NEP-27 fits into a *longue durée* picture of manuscript production.[6] The original dataset included manuscripts or fragments of Quran manuscripts dateable from the tenth to the early fifteenth centuries CE, for a total of 163 luxury Quran manuscripts. 33 of these manuscripts are dated by colophons or inscriptions, while another three have a *terminus ante quem* associated with the deaths of their owners/patrons. The precise production sites of these manuscripts are largely unknown, although most are thought to have been produced in Egypt, Syria-Palestine, Yemen, Iraq, or Iran. For the purpose of contextualizing NEP-27, manuscripts produced before the eleventh century or after the thirteenth century were omitted, leaving a corpus of 90 manuscripts, with 23 dated by colophon and one with a known *terminus ante quem*. While there are many 'working' manuscripts of the Quran with little or no ornament dateable to the period in question, such manuscripts were omitted from this corpus because their production is unrelated to that of luxury manuscripts like NEP-27.

5 As Edward Tufte, the father of data visualization criticism, explains: "the relational graphic – in its barest form, the scatterplot and its variants – is the greatest of all graphical designs. It links at least two variables, encouraging and even imploring the viewer to assess the possible causal relationship between the plotted variables. It confronts causal theories that X causes Y with empirical evidence as to the actual relationship between X and Y." Edward R. Tufte, *The Visual Display of Quantitative Information* (Cheshire, CT: Graphics Press, 1983), 47.

6 I gathered this data by hand from the websites of Sotheby's, Christie's, and Bonhams as well as major museums and libraries and from printed catalogues of several manuscript collections (the Khalili collection, the Chester Beatty Library, etc.) during the spring of 2012. It is by no means exhaustive, but it is sufficient to paint in broad strokes the development of the medium. Compiling the data necessary to create such a quantitative overview may become dramatically easier as museums and archives adopt the tenets of linked open data or similar standards. Whether major auction houses, which have embraced online listings, will have any incentive to do so remains unclear.

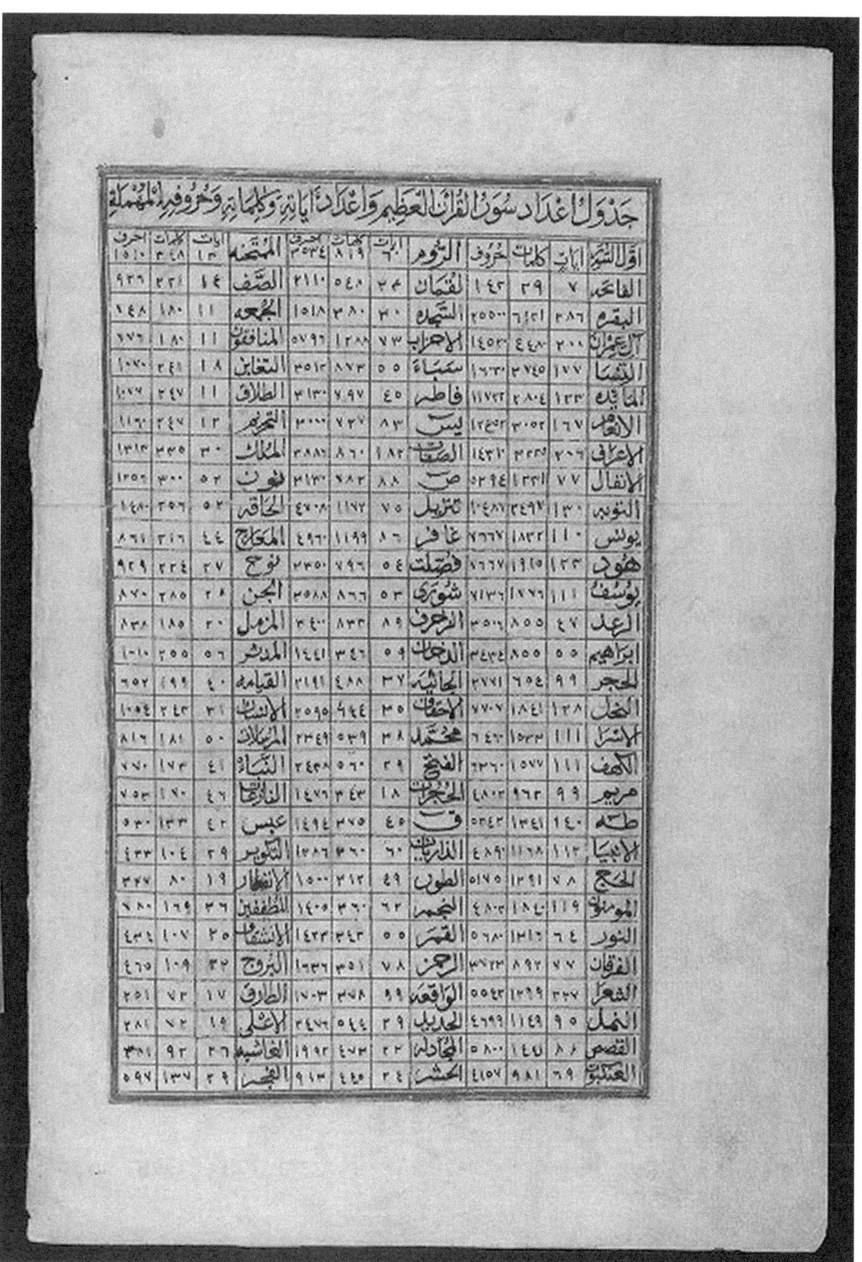

Figure 7.5. Table Quantifying the Verses, Words, and Letters in each Sūra of the Quran. Folio 212 verso, Manuscript of the Quran. Maḥmūd ibn al-Ḥusayn al-Kirmānī, 559/1164, Hamadan, Iran, with later alterations. Ink on paper, 42 × 29.1 cm, University of Pennsylvania Museum of Archaeology and Anthropology, NEP-27. Digital images created by the Penn Libraries (2012).

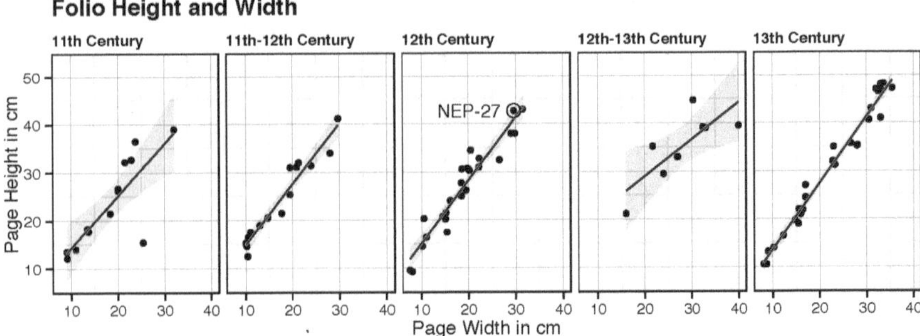

Figure 7.6. Folio Height and Width of Luxury Quran Manuscripts ca. 1000–1300. The ratio of folio height to width of luxury Quran manuscripts was established by the eleventh century and remained largely unchanged over the period in question.

The proportions and sizes of the page, as seen in Figure 7.6, seem to be relatively constant over the centuries leading up to and following that of NEP-27. The manuscript in question is itself one of the larger *muṣḥafs* produced during this time period, although the original sizes and proportions of some manuscripts have been altered over the centuries in the process of rebinding. The number of lines per page is not very closely correlated to page height (Figure 7.7). Luxurious multi-volume manuscripts could contain as few as three lines per page, and more affordable single-volume manuscripts could squeeze in almost forty lines per page, regardless of the physical folio size or the proportions of the page. It may also be interesting to note here that during the eleventh and twelfth centuries, manuscripts seemed to cluster into two groups, one containing three to seven lines per page, and the other containing fifteen to twenty-three lines per page. These two categories seem to merge moving into the thirteenth century, perhaps related to a shift in workshop practice or trends in patronage. To draw more substantial conclusions, it would be necessary to gather many more securely dated examples. Finally, it is clear that the Arabic interlinear gloss of NEP-27 is unique, but that it is related to a group of manuscripts containing Persian interlinear glosses (Figure 7.8).[7] This resemblance is logical enough, considering the production of the book in the Persian-speaking city of Hamadan, Iran, but the fact that the gloss of NEP-27 is in Arabic rather than Persian sug-

7 For a recent study of Persian interlinear glosses from a historical and textual perspective, see Travis E. Zadeh, *The Vernacular Qur'an: Translation and the Rise of Persian Exegesis* (Oxford: Oxford University Press, 2012).

gests that these glosses, even the Persian ones, did not function as straightforward reading aids.

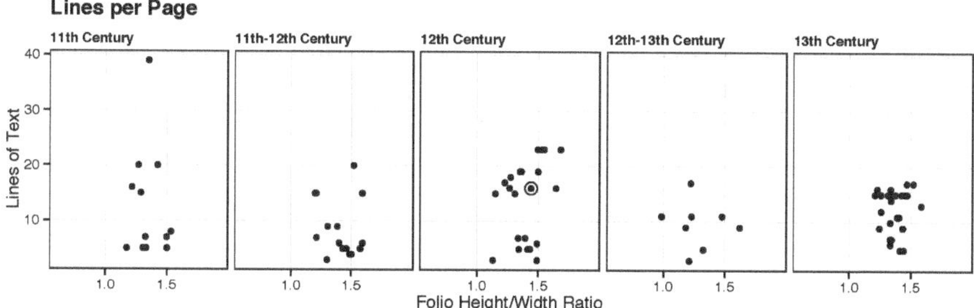

Figure 7.7. Lines of Text per Page in Luxury Quran Manuscripts ca. 1000–1300. The separation between two distinct groups of three to seven-line manuscripts and fifteen to twenty-three-line manuscripts in the eleventh and twelfth centuries becomes blurred in the thirteenth century. With almost forty lines of text per page, the outlier in the graph of the eleventh century is more representative of working manuscripts produced for students and scholars than luxury books.

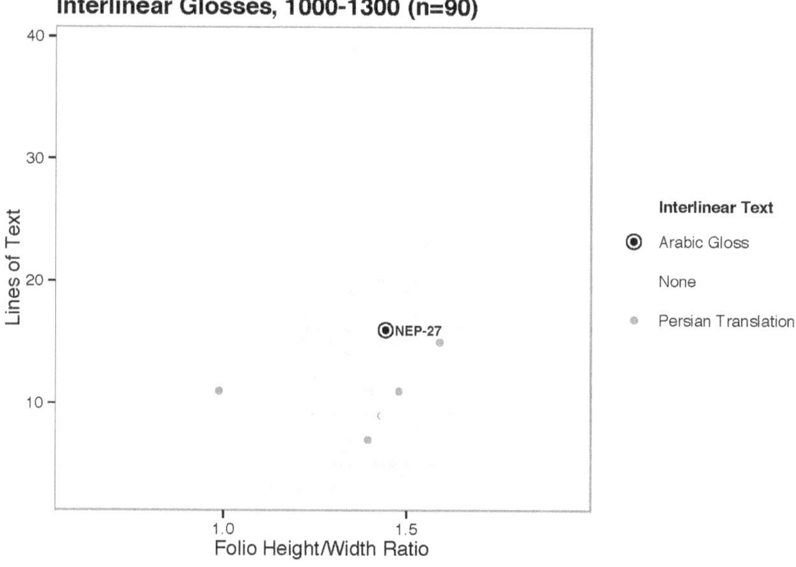

Figure 7.8. Interlinear Glosses in Luxury Quran Manuscripts, ca. 1000–1300. The Arabic gloss of NEP-27 is unique, but may be partially explained by its production in Iran where Persian interlinear translations of the Quran were produced in a number of different luxury formats (seven, nine, eleven, and fifteen lines of text per page).

I also adopted a quantitative approach in my study on the decorative bands that mark the beginning of each of the 114 *sūras* in the Quran (referred to as *fawātiḥ* or *iftitāḥāt*, from the Arabic root for "opening").[8] Towards the end of the seminar, it became clear that, in spite of the colophon naming a single maker of the manuscript, multiple craftsmen had been involved in its production. One of the students in the seminar, Michael Falcetano, produced a typology of four different rosettes used as single-verse markers, which serve as a proxy for four different craftsmen involved in producing the manuscript. Two of these craftsmen in particular completed the single-verse markers for most of the manuscript, with the remaining two craftsmen contributing to only a few pages each. This discovery led to a debate about whether all the illumination in a folio was completed by a single craftsmen, or whether different elements were completed by different craftsmen according to their skill (single verse markers for apprentices, *sūra* headings for more skilled artists). The divide is effectively that between distributed or hierarchical organizations of labor. In the course of examining the *sūra* headings, I observed that one of the single-verse markers was actually integrated into the heading of *Sūrat al-Muzzammil* (Figure 7.9). The presence of a single-verse marker in the ornamental heading of *Sūrat al-Muzzammil* implies that the same artist who decorated the verse markers on a page was also involved in decorating part or all of the *sūra* headings on the same page, but a single instance might also simply be a misleading outlier. I suspected that by breaking the *sūra* headings into their constitutive elements, it might be possible to determine whether these elements correlated with other features on the same page, like the single-verse markers, or strictly with other elements within the *sūra* heading, which would suggest a division of labor at the level of individual elements of the illumination rather than the unit of the page.

I created a spreadsheet on which I recorded the presence or absence of thirty-seven different compositional, palaeographic, and ornamental elements in each *sūra* heading. The goal of this procedure was not to describe every single feature of the manuscript's *sūra* headings, but rather to describe enough features to chart patterns of their variation. Examples of features noted in the survey include the use of broken cursive or *thuluth* and the presence or absence of squares on either side of the main text of the *sūra* heading. I also recorded different approaches to treating vegetal decoration, such as the use of red and white ink, vegetal ornament with very thin stems, and thicker-stemmed vegetal ornament. Other motifs include the use of three dots arranged in a triangle, scattered

8 Adam Gacek, *The Arabic Manuscript Tradition: A Glossary of Technical Terms and Bibliography* (Leiden: Brill, 2001), 59.

Figure 7.9. A Single-Verse Marker in the Heading of Sūrat al-Muzzammil. Detail of folio 196 verso, Manuscript of the Quran. Maḥmūd ibn al-Ḥusayn al-Kirmānī, 559/1164, Hamadan, Iran, with later alterations. Ink and gold on paper, University of Pennsylvania Museum of Archaeology and Anthropology, NEP-27. Digital images created by the Penn Libraries (2012).

throughout the center of the *sūra* heading, or the stylized agglomerations of petals that seem to grow from the edges of the frame of several *sūra* headings. I then visualized this data using an exploratory statistical technique known as principal component analysis (PCA).[9]

PCA is a powerful multivariate technique designed to reveal the most strongly correlated components of a multivariate dataset, which has been used to analyze everything from genetic data to the geochemical properties of archaeological ceramics. It is a particularly useful tool for dimensional reduction – the first two principal components of a multivariate dataset (the two orthogonal eigenvectors that have the highest variance possible) provide a two-dimensional slice through the dataset in which the data is most spread out. Rather than looking at correlations between each of the ornamental motifs and compositional elements individually, PCA visualizes how all of them relate to each other simultaneously in a graph that presents the maximum variance among them. The axes of the graph, the first two principal components, do not correlate with any single variable in the dataset, but instead with latent constructs, also known as hidden variables, that are not directly measured in the data itself. These latent constructs might in turn be related to the division of labor or the artistic training of the craftsmen involved in producing the manuscript. Figure 7.10 consists of

9 Multivariate analysis is a form of statistical analysis defined by its ability to observe and analyze more than one outcome variable. While many statistical analyses are used to test hypothetical correlations and determine the likelihood that these correlations are random, exploratory techniques are more often used to formulate hypotheses that can, in turn, be tested using other types of analyses. In this case, a generalized version of PCA known as multiple factor analysis (MFA) was performed using the FactoMineR statistical package. For more on MFA, see Hervé Abdi and Dominique Valentin, "Multiple Factor Analysis (MFA)," in *Encyclopedia of Measurement and Statistics*, ed. Neil J. Salkind (Thousand Oaks, CA: SAGE Publications, 2007), available at: http://www.utdallas.edu/~herve/Abdi-MFA2007-pretty.pdf.

a graph of the individual *sūra* headings based on the first two principal components. The first principal component, which accounts for twenty-four percent of the variation in the *sūra* headings, is plotted as the x-axis, and the second principal component, which captures almost fourteen percent of the variation (the next largest variance possible that is uncorrelated with the first principal component), occupies the y-axis. In the case of NEP-27, the first principal component captures the broadest stylistic variation within the *sūra* headings: *sūra* headings on the left are less ornamental, while those on the right are more ornate. The second principal component then stretches this linearly-uncorrelated set vertically and represents variation that is uncorrelated with (orthogonal to) the simple-ornate spectrum. This second level of variation is more difficult to characterize, but it seems to be based on compositional elements that are uncorrelated with the presence or absence of ornamental features. For example, headings that are located on the bottom of the page are pulled toward the bottom of the graph, while those that are located on the top of the page are at the top of the graph.

Because most of the variation that is related to the 'style' of the *sūra* headings is captured in the first principal component, clusters of *sūra* headings along the horizontal axis of the graph might indicate different styles. While there are some distinct, smaller clusters, there are not two obvious clusters on the horizontal axis that would correlate with the two craftsmen who completed most of the single-verse markers. The *sūra* headings in Figure 7.10 are color coded based on the single-verse markers that appear on the same page. Two broad groups of similar *sūra* headings (indicated by dotted lines in Figure 7.10) correlate with the two main styles of single-verse markers. If the *sūra* headings associated with the two different craftsmen were homogeneously mixed together, then either both craftsmen produced similarly varied kinds of *sūra* headings or a single craftsmen must have been responsible for the *sūra* headings throughout the manuscript. Instead, Figure 7.10 reveals that the two craftsmen are associated with two distinct concentrations of *sūra* headings at either end of the first principal component (the horizontal axis), with some overlap at the center. Because these two clusters are fairly distinct rather than completely intermingled, there does appear to be a correlation between the type of single-verse marker that appears on a page and the ornamental features that appear within the sura headings on that same page. If these single-verse markers are a reasonable proxy for the different craftsmen who worked on the manuscript, this would mean that most of the time the same craftsmen completed most or all of the ornamental elements on a given folio—from single-verse markers to *sūra* headings.

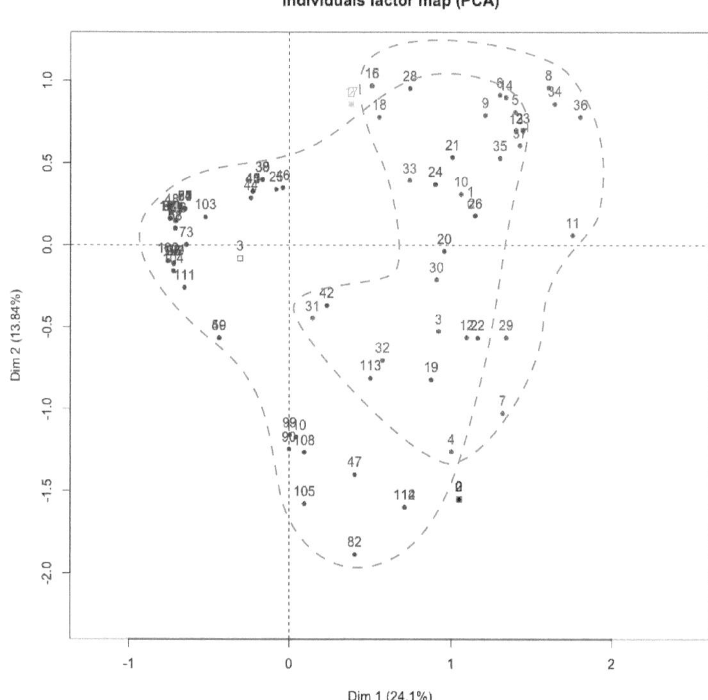

Figure 7.10. Multiple Factor Analysis of Visual Features in the Sūra Headings of NEP-27
The first two principle components of the compositional and ornamental elements in the sūra headings of NEP-27 reveal moderate correlation with the type of single-verse marker that appears on the same folio.

The overlap between the two craftsmen might suggest that there were occasions when both illuminators worked on the same folio.[10]

I also briefly explored the use of clustering algorithms, a data-driven knowledge discovery process that sorts the *sūra* headings into groups based on how similar they are in terms of the presence or absence of different ornamental var-

10 The divergence between the PAM clusters and the single-verse marker clusters merits more investigation. The PAM clusters need not correlate with individual craftsmen and might better represent different models, artistic training, or working methods in the production of the folios in question. A comparative study of living craft traditions could shed much-needed light on these questions.

iables that were recorded.[11] In Figure 7.11, each *sūra* heading is outlined in one of five groups based on the results of a clustering algorithm. The number of clusters to analyze (*k* value) was determined using the "Elbow Method" in which the number of clusters is graphed against the percentage of variance that it explains and a *k* value at or near the graph's trade-off point (or "elbow") is selected. This method produced a *k* value of five, which differs slightly from the four craftsmen that Michael Falcetano proposed, and divides *sūra* headings that appear visually similar into multiple groups. These clusters suggest five distinct but related categories of *sūra* headings (perhaps these might be thought of as models or visual ideals), some of which are closely associated with one of the two illuminators (cluster number five on the left and cluster number three on the right), while others are employed by both of them.[12]

Once this dataset was available, it also became possible to ask questions that I had not anticipated when I began compiling it. For example, how many of the formal elements were actually correlated with the different single-verse markers (proxies for craftsmen), and how many were simply correlated with other features of the *sūra* headings? To ask this question another way—did individual training and preference impact the final *sūra* heading (are motifs associated with specific craftsmen), and if so, how great was this impact relative to that of the conceptual models or visual formulae from which these craftsmen were working?[13] It is possible to quantify these correlations using a statistical technique known as co-occurrence analysis. This technique provides a measurement of the probability that a correlation between features is random, which in turn allows investigators to focus on correlations that are probably meaningful. For the

---

11 Both the definition of a cluster or group and the criteria by which data points are sorted into clusters depends on the type of data that is being analyzed and the particular clustering algorithm selected. This graph was produced using the partitioning around medioids algorithm, which randomly selects a set number of different points (*k*) as the centers of clusters, populates these clusters with the closest data points, and measures the 'fit' of each cluster (generally the similarity of the points to the center point). The algorithm then selects each point within a cluster as the center of a new cluster and compares the fit of the new clusters to that of the old one. If the fit is better, the new center is kept and the process iterates. The algorithm ends when none of the points within a cluster produce a better fit than the current center point.

12 As a process of knowledge discovery, the meaningfulness of these groupings is not inherent in the technique used, but rather in the intersubjective discourse in which otherwise meaningless facts find meaning. For the intersubjective nature of concepts of style (which, for the moment, applies equally to stylistic categories delimited by clustering algorithms that humans might create and use), see Richard Neer, "Connoisseurship and the Stakes of Style," *Critical Inquiry* 32 no. 1 (September 1, 2005): 20–24.

13 Like PCA, this is a data-driven approach rather than a hypothesis-driven inquiry.

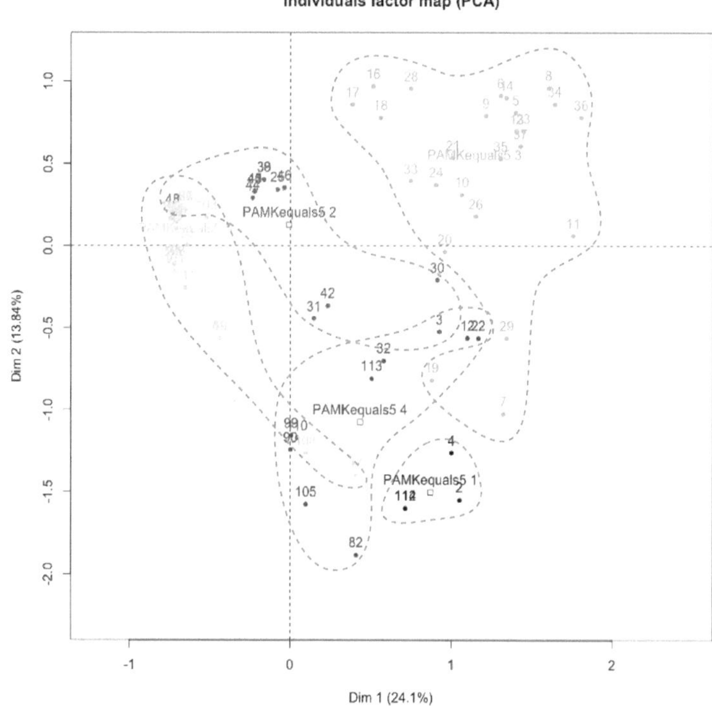

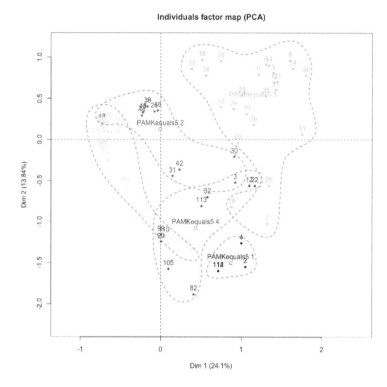

Figure 7.11. PAM Clustering of Sūra Headings in NEP-27 (k=5). Partitioning around medoids clustering of the sūra headings in NEP-27 into five groups based on their compositional and ornamental elements.

purpose of characterizing the different styles of the craftsmen who worked on the manuscript, it is possible to limit this analysis to co-occurrences between different single-verse markers and various elements in the *sūra* headings. A network graph reveals the extent to which elements within the *sūra* headings co-occur with the different single-verse markers, showing significant overlap between the two main scribes that could be a product of similar training, collaboration, or both (Figure 7.12). However, it is also revealing to take into consideration correlations between elements within the *sūra* headings independent of the single-verse marker types, in addition to these markers of individual style. Out of 820 potential correlations between the ornamental motifs of the *sūra* headings and the individual verse markers of NEP-27, co-occurrence analysis reveals that there are sixty-two statistically-significant correlations.[14] Of these sixty-two co-occurrences, twenty-one are negatively correlated (elements that do not appear together), some of which are simply mutually exclusive compositional "formulae" or calligraphic styles. Among the fourty-one positively correlated co-occurrences, just eight are correlations between the single-verse marker type and various formal elements of the *sūra* headings. The remaining thirty-three correlated co-occurrences are strictly among features of the *sūra* headings (Figure 7.13). That is, there is a small group of correlations between artists and *sūra* heading motifs and a larger group of correlations that occur between motifs in the *sūra* headings regardless of the artist.[15] These two numbers are perhaps the most thought-provoking element of this entire analysis. Here we find something that approaches a quantification of the nebulous concept known as style.[16] But what, if anything, does it mean to make the jump from sixty-two statistically significant correlations to the idea that the *sūra* headings of NEP-27 are twenty-seven percent individual style and seventy-three percent shared style?

4. Questions of Style

Proceeding from a quantitative approach, we have stumbled into one of the fundamental methodological debates of of art history. In 1893, Alois Riegl published a book on the development of ornament with the unassuming title *Stilfragen*, translated into English as *Problems of Style*. Riegl traced the development of vegetal ornament from Ancient Egyptian friezes to the Arabesque, arguing that

14 These correlations are based on a correlation matrix created using the cor() function in the R statistical programming language. The resulting correlations were tested to determine their p values using cor.test(), and all p values were adjusted using Bonferroni correction. While many of the other decorative elements correlate quite strongly with the rosette styles, only features considered statistically significant once adjusted with Bonferroni correction were considered for the purpose of discussion. I am especially grateful to Joshua A. Shapiro for his assistance in conducting correlation analysis and his insights into the application of statistical techniques to this material.

15 Shared models and/or training, as well as contributions from artists who did not work on the single-verse markers, may partially explain the divergence between the PAM-clustering results and the clusters derived from the single-verse markers.

16 For an overview of early approaches to quantifying style in digital art history (sometimes referred to as stylometrics, a term that I would reject on the grounds of the word *style*'s inconsistent definition), see Hussein Keshani, "Towards Digital Islamic Art History," *Journal of Art Historiography* 6 (June 2012), available at: http://arthistoriography.files.wordpress.com/2012/05/keshani.pdf.

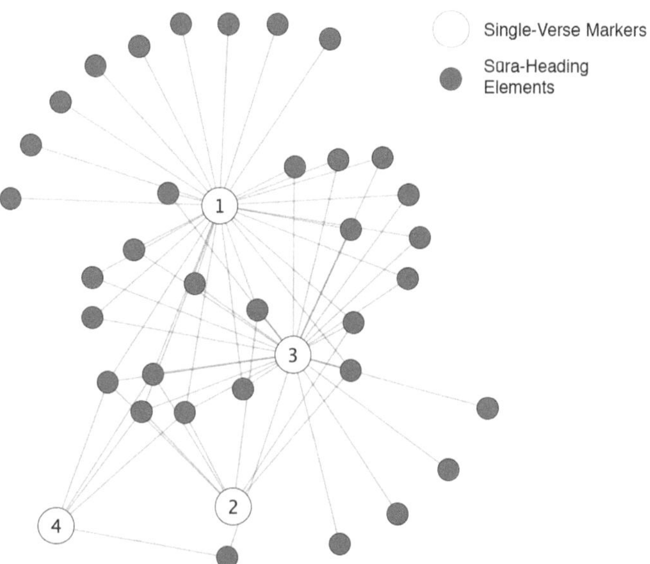

Figure 7.12. Co-occurrences Between Single-Verse Markers (by type) and Visual Features of Sūra Headings in NEP-27. A network graph of the co-occurrences between single-verse marker types and sūra heading elements in NEP-27 reveals similarities of and differences between the sūra heading elements that appear with the two main types of single-verse markers (type 1 and type 3).

changes in the form of apparently meaningless decorative elements actually correlated with shifting cultural mores.[17] One of the first works to take as its primary subject the psychological and artistic expressions of anonymous craftsmen, the

17 I turn to Riegl here because his focus on ornament (and the little critical attention that it has received from the art historical mainstream since) highlights the challenge of creating both analogue and digital methodologies suitable for non-figural Islamic art. For example, projects like Iconclass (http://www.iconclass.nl/home) have created linked open data unique resource identifiers (URIs) for iconographic elements, but these are still of limited use to scholars who focus on fields outside of Europe (the classical canon and Judeo-Christian art). Even if senmurvs and the Burāq are eventually added to Iconclass, historians of Islamic art who study calligraphy or marbled papers (just two examples of highly valued aesthetic production) will need a very different framework for producing useful digital descriptions of their material. We still lack well-defined standards for describing medieval manuscripts produced within the Islamic world, much less the details of ornamental motifs such as those in NEP-27.

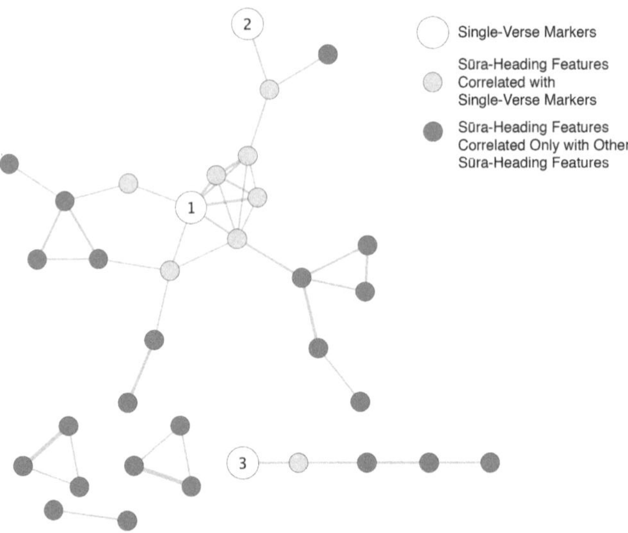

Figure 7.13. Statistically Significant Co-occurrences Among Single-Verse Markers (by type) and Visual Features of the Sūra Headings in NEP-27. Most of the statistically significant co-occurrences are strictly among elements of the sūra headings. Only a few of the co-occurrences between single-verse markers and elements of the sūra headings shown in Figure 7.12 are significant.

book inaugurated a series of debates about what causes similarities between the individual works of an artist or between the works of a group of artists working at the same time. Riegl concluded that there existed a unifying social or ideological force that he called *Kunstwollen*, literally "that which wills art." For a brief period following its publication, scholars, including the noted historian of art Erwin Panofsky, dreamed that *Kunstwollen* could be the key to discovering the a priori principles that structure the historical development of art. Riegl's concept of a driving force of stylistic unity has since been dismantled by some of the most important figures in the field, most notably Ernst Gombrich, who disputed both the essentialist cultural assumptions that underlay the theory and the historicist framework that posited artistic unity as a necessity rather than a contingent product of exceptional interactions between individuals and objects.[18]

In addition to this deconstruction of Riegl's approach to ornament, the concepts of individual and collective (or general) style have also undergone critical revision. Svetlana Alpers has argued that these may better be conceived of as points on a spectrum rather than a dichotomy.[19] The agency of craftsmen (anonymous craftsmen in particular) has frequently been sublimated as a result of the valorization of individuality that shaped the discipline of art history since the Italian Renaissance. Not even Islamic art, with its emphasis on ornament rather than figural decoration in religious contexts, has been spared this disciplinary obsession with individual style, as illustrated by the fame of calligraphers such as Ibn al-Bawwāb. An uncritical quantitative analysis framed in terms of individuality risks reifying the concept. Griselda Pollock's scathing critique of recent work in computational stylistic categorization and the unfortunately named "influence detection" makes it clear that approaching art historical challenges purely from the perspective of computer science can indeed lead to code that perpetuates deprecated art historical methodologies.[20] I would argue, however, that co-occurrence analysis actually provides us with a concrete method with which to locate various works on Alpers' spectrum. The fact that critics and historians have arbitrarily valorized one end of this spectrum should not discourage us from analyzing shared motifs and compositional strategies between artists, but instead caution us against doing the same. This spectrum ultimately reflects the conceptual frameworks and values of art historians today rather than the way visual culture was understood by the people who created and used objects

18 E. H. Gombrich, *The Sense of Order: A Study in the Psychology of Decorative Art* (Ithaca, NY: Cornell University Press, 1979), 183–87.

19 Svetlana Alpers, "Style Is What You Make It: The Visual Arts Once Again," in *The Concept of Style*, ed. Berel Lang (Philadelphia: University of Pennsylvania Press, 1979), 95–117.

20 Griselda Pollock, "Computers Can Find Similarities between Paintings – but Art History Is about so Much More," *The Conversation*, August 22, 2014, available at: http://theconversation.com/computers-can-find-similarities-between-paintings-but-art-history-is-about-so-much-more-30752. The paper in question is actually quite innovative in using a machine learning algorithm trained on search results for different 'styles' of art to categorize images analyzed using variants of the scale invariant feature transform algorithm (SIFT). Its uncritical acceptance of historiographically contingent art historical styles as a meaningful basis for categorization, rather than the clunky and artificial heuristic that they are, by no means invalidates possible uses of such algorithms in a more nuanced context, or indeed as a tool with which to critically rethink the concept of style. See Babak Saleh, Kanako Abe, Ravneet Singh, and Ahmed Elgammal, "Toward Automated Discovery of Artistic Influence," arXiv:1408.3218 [cs], August 14, 2014, available at: http://arxiv.org/abs/1408.3218.

such as NEP-27. Given that among art historians there exists an interest in the social conditions and processes that shaped the production of art, however, this spectrum allows us to consider the nature of artistic training and collaboration at different levels (individual, intra-workshop, and perhaps eventually inter-workshop) and encourages us to consider how, in other times and places, craftsmen were rewarded for their ability to function at a variety of points on this spectrum.

Suggesting that the *sūra* headings of NEP-27 are twenty-seven percent individual style and seventy-three percent shared style provides one way to locate the *muṣḥaf* on Alpers' spectrum (although there are certainly other approaches one might take that would arrive at different values). PCA and co-occurrence analysis provide a consistent and granular methodology with which to parse the interactions between the human agents elided in Riegl's *kunstwollen*. A broader survey of ornament in contemporaneous manuscripts along these same lines could begin to reveal the extent to which motifs are unique to objects or artists or, on the contrary, permeate a larger, shared visual culture. Expanding this survey diachronically would allow historians to analyze at which historical moments or geographical locations workshop practice was systematized and how these systems differed from each other. It might eventually be possible to connect some of these practices to the socio-economic and cultural forces that affected craftsmen, who are often absent from textual sources and the deceptively simple colophons of objects such as NEP-27. These are a few of the new directions of inquiry one could pursue based on the insights provided by a quantitative analysis. This methodology, however, still begs the questions of meaning that have pre-occupied historians of Islamic art, no less than other historians of art, for most of the last century. While this paper has focused on the production of NEP-27, it remains to be seen how we might leverage digital tools to understand how the people who commissioned and used NEP-27 not only produced but also understood its structuring decorative elements. Computational approaches to the history of Islamic art will necessarily combine analyses of textual as well as visual material if these methods hope to speak to such questions.

Bibliography

Abdi, Hervé, and Dominique Valentin. "Multiple Factor Analysis (MFA)." In *Encyclopedia of Measurement and Statistics*, ed. Neil J Salkind. Thousand Oaks, CA: SAGE Publications, 2007. Available at: http://www.utdallas.edu/~herve/Abdi-MFA2007-pretty.pdf.

Allan, James. "Manuscript Illumination: A Source for Metalwork Motifs in Late Saljuq Times." In *The Art of the Saljūqs in Iran and Anatolia: Proceedings of a Symposium Held in*

Edinburgh in 1982, ed. Robert Hillenbrand, 118–26. Costa Mesa, CA: Mazda Publishers, 1994.

Alpers, Svetlana. "Style Is What You Make It: The Visual Arts Once Again." In *The Concept of Style*, ed. Berel Lang, 95–117. Philadelphia: University of Pennsylvania Press, 1979.

Ettinghausen, Richard. "A Signed and Dated Seljuq Qur'an." *Bulletin of the American Institute for Persian Art and Archaeology* IV (1935): 92–102.

Gacek, Adam. *Arabic Manuscripts: A Glossary of Technical Terms and Bibliography.* Leiden: Brill, 2011.

—. *Arabic Manuscripts: A Vademecum for Readers*. Leiden: Brill, 2009.

—. *The Arabic Manuscript Tradition: A Glossary of Technical Terms and Bibliography.* Leiden: Brill, 2001.

George, Alain. *The Rise of Islamic Calligraphy.* London: Saqi, 2010.

Gombrich, E. H. *The Sense of Order: A Study in the Psychology of Decorative Art.* Ithaca: Cornell University Press, 1979.

James, David. *Qur'ans of the Mamluks.* New York: Thames and Hudson, 1988.

James, David Lewis. *The Master Scribes: Qurans of the 10th to 14th Centuries AD.* Nasser D. Khalili Collection of Islamic Art. New York: Nour Foundation in association with Azimuth Editions and Oxford University Press, 1992.

Keshani, Hussein. "Towards Digital Islamic Art History." *Journal of Art Historiography* 6 (June 2012). Available at: http://arthistoriography.files.wordpress.com/2012/05/keshani.pdf.

Loveday, Helen. *Islamic Paper: A Study of the Ancient Craft.* London: Archetype Publications, 2001.

Neer, Richard. "Connoisseurship and the Stakes of Style." *Critical Inquiry* 32 no. 1 (September 1, 2005): 1–26.

Netz, Reviel, ed. *The Archimedes Palimpsest.* Cambridge: Cambridge University Press, 2011.

Pollock, Griselda. "Computers Can Find Similarities between Paintings – but Art History Is about so Much More." *The Conversation*, August 22, 2014. Available at: http://theconversation.com/computers-can-find-similarities-between-paintings-but-art-history-is-about-so-much-more-30752.

Saleh, Babak, Kanako Abe, Ravneet Singh Arora, and Ahmed Elgammal. "Toward Automated Discovery of Artistic Influence." *arXiv:1408.3218 [cs]*, August 14, 2014. Available at: http://arxiv.org/abs/1408.3218.

Tufte, Edward R. *The Visual Display of Quantitative Information.* Cheshire, CT: Graphics Press, 1983.

Wright, Elaine Julia. *The Look of the Book: Manuscript Production in Shiraz, 1303–1452.* Seattle: University of Washington Press, 2012.

Zadeh, Travis E. *The Vernacular Qur'an: Translation and the Rise of Persian Exegesis.* Oxford: Oxford University Press, 2012.

Till Grallert

Mapping Ottoman Damascus Through News Reports: A Practical Approach

This paper introduces a digital workflow and a set of tools to visually scrutinize possible correlations between certain historical phenomena, discourses, and terminologies on the one hand, and geographical locations on the other, by means of browser-based maps that require only minimal prior programming knowledge. The workflow provides historians with a means to quickly check whether references to certain events or certain terms within a large corpus of sources form clusters on a geographic map—as long as the information is available in a somewhat structured and machine-readable form, such as a reference or citation manager.

While the workflow can be applied to scrutinize the distribution of fires, crimes, or road works, it was developed in response to a practical, methodological question of how to investigate the extent to which Damascene and Beiruti newspapers—and particularly the news reports from and about Damascus during the last forty years of Ottoman rule (1875–1914)—perpetuated the state's discourse on the provision of public order (*āsāyış-i ʿumūmī / rāḥat ʿumūmiyya*) for generating legitimate Ottoman statehood. Such a study of linguistic strategies used to delegitimize acts of violence and the perpetrators thereof required a methodology to deal with thousands of newspaper articles from seven newspapers of at least weekly publication and six monthly or fortnightly journals. In the course of the two years that I spent reading these newspapers for a doctoral thesis on the production of public places and public space in late Ottoman Damascus, I increasingly came under the impression that a specific terminology for violent challenges to legitimate Ottoman statehood—such as *mushājara* (quarrel), *munāzaʿa* (riot), or *ashqiyāʾ* (pl. of *shaqī*, brigand, rascal, wretch) and their derivatives—tended to cluster around specific areas in the city of Damascus as well as in the larger province of Syria. After submitting my thesis, I wanted to further scrutinize this impression. But how could I systematically test this hypothesis for a large number of terms without sieving through all the newspaper articles again and without manually locating every relevant toponym on paper maps?

In the perfect world of infinite resources and skills, one would already have a fully coded database of individual historical events and machine-readable transcriptions of sources. In such a case, qualitative coding, semantic and linguistic mark-up of mono-thematic chunks of information, or a combination of both would have already established the link between the historical criteria of interest and geographic locations. Toponyms would function as placeholders for locational data on latitude and longitude stored in a second database. Integrated into a geographic information system (GIS), most analytical queries could be readily displayed and printed. However, in the real world of the humanities, and particularly the field of Middle East studies, we encounter individuals with limited access to resources toiling away in isolation from other researchers as the most common case. As a result, we have to work with partially and inconsistently coded heterogeneous data in databases, most often some sort of reference managing software, whose smallest unit are individual sources instead of events—if we have machine-readable data at all.

This paper elaborates how one can nevertheless produce meaningful (and sometimes visually appealing) maps that visualize the analytical questions at hand with a relatively low level of programming skill and within a reasonable amount of time. To achieve this goal, the aim is to re-purpose software already in use (e. g., a reference manager) and to employ file formats and programming languages that maintain a high level of human readability, are well established and widely used, and are suited for most tasks at hand. In addition, the number of file formats and programming languages should be kept as small as possible, and preference should be given to software and formats that are distributed as either open source or under a creative commons license. In other words, the workflow presented in this paper ensures ease of use, low additional costs and programming efforts, and long-term data accessibility, including human readability.

The languages and formats thus chosen were—and here one cannot avoid some technical acronyms—XML and its siblings XSLT and XPath for storing and processing data, JSON for serving the data to the open-source mapping tool SIMILE Exhibit 3, and HTML (including CSS) for displaying the results.[1] All of these formats are recommended standards established by the World Wide Web Consortium (W3C)[2]—with the exception of JSON, which is an Ecma

1 For the current specifications of the Extensible Markup Language (XML), Extensible Stylesheet Language Transformations (XSLT), and the XPath data model, see http://www.w3.org/TR/xml11/; http://www.w3.org/TR/xslt20/; and http://www.w3.org/TR/xpath-datamodel/. For the specification of the JavaScript Object Notation (JSON), see http://www.json.org/. For the latest specifications of the Hypertext Markup Language (HTML) and Cascading Style Sheets (CSS), see http://www.w3.org/TR/html/ and http://www.w3.org/TR/CSS2/. For Exhibit 3.0, see http://simile-widgets.org/exhibit/ and section four below.
2 http://www.w3.org/

standard[3]—and can be displayed and edited with the simplest text-editing software already present on one's computer. All of the most widely adopted reference managing software applications, such as Zotero, EndNote, Citavi, Bookends, Mendeley, Sente, etc., can export data as XML.[4] Processing the XML with XSLT stylesheets requires an interpreter, of which there exists a myriad of free software implementations that meet the established criteria. As I already had a license for and experience with one of the major proprietary XML editors, oXygen, I opted for this software instead of an open-source alternative.[5]

It must be kept in mind that 'digital' does not mean 'fully automated'. Indeed, as we will see, the suggested workflow involves many steps that can only be partially automated, since they depend on the human capacity for judgment and comprehension of implicit information. The only actual programming —that is, serialized transformations of data and automated generation of new data points—is done with XSLT stylesheets. It is far beyond the scope and intent of the present chapter to provide an introduction to XSLT or, for that matter, XML, XPath, HTML, CSS, JSON, etc. These can be found in the referenced links and citations. Instead, the paper focuses on the general steps necessary for correlating toponyms and geocoded locations with some historical data of interest to the researcher, using the example of the geographic distribution of references to *ashqiyāʾ*, and presents a concrete tool for visualizing the mashed-up data on a map. However, the detailed examples provided in this paper should allow even those readers who have never before seen XML or a website's underlying HTML to follow the discussion and to remove some of the menace of 'programming'. In a similar vein, I will not present the minute details and idiosyncrasies of my XSLT stylesheets. Interested readers can scrutinize, download, and—if I am

3 The "European Computer Manufacturers Association" (Ecma) changed its name to "Ecma International— European association for standardizing information and communication systems." Its adoption of JSON as Standard ECMA-404 can found at: http://www.ecma-international.org/publications/standards/Ecma-404.htm/.

4 Zotero is the only open and free reference manager in this list and supports Windows, OSX, and Linux. It can be downloaded at: https://www.zotero.org/. EndNote (http://endnote.com/) is part of the Thomson Reuters publishing company and probably the most well-known and most widely adopted reference manager within academic institutions. It supports Windows, OSX, and iOS. Among those applications mentioned, Mendeley (http://www.mendeley.com/) supports the broadest range of operating systems (Windows, OSX, Linux, iOS) and emphasizes the collaborative nature of academic reading practices, but its acquisition by the publishing company Elsevier in 2013 has been met with criticism. Citavi (http://www.citavi.com/) is a Windows-only application, while BookEnds (http://www.sonnysoftware.com/) and Sente (http://thirdstreetsoftware.com/) support only Apple's OSX and iOS.

5 http://www.oxygenxml.com/

lucky—improve them on the code-sharing website GitHub.[6] I have made sample data as well as a visualization of the geographical distribution of references to *ashqiyā'* publicly available online for the reader's perusal.[7] Finally, special attention is paid to the critical evaluation of every technology's and methodological approach's implications for the analytical question at hand.

1. Starting from a Database of Sources

My research into the history of public space(s) and contentious repertoires is based in large part on systematic readings of two Damascene and four Beiruti newspapers, with occasional recourse to other newspapers and journals from Beirut, Cairo, Damascus, and Istanbul between 1875–1914. Comprehensive collections of any of the three Damascene newspapers, *Sūriye*, *Dimashq*, and *al-Shām*, published before 1908 are yet to be discovered,[8] but the press in the neighboring city of Beirut carried articles about and from Damascus on a regular basis, and copies survived in a number of libraries and archives. Therefore I employed the Beiruti newspapers *Ḥadīqat al-Akhbār* (1881–88, a semi-official publication of the province of Syria), *al-Bashīr* (1875–1914, a Jesuit publication), *Lisān al-Ḥāl* (1877–1914, published by Khalīl Sarkīs), and *Thamarāt al-Funūn* (1875–1895, 1908, published by *Jamʿiyyat al-Funūn*, ʿAbd al-Qādir al-Qabbānī, and Aḥmad Ḥasan Ṭabbāra) in addition to the Damascene publications *Suriye* (1882–88, 1899–1902, the official provincial gazette) and the daily newspaper *al-Muqtabas* (1908 onwards, published by Muḥammad Kurd ʿAlī).[9] Throughout

6 https://github.com/tillgrallert/MappingOttomanDamascus2014/

7 The code can be found at: https://github.com/tillgrallert/MappingOttomanDamascus2014; a live example is hosted at: https://tillgrallert.github.io/MappingOttomanDamascus2014/.

8 *Sūriye* was the official gazette of the province, and the two other papers were owned and operated by the staff of the provincial printing press; Ami Ayalon, *The Press in the Arab Middle East: A History* (New York: Oxford University Press, 1995), 28–46. For lists of published Arabic journals and newspapers, see Fīlīb Dī Ṭarrāzī, *Tārīkh al-ṣiḥāfa al-ʿarabiyya: Yaḥtawī ʿalā akhbār kull jarīda wa-majalla ʿarabiyya ẓaharat fī l-ʿālam sharqan wa-gharban maʿa rusūm aṣḥābihā wa-l-muḥarrirīn fīhā wa-tarājim mashāhīrihim* (vols. 1–3; Bayrūt: al-Maṭbaʿa al-adabiyya, 1914); Fīlīb Dī Ṭarrāzī, *Tārīkh al-ṣiḥāfa al-ʿarabiyya: Yaḥtawī ʿalā jamīʿ fahāris al-jarāʾid wa-l-majallāt al-ʿarabiyya fī l-khāfiqīn mudh takwīn al-ṣiḥāfa al-ʿarabiyya ilā nihāyat ʿām 1929* (vol. 4; Bayrūt: al-Maṭbaʿa al-amīrikāniyya, 1933); Mihyār ʿAdnān al-Mallūḥī, *Muʿjam al-jarāʾid al-sūriyya 1865–1965* (Dimashq, 2002).

9 The sample also includes some small print-runs of the Beiruti newspaper *al-Janna* and the monthly journals *al-Jinān*, *al-Maḥabba*, and *al-Ḥasnāʾ*—also published in Beirut—as well as *al-Ḥaqāʾiq* and *al-Muqtabas* from Damascus. Years in brackets represent the print runs consulted.

the years under survey, letters from readers and correspondents were the common form of reporting from places other than a newspaper's printing location. Letters from Damascus were particularly frequent. Despite various gaps and irregularities in the density of reports, we have more or less weekly accounts of Damascene events over the course of 40 years. This vast body of 3,000-odd regular reports provides us with a yet untapped source of the social and political history of Damascus, often reporting events and details not covered by either the consular reports or much later written memoirs.[10]

Metadata—including excerpts, partial transcriptions and translations, and images of all articles—were manually entered into a relational database parallel to and during the reading at libraries and archives. This process included some semantic mark-up of persons and locations with simple XML tags (`<persName>` and `<placeName>`), which happen to conform to the Text Encoding Initiative's flavor of XML (TEI P5).[11] In a second step, every article was coded with keywords for topic, type of publication, referenced locations, etc.

Due to its ease of use and easy customization of the underlying database as well as the graphic user interface (GUI), I employ the off-the-shelf reference managing software Sente, running on Apple's OS X and iOS operating systems.[12] Sente stores all data in an open-source SQLite database,[13] which can be queried through Sente's GUI or any tool able to manipulate SQLite databases. Individual references can be tagged, and tags can be organized in hierarchical ontologies. In addition, the entire database or the result of any query can be exported as an XML file. Using proprietary software always poses the danger of trapping one's most valuable asset, the research data. Sente's reliance on an open-source database for storing the data and the possibility to export all data in a well-understood, structured, and open format, such as XML, ensures that the research data can be accessed without any loss of information at any given moment and without continued access to Sente itself. For the purpose of the present

---

10 For more information on the sample, the publication history of individual titles, and the history of the press in late Ottoman Damascus and Beirut, see Till Grallert, "To Whom Belong the Streets? Property, Propriety, and Appropriation: The Production of Public Space in Late Ottoman Damascus, 1875–1914" (Ph.D. diss., Freie Universität, Berlin, 2014), 16–20, 40–94. My current research project is concerned with the genealogy of food riots in the Middle East between the eighteenth and twentieth centuries.

11 On the TEI, see http://www.tei-c.org/index.xml. On the TEI P5 XML guidelines and schema, see http://www.tei-c.org/Guidelines/P5/.

12 http://www.thirdstreetsoftware.com.

13 http://www.sqlite.org.

paper, the basis for all further manipulations and processing of data is the Sente-generated XML output.

Figures 8.1 and 8.2 show the same information—an article from an anonymous reader-cum-correspondent of the Beiruti newspaper *Lisān al-Ḥāl* in Damascus, dated 31 May and published on 5 June 1884, reporting on bandits (*ashqiyāʾ*) from the quarter of Mīdān attacking a caravan from the Jabal Ḥawrān just outside the city gates—within Sente's GUI and as XML export.

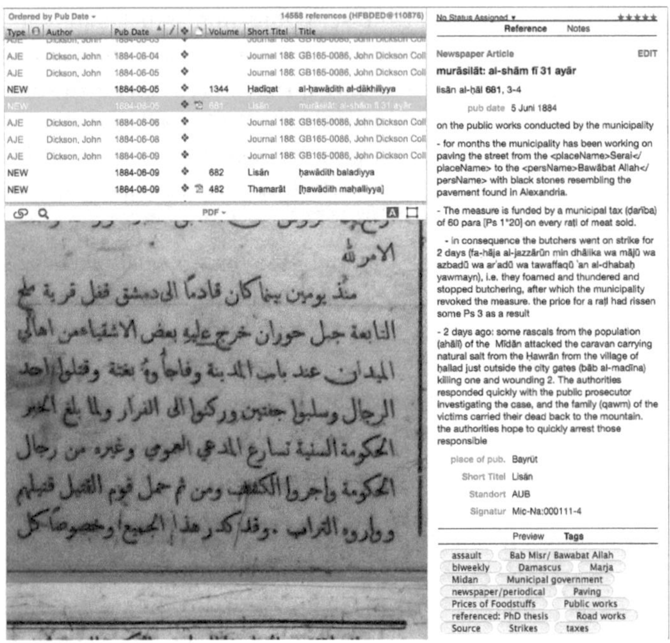

Figure 8.1. Lisān al-Ḥāl 5 Jun 1884 (#681) as displayed in Sente's GUI.

Figure 8.1 shows a list of chronologically sorted references in the upper section of the main panel of Sente's GUI. To the right, one can find detailed bibliographic information on the selected reference, including an English summary of the article's content, as well as a number of tags describing both meta-information on the article and some of its content in the lower section. A digitized image of the article is displayed below the reference list. Note that the summary mixes English and transliterations of Arabic without any computer-readable marker to distinguish between the two. Note also that the summary contains some semantic mark-up of toponyms inside the `<placeName>` tags. Figure 8.2 presents the same information as a tree of XML nodes:

```
<tss:senteContainer version=”1.0” xmlns:tss=”http://www.
thirdstreetsoftware.com/SenteXML-1.0”>
  <tss:library>
    <tss:references>
      <tss:reference>
        <tss:publicationType name=”Newspaper article”/>
        <tss:dates>
          <tss:date day=”5” month=”6” type=”Publication” year=”1884”/>
          <!-- ... -->
        </tss:dates>
        <tss:characteristics>
          <tss:characteristic name=”articleTitle”>murāsilāt: al-shām
          fī 31 ayār</tss:characteristic>
          <tss:characteristic name=”publicationTitle”>lisān al-ḥāl
          </tss:characteristic>
          <tss:characteristic name=”abstractText”>on the public works
conducted by the municipality&lt;br&gt;- for months the municipality
has been working on paving the street from the Serai to the Bawābat
Allah with black stones resembling the pavement found in Alexandria.
&lt;br&gt;- The measure is funded by a municipal tax (ḍarība) of 60
para [Ps 1”20] on every raṭl of meat sold. &lt;br&gt; - in consequence
the butchers went on strike for 2 days (fa-hāja al-jazzārūn min
dhālika wa mājū wa azbadū wa arʿadū wa tawaffaqū ʿan al-dhabaḥ
yawmayn), i.e. they foamed and thundered and stopped butchering,
after which the municipality revoked the measure. the price for a
raṭl had rissen some Ps 3 as a result&lt;br&gt;- 2 days ago: some
rascals from the population (ahālī) of the Mīdān attacked the caravan
carrying natural salt from the Ḥawrān from the village of ḥallad just
outside the city gates (bāb al-madīna) killing one and wounding 2. The
authorities responded quickly with the public prosecutor investigating
the case, and the family (qawm) of the victims carried their dead
back to the mountain. the authorities hope to quickly arrest those
responsible</tss:characteristic>
          <tss:characteristic name=”language”>arabic
          </tss:characteristic>
          <tss:characteristic name=”pages”>3-4</tss:characteristic>
          <tss:characteristic name=”publicationCountry”>Bayrūt
          </tss:characteristic>
          <tss:characteristic name=”rating”>5</tss:characteristic>
          <tss:characteristic name=”UUID”>E51A2AE9-2C55-411F-B813-
          0D802281A229</tss:characteristic>
          <tss:characteristic name=”volume”>681</tss:characteristic>
          <tss:characteristic name=”Signatur”>Mic-Na:000111-4
          </tss:characteristic>
          <!-- ... -->
        </tss:characteristics>
        <tss:keywords>
          <tss:keyword assigner=”Sente User BachPrivat”>Bab Misr/
          Bawabat Allah</tss:keyword>
          <tss:keyword assigner=”Sente User BachPrivat”>Damascus
          </tss:keyword>
          <tss:keyword assigner=”Sente User BachPrivat”>Marja
          </tss:keyword>
```

Figure 8.2. The same data as Sente XML. [Part 1/2]

```
        <tss:keyword assigner="Sente User BachPrivat">Midan
        </tss:keyword>
        <tss:keyword assigner="Sente User BachPrivat">Municipal
        government</tss:keyword>
        <tss:keyword assigner="Sente User BachPrivat">Prices of
        Foodstuffs</tss:keyword>
        <tss:keyword assigner="Sente User BachPrivat">Public works
        </tss:keyword>
        <tss:keyword assigner="Sente User BachPrivat">Road works
        </tss:keyword>
        <!-- ... -->
      </tss:keywords>
      <tss:attachments>
        <tss:attachmentReference type="PDF (Portable Document
        Format)">
          <URL xmlns="">file://localhost/<!-- ... -->/SenteLibrary.
          sente6lib/Contents/Attachments/!%20Unknown%20
          Author(s)/1884%20lis%C4%81n%20al.pdf</URL>
        </tss:attachmentReference>
      </tss:attachments>
    </tss:reference>
  </tss:references>
 </tss:library>
</tss:senteContainer>
```

Figure 8.2. The same data as Sente XML. [Part 2/2]

Each reference in the reference list of Figure 8.1 is represented by a <tss:reference> node (also called 'elements' in XML parlance). Inside this node one finds various child nodes that provide a detailed description of the reference: <tss:dates> and its descendants provide publication dates as well as timestamps for edits. Most of the bibliographic data is found in <tss:characteristic> nodes with a 'name' attribute that describes their function: issue and volume numbers, publication and article titles, page numbers, and place of publication as well as content. A <tss:keyword> node stores the tags, and the link to the attached image of the article is provided in the <tss:attachment> node.

The available data itself is imperfect insofar as the categories of 'news report' and 'newspaper article' are fuzzy in the context of the late nineteenth-century Arabic and Ottoman press. During most of the period under study, newspapers did not mark individual articles with a heading. Sections of news reports were marked as "local news" (variably titled *akhbār maḥalliyya*, *ḥawādith maḥalliyya*, *ḥawādith baladiyya*, *ḥawādith dākhiliyya*, or just *maḥalliyya*) or "regional news" (labeled *akhbār al-jihāt*, *al-jihāt*, *akhbār al-wilāya*, *ḥawādith al-wilāya*), with small graphic marks of boundaries between reports. Consequently, the granularity of capturing individual articles varies across the sample, between newspapers as well as over time. Opinion pieces and editorials were almost entirely excluded from the sample.[14]

Secondly, while human beings are used to multilingual contexts and implicit information, computers are not. A research database uniting sources in more than one language and more than one script—including a mix of translations and different transcriptions of languages into multiple scripts—resists any attempt of 'catch-it-all' searches for literal strings.[15] Explicit semantic mark-up is thus the only way to disambiguate the source texts and make them accessible to computational analysis.

Thirdly, the semantic mark-up and the ontology for tagging sources evolved —and in any real-world research project, they commonly evolve—over the course of the data-capturing process. This means that the density and quality of mark-up varies across the sample. The semantic mark-up of persons and locations within Sente is far from complete. Due to available tools further down in the workflow, the original semantic mark-up aimed at establishing every relevant string (i. e., a name of a person or place) only once, instead of marking every occurrence of each individual string.[16]

2. Establishing a List of Geocoded Locations

In order to display places on a map, toponyms must be associated with locations —for example, by providing geographic information on latitude and longitude (geocoding). The first step in this process involves extracting all relevant toponyms from the research database and organizing them by the places they signify. Second, these places must be geocoded.

---

14 This approach presupposes that, by specifically focusing on news reports instead of opinion pieces and editorials or other canonical works, it is possible to grasp a broadly accepted everyday usage resonating with the contemporaneous reading audience as a matter-of-fact description. The focus here is the resilience of certain terms and the gradual shifts of semantics instead of the programmatic ruptures and utopian spaces of political ideologies.

15 A computerized solution for this dilema in the form of natural entity recognition (NER) is presently only available for major European and East Asian languages. One of the most well-known ready-to-use implementations is the Stanford NER, developed by The Stanford Natural Language Processing Group. It is distributed under GNU General Public License and can be downloaded at: http://nlp.stanford.edu/software/CRF-NER.shtml.

16 I wrote further XSLT stylesheets to extract every marked-up string, to process them, and to finally use them for a natural entity recognition, which, if run on the original Sente XML, automatically tags every occurrence of these strings with the appropriate mark-up.

2.1 Extracting the Toponyms and Organizing a Hierarchy of Places

In a best-case scenario, the semantic mark-up of the research data would already differentiate between the personal name 'Paris' and the toponym 'Paris', to use a common example. More precisely, the semantic mark-up would differentiate between all individual persons named 'Paris', such as the well-known heiress to the Hilton hotel chain, and places of the same name, such as the capital of France. On the other hand, such mark-up would also go beyond the literal string in Latin script and note that an Arabic reference to *bārīs* in the newspaper *Lisān al-Ḥāl* concerned the latter. Yet the most common scenario for historians of the Middle East, as outlined in section one, are databases with partially implemented semantic mark-up and an inconsistent tagging ontology.

Thus, an ontology of places, including all their known names in the languages relevant to the research project, was established by:

a) extracting the tagging ontology from the Sente SQLite database;
b) extracting all strings marked as `<placeName>` from the XML library file exported from Sente using XSLT[17];
c) manually adding additional highly likely or known spellings and toponyms missing from either a) and b).

The resulting list of places was then organized into a hierarchy following the Ottoman administrative divisions at use during the time under study and local spatial organization as presented in the sources themselves (i.e., the neighborhood of ... in the quarter of ... in the *thamn*/ *nāḥiye* of ...).[18]

Following the general considerations as to the preference of open and widely accepted standards and the availability of the research data as an XML file, the ontology of places was also implemented in XML. There are myriad XML schemas for storing and processing geographical data. I chose to implement the ontology in the Text Encoding Initiative's TEI P5 XML flavor, due to my familiarity with it. TEI is specifically tailored to the semantic mark-up of textual sources and

---

17 I made the stylesheet available at: https://github.com/tillgrallert/MappingOttomanDamascus2014/blob/xslt/master/Sente2Tei%20extract%20placeName.xsl.

18 The organization into strictly hierarchical XML nodes following administrative divisions on the ground is inherently ahistoric on the higher levels. Provinces (*vilāyet*), districts (*sancak*, *mütessarıflık*), and counties (*kaza*) were repeatedly reorganized, and XML is particularly ill-suited to model such changes. Lower administrative units and the local spatial organization into alleys, streets, neighborhoods, or quarters, on the other hand, were rather stable.

offers full support of Unicode characters. It is also the quasi-standard for many digital edition projects, which made it a natural choice.[19]

TEI P5 provides a <listPlace> container element, which can contain further <listPlace> and <place> elements that allow for a representation of administrative divisions. Each <place> element should contain at least one <placeName> element, specifying the toponym, and a <location> element to record information on the geographic location, such as a postal address or, in our case, a combination of latitude and longitude values. As we have no information on the locations yet, the <location> tag will be populated in the next step.

```
<tei:listPlace type="province" xmlns:tei="http://www.tei-c.org/ns/1.0">
    <tei:listPlace type="district">
        <tei:listPlace type="county">
            <tei:listPlace type="town">
                <tei:place type="town">
                    <tei:placeName xml:lang="ar-Latn-x-
ijmes">Dimashq</tei:placeName>
                    <tei:placeName xml:lang="ota-Latn-x-ijmes">Şām-i
şerīf</tei:placeName>
                    <tei:placeName xml:lang="tr">Şam-i şerif</tei:placeName>
                    <tei:placeName xml:lang="en">Damascus</tei:placeName>
                    <tei:placeName xml:lang="de">Damaskus</tei:placeName>
                    <tei:placeName xml:lang="fr">Damas</tei:placeName>
                </tei:place>
            </tei:listPlace>
        </tei:listPlace>
    </tei:listPlace>
</tei:listPlace>
```

Figure 8.3. Various known toponyms for the city of Damascus, recorded in a hierarchical ontology in TEI P5 XML. Note that information on languages and scripts is recorded in the "xml:lang" attribute.

2.2 Geocoding the Places

While there is no shortage of gazetteers of toponyms and their respective locations on the planet for the contemporary world and for languages written in Latin script, and while there are notable efforts to provide such tools for the study of the Roman and Hellenistic worlds of antiquity,[20] such historical gazet-

---

19 On the TEI, see http://www.tei-c.org/index.xml. On the TEI P5 XML guidelines and schema, see http://www.tei-c.org/Guidelines/P5/.

20 The Pleiades project (http://pleiades.stoa.org/) is probably the most well known. Pleiades+ extendes this gazetter with further toponyms from the GeoNames database (http://www.geonames.org/). The Pelagios project (http://pelagios-project.blogspot.com/), whose current phase

eers are completely absent for the Ottoman Empire, *Bilād al-Shām*, and the larger Eastern Mediterranean between antiquity and the twentieth century. Therefore, the places established in section 2.1 had to be either manually geocoded using a paper map or through one of the ubiquitous online mapping tools, such as the commercial services offered by Google,[21] Yahoo,[22] or Microsoft[23] and the non-profit and community-driven projects of OpenStreetMap[24] and WikiMapia,[25] to name but a few. In addition, one can query online databases, such as GeoNames,[26] for the locations of toponyms.

Due to the (still growing) number of places in a never-finished research database and the aspired future interoperability of the ontology with the semantic web, (semi-)automatic geocoding was preferred over purely manual coding. GeoNames is licensed under a creative-commons attribution license, is free to use, and provides full-Unicode support, including Arabic. The database can be downloaded in its entirety or queried through a large number of application programming interfaces (APIs) that return data as XML.[27] This made GeoNames the perfect choice for the task at hand.

A XSLT stylesheet[28] queries the GeoNames database through the search API for the latitude and longitude of each place in the ontology produced in section 2.1 as well as for additional toponyms not yet available in the ontology. The first query for the example from Figure 8.3 would be http://api.geonames.org/search?name=Damascus&maxRows=1&style=FULL&lang=en&username=demo,[29] which returns the XML node shown in Figure 8.4.

---

will also include early Islamic sources, provides tools to tag any input source with historical toponyms provided by online gazetteers such as Pleiades. Another noteworthy example is the Index Anatolicus (http://nisanyanmap.com/). See also Maxim Romanow, "al-Thurayya: an Islamic Supplement to Pleiades," *al-Raqmiyyāt Blog*, 17 Mar 2014, available at: http://alraqmiyyat.org/2014/03/al-thurayya-an-islamic-supplement-to-pleiades/.

21 http://maps.google.com

22 http://maps.yahoo.com

23 http://www.bing.com/maps

24 http://www.openstreetmap.org

25 http://wikimapia.org

26 http://www.geonames.org

27 For a list of available APIs and their various options, see http://www.geonames.org/export/ws-overview.html.

28 I made the stylesheet available at: https://github.com/tillgrallert/MappingOttomanDamascus2014/blob/master/xslt/Tei2GeoNames2Tei.xsl.

29 Note that it might be necessary to register for a free username, as the allowed frequency for using the API is otherwise severely restricted. GeoNames provides the functionality to add further locations likely to be present within the research database. Through its "nearby?" API, one can search for various types of locations within a certain radius of any given point on the map,

```
<geonames style="FULL">
    <totalResultsCount>228</totalResultsCount>
    <geoname>
        <toponymName>Damascus</toponymName>
        <name>Damascus</name>
        <lat>33.5102</lat>
        <lng>36.29128</lng>
        <geonameId>170654</geonameId>
        <countryCode>SY</countryCode>
        <countryName>Syria</countryName>
        <fcl>P</fcl>
        <fcode>PPLC</fcode>
        <fclName>city, village,...</fclName>
        <fcodeName>capital of a political entity</fcodeName>
        <population>1569394</population>
        <alternateNames>Al-Sham,Al-
Shām,Cham,DAM,Damas,Damasc,Damasco,Damascu,Damascus,Damasek,Damask,Damask",Da
maskas,Damasko,Damaskos,Damaskus,Damaszek,Damašek,Dammeseq,Dimaejk,Dimashk,Di
mashk al-Sham,Dimashk al-Shām,Dimashq,Dimeshki esh Sham,Dimishq,Dimäjk,Esh
Sham,Esh Shām,Sam,da ma shi ge,damaseukuseu,damasukasu,dmshq,dmsq,drmswq,Şam,
Δαμασκός,Дамаск,Дамаскъ,Димишк,Դամասկոս,דמשק,دمشق,ܕܪܡܣܘܩ,ደማስቆ,ダマスカス,大马士革
,다마스쿠스</alternateNames>
        <elevation/>
        <continentCode>AS</continentCode>
        <adminCode1 ISO3166-2="DI">13</adminCode1>
        <adminName1>Damascus City</adminName1>
        …
        <alternateName lang="am">ደማስቆ</alternateName>
        <alternateName lang="ar">دمشق</alternateName>
        <alternateName lang="bg">Дамаск</alternateName>
        <alternateName lang="bs">Damask</alternateName>
        <alternateName lang="ca">Damasc</alternateName>
        <alternateName lang="cs">Damašek</alternateName>
        …
        <timezone dstOffset="3.0" gmtOffset="2.0">Asia/Damascus</timezone>
        <bbox>
            <west>36.09593</west>
            <north>33.67277</north>
            <east>36.48662</east>
            <south>33.34763</south>
        </bbox>
        <score>106.7225112915039</score>
    </geoname>
</geonames>
```


Figure 8.4. The GeoNames entry for the city of Damascus, as returned by the API call.

The information on the location and additional toponyms is extracted from the `<lat>`, `<lng>`, and `<alternateName>` nodes of the resulting XML (Figure 8.4) and integrated into the original TEI ontology (Figure 8.3). To record the specific entry in the GeoNames database as the source of the information, an @xml:id attribute based on the `<geonameId>` of the query result is added to the `<place>` element (Figure 8.5).

---

e. g., for mosques at a distance of less than 3 km from Marja Square, which would cover the entire area of Damascus in late Ottoman times.

```
<tei:listPlace corresp="#lgn170654" type="province"
xmlns:tei="http://www.tei-c.org/ns/1.0">
    <tei:listPlace corresp="#lgn170654" type="district">
        <tei:listPlace corresp="#lgn170654" type="county">
            <tei:listPlace corresp="#lgn170654" type="town">
                <tei:place type="town" xml:id="lgn170654">
                    <tei:placeName type="toponym">Damascus</tei:placeName>
                    <tei:placeName xml:lang="ar-Latn-x-
ijmes">Dimashq</tei:placeName>
                    <tei:placeName xml:lang="ota-Latn-x-ijmes">Şām-i
şerīf</tei:placeName>
                    <tei:placeName xml:lang="tr">Şam-i şerif</tei:placeName>
                    <tei:placeName xml:lang="en">Damascus</tei:placeName>
                    <tei:placeName xml:lang="de">Damaskus</tei:placeName>
                    <tei:placeName xml:lang="fr">Damas</tei:placeName>
                    <tei:location>
                        <tei:geo>33.5102,36.29128</tei:geo>
                    </tei:location>
                </tei:place>
            </tei:listPlace>
        </tei:listPlace>
    </tei:listPlace>
</tei:listPlace>
```

Figure 8.5. Updated TEI ontology of places.

While GeoNames commonly returns correct results and avoids the bias for locations within the United States shown by Google's and other mapping tools,[30] the correct location must be manually confirmed in cases of two or more locations with a similar name. In addition, many smaller locations or places no longer existing, such as neighborhoods and souks inside the city of Damascus, are not (yet) listed in the database. To correct the data and quickly retrieve geo-spatial data for visually established locations, I employ Google Earth,[31] which can ingest data from XML files adhering to the KML standard.[32] A simple XSLT stylesheet maps the TEI XML of Figure 8.5 to a KML file, which can then be imported into Google Earth[33] (Figure 8.6).

Finally, Google Earth's GUI allows to manually add 'placemarks' to the map and to display the relevant geospatial information. This information can either

30 For instance, if not accompanied by the qualifier 'Italy', Google's ChartWrapper maps 'Naples' to Florida. ChartWrapper is part of the visualization API; see https://developers.google.com/chart/interactive/docs/reference.

31 Google Earth software is free to use and available for Windows, OSX, and Linux: http://www.google.com/earth.

32 KML was originally developed by Google as "Keyhole Markup Language" and then submitted to and approved by the Open Geospatial Consortium; see http://www.opengeospatial.org/standards/kml/.

33 I made the stylesheet available at: https://github.com/tillgrallert/MappingOttomanDamascus2014/blob/master/xslt/Tei2Kml.xsl.

```
<kml:kml xmlns:kml="http://earth.google.com/kml/2.0">
    <kml:Document>
    ...
        <kml:Placemark xml:id="lgn170654">
            <kml:name>Dimashq</kml:name>
            <kml:Point>
                <kml:coordinates>36.29128, 33.5102</kml:coordinates>
            </kml:Point>
        </kml:Placemark>
        ...
    </kml:Document>
</kml:kml>
```

Figure 8.6. A KML <kml: Placemark> node for the toponym *Dimashq* and its latitude and longitude.

be manually transferred or exported as KML, which can then be transformed to TEI XML and integrated into the ontology through another XSLT stylesheet.[34]

3. Mashing Up the Data

The next step is the actual analysis of whether a certain discourse or a particular vocabulary—the example for the current paper is the discourse on legitimate rule and violence and its vocabulary of *ashqiyāʾ*, etc.—correlate with particular locations. In technical terms, we aim at establishing links between certain criteria within the research database (Sente XML) and the geospatial data in the ontology of places (TEI XML). The output is a count of instances of the search criteria per location. The relationship between locations and the number of references can be recorded in various ways; the format and level of detail are ultimately governed by the requirements of the chosen solution for visualizing the data.

The process involves two steps, both of which are done with XSLT stylesheets:

a) Establishing a sub-sample of references/sources inside the XML research database that meet the criteria, for instance, all sources that contain references to all known forms and derivatives of the Arabic word *shaqī*, e. g., the plural *ashqiyāʾ*, the Ottoman-Turkish variants of *şakī* and *eşḳıyā*, as well as their possible English translations as *brigand*, *rascal*, *wretch*, *villain*, etc. Including English translations is necessitated by the imperfections of the research database, as out-

34 I made the ontology of toponyms available at: https://github.com/tillgrallert/OttomanDamascus/blob/master/LocationsMaster.TEIP5.xml.

lined in section one, which might not contain transliterations in every instance of *ashqiyā*, but only an English summary.[35]

b) Establishing the number of references within this subset that refer to any one of the known toponyms for every location of the ontology. This latter step represents some sort of a named entity recognition, insofar as it associates every instance of the strings 'Damascus', 'Dimashq', 'Şām-i şerīf', etc., in the research database (including the geographic tags mentioned above) with the city of Damascus and a combination of values for latitude and longitude (33.5102, 36.29128).[36] The most simple—although not necessarily the most useful—notation of the result would be comma separated values (CSV):

```
Toponym, latitude, longitude, number of references to "ashqiyā'"
Dimashq, 33.5102, 36.29128, 88
```

Both steps involve a number of possible and likely errors, the extent of which cannot readily be quantified. The quality of step a) is mainly determined by the quality of the data-recording process and the search query. While it might not produce false positives, it will generate an unspecified number of false negatives: information present in the sources might not have been recorded, and spelling errors, particularly in transcriptions, might pass unregistered.

The error margin of step b) is much higher, as, in addition to the shortcomings of the data that hampered step a) with false negatives and which also apply here, it will produce false positives in cases of sources that cover more than a singular topic and in cases of ambiguous toponyms. Since the size of the geographic area (mostly the Ottoman provinces of Syria and Beirut) and the number of recorded toponyms in the ontology are both rather small and clearly focussed on Damascus and its surroundings, duplicate toponyms did not yet appear. Confusion between terms that designate places, persons, etc.—such as the common example 'Paris'—is not likely to occur in Arabic and can be omitted as a source of errors.[37]

---

35 As this chapter is concerned with establishing the mapping of the correlation between the search criteria and geographic locations, the search queries to establish matching sub-samples of my database will not be covered here.

36 I made the stylesheet available at: https://github.com/tillgrallert/MappingOttomanDamascus2014/blob/master/xslt/Tei2GeoNames2Tei.xsl.

37 Geographic names that involve some sort of personal names or group identities are usually prefixed by a typological specification or marked as female generic nouns: i.e., *maḥallat al-yahūd* ("the Jewish Quarter"), *jamīʿ Mūrad Bāshā* ("the Mosque of Murad Pasha), *al-dārwishiyya* (referring to the Mosque of Darwish Pasha), etc.

Some false positives can be averted based on linguistic structures and our knowledge of the recording process: if records in the research database were structured by topic, for instance through inserting paragraphs and additional graphical markers (see Figure 8.1), one can limit the query that correlates search criteria with toponyms to paragraphs. In a similar vein, the query can be limited to sentences or a maximum range of words allowed between the search criteria and the toponyms. False positives caused by geographic tagging of poly-thematic entries in the database can only be averted by ignoring the tags altogether. This, in turn, however, would produce false negatives in cases of implicit locations that were recorded in the tags, but which are absent from the text of the reference. Altogether, the results should be taken with a grain of salt and be read as orders of magnitude instead of precise quantitative measurements.

4. Visualizing / Mapping the Data

The final task is to visualize the correlations between topics/vocabularies and locations on a map and in a meaningful way, such as color and/or size. The tool chosen for visualizing the data is the free and open-source Exihibit 3.0 SIMILE widget (Exhibit), which, inter alia, provides a JavaScript mapping tool that can display locations and additional information on base layers provided by Google maps and, through additional plug-ins, OpenStreetMap in any modern web-browser.[38] Thus, it utilizes available programs and server-side computing instead of providing another layer of complexity through additional software. All it needs is an HTML page that calls the Exhibit JavaScript framework and a JSON data source in its header (Figure 8.7). The display is then manipulated right inside the HTML code by a small variety of commands specific to Exhibit and can be styled with regular CSS. The only shortcoming of this solution is that the ease of use requires continuous Internet access.

4.1. The JSON Data Source

Exhibit requires a well-formed JSON file as data source, which can be imagined as a verbose description of a table with each cell being individually and coher-

38 http://simile-widgets.org/exhibit/. Apart from mapping, Exhibit provides search and filtering tools as well as interactive timelines. Simile widgets were originally developed by the MIT's SIMILE project; see http://simile.mit.edu/.

```
<html xmlns:ex="http://api.simile-widgets.org/exhibit/3.0.0/"
xmlns="http://www.w3.org/1999/xhtml">
    <head>
        <meta http-equiv="Content-Type" content="text/html; charset=UTF-8"/>
        <title>ashqiyā' between 1858 and 1917.</title>
        <link href="http://www.simile-widgets.org/styles/common.css"
rel="stylesheet" type="text/css"/>
        <link href="simileData-ashqiya'.js" rel="exhibit-data"
type="application/json"/>
        <link href="http://api.simile-
widgets.org/exhibit/3.0.0/extensions/map/map-extension.js" rel="exhibit-
extension" type="text/javascript"/>
        <script src="http://api.simile-widgets.org/exhibit/3.0.0/exhibit-
api.js"/>
    </head>
    <body>
        ...
    </body>
</html>
```

Figure 8.7. `<link>` nodes in the HTML header that load the Exhibit JavaScript framework and the data source.

ently named. But Exhibit makes no requirements as to a specific terminology. Thus, we format the information on place (identified by one of the associated toponyms), type of entity (e.g., 'quarter', 'street', etc.), geographic location, and the number of references that met the particular search criteria produced in 3.b) as shown in Figure 8.8.

```
{
    "items":[
    {
        "label":"Dimashq",
        "type":"town",
        "typeCode":"3",
        "latlng":"33.5102, 36.29128",
        "events":"88",
        "eventType":"ashqiyā'"
    }]
}
```

Figure 8.8. The association of the toponym *Dimashq* and its latitude 33.5102 and longitude 36.29128 with the number of 88 references to *ashqiyā'* as a JSON array.

4.2 The Display / Widgets

Exhibit can display and visualise the JSON data source in various ways. Each display is called a 'view' and represented by a `<div>` inside the HTML page. Using the 'ex'-namespace, attributes added to the `<div>` specify and manipulate the displayed data as well as the display. We commence displaying a base-layer provided by Google maps, to which we add clickable dots for each location in our JSON data source (Figure 8.9).

```
<div ex:role="view"
        ex:viewClass="Map"
        ex:center="33.509166, 36.310154"
        ex:zoom="15"
        ex:mapHeight="580"

        ex:label="events"
        ex:latlng=".latlng"

        ex:shape="circle"
        ex:colorLegendLabel="Location type"
        ex:colorCoder="type-color"
        ex:colorKey=".typeCode"
        ex:sizeLegendLabel="Events"
        ex:sizeCoder="events-size"
        ex:sizeKey=".events">
</div>
```

Figure 8.9. The <div> tag with attributes specifying the view.

The first section of attributes defines the display as a map, provides a point at the center of the displayed map, a zoom-level, and a size for the map. The second and third sets of attributes link the functions of the Exhibit display to the entries in the JSON data source.

By default, Exhibit provides all available information on each item in the data source, represented by a dot on the map, upon clicking on the dots. Yet, useful as equally shaped, sized, and colored dots on a map might be to reveal geographical clustering, the information we are actually interested in displaying is still missing from the map: the number of references inside our database that met the search criteria per location. The most intuitive display would be areas (instead of dots) whose size corresponds to the displayed information. In addition, a color scheme for administrative divisions might further support easy readability of the map. Both functions are provided through another class of Exhibit's <div>s, a 'coder' (Figure 8.10). The coders are already linked in Figure 8.9.

```
<div ex:coderClass="ColorGradient"
        ex:gradientPoints="1, #FF0000; 2, #FFA500; 3, #FFFF00; 4, #008000; 5,
#0000FF; 6, #800080"
        ex:role="coder"
        id="type-color"/>
<div ex:coderClass="SizeGradient"
        ex:gradientPoints="1, 10; 5,30; 30,60; 100, 100"
        ex:role="coder"
        id="events-size"/>
```

Figure 8.10. "coder" <div>s that specify the display of values associated with individual locations on the map.

These coders specify that a minimal value of one report mentioning *ashqiyāʾ* shall be displayed as a circle of ten pixels in diameter, while the maximal value of 100 reports shall result in a circle of 100 pixels in diameter. Note that the size gradient is non-linear. The color corresponds to six administrative levels in discrete steps from the street (encoded as "1"), which are displayed in red (#FF000), to purple (#800080) circles signifying provinces of the Ottoman Empire after 1888. When the final code is loaded in a web-browser, the resulting map for the *ashqiyā'* sample is shown in Figure 8.11.

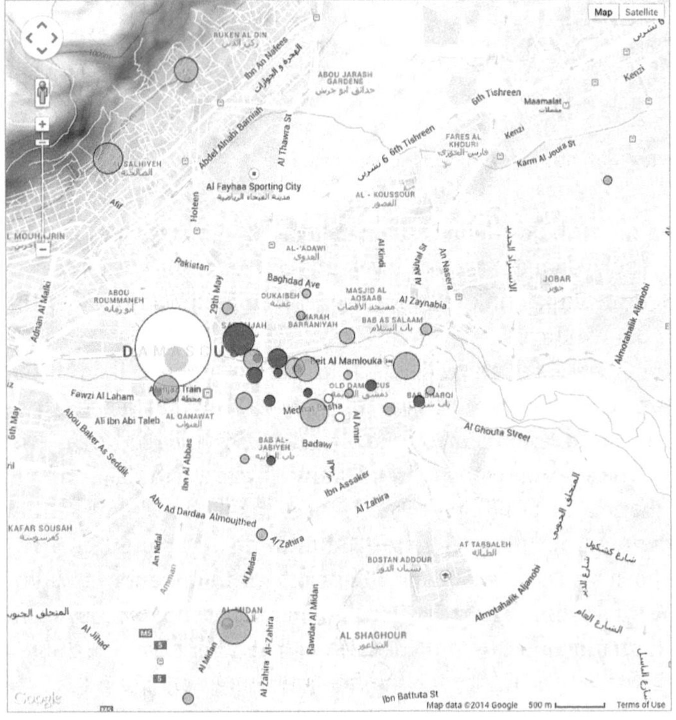

Figure 8.11. The Exihibit map view with circles whose size indicates the number of reports mentioning a specific criterion and whose color corresponds to administrative levels.

Additional Exhibit views allow us to further explore the data source by limiting the display through various search criteria, which might result in a website that looks like Figure 8.12.

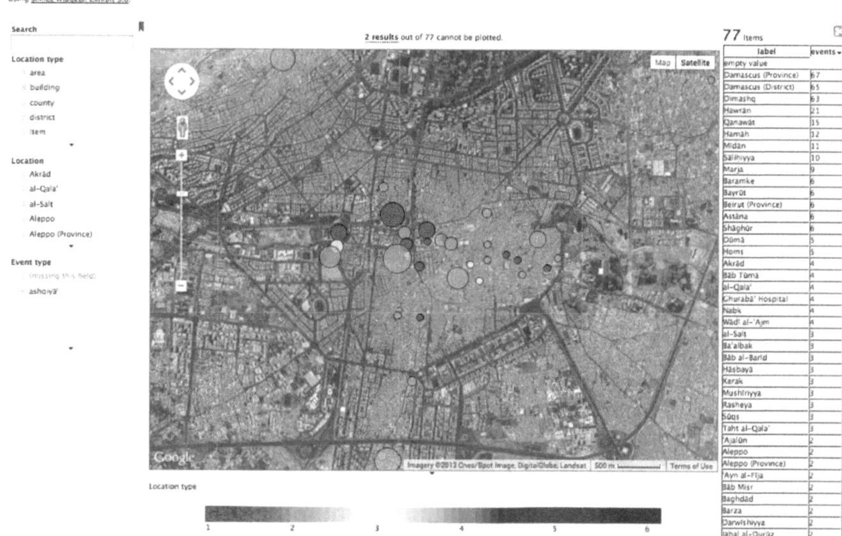

Figure 8.12. The final webpage, adding various views to the map that allow for browsing and limiting the displayed data by various criteria.

5. Conclusion

The suggested workflow provides a highly flexible visualization framework for quickly testing possible correlations of historical data points and geographical locations. Once set up, the geocoded ontology of places and toponyms as well as the XSLT stylesheets can be re-used, and maps can be produced almost instantaneously. The workflow is scalable to very large datasets of tens of thousands of sources. Quantitative increases in the amount of data and qualitative improvements of already existing data—be it improved semantic mark-up of the sources or further entries to the ontology of places—will have an immediate impact on the quality of the produced maps without tinkering with the XSLT stylesheets.

The visualization can help to detect geographic clustering that might otherwise remain shrouded—particularly in large data sets that have been accumulated over longer periods and whose meticulous details have slipped from the historian's memory. Yet the outcome must be taken with a grain of salt, and seemingly apparent correlations must then be further scrutinisezd through more traditional methods of much closer reading. The visualization generates a dangerous sense of exactitude that obfuscates the inherent fuzziness of the categories, toponyms, or locations: once represented on a map, everything is unambiguously located and defined. While the quality of the map is heavily dependent on the type of sources—on their granularity, on the degree of their internal heterogeneity, and, not least, on the quality of metadata collection—this level of ambiguity is absent from the map itself.

Keeping these shortcomings in mind, what, finally, are the outcomes of a spatial analysis for the exemplary research question in the introduction to this paper? To what extent did newspapers and particularly the news reports from and on Damascus between 1875 and 1914 perpetuate the state's discourse on the provision of public order (*āsāyış-i ʿumūmī / rāḥat ʿumūmiyya*) for generating legitimate Ottoman statehood?

Whereas newspapers were rife with reports on petty and violent crime—mostly theft and robbery—they remained significantly silent when it came to violent public action or chose to report such action only by denying it had ever occurred. In addition, they took recourse to a euphemistic and generic language, preferring the "incident" (*ḥāditha* and *waqāʾiʿ*) for all sorts of unpleasant events over the more explicit statements of opposition and violence, such as *mushājara* (quarrel) or *munāzaʿa* (riot). "Bandit" (*shaqī*, pl. *ashqiyāʾ*) became the preferred label for any person engaged in violence potentially threatening the legitimacy of the ruling state. Also, as criminalized subjects and in accordance with the Penal Code, all such persons were stripped of their honorific titles and salutations (e.g., Muḥammad ibn ʿAlī instead of Muḥammad Efendi Bey). Only some of these omissions and linguistic markers can be attributed to the regime of censorship and the press laws increasingly regulating permissible news content in the later years of Abdülhamid II's reign, with the aim of preventing anything that could instigate fear and anxiety (*takhdīsh al-adhhān*) among the population and thus threaten the established order. Rather, being mutually dependent, and as many publishers were at one point or another employees of the state, the state and the press joined forces in a common modernizing project with an ever-expanding state at its core.[39]

A spatial analysis of the discourse on violence reveals insights into the making of a specific (and idealized) urban identity as set against a violent 'other'. The

---

39 See the second chapter, especially pp.92–94, 287–89 of Grallert, "To Whom Belong the Streets?"; c.f. Maurus Reinkowski, *Die Dinge der Ordnung: eine vergleichende Untersuchung über die osmanische Reformpolitik im 19. Jahrhundert* (München: Oldenbourg, 2005), 233 ff., for a discussion of the Ottoman terminology of law and order and how the discourse on *āsāyış* dwelt on the provision of security (*emeniyet*) for the purpose of general tranquility and welfare (*rāḥat, istirāḥat*).

locus of the civilized, progressive, and essentially peaceful urban centre's 'other' are the geographic and socio-ethnic margins of the province of Syria and the fringes of Ottoman society. *Geographically*, these margins are mostly located to the south of Damascus: the deserts of the East, the Lajā, and most prominently the Ḥawrān (including Jabal Durūz, Jabal Ḥawrān, and Qunayṭra and the plains to the west of it). These areas are of a vexing duality of a distant-present/known-unknown: on the one hand, and for most townspeople, they were as far away as any other place they had never been to. On the other, they were highly present in everyday stories and news reports. At the *socio-ethnical* margin, Druze, Bedouins, and Circassians are the loci of violence. The opposition between the sedentary, urban population and the villains from the periphery culminates in a linguistic dichotomy of "the populace" (*al-qawm*) on the one hand, and the Bedouins on the other. Armed Bedouins and Druze of the south become the epitome of the vicious (semi-)nomadic bandits (*ashqiyā'*) threatening the urban "flock" under the protection of the Ottoman authorities.[40] Accordingly, an opinion piece from Damascus in 1881 was titled *al-waṭan wa ashqiyā' al-durūz*—the homeland and the Druze bandits.[41]

Bibliography

Ayalon, Ami. *The Press in the Arab Middle East: A History.* New York: Oxford University Press, 1995.

Grallert, Till. "To Whom Belong the Streets? Property, Propriety, and Appropriation: The Production of Public Space in Late Ottoman Damascus, 1875–1914." Ph.D. dissertation, Freie Universität, Berlin, 2014.

al-Mallūḥī, Mihyār ʿAdnān. *Muʿjam al-jarāʾid al-sūriyya 1865–1965.* Dimashq, 2002.

Reinkowski, Maurus. *Die Dinge der Ordnung: eine vergleichende Untersuchung über die osmanische Reformpolitik im 19. Jahrhundert.* München: Oldenbourg, 2005.

Ṭarrāzī, Fīlīb Dī. *Tārīkh al-ṣiḥāfa al-ʿarabiyya: Yaḥtawī ʿalā akhbār kull jarīda wa-majalla ʿarabiyya ẓaharat fī al-ʿālam sharqiyyan wa-gharbiyyan maʿa rusūm aṣḥābihā wa-l-muḥarrirīn fīhā wa-tarājim mashāhīrihim.* Vols. 1–3. Bayrūt: al-Maṭbaʿa al-adabiyya, 1913–14.

40 This othering of Bedouins and Druze, as well as the population of the Ḥawrān, also becomes evident by looking at the numbers of newspaper articles referring to these two groups in conjunction with violent events of some sort and those which do not mention violence. For both groups, the ratio is about two to one: only one third of all articles referring to Bedouins and Druze did so in non-violent contexts.

41 *Thamarāt al-Funūn*, 14 Mar 1881 (#322).

—. *Tārīkh al-ṣiḥāfa al-ʿarabiyya: Yaḥtawī ʿalā jamīʿ fahāris al-jarāʾid wa-l-majallāt al-ʿarabiyya fī al-khāfiqīn mudh takwīn al-ṣiḥāfa al-ʿarabiyya ilā nihāyat ʿām 1929.* Vol. 4. Bayrūt: al-Maṭbaʿa al-amīrikāniyya, 1933.

José Haro Peralta and Peter Verkinderen[1]

"Find for Me!": Building a Context-Based Search Tool Using Python

The last decade has seen the beginning of what could become a methodological revolution in the fields of Arabic and Islamic Studies with the appearance of large collections of digitized classical Arabic texts.[2] The aim of this chapter is to show that open-source tools can be developed by researchers to utilize the existing collections of digital texts more comprehensively. We will focus on the possibilities that easy-to-learn but powerful programming languages like Python offer for advanced search operations. The authors of this chapter use Python for historical research with early Islamic texts and have built an open-source textual analysis toolkit, released under the name Jedli. In the second part of this chapter, we will present the basic building blocks of the Jedli program, with special focus on its context search function. We hope the ideas presented in this chapter can serve as an inspiration for other researchers to build more complex tools for textual analysis.

Jedli was developed within the framework of the research project "The Early Islamic Empire at Work: The View From the Regions Toward the Center," which is based at the University of Hamburg and funded by the European Research Council. This project aims at providing a better understanding of the political and economic structures of the Islamic Empire during its first three centuries by looking at the working mechanisms of five key regions (Fārs, Ifrīqiya, al-Jazīra, Khurāsān, and al-Shām).[3] Although the study of material culture (exemplified in coins and archaeological remains) forms an important part of the project, its

---

1 ERC project, "The Early Islamic Empire at Work—The View from the Regions toward the Center," University of Hamburg. The research leading to these results has been possible thanks to funding from the European Research Council under the ERC Advanced Grant no. 340362. We express our gratitude to all members of the project for providing useful feedback during the development of the Jedli toolkit as well as to the participants in the "Textual Corpora and the Digital Islamic Humanities" workshop at Brown University (October 17–18 2014), who made important suggestions and remarks on a preliminary version of this article. Special thanks go to our colleague Hannah-Lena Hagemann, whose comments and criticism contributed notably to improve the arguments developed in this article.

2 By 'digitized texts' we do not mean scanned PDFs of text editions, but texts which have been produced directly in a digital format, normally using a double-keying method (i.e., two typists type the same text independently, and the two texts are then compared to filter out typos).

3 See the project website: http://www.islamic-empire.uni-hamburg.de/.

main component is the analysis of textual primary source material, which is combed for information on the administration, economy, and elites of the key regions. The relevant text corpus consists of a large number of 'literary' (in the sense of non-documentary) texts that were written between the eighth and the thirteenth centuries CE and belong to different genres (historiography, geography, law, prosopography, and others).

The sheer magnitude of the corpus, the large scope of the research questions, and the limited research time available call for a strategy to retrieve information from the texts faster and in a more targeted way than is usually possible with traditional means of textual research, such as browsing through the indexes of edited works. This strategy makes use of the opportunities offered by digitized texts.

Collections of digitized Arabic texts began to appear in the 1990s, starting with digitized Qurans and *ḥadīth* works. The first of these collections appeared on CD-ROMs, but the most important ones are now available online.[4] The largest and most developed collection is currently al-Maktaba al-Shamela (http://www.shamela.ws), which has been online since 2005.[5] This digital library contains more than 6,500 books, divided into 76 categories. Not only does al-Maktaba al-Shamela have the largest collection of books, it also has an online platform (http://www.islamport.com), which allows a basic search across all the books within a specific category, and a dedicated desktop program, developed to read and search the collection. The desktop program offers an advanced search engine, which allows users to search for multiple words at a time, using OR and AND operators, in one or more books in the library. The latest version of the search engine also has options for disregarding different combinations of *alif-hamza* and dotted and undotted final *yā*'s and *tā' marbūṭa*s.

Although the inbuilt tools of some of these digital libraries can be used for complex searches in one or more documents, the existing programs are very rigid and do not give researchers control over what they can do with the texts. Digitized texts offer new research opportunities that were unthinkable with printed texts, but even simple tasks such as word counting, let alone more advanced operations, such as an analysis of vocabulary diversity, are not possible

4 For an overview of the most important websites, see http://islamichumanities.org/resources/. Some text collections, such as al-Jāmiʿ al-Kabīr, are still distributed on physical data carriers like flash drives and hard disks.

5 The first version of the program (April 2005) did not have a designated website but was distributed on the Ahl al-Hadeeth forum (www.ahlalhdeeth.com [sic]). The library moved to its own website in 2006.

with the tools offered by digital libraries. Moreover, search results cannot be exported for analysis and visualization in maps or graphs.

It must be added that the text collections also have a number of problems. In his presentation "Collections of Text vs. Textual Corpora, or What We Have and What We Need" at the Textual Corpora and the Digital Islamic Humanities Workshop in 2014 (October 17–18, Brown University),[6] Maxim Romanov pointed out that the currently available collections of digital texts are ill-suited for computational analysis: they aim at reproducing physical books rather than creating truly digital editions of the texts; their scope is limited, often on an ideological basis; the grouping into literary genres is inflexible and sometimes unhelpful; and metadata is incomplete and cannot be updated. We could add that the quality of the digitization is variable and not always based on high-quality editions. Moreover, the critical apparatus and footnotes are not dealt with in a consistent way.

Even if the collections of books that these digital libraries contain leave much to be desired, they do offer large quantities of digitized texts, including many of the most important sources for early Islamic history. These texts can be exported and converted to a format suitable for computational processing, such as .txt files. Once this is done, researchers can overcome the limitations of the tools offered by the above-mentioned digital libraries by building their own tools in a way that suits their needs.

The authors of this article have used the programming language Python to build a number of tools designed to find and retrieve information relevant to our research questions from Arabic texts. Programming languages are basically languages designed to communicate instructions to computers (and other machines). Python offers the advantage of being a a dynamic language, which means that a piece of code can be written and tested immediately, allowing for an interactive development experience of trial and error that eases the learning curve considerably. Python also contains a number of modules that are very suitable for textual analysis.

One of these modules that we are going to use extensively in this article is the RE (Regular Expressions) module. A regular expression is a sequence of characters that defines a pattern. This pattern can be used to search, select, and replace sequences of characters in a text.[7] For example, if we want to find the word

6 For the workshop program, see http://islamichumanities.org/workshop-2014/

7 For a gentle introduction to regular expressions, see Michael Fitzgerald, *Introducing Regular Expressions* (Sebastopol, CA: O'Reilly Media, 2012). More advanced coverage of this topic can be found in Jeffrey E. F. Friedl, *Mastering Regular Expressions* (Sebastopol, CA: O'Reilly

'color' in a text, but we do not know whether it is written in American or British spelling, we can use the following regular expression to match both forms:

```
colou?r
```

The question mark indicates that the preceding token (i.e., the 'u') may or may not be there. Therefore both 'colour' and 'color' will match this pattern.

1. Jedli's Main Functionalities

The authors of this chapter have built a data-mining toolkit for Arabic texts that consists mainly of three functions, namely an indexer, a context search function, and a highlighter. We will explain how these functions work, providing examples of how we use them in our own work. We will also suggest how researchers working on different topics might benefit from using these tools. In the second part of the chapter, we will focus on their technical aspects.

The first tool, the 'Indexer', lists all the pages in which a word appears. It can be used to search for one word at a time or be fed with a whole checklist of words, and it can undertake the search within one or more sources at the same time. Furthermore, it can either return a simple list of page numbers, or —for every page number—the surrounding context in which the word is found.

The main advantage of this function over manually searching for words in indexes of printed volumes is obviously its time-saving effect: the more words one needs to look up, and the more volumes one needs to search, the more time is saved. The Indexer is also more accurate than traditional indexes. In a test using the index of the *Bibliotheca Geographorum Arabicorum*,[8] a collection of exemplary editions of Arabic texts, the Indexer found significantly more results per search word than the printed index.

Furthermore, this Indexer is more powerful and flexible than any of the in-built search tools in the above-mentioned digital libraries, which all have indexing functions that can index a word in multiple sources at the same time. For one, it allows the user to index not only one term at a time, but also to feed it a checklist of search terms, which can be re-used and adjusted at any time. This is very convenient, since new relevant search terms may turn up while

Media, 2006) and in Jan Goyvaerts and Steven Levithan, *Regular Expressions Cookbook* (Sebastopol, CA: O'Reilly Media, 2012).

8 Michael Jan de Goeje, ed., *Bibliotheca Geographorum Arabicorum* (8 vols.: Leiden: Brill, 1870–94).

going through the results of the first search; these new search terms can then simply be added to the checklist for further indexing operations. Using regular expressions, one can restrict the number of results, excluding instances that are unlikely to be relevant. If we are looking for references to the province of Fārs, for example, we might want to leave off the 'outcomes list' instances of the *nisba* 'al-Fārisī' or cases in which the search word is preceded by numbers (as the text is more likely talking about horsemen, *fāris*). Moreover, regular expressions can also be used to define patterns that account for different spellings of words.[9]

The Indexer also gives the user full control over the output of the results: it can either return a simple list of page numbers or also include the contexts in which the word appears. The user can define how many context words before and after the search word are needed in order to determine if a result is relevant. One could also adapt the Indexer to define the context based on criteria other than number of words, e.g., punctuation, a number of lines in a poem, the beginning and end of a biography in a biographical dictionary, or an *isnād* in *ḥadīth* works. In addition, the Indexer saves the results for further reference, currently in an HTML document, but it can easily be adapted to output the results in a format that can be used for further analysis and visualization. For instance, the results of a search could be saved in a .csv document,[10] which can then be used to produce a graph so as to visualize how the results are spread over a selection of sources in order to spot patterns. If the search involves toponyms and is combined with a database of coordinates, it would also be possible to produce a map-based visualization of how different regions of the Islamic Empire are represented in a selection of texts.

The second tool we built is the 'Context Search' function. This tool was developed in the first instance to find information about the governors of our project's five key provinces. The number of sources that can provide information about this is very large, and going through all of them with the help of the Indexer would still require an enormous amount of time. We wanted to develop an approach that would allow us to gather some initial data quickly so we could start working on research hypotheses sooner.

9 To give only a few examples: defective spellings, different combinations of *alif* and *hamza*, dotted and undotted *tāʾ marbūṭa*s, and final *yāʾ*s. See the second part of the article for practical examples on how to build such regular expressions.

10 CSV stands for 'comma-separated values'; it is a common file format that is used to store tabular data in plain text form. Each line of the file contains a record, and each record has the same number of fields, separated by commas (or other delimiters).

The basic idea behind the Context Search function is that relevant information about a certain topic can be found if we can figure out in which kinds of contexts (as defined by their vocabulary composition) it is likely to appear. The Context Search function gives options to define contexts based on their length (number of words), which terms must appear in them, and even which words should not appear in them.[11] These checks are undertaken by feeding the function with checklists of words. It is therefore very important to build up these checklists carefully in order not to overlook relevant search results.

How we proceeded in our search for governors will illustrate how this tool can be used. In a first step, we used the Indexer to look up all contexts in which the name of a province was mentioned in one source. We then manually selected those search results that were related to governors. In a next step, we analyzed the vocabulary composition of these search results and identified the 'trigger words' in these contexts, on the basis of which we (consciously or unconsciously) had decided that the text fragment talks about a governor. The most effective trigger word was found to be *ʿalā* in combination with the name of the province (e.g., *ʿalā Ifrīqiya*, "in charge of Ifrīqiya"). Other trigger words included *wālī, wallā, wilāya, waliya, aqarra, ʿazala, ghalaba, fī yad, istakhlafa, ʿāmil*, and *dīwān*. These trigger words were put in a checklist, in a .txt document. We also analyzed how close to the name of the province these trigger words were located in order to define a word range that would limit irrelevant context while not excluding relevant context.[12] This word range is partly dependent on the verbosity of the author: in the case of the –very concise– *Taʾrīkh* of Khalīfa b. Khayyāṭ, the most effective word range consisted of eight words before and after the name of the province. More verbose authors such as al-Ṭabarī might require larger contexts.

The Context Search function first runs the Indexer to find all instances of the main search word in the text, setting a word range for the context. Instead of immediately outputting all the search results into a list of page numbers and text snippets, as the Indexer does, the Context Search has an intermediary step: it

11 Al-Maktaba al-Shamela's program allows the user to run a search with multiple search words, which can be connected with AND and OR operators. This is helpful, but the basic search unit in al-Maktaba al-Shamela is the page, which is not the most meaningful unit for textual analysis: on the one hand, the search words might be spread over more than one page, in which case our multiple-word search would not score a hit; and on the other hand, a page contains up to 3,000 characters, which means that it is very possible that the search words, even if they are on the same page, do not belong to the same context.

12 The Context Search could also be adapted to use other types of context range, as described above.

checks whether one or more of the trigger words from our checklist appears in the context. Regular expressions can again be used to account for different spellings of both the main search word and the trigger words and to allow for specific prefixes and suffixes to appear attached to these words but not to other characters. If a trigger word appears in the context, the result is put in the list of final outcomes; if none of the trigger words appear in the context, the result could be put into a separate list of 'probably irrelevant contexts' or immediately discarded. This is an interactive process; carefully checking the output results for irrelevant contexts in the 'relevant' list (and vice versa), and tweaking the checklist and the word range accordingly, will lead to ever better results.

One could also add another checklist of words that signal a context that is very unlikely to be relevant. If we use the Context Search function to look for governors of Fārs, for example, we can put expressions such as *alf fāris, miʾat fāris*, etc. (which refer to cavalry and not to the province) into this list. The Context Search function could then send contexts in which words from this list occur to the irrelevant results list, if no other mention of Fārs is made in the same context.[13]

Finally, the Context Search function can also be adapted so it can be fed with a checklist of main search words instead of only one main search word. For example, in the case of our own research, that checklist might include the names of the five key provinces of our project (Ifrīqiya, al-Shām, al-Jazīra, Fārs, and Khurāsān). The function would then search for information about the governors of all of these provinces at the same time.

The Context Search function is suitable for spotting passages in the sources that potentially contain information about certain topics, so long as these passages can be defined by the presence of specific vocabulary. It could, for example, be used to find information about the prices of certain products in a number of sources. In this case, the main search word might be the term *dīnār* or a checklist of main words that contains a number of currency units, including *dirham*, *qīrāṭ*, and others, together with their plural forms. Another checklist might contain a list of products whose prices we want to know, such as *ḥinṭa*, *shaʿīr*, or *khubz*.

The third function of the Jedli toolkit, the 'Highlighter', marks search words in a text with a user-specified background color. If we want different words to be highlighted in different colors, we can feed the Highlighter with different lists of

13 More checklists could be added, each with different rules for discarding and including contexts. The checklist mentioned in this paragraph's example acts on the main search word; we could, for example, build a third checklist that interacts with the trigger words of the first checklist.

words and apply a different color to each one of them. As with the Indexer, regular expressions can be used to reduce the number of irrelevant results. This function is useful when we want to read through a whole text but pay special attention to those passages that contain a number of keywords that are particularly relevant for our research.

The Highlighter was designed to mark toponyms belonging to the five key provinces of our project in the sources. Each researcher compiled a list of places in their province. These lists were fed to the program, which then produced documents of the sources in which the selected words were highlighted. In the case of toponyms that can apply to different places of the Islamic Empire (e.g., al-Sūs in the Maghrib and in Khūzistān) or could figure in some contexts as something other than a toponym (e.g., Fārs and *fāris*), they were moved to a second list that was highlighted in a different color within the text. A third list was also made, which contains words that often appear in conjunction with words from the second list in contexts where these words are not the toponyms in the province we are looking for (e.g., Khūzistān for al-Sūs, and *alf*, *miʾa*, etc. for *fāris*). This is a process of trial and error: once the Highlighter is run on a text, irrelevant contexts can be spotted in which a specific word is marked. This word can then be moved to the second checklist and these specific contexts analyzed to see whether there are words connected to the search word that signal the context is irrelevant. These signal words can then be added to the third checklist. The result is that one can scroll through a text and identify relevant passages in the blink of an eye, based on the color-coding.

The Highlighter can of course be used to highlight words other than toponyms. It is useful in many of the same cases as the Context Search function, but it can also be used to highlight structural elements of the text in order to make it easier for the reader to navigate the text. In a chronicle, for instance, one could highlight expressions that refer to years or dates in general; one could also highlight words that frequently appear in *isnād*s (e.g., *ḥaddatha*, *akhbara*) so that one immediately sees where a new *ḥadīth*/*khabar* starts.

The output of the Highlighter function is an HTML document that can be opened with any browser. The Highlighter inserts tags around the words to be highlighted, which the browser translates into color. As an additional feature, the program can attach a special symbol (e.g., '$') to every word from the checklists. This symbol is not visible in the text,[14] but it can be searched for, which facilitates reaching those text passages that contain highlighted words. Google

14 In the source code of the HTML document, the symbols are enclosed by tags with the <hidden> attribute to prevent it from displaying in the browser.

Chrome has a useful feature that can be used in conjunction with the Highlighter: when conducting a search with Chrome's built-in search function (Ctrl + F), the browser indicates the location of every search result in the document with a small yellow mark in the scrollbar to the right of the screen. If the hidden symbol is searched for, all sections of the document that contain highlighted words will be indicated in the scrollbar.

The tools we have described above have been made available to researchers in the Jedli toolkit. This toolkit has been released in two forms: one is a set of simple Python scripts that researchers can easily adapt to their own needs by adjusting the code. The other form of Jedli is designed for researchers who are not (yet) willing to interact with programming languages and scripts, but still want to use the powerful search capabilities of Jedli. Its graphical user interface,[15] with its buttons and input fields (see figures 9.1 and 9.2), looks like any other desktop program and does not confront the user with its underlying scripts. On the downside, the program with graphical user interfaces is more difficult to modify and tune to the specific needs of other researchers.

The remainder of this article is intended as an introduction to some of the possibilities that Python and regular expressions offer for the development of tools for textual analysis. It will take the guise of a tutorial on how to build simplified versions of the Indexer and Context Search functions described above. It is not intended as a full-blown introduction to Python,[16] but will build up the argument from very simple operations and explain all pieces of code in a way that should be understandable for people without previous programming experience. All the code examples in this article are available online (https://github.com/jedlitools/find-for-me).

---

15 The graphical interface of the Jedli toolkit is implemented using the tkinter library, which forms part of the standard package of Python. In order to learn more about this library and how to use it, see the following books: Mark Lutz, *Programming Python* (Sebastopol, CA: O'Reilly Media, 2013), 355–767; Bhaskar Chaudhary, *Tkinter GUI Application Development* (Birmingham: Packt Publishing, 2013).

16 For this, see any of the references mentioned by the Python Foundation at https://wiki.python.org/moin/IntroductoryBooks (modified May 24, 2015) as good starting points for learning the language. Especially recommended is Mark Lutz, *Learning Python* (Sebastopol, CA: O'Reilly Media, 2013).

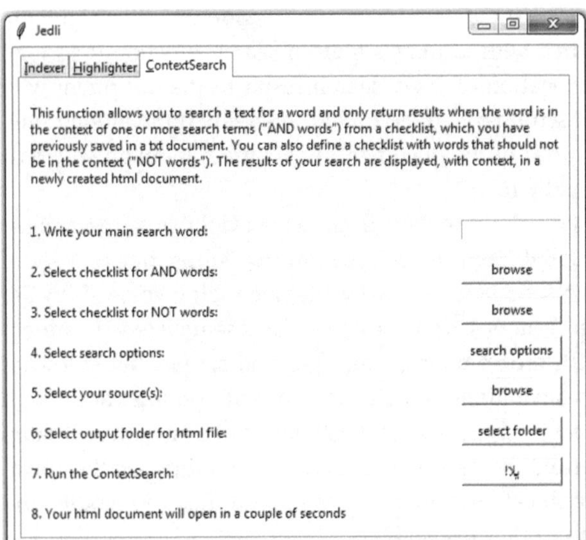

Figure 9.1. Jedli's Graphical User Interface—main screen (February 2015)

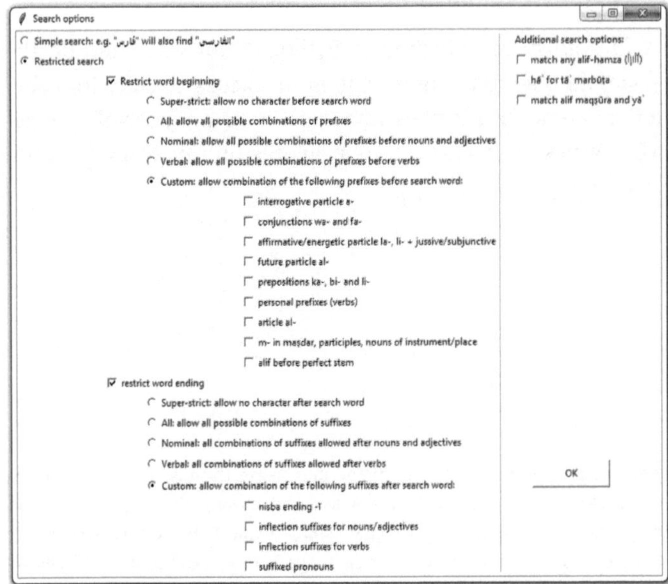

Figure 9.2. Jedli's Graphical User Interface—search options screen

2. Basic Python Operations

In order to use Python, it needs to be installed on the computer.[17] Once Python is installed, we can start using it by clicking the icon of Python's interactive interpreter, called IDLE, in the Start menu. IDLE functions basically like a text editor that assists in writing code.[18]

Once we open IDLE, we have to create a new Python file by pressing Ctrl+n (or using the menu: File > New File) and save it in a new folder. In order to make things easier, we advise placing all the Python files and the texts that we are going to analyze with them in the same folder.[19] For the examples in this article, we will use two texts: al-Balādhurī's *Futūḥ al-buldān* and Khalīfa b. Khayyāṭ's *Ta'rīkh*, which can be downloaded to the recently created folder from the following website: https://github.com/jedlitools/find-for-me. Other texts can also be used for experimentation.[20]

The first step in analyzing a text is 'opening' the text file, i.e., loading it into memory so that it is accessible to the program for processing. Using the "baladhuri_futuh.txt" file as an example, we can open the file with this line of code:

Code sample 1: ex1_basic_funcs.py

```
text = open('baladhuri_futuh.txt', mode='r', encoding='utf-8').read()
```

In this case, we assign the full text of the *Futūḥ* to a variable named `text`, using the = sign. Variables are basically empty memory containers in which values can be stored. Once a value is assigned to a variable in a Python file, we can refer to this variable at any point within the same file. This means that, as long as we keep working within this same Python file, any time we use the variable

---

17 For the Windows operating system, the installation package can be downloaded from the following URL: https://www.python.org/downloads/release/python-340/. Python comes preinstalled on the Mac OS and most Linux distributions. However, it must be noted that in this article we use Python 3.4. In case the reader has an older version, we advise updating it so the code that we will present here is fully compatible. For more on how to install Python, see the webpage of the Python Foundation or Lutz, *Learning Python*, 1421 ff.

18 For more on IDLE, see Lutz, *Learning Python*, 73 ff.

19 If the .txt files are in a different folder, the directory path where the .txt files reside has to be specified so the program can find them.

20 Additional texts can be downloaded from al-Maktaba al-Shamela in .epub format (by clicking on the mobile phone icon). This format must then be converted to .txt format using a converter such as Calibre or the converter that is distributed with the Jedli toolkit.

`text`, we will be referring to the *Futūḥ* of al-Balādhurī.[21] We can name variables in almost any way we want;[22] we could, for example, have opted also for `baladhuri`, `futuh`, or `source` instead of `text`.

`open()` is a built-in Python function that requires at least one argument (the name of the file we want to open, in this case 'baladhuri_futuh.txt') and admits a number of flags (optional parameters). Arguments and flags are written between the parentheses and separated by commas. The two flags that are of interest for us here are the `mode` and the `encoding` flags. With the `mode` flag, we specify whether we want to open the file for 'reading' (`r` – the function is set to this by default) or for 'writing' (`w`).[23] The `encoding` flag is of fundamental importance when working with non-English texts, since it specifies which protocol the function must use to interpret the characters in the text. In this case, we use the Unicode protocol utf-8. Note that the filename and the flags are all enclosed between quotes; single or double quotes (`' '` or `" "`) can be used for this.

The `.read()` at the end of the line is a method of `open()`; it specifies that the program should load the text from the text file in memory as a string object, i.e., as one continuous sequence of characters. Any change the program makes to the text loaded into the memory will not affect the original text in the .txt file, since we are only working with a representation of it loaded in the memory of our computer.

Now the text is available for any kind of analysis we want to perform. To get an idea of what the text looks like, we can print it. Printing the entire text could overload the interpreter, so we will print only a 'slice' of the text:

Code sample 2: ex1_basic_funcs.py (continued)

```
print(text[0:500])
```

This will print the first 500 characters of the text. In order to run the code, hit the F5 button. IDLE will ask to save the changes made in the file first; after clicking

21 This also means that if we open a new Python file and want to work with the same text, we have to load it in memory and assign it to a variable again, as we did here. There is more to this topic than we can cover here; for more information on how variables work in Python, see Lutz, *Learning Python*, 339 ff.

22 Only alphanumeric characters (numbers and letters) are allowed in the name of the variable. No spaces are allowed (use underscore instead). By convention, we write variable names in lower case; variable names should not be preceded or followed by underscores.

23 It also allows for some additional options that do not concern us here. See Lutz, *Learning Python*, 122 ff and the Python documentation at "2. Built-in Functions, open," last modified May 23, 2015, available at: https://docs.python.org/3.4/library/functions.html#open.

OK, a new window (called the 'shell') will pop up, and the text will be printed there.

We use square brackets behind the variable to refer to the position of the characters that we want to print in the text. This is called slicing. Square brackets can also be used to select one single character of the text (e.g., `text[0]` would print the first character of the text); this is called indexing.[24]

Another simple text operation is calculating how many characters it contains; we can do this with this line of code:

Code sample 3: ex2_basic_funcs.py

```
print(len(text))
```

Pressing F5, we can see that our text contains 723,413 characters. Here we have used the `len()` function, which counts how many elements an object contains.

2.1 Basic Search

To check how often a word appears in the text, or where, we have to import the `re` (Regular Expressions) module. Importing this module in Python is as easy as typing:

Code sample 4: ex3_basic_search.py

```
import re
```

Importing modules is usually done in the very first lines of the code. Like variables, once we import a module in a Python file, it remains available as long as we keep working within the same file. If we want to use this module in a different Python file, we must make the `import` statement at the very beginning of our code. Here, we will be using the function `findall()` from the `re` module, which searches for all the string sequences in the text that conform to a defined pattern. In order to ensure that Python can find the function `findall()` in the module `re`, we have to write `re.findall()`:

24 Index and slice notation in Python always starts with 0. That is, the first element of a string or list (or any other indexable object) is 0, not 1. On the other hand, the last index number in a slice refers to the character before which the slice will be cut off: in our example [0:500], the last character of the slice will be character no. 499, i.e., the 500th character, since we start counting from 0.

Code sample 5: ex3_basic_search.py
```
results = re.findall('البصرة', text)
print(results)
```

We store the outcome of the operation in the variable `results`. The `findall()` function takes two arguments: the first is the pattern we are searching for, and the second is the string in which the function should find this pattern. In our case, the pattern is the literal string "البصرة".

The result of hitting F5 is a list of every word that matches the pattern we have set. Notice that lists in Python are always symbolized by square brackets, and that since our list is a list of strings, every instance in the list is enclosed in quotes. In this case, because our pattern was unambiguous, we end up with a list of repetitions of the search word, one repetition for every time it is present in the text. This is arguably not extremely helpful in this form, but we will presently see how we can use the `findall()` function in more meaningful ways. We could, for example, count how many times the word is mentioned using the `len()` function that we already encountered before:

Code sample 6: ex4_basic_search.py
```
print(len(results))
```

This will print the number of times the search word is mentioned in the text. The power of regular expressions shows better when we build less 'literal' patterns, that is, when we use special symbols to build patterns in a more abstract way. For example, the symbol `\w` stands for any 'word character', which means any letter or digit (so-called alphanumerical characters). This allows us to build a rough regular expression to count all the words in the text:[25]

Code sample 7: ex5_list_of_words.py
```
list_of_words = re.findall(r'\w+', text)
print(len(list_of_words))
```

In regular expressions, the backslash is used to escape (i.e., overrule) the default meaning of a character and give it a different meaning. In the piece of code above, the backslash escapes the literal meaning of the letter `w`, and `\w` refers to any alphanumeric character. Some characters have a special meaning in reg-

25 Note that the code samples in this chapter build on the previous code. If the reader keeps working within the same Python file, this should not be a problem. If a new Python file is opened, it is necessary to import the `re` module in the first line of the code and to assign the *Futūḥ* of al-Balādhurī to the variable text again.

ular expressions by default. For example, a dot always stands for 'any character'; in this case, the backslash escapes this meaning, so that \. refers to a full stop. This use of the backslash may confuse the Python interpreter. It is therefore highly recommended to write an `r` before all regular expressions that include backslashes; this signals to Python to interpret the string as raw literals and removes any confusion over the backslashes.[26]

The plus sign signifies one or more repetitions of the preceding token; in our case, it will match any 'word character' until it reaches a non-word-character, which could be a space, a line break, or a punctuation mark, for instance. There are better ways to count words in a text,[27] but this is good enough for a first experimental approach. Our outcome is 179,788 words.

In order to get an impression of how Python identifies words in the text with the `\w` regular expression, we could print a 'slice' of the list of words, for example the first 50 words:

Code sample 8: ex6_list_of_words.py
```
list_of_words = re.findall(r'\w+', text)
print(list_of_words[:50])
```

We have again used slice notation (see code sample 2), in this case applied to a list. Note that on this occasion, we used the notation `[:50]`, which is identical to `[0:50]`. We can transform this list into a set, which is another Python object similar to the list, but which contains only one instance of every element (that is, it eliminates duplicates), and it does not store its elements in any particular order. It could serve as a rough approximation to know how many unique words the text contains (taking into account all the warnings given in footnote 27 about the inaccuracy of the approach taken here for word counting). We do this with these two lines of code:

Code sample 9: ex7_unique_words.py
```
unique_words = set(list_of_words)
print(len(unique_words))
```

---

26 See the Python documentation on "Regular expression operations" on this phenomenon (https://docs.python.org/3.4/library/re.html). On raw strings, see Lutz, *Learning Python*, 196–98.

27 Because the `\w` regular expression matches any alphanumerical character, in this case, we also count numbers as words. Note also that this function does not identify prefixes that are attached to words (such as the conjunction *wa-)* as separate words. For a more accurate approach, use the tokenizer that is distributed with the Natural Language Toolkit (NLTK), as discussed below.

Our outcome is 19,781.

For many research topics, keywords can be identified that allow us to select relevant passages in primary sources. Counting how frequently such words appear in a text can be useful at the beginning of a research project, when we want to select those texts that can potentially provide more information about the topic we want to study. A useful function in this context would be one that tells us how frequently a word appears in a text. The following lines of code do exactly that:

Code sample 10: ex8_word_frequency.py

```
word = 'فرضة'
word_instances = re.findall(word, text)
freq_word = len(word_instances)
freq_word = str(freq_word)
print(word + ' appears ' + freq_word + ' times in this text')
```

Testing this code (hit F5) with the *Futūḥ al-Buldān* of al-Balādhurī, we get the following outcome:

```
فرضة appears 2 times in this text
```

The first thing we do in this piece of code is to assign the string فرضة to the variable word. Then we use this variable in the `findall()` function, in order to search for فرضة in al-Balādhurī's *Futūḥ*, which is assigned to the variable `text`. We also use the `len()` function to count how many outcomes the search returns, and we store this value in the variable `freq_word`. In order to output the results to the Python shell, we use the `print` statement, which in this case uses the + sign to concatenate sequences of strings, including the string فرضة, which is stored in the variable `word`. Notice that the `len()` function always returns an integer (a data type different from string), so in order to be able to concatenate the value of the variable `freq_word` with the other strings in the `print` statement, we first need to convert it from integer to string, for which we use the function `str()`.

We can transform this code into a function so we can re-use it at a later point in the file. The following piece of code shows how to do it:[28]

Code sample 11: ex9_word_counter.py

```
def word_counter(search_word, search_text):
    freq_word = len(re.findall(search_word, search_text))
```

28 In IDLE, lines can be indented with the command Ctrl +].

```
freq_word = str(freq_word)
print(search_word + ' appears ' + freq_word + ' times in this text')
```

Functions are defined in Python with the def ('define function') statement, which must be followed by the name we want to give our function as well as parentheses and a colon. The parentheses can be empty, or they can contain the arguments needed for the function to work properly. In this case, the arguments are two variables, which we called search_word and search_text. These variables are then used in the body of the function: search_word will be the search pattern in the findall() function, and search_text will be the string to be searched in that same function. The actual names of the variables are not important, as long as we keep the same names in the body of the function when we refer to them.

Now we can start using ('calling') this function whenever we need it:

Code sample 12: ex9_word_counter.py

```
word_counter('فرضة', text)
word_counter('البصرة', text)
```

As can be seen in this example, we 'call' the function by writing its name and specifying the variables of the function. Note that the variables in the function call follow the same order as the variables in the function definition: search_word will be فرضة in the first function call and البصرة in the second; search_text will be the text variable to which we assigned above al-Balādhurī's *Futūḥ al-Buldān.*

2.2 Generating an Index

With all of these concepts and tools under our belt, we are now ready to extend the capabilities of these functions so they tell us also where exactly the word appears in the text—that is, we can build a simple index generator.

In order to generate an index, we need to find the word or expression we search for and the page reference. The findall() function from the re module that we have already encountered will serve our purposes for this task well. We have already seen how to find a word in a document using that function. The tricky part in this case is figuring out how to find both the word and its related page number in a single search.

If we have a look at the .txt document,[29] we will see that the pagination follows a very clear pattern, which looks like this:

الجزء: 1 ¦ الصفحة: 263

This pattern is followed throughout the document, and therefore we can describe it in a regular expression: we first have the Arabic word for volume (الجزء), followed by a colon, a white space, one or more digits that represent the volume number, another white space, a broken bar, another white space, the Arabic word for page (الصفحة), colon, again a white space, and finally one or more digits that represent the page number. Digits are symbolized in regular expressions by `\d`, and as we have already seen, the + sign can be used to indicate a repetition of the same token. If we want to express 'one or more digits', we write `\d+`.

If we try to write this regular expression, we will run into a problem with the IDLE editor, because mixing (right-to-left) Arabic and (left-to-right) Latin characters in the code will mess up its display, rendering it unreadable:

```
الجزء: \d+ الصفحة ¦: \d+
```

One solution to deal with this is to assign the Arabic letters to variables and substitute them in the regular expression, using the + operator to concatenate the strings, as we have seen before:

Code sample 13: ex10_index_generator.py

```
juz = 'الجزء:'
safha = 'الصفحة:'
page_regex = juz + r' \d+ ¦ ' + safha + r' \d+'
```

Now that we know how to find page numbers and how to search for words, we need to find a way to connect these two elements. We can do this by including in our regular expression our search word, the `page_regex`, and all the characters in between. Such a regular expression would look like this:

```
search_regex = word + r'.+?' + page_regex
```

As we have seen above, the dot is a special character that matches any character. The question mark tells the regular expression not to be greedy, that is, to stop at

29 We recommend using the text editor EditPad Pro (http://www.editpadpro.com/, only available for Windows) for this, since it can handle large .txt documents better than other text editors.

the first match of the `page_regex` it encounters. With this regular expression, the result of our search would be a block of text that starts with the search word and ends with the page number of the page on which the search word was found. However, what we really want in the final result is just the page number. To achieve this, we add parentheses around the elements of the regular expression we are interested in, which will ensure that only those elements will be included in the list of results produced by the `findall()` function. Because these parentheses 'capture' the elements they contain, they are called capturing groups in regular expressions. The resulting function would look like this:

Code sample 15: ex11_index_generator.py

```
def index_generator(word, text):
    juz = 'الجزء:'
    safha = 'الصفحة:'
    page_regex = juz + r' \d+ | ' + safha + r' \d+'
    search_regex = word + r'.+?(' + page_regex + ')'
    pagination = re.findall(search_regex, text, re.DOTALL)

    return pagination
```

As we have seen before, regular expressions in Python are always strings, and we can concatenate strings by using + signs. Note that the brackets of the capturing group need to be put between pairs of quotes, because they are part of the search regex (short for regular expression) string; the variables need to be outside of the quotes, however, because otherwise Python will consider them literal strings.

This function contains two new elements that need a short explanation: the first is the use of the flag `re.DOTALL` in the `findall()` function. We said before that the dot in a regular expression matches any character, but in fact, it matches any character except a newline, which is represented by the `\n` character in a string. If we include the flag `re.DOTALL` in the `findall()` function, the dot will match anything, including the newline character. The second is the `return` command. Contrary to the `print` statement, which outputs the result of the function directly to the Python shell, the `return` command returns the result of the function (in this case, the list `pagination`), so we can assign it to a variable and use it later in our code. We can now call our new function—adding between its parentheses the two arguments it needs: the search word and the reference to our text—and print the outcomes:

Code sample 16: ex11_index_generator.py

```
index = index_generator('فرضة', text)
print(index)
```

For the word *furḍa*, the `index_generator()` will return the following outcome:

```
['الجزء: 1 ¦ الصفحة: 333', 'الجزء: 1 ¦ الصفحة: 286']
```

In case the word we are looking for appears very frequently in the text, the list of results will look cluttered. It would be better if we printed every search result on a new line. This is easily done with the following piece of code:

Code sample 17: ex12_index_generator.py

```
index = index_generator('فرضة', text)
for page in index:
    print(page)
```

Here, we use a `for` loop. In a `for` loop, the header line of the `for` statement ends with a colon, and the line(s) that belong to its scope are indented. Note that we use `page` here as a variable to refer to every element in the index list, but we could have given this variable any other name. We can read the statement as: 'print every element in `index`'. This is the result if we run the `index_generator()` now:

```
الجزء: 1 ¦ الصفحة: 333
الجزء: 1 ¦ الصفحة: 286
```

Loops are very powerful and allow us to make our index function much more useful in a number of ways. For example, they allow us to search for several words at the same time:

Code sample 18: ex13_index_more_words.py

```
search_words = ['الكوفة', 'البصرة', 'فرضة']
for word in search_words:
    index = index_generator(word, text)
    print(word)
    for page in index:
        print(page)
```

This will make an index for every word in the list `search_words`. We can take this approach a step further. Instead of using a list of search words defined within our Python code, we could write the words we want to search for in a separate file, e.g., a .txt file. This would be especially convenient if we were to handle a large list of words. Such a file can be accessed by Python with the `open()` function we used before (see code sample 1) and its list of words assigned to a variable. For this, we have to open a text editor and write every search word on a new line (without leaving empty lines between them). Then we save the file in the folder with our source file (in our case, the al-Balādhurī text file), making sure we give the file a .txt extension (which is the default in a text editor).[30] We name this document "checklist.txt." The following lines of code show how to access the checklist and build an index of its words:

Code sample 19: ex14_index_checklist.py

```
search_words = open('checklist.txt', mode='r',
               encoding='utf-8-sig').read().splitlines()
for word in search_words:
    index = index_generator(word, text)
    print(word)
    for page in index:
        print(page)
```

The `open()` function loads the entire document as one string into memory. The encoding name in this case is 'utf-8-sig', which is here necessary in order to drop a byte order marker sequence that would otherwise appear attached to the first word in the list.[31] Notice the `splitlines()` method added at the end of the `open()` function. This method builds a list in which each line of the original document is an individual element. Since we wrote every search word on a new line, each search word from our checklist document is now stored as a separate element in the `search_words` list.

We can go even further: instead of indexing these search words in one text at a time, we could index them in a collection of texts stored in a specific directory or folder. For this, we first need to create a sub-directory within the directory in which we work and store in it all the sources in .txt format that we want to index. We call this directory 'sources'. The following code shows how to build an index of all the words contained in the checklist.txt file for each of the texts stored in the sources directory:

Code sample 20: ex15_index_directory.py

```
import os

search_words = open('checklist.txt', mode='r',
               encoding='utf-8').read().splitlines()

for filename in os.listdir('sources'):
    text = open(filename, mode='r', encoding='utf-8').read()
```

---

30 You can download a sample checklist from: https://github.com/jedlitools/find-for-me
31 For more on byte order markers, see Lutz, *Learning Python*, 1201 ff.

```
    print(filename)
    for word in search_words:
        index = index_generator(word, text)
        print(word)
        for page in index:
            print(page)
```

In this piece of code we import a new module, called `os` ('operating system'), which contains a function named `listdir()`. This function builds a list of all the file names in the directory specified as an argument for the function, in our case `sources`. For every file in the list, we first load the text into memory, then print the name of the file, and finally index each of the words from the checklist.txt file (assigned to the variable `search_words`) in that text. Then the program moves on to the next file in the folder, until it reaches the last file.

2.3 Enhanced Search[32]

One problem with searching Arabic texts is that they include diacritics, such as vowels, *shadda*s, and the like, in an unpredictable way. Since these diacritics are represented by separate characters in the text, their presence can sabotage our searches. The easiest way to deal with this problem, if we are not specifically interested in the vowels, is to temporarily remove all of them from the text loaded in memory. We can do this by using the `sub()` function from the `re` module, which allows us to replace one string with another. In our case, we will replace all the diacritics with empty strings (which are coded in Python by a pair of quotes with nothing in between):

Code sample 21: ex16_denoise.py

```
denoised_text = re.sub(r"ó|ó|ȯ|ő|ọ|ọ|ȯ|ő|-", "", text)
```

In addition to the diacritics, we also included the *kashīda* character.[33] As can be seen, all diacritics are separated by the pipe (|) symbol, which in regular expressions signifies the `or` operator. Removing the diacritics from the text makes

32 The discussion that follows draws heavily on regular expressions-related concepts. For further clarification on any of these concepts, see the references mentioned in note 7.
33 The *kashīda* is the character used to elongate (*taṭwīl*) Arabic characters, e.g. in بـــــسم الله.

searching for words and expressions easier, since we do not have to account for all possible vowelizations of the words.[34]

So far, we have used regular expressions in a limited way, searching only for simple strings. This may not be a problem if we search for words that form a unique sequence of characters, like البصرة, but it would not return good results if we looked for a word like حكم. Running the `word_counter()` function that we built before (code sample 11) with the string حكم in the *Futūḥ al-buldān* returns 112 hits. The problem is that these hits also include many potentially undesirable outcomes, such as الحكم, أحكم, أصالحكم , حكمة and so forth, because these words also contain the string حكم.

In order to limit our search results only to the words we are interested in, we need to use more complex regular expressions. For example, if we only wanted all instances for the word حكم, we could use the expression `\b`, which identifies boundaries around the word. The expression `\bحكم\b` implies that no alphanumeric character can precede the *ḥā'* or follow the *mīm*. As previously stated, when we write regular expressions that contain special characters, we have to write an `r` before the opening quotes of the regex string, like this:

Code sample 22: ex17_word_boundaries.py

```
word = r"\bحكم\b"
word_counter(word, text)
```

This returns only 10 results. However, in Arabic, a number of prefixes and suffixes can be attached to a word without actually altering its meaning, so we may want to include in our list of results all instances of the word with those affixes. For instance, if we also want to include the word when it is preceded by the conjunction *wa-*, we can use this regular expression: `\bو?حكم\b`. It will first look for a word boundary, then zero or one occurrences of a *wāw*, then the string حكم, and finally another word boundary. The question mark after the *wāw* serves to make the conjunction optional, that is, to search for the word both with and without it. If we run the `word_counter()` function with this new regular expression, we obtain 12 results (*ex18_prefixes_conjunctions.py*).

If we also wanted to include the prefix *fa-*, we can use the pipe (|) character, which symbolizes the `or` operator, between the prefixes: `و|ف`. To make the presence of the prefixes optional, we will need to group them between parentheses, followed by the question mark: `(و|ف)?`. As we have seen before, however, the parentheses form a capturing group, which means that only the elements within

34 See Maxim Romanov, "Python Functions for Arabic," *al-Raqmiyyāt: Digital Islamic History*, January 2, 2013, available at: http://maximromanov.github.io/2013/01-02.html.

the parentheses will be returned as an outcome. We therefore need to include the prefixes in a non-capturing group, which is formed by placing a question mark and a colon after the opening parenthesis: `\b(?:و|ف)?حكم\b`. This regular expression yields 16 results (*ex19_prefixes_conjunctions.py*).

Building on this regular expression, we can now build an expression that includes all the personal prefixes that حكم as an imperfect verb can have, in addition to the conjunctions *fa-* and *wa-*. Since we can have only one of the conjunctions combined with one of the personal prefixes, we just have to add an optional group with the verbal prefixes after the conjunctions in our regular expression: `\b(?:و|ف)?(?:أ|ت|ي|ن|ا)?حكم\b`. This time, the function returns 22 results (*ex20_prefixes_verbs.py*).

If we take into account that prefixes in Arabic always appear in the same relative order, as shown in Table 9.1, we can build a regular expression that uses optional non-capturing groups to define the most frequent combinations of prefixes. Such a regular expression could look like this (*ex21_prefixes_all.py*):

`\bأ?(?:و|ف)?ل?س?(?:ك|أ|ت|ي|ن|ا|ال|ب|ل)?(?:ال|لل)?(?:إ|م|ا)?حكم\b`

Another approach would be to group all prefixes together in one non-capturing group and to define the maximum number of possible combinations among them by using curly brackets—for example: `\b(?:ا|ن|ي|ت|س|أ|ال|ل|ك|ب|ف|و|م){0,6}حكم\b` (*ex22_prefixes_all.py*). Both regular expressions in ex21 and ex22 return the same number of outcomes (93), but the latter regular expression is approximately 15 percent faster.

Using similar regular expressions, we can also deal with the suffixes. Table 9.2 shows the most frequent combinations of suffixes. In this case, we put the optional groups after the search word (ex23_suffixes_all.py):

`\bحكمي?(?:ت|ا|ي|وا|ات|ن|تم|تمو|تما|تن|تا|نا|وا)?ن?(?:ة|ى|ني|ي|نا|ك|كم|كما|كن|ه|ها|هم|هن|هما)?\b`

As with the prefixes, another approach would be to group all suffixes together and indicate between curly brackets how many of them can be combined at the same time (ex24_suffixes_all.py):

`\bحكم(?:و|ن|ه|ى|ا|تما|ها|نا|ت|تم|هم|كم|ة|كما|تمو|كن|هما|ي|وا|ني|ات|هن|تن|ك|تا){0,4}\b`

Both regular expressions return 19 results.

We could now assign these regular expressions for suffixes and prefixes to variables, which we can concatenate with the search string using the + sign:

Code sample 23: ex25_affixes_all.py

```
pre_all = r"(?:ا|ن|ي|ت|س|أ|ال|ك|ل|ب|ف|و){0,6}"
su_all = r"(?:و|ن|ه|ى|ا|تما|ها|نا|ت|تم|هم|كم|ة|كما|تمو|كن|هما|ي|وا|ني|ات|هن|تن|ك|تا){0,4}"
search_regex = r"\b"+pre_all+"حكم"+su_all+r"\b"
```

Table 9.1: Relative order of prefixes in Arabic

<table>
<tr><th>1</th><th>2</th><th>3</th><th>4</th><th>5</th><th>6</th><th>7</th><th></th></tr>
<tr><td>interrogative particle</td><td>conjunction</td><td>affirmative/ energetic particle la-
li- + jussive /subjunctive</td><td>future tense particle</td><td>preposition li-, bi-, ka-
personal prefixes (verbs)</td><td>article</td><td>participle / maṣdar prefix mu-
noun of instrument / place m-
perfect prefix i-</td><td>[stem prefixes (verbs)][a]</td></tr>
<tr><td>أ</td><td>و|ف</td><td>ل</td><td>س</td><td>ك ب|ل|أ|ت|ي|ن|ا</td><td>ال</td><td>ا|م|إ</td><td>[أ|ت |ن |است]</td></tr>
</table>

Categories in columns one to seven can be combined; prefixes inside the same categories are mutually exclusive.

[a]Since verbal stems are not only determined by prefixes, but also by infixes, we would opt to make a separate search word for every verbal stem we look for.

There is still another problem when dealing with digital Arabic texts, which is that *hamza*s, *madda*s, and *waṣla*s are not written in a consistent way. Since these combinations have their own Unicode representations, they are considered separate characters in our searches. For example, if we search for the word أصغر with *hamza* in the *Ta'rīkh* of al-Ṭabarī, we obtain 43 outcomes. However, the text also contains an additional 27 instances of the word اصغر written without the *hamza*, which did not show up in our list of results for أصغرwith *hamza*.

Table 9.2: Relative order of suffixes in Arabic

<table>
<tr><th></th><th>suffix type</th><th>suffix type Arabic</th><th>combined suffixes</th></tr>
<tr><td>1</td><td>nisba -ī</td><td>ي</td><td>ي</td></tr>
<tr><td>2</td><td>female ending tā’</td><td>ت</td><td rowspan="4">ت|ا|ي|و|ات|ن|تم|تمو|تما|تن|تا|نا|وا</td></tr>
<tr><td></td><td>female ending alif</td><td>ا</td></tr>
<tr><td></td><td>nominal inflection suffixes without nūn</td><td>ا|ي|و|ات</td></tr>
<tr><td></td><td>verbal inflection suffixes without indicative-specific nūn</td><td>ت|ا|ي|و|ات|ن|تم|تمو|تما|تن|تا|نا|وا</td></tr>
<tr><td>3</td><td>verbal inflection final nūn</td><td>ن</td><td rowspan="2">ن</td></tr>
<tr><td></td><td>energetic suffix -anna</td><td>ن</td></tr>
<tr><td>4</td><td>tā’ marbūṭa, alif maqṣūra</td><td>ة|ى</td><td rowspan="3">ة|ى|ني|ي|نا|ك|كم|كما|كن|ه|ها|هم|هن|هما|ن</td></tr>
<tr><td></td><td>pronominal suffixes</td><td>ني|ي|نا|ك|كم|كما|كن|ه|ها|هم|هن|هم</td></tr>
<tr><td></td><td>nominal inflection final nūn</td><td>ن</td></tr>
</table>

Categories in rows one to four can be combined; suffix types within the same category are mutually exclusive so they cannot be combined.

There are two ways to deal with this problem, so that our searches yield all the results we want. One is similar to what we did with the short vowels: replace all combinations of *alif*s with *hamza*s, *madda*s, or *waṣla*s in the text by simple *alif*s, using the `sub()` function from the `re` module that we have already used:

Code sample 24: ex26_alifs.py

```
modified_text = re.sub("أ|إ|آ|ٱ", "ا", text)
```

If we perform this operation, there will be no more combinations of *alif* with *hamza*, *madda*, or *waṣla* in the text, so we would only have to search for اصغر without *hamza* to obtain all 70 results.

Another option is to act on the level of the search word rather than the searched text: we could make explicit that we are searching for any of the *alif* combinations:

Code sample 25: ex27_alifs.py

```
search_results = re.findall("[أآإا]صغر", text)
```

The square brackets in a regular expression define character classes, which will match any of the characters inside the brackets. This regular expression also yields 70 results in the text of al-Ṭabarī.

The *tā' marbūṭa* and the *alif maqṣūra* suffer from similar problems as the *alif* in our texts: sometimes the dots above a *tā' marbūṭa* or the dots under a *yā'* are left out, and sometimes the *alif maqṣūra* is dotted. We can use the same two strategies as with the *alif*s to deal with these problems.[35]

2.4 Contextual Search

We will now show the basics of a search function that allows the user to define the context in which search words should occur.[36] In order to illustrate how we implemented the `context_search()` function of the Jedli toolkit, we will use here the case of Ifrīqiya in the *Ta'rīkh* of Khalīfa b. Khayyāṭ as an example.

The first thing we need to do is to create a new .txt file (using a text editor), which we might call governors_checklist.txt, and save it in the same directory in which we store our Python files. In this document, we have to write down the list of trigger words related to governmental functions mentioned at the beginning of this article, one word in each line (avoiding empty lines), as we did when we created the checklist.txt file (code sample 19).[37] Then we have to load the text of Khalīfa's *Ta'rīkh* into memory and assign it to a variable, just as we did before with the text of al-Balādhurī. We will also remove its vowels so our searches can work effectively:

Code sample 26: ex28_context_search.py

```
import re
```

35 We could replace all instances of the *tā' marbūṭa* in the text with a *hā'* without dots, and all instances of *alif maqṣūra* with normal *yā'* with the following regular expressions:

```
modified_text = re.sub("ة", "ه", text)
modified_text = re.sub("ى","ي", text)
```

If we want to do the change on the level of search, we can use the following regular expressions:

```
search_results = re.findall("البصر[ةه]", text)
search_results = re.findall("مول[ي]", text)
```

36 See above for more on this function.

37 You can download the .txt file containing the list of words from https://github.com/jedli-tools/find-for-me.

```
text = open('khalifa_tarikh.txt', mode="r", encoding="utf-8").read()
text = re.sub(r"ó|ó|ó|ő|ọ|ọ|ȯ|ő|-", "", text)
```

This piece of code nicely illustrates how a variable works like an empty box. Assigning the `open()` statement to the variable text, we put Khalīfa's text into the box; then we take it out of the box to remove all vowels with the `sub()` operation and put the modified version back into the same `text` box.

The next thing we need is to write a function that returns a list of words from the governors_checklist.txt file. The following code, based on what we saw in code sample 19, does the job:

Code sample 27: ex28_context_search.py

```
def search_words(checklist):
    search_words = open(checklist, mode='r',
          encoding='utf-8-sig').read().splitlines()
    return search_words
```

Notice that we use here the `return` command instead of the `print` statement, as we did in code sample 15. Now we have to find a way to connect each of the terms from the checklist with the name of the province we are interested in. In order to facilitate this task, we will search first for all contexts in which the name of a region appears, and then check whether in those contexts we can find one of the words from the checklist. But first, we have to figure out how long the context should be—that is, how many words around the name of the region we should retrieve from the text to make sure that government-related words are going to appear in it, in those cases in which the chronicler is giving information about the governors of the region.

In our analysis of Khalīfa's text, we found that the optimal context length for this consists of eight words on both sides of the search word (the name of the region in this case). In order to define words, we will use a regular expression with a pair of special characters: `\s` and `\S`. The former refers to any whitespace character (space, tab, etc.), the latter to any character that is not a whitespace (which will include not only word characters, but also line breaks, punctuation marks, and the like). Essentially, we are defining words here as sequences of one or more non-whitespaces followed by one or more whitespaces.[38] The following

38 Note that this assumption would not be valid for linguistic analysis, because the definition of 'word' that we use here also includes punctuation marks and other non-alpha-numeric characters.

regular expression would capture a context of zero to eight words around a variable called `region`:

Code sample 28: ex28_context_search.py

```
r"(?:\S+\s+){0,8}"+region+r"(?:\s+\S+){0,8}"
```

Note that we expect the variable `region` to be preceded and followed by a whitespace; for this reason, the `\s` and `\S` characters in the regular expression appear in reversed order on both sides of the variable `region`.

In order to substitute the Arabic word for Ifrīqiya with the variable `region` within the regular expression developed above, we have to take into account that this name can appear under a number of variants in Arabic texts: the *alif* might bear the *hamza* either above or below, or not bear a *hamza* at all; the word might end either in a *tā' marbūṭa*, which might bear the dots or not, or in an *alif*. Besides, it is possible that the word is preceded by a conjunction and/or a preposition. This is therefore a good case in which we can apply the techniques described above to deal with these kinds of situations:

Code sample 29: ex28_context_search.py

```
region = r"[وفبل]{0,2}"+r"[اإأآ]" +"فريقي" +r"[اةه]"
```

Now we can use the function `findall()` from the `re` module in order to retrieve from the text all contexts in which the word Ifrīqiya appears. The following piece of code achieves this:

Code sample 30: ex28_context_search.py

```
def context_search(region, checklist):
    gov_words = search_words(checklist)
    regex = "(?:\S+\s+){0,8}"+region+"(?:\s+\S+){0,8}"
    contexts = re.findall(regex, text, re.DOTALL)
    outcomes = []
    for passage in contexts:
        for word in gov_words:
            pre_all = r"(?:ا|ن|ي|ت|س|أ|ال|ك|ل|ب|ف|و){0,6}"
            su_all = r"(?:و|ن|ه|ى|ا|تما|ها|نا|ات|تم|هم|كم|ة|كما|تمو|كن|هما|ي|وا|ني|ات|هن|تن|ك|تا){0,4}"
            regex_w = r"\b" + pre_all + word + su_all + r"\b"
            if len(re.findall(regex_w, passage)) > 0:
                passage_page = index_generator(passage, text)
                passage = re.sub(r"\n", " ", passage)
                outcomes.append((passage, passage_page))
                break
    return outcomes
```

We use the `search_words()` function we defined above to assign the list of words related to governors to the variable `gov_words`. Then we use the regular expression we defined before in code sample 28 to identify all the contexts in which the name of the region appears. We store the outcomes of our search in the variable `results`. Then we create an empty list, named `outcomes`, which we will presently use to store the final results of our function. After that, we check for each of the passages in the `results` list to see whether they contain any of the trigger words[39] from the `gov_words` list. For this, we have to use two `for` loops—one to step through all the passages stored in the variable `contexts`, and another to iterate through each of the words in the `gov_words` list; an if statement checks if the condition is met.[40] If the `findall()` function finds at least one instance of a trigger word in the passage, we use the `index_generator()` function we defined in code sample 15 to find its page number. We then use the `append()` method to add to the `outcomes` list a tuple[41] that contains two elements: the passage itself and the page number. In case a passage contains more than one of the words from the `gov_words` list, it would be added to the `outcomes` list once for every word, because the `if` statement is performed for each word in the `gov_words` list. In order to avoid this, we use a `break` statement, which will stop the `for` loop that steps through the `gov_words` list as soon as the condition is met once and the passage has been added to the `outcomes` list.

In order to call the `context_search()` function, we have to add the required arguments between the parentheses: the name of the region (in our case, the regex formerly defined and stored in the variable `region`) and the name of the file containing the list of words related to governors. The function will return the variable `outcomes`, which must be stored in another variable (here `governors`) so we can print the results:

Code sample 31: ex28_context_search.py

```
governors = context_search(region, 'governors_checklist.txt')
```

39 We use the regular expressions for the prefixes (`pre_all`) and suffixes (`su_all`) that we developed earlier to include possible combinations of affixes that can appear around the trigger words.

40 On the '`if`' statement, see Lutz, *Learning Python*, 320 ff.

41 A tuple can be described as a list that is locked: it is immutable; its elements cannot be changed. Contrary to a list, which is enclosed in square brackets, a tuple is always between parentheses.

If we print the variable `governors`, we will get a list of all the tuples containing the relevant passages and their page numbers that the function has returned. This output is not very readable. In order to produce a more user-friendly formatting, we can print these values in the following way:

Code sample 32: ex29_context_search.py

```
e=1
for s, p in governors:
    print(e, "\n", s, "\n", p, "\n\n")
    e = e+1
```

We use a for loop to step through each of the tuples contained in the list returned by the `context_search()` function. We assign variables for each of the two elements in the tuple (`s` for the passage, `p` for the page) and print these separately, putting line breaks (`\n`) in between. This is called value unpacking, and it allows us to handle separately the elements contained in a tuple.[42] We can also number the results by introducing a new variable, `e`, to which we initially assign the value 1, and increment its value by another unit for every step in the loop.

The current version of the Jedli toolkit allows the user to undertake contextual searches in this way, although we are currently working on an enhanced definition of context that will allow the user to search for more complex contexts. In the Jedli toolkit, the results are not printed to the Python shell, but saved as an HTML file that we can then open with a browser. In the HTML file, the search and trigger words are highlighted in different colors.

3. Conclusions

This article has introduced a number of basic functions that can be developed in Python as building blocks for the implementation of a fairly complex context search function. These building blocks are also core elements of the Jedli toolkit for the textual analysis of Arabic works. The reader of this article will now hopefully understand the Jedli toolkit code without graphical interfaces and be able to adapt it to their own needs and contribute to its improvement. Alternatively, the reader could use these building blocks to develop their own code for textual analysis.

---

42 This is just an extended way of making variable assignments. For more on value unpacking, see Lutz, *Learning Python*, 341 ff and 396 ff.

Jedli is a basic toolkit for textual analysis, but it represents a first step in the development of more complex tools for more advanced analyses of medieval Arabic texts. One possible direction in the enhancement of Jedli could be to integrate it into existing third-party libraries for Python for complex textual analysis. One such library is the Natural Language Toolkit (NLTK), developed originally by Steven Bird (University of Melbourne), Edward Loper (BBN Technologies), and Ewan Klein (University of Edinburgh).[43] This library includes tools such as a complex tokenizer, stemmers, and several others that allow us to perform lexical or word frequency analysis as well as parts-of-speech tagging, to name just a few. With the help of these tools and a few more lines of code, for example, it is possible to build a simple program that analyzes and measures the degree of similitude between two or more different texts.[44] More specialized libraries are also available that let us perform more complex tasks, such as topic modeling.[45]

Future development in this direction could lead to the implementation of complex analytical tools for linguistic analysis and textual criticism. As a single algorithm can perform the same analysis over and over again through large collections of texts, this approach could allow us to reach a better understanding of the chroniclers' sources, something on which the authors and compilers of the extant text corpus often provided no information. It could also shed light on how traditions were transmitted and modified over time, how words developed new meanings, or how the style of language employed by medieval authors varied according to chronology, geography, or literary genre.

Bibliography

Bird, Steven, Ewan Klein, and Edward Loper. *Natural Language Processing with Python.* Sebastopol, CA: O'Reilly Media, 2009.

Chaudhary , Bhaskar. *Tkinter GUI Application Development.* Birmingham: Packt Publishing, 2013.

de Goeje, Michael Jan, ed. *Bibliotheca Geographorum Arabicorum.* 8 vols. Leiden: Brill, 1870–94.

43 The best available introduction to the NLTK is Steven Bird, Ewan Klein, and Edward Loper, *Natural Language Processing with Python* (Sebastopol, CA: O'Reilly Media, 2009). See also the website of the NLTK project: http://www.nltk.org/.

44 Willi Richert and Luis Pedro Coelho, *Building Machine Learning Systems with Python* (Birmingham, Packt Publishing: 2013), 57 ff.

45 Ibid., 75 ff.

Goyvaerts, Jan, and Steven Levithan. *Regular Expressions Cookbook.* Sebastopol, CA: O'Reilly Media, 2012.

Fitzgerald, Michael. *Introducing Regular Expressions.* Sebastopol, CA: O'Reilly Media, 2012.

Friedl, Jeffrey E. F. *Mastering Regular Expression.* Sebastopol, CA: O'Reilly Media, 2006.

Lutz, Mark. *Learning Python.* Sebastopol, CA: O'Reilly Media, 2013.

Lutz, Mark. *Programming Python.* Sebastopol, CA: O'Reilly Media, 2013.

Python Software Foundation. *Python 3.4.3 Documentation.* Last modified May 25, 2015. Available at: https://docs.python.org/3/tutorial/.

Richert, Willi, and Luis Pedro Coelho. *Building Machine Learning Systems with Python.* Birmingham, Packt Publishing: 2013.

Romanov, Maxim. "Python Functions for Arabic." *al-Raqmiyyāt: Digital Islamic History,* January 2, 2013. Available at: http://maximromanov.github.io/2013/01-02.html.

Joel Blecher

Pedagogy and the Digital Humanities: Undergraduate Exploration into the Transmitters of Early Islamic Law

The present volume has attempted to shed light on how the various methods and approaches emerging under the umbrella of the digital humanities hold great promise for graduate students, faculty, and independent researchers in Islamic studies. This essay goes a step further by arguing that digital humanities projects also hold great promise for instructors of Islamic studies in the undergraduate classroom. Although faculty who teach in other areas of the undergraduate humanities curriculum have been incorporating such projects into their syllabi for years, instructors of Islamic studies have, until now, been slow to follow suit. Although there may be several factors that explain this state of affairs, the principal obstacle for undergraduates in the North American context is plain to see: the paucity of sources in English. While this impediment remains a constraint for all but a rare few undergraduates who have a reading knowledge of an Islamicate language, the recent publication of a number of English translations of key Islamic texts has begun to open the door for digital humanities projects in the undergraduate context.

The present chapter documents one such project on the transmitters of early Islamic law, undertaken by twelve undergraduates of mixed years in an introductory-level survey on the origins of Islamic civilization at Washington and Lee University's Department of History.[1] Students in the course combined the traditional tools of historical inquiry with computational tools to explore, picture, and develop new insights into the political, social, and cultural history of the transmission of early Islamic law. Practically, this meant students undertook close readings of primary sources and critical reviews of secondary literature while also mining data, creating a database, and using online visualization software.

---

1 The course was made possible by a Digital Humanities Incentive grant at Washington and Lee University. I would like to thank Jeff Barry and Brandon Bucy for their assistance and also acknowledge the hard work of the students enrolled in History 171, "Islamic Civilization: Origins to 1500" in the fall of 2014: Jacob Barr, Thomas Claiborne, Amanda Dixon, Rowan Farrell, Alice Kilduff, Zejun Lu, Riley Messer, Lucas Payne, Matthew Sackett, Jerry Schexnayder, Chapman Sklar, Andrew Watson, and Pearson Wolk. Lastly, I would like to thank A.D. Goldman for his advice in designing the project.

The source for the study was an English translation of ʿAbd al-Ḥayy al-Laknawī's (d. 1886–7) biographical dictionary of the transmitters of one of the earliest canonical sources of Islamic law, the *Muwaṭṭaʾ* (*The Well-Trodden Path*), a collection of more than 1700 reports (*ḥadīth*s) attributed to Muhammad, his companions, and the pious transmitters of the following generation.[2] These reports address almost every area of Islamic law, including purity, divorce, offenses, and so on. Biographical dictionaries like al-Laknawī's belong to a genre of writing that emerged in the classical period of Islamic civilization and detailed the lives of these transmitters, in part to allow élite audiences to evaluate the trustworthiness of each transmitter and, by extension, the authenticity of the *ḥadīth*. The compiler of this collection, Mālik ibn Anas (d. 795), narrated each of these reports by a chain of oral transmission to their sources, typically three or four degrees between him and Muhammad, Muhammad's companions, or those who followed them by a generation. As a consequence, Laknawī's biographical dictionary offers biographies of approximately 500 transmitters from the first two Islamic centuries. The entries in this work often include transmitters' death dates and locations of residence or migration, so that *ḥadīth* critics could evaluate whether each chain of transmission was historically plausible. Entries also indicate transmitters' gender and frequently their tribal lineage. Additionally, but with less frequency, some entries reported whether the transmitter was known to have converted to Islam, what their occupation was, and whether they were a partisan (*shīʿa*) of ʿAlī, a companion of the Prophet, a member of the generation that followed the companions, or were descended from a client (*mawlā*, a non-Arab Muslim dependent on an Arab patron). Lastly, entries would sometimes preserve remarks of praise or doubt concerning transmitters' trustworthiness.

The project was intended to show students how to do historical research 'from farm to table' and unfolded in four broad phases: planning, collection, cleanup, and visualization. After I consulted with colleagues and a team of university librarians to plan the project, students worked as a single group to extract data from Laknawī's biographical dictionary and enter it into a master- database they created. They formed several small groups to clean up the data they collected by standardizing transliterations and place names, converting dates from *hijrī* to Gregorian, and so on. Lastly, they worked as individuals to visualize and analyze patterns in the data, placing their findings in the context of the broader

2 See the appendix of Mālik ibn Anas and Muhammad ibn al-Ḥasan al-Shaybānī, *The Muwaṭṭaʾ of Imam Muḥammad*, trans. Abdassamad Clarke (London: Turāth Publishing, 2004), 471–571. The translation was based on ʿAbd al-Ḥayy al-Laknawī, *al-Taʿlīq al-mumajjad li-Muwaṭṭaʾ al-Imām Muḥammad*, ed. Taqī al-Dīn al-Nadwī (Damascus: Dār al-Qalam, 1991).

topics surveyed in the course, such as the transformations brought about by the early Islamic conquests and evolutions in the transmission of Islamic religious and legal authority.

Is Laknawī's biographical dictionary reliable as a historical source? This was a question I posed to the students, and one that created an important teaching moment regarding the practice of history and historiography. After some debate, students were able to justify the merit of the project without fully settling the question of reliability: even if the point were granted that Laknawī's dictionary did not preserve the precise number of transmitters who were women, converts, partisans, companions, clients, and so on, it did preserve a precise number of transmitters who were reported by scholarly authorities to have been women, converts, partisans, companions, clients, and so on. To this end, students would often remind one another that their data did not represent 'converts' or 'partisans', but 'transmitters reported to be converts' or 'transmitters reported to be partisans'. Nevertheless, the outcome still shed light on the construction of authority in early Islamic law.

Since the project was semester-long, the workloads for both the students and the instructor were very manageable. For most of the term, the project felt as if it were running itself, often enriching but never intruding on the broader survey course. Students made a little progress each week, either on data collection, cleanup, or visualization, but still had time to do the assigned readings and write a mid-semester and a final paper. Having support from the university librarians was crucial in keeping the workload manageable for the instructor, and any instructor would be wise to make sure there is knowledgeable technical assistance in place before embarking on such a project.

1. Before Class: Planning the Project

Before students were able to collect data from Laknawī's dictionary, I worked with a team of four librarians to brainstorm what tools would be most appropriate for the project. Initially I had proposed that students use a shared spreadsheet (such as the Sheets application available through Google Drive) to enter the data. In that case, the preparation phase would have simply involved labeling the columns to indicate what information we wanted—name, death date, gender, and a range of other items—and students would have entered the appropriate information directly into the table. This plan could have worked, but it seemed to me that confusion might arise if a number of students were editing the document simultaneously. The librarians and I were also concerned that typographical errors might be more likely to be introduced into the spreadsheet if the database grew unwieldy in size. Our priority was to enable students to devote their focus to reading and analyzing the primary sources, not managing these kinds of technical difficulties.

Brandon Bucy, a senior academic technologist at Washington and Lee, proposed an alternative that avoided those problems. Using a simple HTML design program, Brandon suggested we build an online form in which students could enter the data as if they were answering an online questionnaire. Among other questions, the form could ask: What is the transmitter's full name? What gender is the transmitter? What location of residence was the transmitter associated with? To help streamline the data, each question either had multiple-choice radio buttons or a textfield for a short answer, with examples modeling the desired format of the answer. In some cases, if students did not know the answer to a specific question, they were instructed either to leave the box blank or type 'unknown'.

The data collected using the form could be easily exported into a spreadsheet for students to manipulate later. Since students had to sign in with their university username and password in order to access the form, the other added benefit was that the form would automatically tag entries with the name of the student who submitted it, which was useful for evaluation and grading.

Although the form promised a far easier data entry system for students, it was not without its own kinks. For one, I insisted that the form be able to accept diacritics and special characters (for *hamza* and *ʿayn*), which the form did not accept in its default setting. Brandon solved this problem by enabling the form to accept a Unicode font. Nevertheless, a worry remained: the form could now record diacritics, but would students who had little experience using diacritics be able to input them from their personal computers? To anticipate these problems, we provided links to a tutorial on how to input diacritics on a Macintosh or PC. We also provided the relevant diacritics and special characters at the top of the questionnaire, so that students could work at any computer and simply copy and paste any character they needed.

2. The First Six Weeks: Creating a Master Database

By the second week of class, as students were embarking on their survey of early Islamic history, they were each assigned six to eight pages out of the approximately 100-page dictionary that cataloged the approximately 500 transmitters of the *Muwaṭṭa*ʾ in alphabetical order. Since the length of each entry varied from a few lines to a page, dividing the source up by pages rather than entries or letters of the alphabet distributed the labor of data collection and data entry most fairly. By the end of each week, students were expected to submit a form for about two pages of transmitters, with the goal of finishing their section of the dictionary by week six of the course. Students used the form to record the transmitter's name, gender, and, when provided, death date, alternate death dates, tribe or clan, occupation, and known locations of residences. Students were also asked to collect other identity markers associated with them. With 'yes' or 'no' radio buttons, students were asked to record whether Laknawī indicated whether the transmitter was a companion, a follower, a partisan of ʿAlī, a member or descendent of the *anṣār*, a *mawlā*, or a convert. If they answered 'yes' to the convert question, a one-line textfield allowed students to note the former religion with which that transmitter was known to have been associated. At the end of each entry, students had the opportunity to add any other notes, qualifications, or remarks they thought might be worth recording in the database.

Some class time was required to help train students to collect and enter data correctly. I provided an in-class overview of the basic rationales behind transliteration—the significance of *hamza* and *ʿayn*, the difference between *h* and *ḥ*–as well as common markers of gender, such as ibn/Abū, bint/Umm, and common patterns in Arab *nisba*s. This conversation, while sparked by the digital humanities project, helped to unlock broader themes in the conception of genealogy in classical Arabic culture and taught beginning students how to better understand the names in the scholarly literature and historical sources they were encountering in other parts of the class. Students were asked to try collecting and entering data from one or two 'pilot' entries as homework, so that any difficulties could be clarified during our next class meeting.

One minor problem with the form, which could have been easily rectified but was not, was that students could not confirm that the data they had entered was correct. Technically, there was a way they could search the data they themselves had entered, but this was a relatively cumbersome process. A confirmation page prior to finally submitting the data would have likely reduced typographical errors and other data misfires that would later need to be addressed during the clean-up phase.

Participation in the creation of the database was worth ten percent of their overall grade. Students were told they would be evaluated on their accuracy, attention to detail, and participation. If students produced more than ten accurate and detailed entries per week, they stood to gain extra credit. I randomly sampled students' entries for the purposes of quality control and evaluation.

The data collection and entry phase proceeded with greater-than-expected efficiency. Several students finished well before week six. Although some waited until week four or week five to accelerate their data collection and entry, all twelve students finished on time, and the master database was completed by the end of week six.

Throughout this phase, students would frequently come to class with peculiar and entertaining anecdotes and stories about the biographies of the transmitters they had studied that week. They would just as frequently connect a historical place (such as Kūfā) or a historical figure (such as ʿUmar II) with the same location or person they had encountered through the digital humanities project. In retrospect, these connections could have been made even more explicit, perhaps with a dedicated five-to-ten-minute discussion of an entry each class or each week. After all, these conversations were precious opportunities to connect the primary research students were performing with the secondary historical literature they were surveying.

3. Weeks Six to Ten: Drafting Visualizations and Cleaning Up the Database

After the midterm exam and a short fall term break, I met with Jeff Barry, an associate university librarian at Washington and Lee, to discuss the visualization tools that would work best to achieve the goals of the project. We were looking for something both practical and appealing to students of history. We had corresponded previously to consider the advantages and disadvantages of using the built-in graphing features offered by Microsoft Excel. On the one hand, it was a commonly accessible program, and one which students would no doubt be able to use in other contexts or settings beyond the humanities classroom. On the other hand, Excel had been designed to visualize certain kinds of quantitative data, but was limited in displaying the patterns in networks and relationships across time and space that this data called forth. Inspired, in part, by the "Mapping the Republic of Letters" project at Stanford University,[3] Jeff and I decided to forgo Excel in favor of two on-line visualization tools that held greater promise in visualizing networks, timelines, and maps: Palladio, designed by a

3 See http://republicofletters.stanford.edu, last accessed January 10, 2015.

research lab called Humanities + Design at Stanford University; and RAW, designed by the DensityDesign research lab in Milan, Italy.[4]

Importing the master database into Palladio and RAW was very quick—a simple drag-and-drop or cut-and-paste was all that was needed—but an unforeseen problem immediately presented itself: the data badly needed to be 'cleaned up'. The form, we naively believed, had been designed in a way that would require only minor corrections on particular entries. In fact, there were a large number of cleanup tasks to perform on our database before we would be able to use it.

Jeff attempted to clean up some of the data himself (for example, by standardizing spellings for Medina, Medinah, and Madīnah), but we soon realized that cleaning up the data entailed much more than this. Following our discussion, it occurred to us that it would not only be more efficient to have students work in groups to perform the cleanup, but students could also use the cleanup to learn how to weigh advantages and disadvantages when standardizing certain areas of the database that they would later analyze for their individual projects. Incorporating a data-cleanup activity into the assignment also taught students a critical lesson that we ourselves had overlooked: cleanup was an essential part of any data-collection and data-mining project.

Rather than breaking the students up into groups and arbitrarily assigning cleanup tasks, I took time from one of our first class meetings after the fall break to have students import the raw data into Palladio and RAW, experiment with visualizing the data, and think through for themselves what in our data needed to be cleaned up. Jeff came to our class to introduce the web applications to the students, demonstrate some examples, clarify any questions, and make himself available in the future should students have technical questions. By experimenting and visualizing certain patterns and correlations in the data, students not only began to acclimate themselves to the idiosyncrasies of Palladio and RAW, but they saw right away where the shortcomings in the data were. For example, Palladio's map function did not work with our raw data, since cities had been identified by their historical names rather than by latitudinal and longitudinal coordinates. Students saw for themselves that a cleanup would require them to create a new column in the spreadsheet and add the relevant latitudinal and longitudinal coordinates.

Two other minor issues caught students' attention. First, our data had recorded dates according to the Islamic calendar, but some students thought it

---

4 For Palladio, see http://palladio.designhumanities.org/; for RAW, see http://raw.densitydesign.org/, last accessed January 10, 2015.

would be useful to add a column that presented dates according to the Gregorian calendar. Second, the data collected on occupations had multiple transliterations for *qāḍī* and *faqīh* (judge and jurist) and sometimes listed multiple occupations for the same transmitter, such as *ʿālim* (scholar) and *ḥāfiẓ* (Quran scholar). It was later suggested that, because the column containing reported occupations was so small (forty data points or less), the cleanup group might consolidate particular occupations into larger occupational classes, such as political, scholarly, military, mercantile/artisanal, and miscellaneous.

The stickiest issue involved the column that contained data on tribes and clans. Laknawī's original entries sometimes indicated that transmitters were affiliated with multiple tribes. In these cases, students had entered both tribes in the same column. Likewise, in cases where Laknawī indicated information on both tribe and clan, students included both identity markers in the same column. This was a design flaw in the online form, which did not include multiple textboxes for students to enter tribe, alternate tribe, and clan. This was in addition to the fact that students were already struggling to discern whether the *nisba* was indicating a tribe, a clan, a place name, an occupation, or all of the above. The resulting data was so confusing that many students in the class thought it might be better to leave our tribe/clan column for future generations of students to clarify and analyze. A small group of students, however, inspired to explore tribal and clan identity markers, wanted to take on the challenge of cleaning up the data.

After attempting to construct a draft of their visualization by working through the data with RAW and Palladio for a week, we met again and discussed what cleanup groups were necessary. Students proposed four cleanup groups: dating, place names, occupations, and tribe/clans. Since some of the cleanup groups were more demanding than others, students organized themselves into cleanup committees of two, three, or four. From that class meeting onwards, each cleanup committee would report to me any progress they made or obstacles they faced during the cleanup.

The group focusing on tribe and clan faced the toughest challenge. This small group agreed to return to Laknawī's dictionary, hone their skills at distinguishing tribes from clans, and then reenter data about tribes and clans in different columns. In order to accomplish their task, students sought a reference list in English of Arabian tribes of the first two Islamic centuries, which is the period most germane to the transmitters in Laknawī's biographical dictionary. Students initially attempted to use a list of Arab tribes compiled on Wikipedia, but found the wiki-list to be a jumble of inconsistent transliterations, clans, regions, and time periods.[5] After some consultation with me, students chose to rely on the table of contents of Werner Caskel's German translation and analysis of Ibn al-Kalbī's *Jamharat al-Nasab.*[6] This table, while not comprehensive, contained the names of the key Arabian tribes from the period, divided by those with origins in the North and the South of the Arabian Peninsula. Once students learned to convert Caskel's German transliteration into one with which they were more familiar, they were able to clean up the column in the spreadsheet to provide reliable and useful data on tribes and clans.

4. Weeks Eleven and Twelve: Editing, Revising, and Presenting Final Drafts

During weeks ten and eleven, students crafted and workshopped drafts of their visualizations. They were instructed to present one, two, or at most three slides that visualized the data they collected on the transmitters of the *Muwaṭṭaʾ*. If they intended to present more than one slide, the slides were expected to be thematically connected or suggest a useful comparison or contrast. They were also allowed to choose to use two or three different tools to visualize the same data, if the two tools demonstrated a useful comparison or contrast (for example, a RAW alluvial graph and a Palladio map of the same variables).

In one class exercise, students grouped into pairs to assess one another's drafts in terms of originality, clarity, accuracy, and overall effectiveness. They offered sources and suggestions with which to improve their analyses. Every five to ten minutes they switched pairs, and in doing so, they got to preview, provide, and receive feedback on one another's digital humanities projects. Students paired with me during this time as well, so that I could offer my own advice and suggestions.

In the final week, students were expected to present their final digital humanities projects and field questions from the audience. Typically this was divided up into three to five minutes of presentation and five to seven minutes of discussion. During the presentation, as well as in the final written project, students were expected to briefly address what historical factors they thought best explained the patterns in the data they found as well as any corroborating

5 See "Tribes of Arabia," Wikipedia, http://en.wikipedia.org/wiki/Tribes_of_Arabia, last accessed January 10, 2015.
6 See Werner Caskel, Ǧamharat an-nasab : *das genealogische Werk des Hišam Ibn Muḥammad al-Kalbī*, vol. 2/2 (Leiden : E. J. Brill, 1966), *i*.

evidence in other historical sources. They were told to clearly indicate any inconsistencies in the data or the visualization and to footnote any sources used to collect or explain the data. Students listened to questions and feedback from their peers and then from me. They were able to take that feedback to revise their final projects before they handed them in at the end of the final week. The visualization, written analysis, and presentation was worth 25 percent of their final grade.

5. Sample Projects, Findings, and New Avenues

The first example is an alluvial graph, generated with RAW, created by Jake Barr, a junior at Washington and Lee.[7] Jake sought to compare the number of women and men who were reported to have been companions or followers in Laknawī's biographical dictionary. This was a simple but effective way of tracking the changing status of women's authority in the transmission of *ḥadīth* across the first two generations following the rise of Islam. While RAW was colorful, user-friendly, and good for displaying broad patterns in the data, it did not generate a title or the number of transmitters, which Jake had to manually add using another word- or image-processing program. Moreover, the alluvial graph, while an excellent tool for experimentation and stumbling across unexpected findings in the master database, can be counter-intuitive to read for those unfamiliar with it. The alluvial graph is not the only graph that RAW generates, and it is possible that another kind of graph could have more clearly communicated Jake's point. In future iterations of the course, students will receive greater direction on how to choose an appropriate graph for their findings during the editing and revision phase.

Read from left to right, Jake's graph shows that while men outnumbered women overall (a ratio of 174:25), women's authority as transmitters of *ḥadīth* dropped precipitously from the generation of the companions of Muhammad (a ratio of 81:21) to the generation that followed (a ratio of 93:3). Jake speculated that the professionalization of *ḥadīth* transmission during this period may have played a role in diminishing women's participation, a hypothesis that has been confirmed by recent work in the field with larger sample sizes.[8] By collecting this data and then visualizing it, Jake was able to demonstrate a nuanced point:

---

7 Jake Barr, "Visualization" (presentation at Washington and Lee University, Lexington, VA, December 12, 2014).

8 See Asma Sayeed, *Women and the Transmission of Religious Knowledge in Islam* (Cambridge: Cambridge University Press, 2013), 63–107.

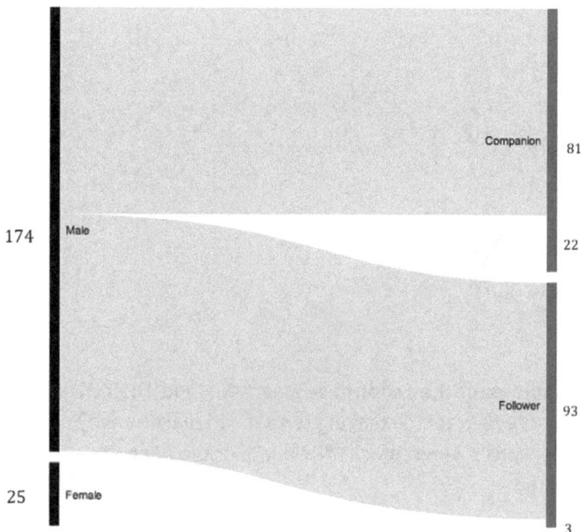

Figure 10.1. The Distribution of Male and Female Transmitters Among the Companions and the Followers. Created by Jacob Barr. RAW Alluvial graph of male and female transmitters who were reported to be companions or followers in Laknawī's biographical dictionary of the *Muwaṭṭa'*. The left side shows the total number of male and female transmitters. The right side of the graph shows how male and female transmitters are distributed among companions and followers.

women's participation, while quantitatively less than men from the outset, was dynamic across time.

Our second example comes from Amanda Dixon, a senior and a history major at Washington and Lee.[9] Amanda was also interested in women who were followers, but she added another variable: place. Amanda used Palladio to generate a graph of followers that displayed connections between the gender of the follower and the places with which they were associated.

In the graph above, Amanda created two nodes in dark grey: male and female transmitters who were followers. The size of the node reflects the relative size of the sample, which is why the node symbolizing male followers is larger than the one for female followers. Next, she commanded Palladio to link places associated with those followers in subnodes, shaded light grey. Amanda observed that male followers were routinely associated with Medina as well as pla-

9 Amanda Dixon, "Gender and Location in the Companions and Followers" (presentation at Washington and Lee University, Lexington, VA, December 12, 2014).

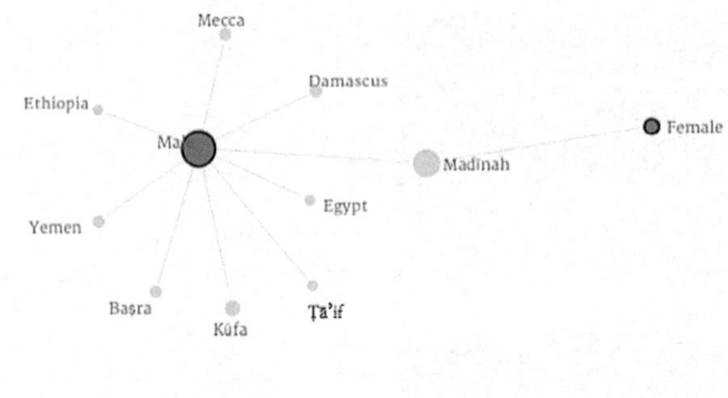

Figure 10.2. Male and Female Transmitters of the Follower's Generation and Their Places. Created by Amanda Dixon. Palladio network graph displaying female and male transmitters who were reported to be "followers" in Laknawī's biographical dictionary of the *Muwaṭṭa'*, linked to places with which they were associated.

ces in territories newly captured by the Muslim conquests of Sassania and Byzantium. Meanwhile, female followers who transmitted *ḥadīth* were only known to have been associated with a single place—Medina. During the generation of the followers, then, Medina was the only city that linked both men and women in the transmission of authoritative *ḥadīth*, at least with respect to the transmitters of Mālik's *Muwaṭṭa'*. Amanda's visualization confirms what recent scholarship has shed light on in larger sample sizes: women's decline in the participation of *ḥadīth* transmission during the era of the followers correlated with social and legal restrictions on women's travel and mobility across the nascent Islamic world.[10]

Our third example was created by Rowan Farrell, a freshman in her very first semester at Washington and Lee.[11] Rowan made use of Palladio's timeline tool to look at the trends in the distribution of transmitters' reported occupations across time.

Rowan had a very small sample size to work with: under forty transmitters in Laknawī's biographical dictionary were reported to have had occupations. Nevertheless, Rowan's visualization suggests some intriguing trends that may provide an avenue of research for future scholars. For one, the most recent death date for transmitters of the *Muwaṭṭa'* who were reported to have held political

---

10 Sayeed, *Women and the Transmission of Religious Knowledge in Islam*, 101–7.

11 Rowan Farrell, "Final Data Analysis" (presentation at Washington and Lee University, Lexington, VA, December 12, 2014).

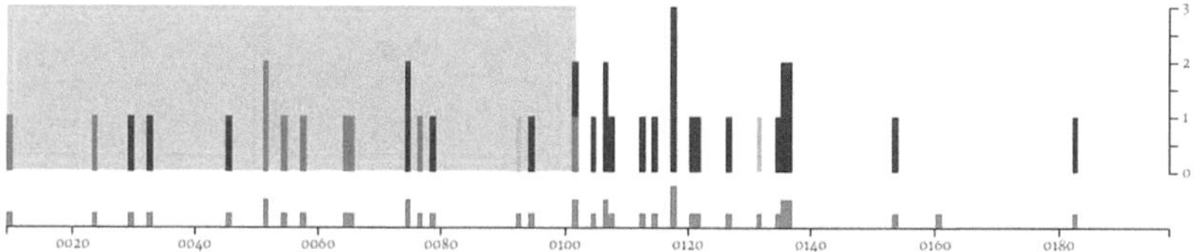

Figure 10.3. The Distribution of Transmitters from Laknawī's Biographical Dictionary with Reported Occupations from 0–185 AH. Created by Rowan Farrell. The darkest grey bars indicate transmitters holding scholarly positions (*qāḍī, faqīh, ʿālim*, etc.). The medium grey bars indicate transmitters who were reported to have held political or administrative positions. The period in which *ḥadīth* transmitters who were reported to have held political or administrative positions lived is further highlighted by the blue or dark grey swath on the left (0–100 AH). The lightest lines represent three transmitters, all of whom were reported to have been merchants, two of whom were reported to have served as soldiers and servants.

or administrative positions is 100 AH, after which point we begin to see the largest clusters of death dates for transmitters who were identified with a scholarly title, such as a jurist (*faqīh*) or a Quran memorizer (*ḥāfiẓ*). Rowan hypothesized that the decline of political authorities as *ḥadīth* transmitters and the rise of scholarly authorities correlates with changing attitudes brought about by macro-political shifts from the era of the 'rightly guided' to the nascent Umayyad dynasty. It is one thing to read about the dynamic relationship between political authority and religious authority in a textbook survey of Islamic history, but it is quite another thing to discover and visualize these patterns firsthand in the data, precisely as Rowan did.

Our last example was created by Alice Kilduff, another student in her first semester of college.[12] Alice's project was more challenging, since it involved tribal and clan affiliations. At its heart, however, her project was an attempt to answer a simple question: With which tribes were *mawlā*s who transmitted *ḥadīth* in the *Muwaṭṭaʾ* affiliated? Alice used RAW to create a Circular Dendrogram to visualize the data.

Alice worked hard with the tribal and clan cleanup subcommittee, so she was familiar with the promises and perils of the data on tribes and their clans. The sample size was relatively small, as students had only been able to identify about a fifth of Laknawī's 500+ transmitters' tribal affiliations. Many clans had been left unidentified. There were also some transmitters whose tribal

12 Alice Kilduff, "Māwla Status and Tribal Identification Among *Muwatta* Transmitters" (presentation at Washington and Lee University, Lexington, VA, December 12, 2014).

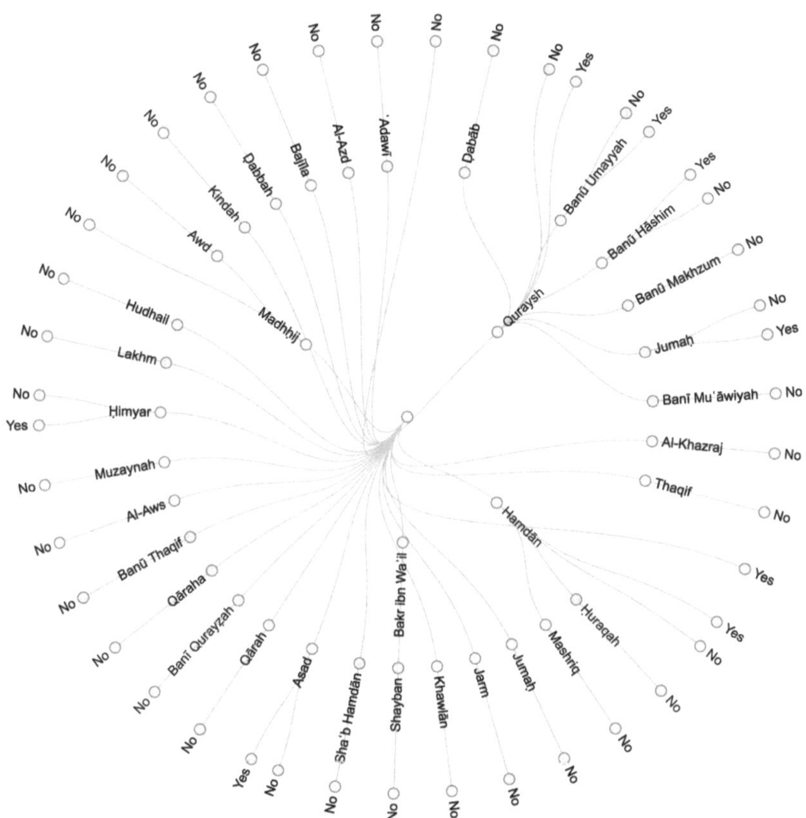

Figure 10.4. *Māwla* Status and Tribal/Clan Identification Among *Muwaṭṭa'* Transmitters. Created by Alice Kilduff. The first nodes closest to the center represent reported tribes. Secondary nodes, if included, represent any known clans or sub-tribes. The outer nodes represent whether the transmitter was reported to be or to be descended from a non-Arab Muslim client of an Arab tribe, called a *mawlā*. Any blank nodes indicate transmitters whose affiliation has yet to be identified.

affiliation was unknown who were identified as *mawlā*. In the end, Alice found that four prominent tribes had patronized *mawlā*s who transmitted or had descendants who transmitted *ḥadīth* in the *Muwaṭṭa'*: the Quraysh, the Hamdān, the Asad, and the Ḥimyar. The Quraysh were the most reported tribal affiliation overall, so it is not surprising to find *mawlā*s and descendants of *mawlā*s among their ranks. Future research may venture an educated guess as to why *mawlā*-transmitters emerged from the Hamdān, the Asad, and the Ḥimyar, rather than other tribes. Nevertheless, Alice's visualization shows how much Laknawī's biographical dictionary has to teach us about the role of status and tribe in the construction early Islamic religious authority.

6. Future goals

In my upper-level course on Islamic law, I once asked students to use Laknawī's biographical dictionary in translation to evaluate the scholarly genealogy of a *ḥadīth* of their choosing from the *Muwaṭṭa*ʾ. Did the death dates appear plausible to them? What was the relative trustworthiness of each transmitter reported to be? Did that *ḥadīth* appear to travel from place to place, or did it stay in Medina throughout its life? The project helped bring alive an aspect of the text students often glossed over—the chain of transmission (*isnād*)—and they wondered whether a larger-scale project could offer insights into networks of transmitters and Mālik's compilatory choices. Such a project could ask even bigger questions: What was the frequency of repeated chains of transmission? Who were the most frequently referenced transmitters of the *Muwaṭṭa*ʾ? How often did Mālik use prophetic reports versus companion reports? What was the average, median, or modal gap in death dates between transmitters? Were certain areas of the law a site of activity for female transmitters? Were certain chapters in the *Muwaṭṭa*ʾ the domain of transmitters with affiliations to a certain place, tribe, or occupation? And yet, how could we answer these questions without poring over the *Muwaṭṭa*ʾ from cover to cover and collecting data on each chain of transmission? Entering data on each transmitter this way would be too tedious, we thought, as many transmitters made repeated appearances.

As I wolfed down a *quattro stagioni* at Crozet's famous pizzeria in Charlottesville, I explained this problem to Aaron Goldman, a friend, colleague, and computational biologist at Oberlin College. Aaron was used to running a computational genomics lab with undergraduates and offered a simple suggestion to make the project manageable. "All you need to do is create a master database," he said between bites. Once a database was created, he imagined, students could go on to perform a larger project, copying and pasting the transmitter's information for each link in the chain they were recording.

A year later, we now have the basic scaffolding of this master database. Future iterations of this course will continue to clean up the database accordingly, build upon it, and repurpose it to investigate some of those bigger questions I outlined above. Future students will be able to study an individual chapter in the *Muwaṭṭa*ʾ, such as the chapter on "Marriage," record its *ḥadīth*s' chains of transmission, and then investigate any patterns that emerge in the links between these chains, including, but not limited to, the following:

- Variation in the gaps in death dates between links in the chain
- Apparent 'movement' within chains of transmission, from transmitters in one location to transmitters in another location
- Apparent 'movement' within chains of transmission, from transmitters of one tribe to transmitters from another tribe
- Variation in the length of chains of transmission
- Frequency of repeated chains of transmission
- Frequency of repeated transmitters
- Frequency of chains with female transmitters
- Frequency of chains with transmitters who are identified as *mawlā*, *shīʿa*, *anṣār*, or convert
- Frequency of chains with transmitters who are identified with scholarly or political occupations
- Frequency of prophetic reports versus companion reports

Once students have collected this kind of data on the chapter on "Marriage," they can then begin to collect data on other chapters, such as "Divorce" or "Prayer," and then compare and contrast chapters with one another. Future projects will also make use of mapping software to track the movement of *ḥadīth* across geographical space or networks of transmitters.

Another area of Laknawī's biographical dictionary that remains to be collected and explored in our database is the matter of trustworthiness. In many entries, Laknawī makes mention of the transmitter's trustworthiness, often by quoting another authority who thought favorably or unfavorably of the transmitter. While this may tell us more about what words of praise or doubt Laknawī chose to include in the dictionary than what Mālik's own choices were in compiling the *Muwaṭṭaʾ*, that data would have much to teach scholars about how often transmitters of the *Muwaṭṭaʾ* were praised and what keywords were used most frequently in their evaluation. We could then take that data to the chains of transmission in the chapters of the *Muwaṭṭaʾ* itself and investigate, for example, whether there is any correlation between the most frequently praised transmitters and other variables, such as tribe, gender, occupation, or frequency of citation.

Digital humanities projects in Islamic studies hold great promise for undergraduate teaching. In some ways, the study of *ḥadīth*, rich with biographical data and networked chains of transmission, is ideally suited for it. As more *ḥadīth* collections like the *Muwaṭṭaʾ* and its appended biographical dictionary are translated into English, more and more data collection and visualization projects will become available to and manageable by undergraduate scholars in Islamic studies. Our hope is that this database of the transmitters of the *Muwaṭṭaʾ*, created by these students and others, may someday be freely available for other scholars and the general public to interface with online. In doing so, broader audiences may discover their own insights into the complex intersections of social life and religious authority that these texts contain.

Bibliography

Caskel, Werner. *Ǧamharat an-nasab: das genealogische Werk des Hišam Ibn Muḥammad al-Kalbī.* Leiden: E. J. Brill, 1966.

Ibn Anas, Malik, and Muhammad ibn al-Ḥasan al-Shaybānī. *The Muwaṭṭa' of Imam Muḥammad.* Translated by Abdassamad Clarke. London: Turāth Publishing, 2004.

Sayeed, Asma. *Women and the Transmission of Religious Knowledge in Islam.* Cambridge: Cambridge University Press, 2013.

Dwight F. Reynolds

From Basmati Rice to the Bani Hilal: Digital Archives and Public Humanities[1]

Basmati rice, a variety of rice grown in the northern regions of the Indian subcontinent, has been a basic foodstuff in that area for centuries, perhaps even millenia. The world therefore reacted with no small amount of astonishment when, on September 2, 1997, the US patent office issued a patent to RiceTec, Inc. (Texas) for "basmati rice lines and grains."[2] The language of the patent was so broadly worded that it brought almost immediate international condemnation. The case proved all the more surprising and ironic when it turned out that the primary shareholder of RiceTec was Prince Hans-Adam II of Lichtenstein. Thus the nominal ruler of a principality of some 35,000 inhabitants, measuring approximately 62 square miles, and with the highest GDP per person in the world when adjusted by purchasing parity, was laying legal claim to a traditional foodstuff from a region that is home to more than a billion people and encompasses over a million square miles. In the face of widespread protests, RiceTec withdrew and/or lost most of its broader claims to "basmati rice," but was in 2001 granted a patent for three specific new sub-varieties that it had developed. Similar patents, however, have also been issued in the US for such basic botanical materials as turmeric (the common spice) and in the European Union for neem (*Azadirachta indica*, the tree from which neem oil is extracted and then used in the manufacture of cosmetics and in many different cures practiced in Ayurvedic and South Asian folk medicine).[3]

One of the most interesting reactions to these events, however, was the establishment in India of an open digital archive of traditional knowledge (the Traditional Knowledge Digital Library or TKDL), which combines the usual archival goals of collection and preservation with a very openly political motivation—to fight off patent piracy ("biopiracy"). It seeks not only to preserve, salvage, and provide access, but also to document and protect, oral culture and traditional

1 This paper was originally delivered as the keynote address at Brown University, at the conference *The Digital Humanities + Islamic & Middle East Studies*, on October 25, 2013.

2 I wish to express my thanks to Sabra Webber, who first called this case to my attention. See Sabra J. Webber, *Folklore Unbound: A Concise Introduction* (Long Grove, IL: Waveland Press, 2015): 116–17.

3 Cormac Sheridan, "EPO Neem Patent Revocation Revives Biopiracy Debate," *Nature Biotechnology* 23 (2005):511–12.

knowledge from a Western capitalist system that seeks to privatize even basic natural materials.[4] This archive serves as an excellent starting point from which to examine both the new capacities of digital archives to preserve oral cultural materials and their ability to play a very public and important role in the arts and humanities. The Middle East and the broader Islamic world are home to thousands of oral, folk, and popular traditions that currently exist in a very precarious state, threatened by the advent of the mass media within their own societies on the one hand and the globalization of culture on the other. Only a handful of these traditions have been studied by scholars, and the results of research conducted by Western scholars often remain completely inaccessible to the societies that created them, locked away in archives and libraries housed in Western universities and museums.

This essay examines the potentially very positive role that digital archives can play in documenting and preserving such traditions, particularly in innovative new multi-media formats, but also imagines digital archives as a way for scholars of Middle East and Islamic Studies to give back to the world the fruits of their research (whether or not this is focused on oral traditions) and a means of playing a much greater role in public humanities. Given the current political turmoil in the region, there is a tremendous need for academics and scholars to help promote cultural understanding and disassemble stereotypes by highlighting elements of Middle Eastern and Islamic culture other than the purely political, religious, or economic images that currently dominate the public sphere. In short, I wish to argue that scholars of Middle Eastern and Islamic studies can and should make more concerted efforts to engage in the work of public humanities in order to reach beyond the narrow academic circles of our fellow scholars and the only slightly broader circle of our students in order to reach and engage a more general public.

1. Digital Archives and Digital Humanities

Within the extraordinarily rapidly expanding world of digital humanities, the lion's share of attention up to this point has been focused on the creation and multiple uses of various forms of databases, textual corpora, and 'big data'. The past decade-and-a-half has witnessed the production of countless new compilations and databases, along with an expanding array of methodologies for extracting new information from them. Islamic and Middle Eastern studies have

4 See http://www.tkdl.res.in/tkdl/langdefault/common/Home.asp?GL=Eng.

not been in the forefront of this movement, in no small part due to the difficulties encountered in developing even such basic tools as OCR for Arabic script, but the impact on the field is growing day by day.[5] The ready availability of 'digitized collections' of texts has already resulted in a vastly expanded capacity to search bodies of texts for specific terms, proper names, and longer passages. Basic tasks such as identifying the author of a particular line of verse or tracing the re-use of a quotation in later works have already become almost instantaneous, instead of taking weeks of painstaking research. The results, however, can sometimes be mixed or even misleading. As we all know, searches for full phrases or less common names and terms are very fruitful (for example, the name of the medieval singer Ziryāb—although his name is also a type of bird, the citations are easily sifted through and separated). On the other hand, a basic search for the highly specialized type of medieval literary collection known in Arabic as a *safīna* is far less useful, since the term is normally used to mean a boat or ship, and only on rare occasions does it appear in reference to 'a personal collection of poems and/or anecdotes'; separating out the handful of significant passages from the tens of thousands of occurrences of the term in its other meanings is scarcely worth the effort, and even a search for clustered or closely occurring terms does not produce much better results. In other words, not all tasks have been greatly simplified or sped up . . . yet.

One of the current weaknesses of these 'digitized collections' that is beginning to be widely recognized is that little care has been taken to use reputable or high-quality editions of the texts that are included, which means that large searches, where researchers do not take (or simply do not have) the time to examine each text individually, are being conducted using an odd amalgamation of texts of widely varying quality. In many instances, it is precisely the odd and less scholarly editions that are being chosen by the compilers of these collections in hopes of avoiding copyright battles. This means that in some cases we are essentially producing highly sophisticated searches of poor quality data. We can only hope that as these collections grow and develop over time, there will also be an increased scholarly voice in the selection of which editions are included or, alternatively, perhaps with the development of reliable OCR, that multiple editions of texts will be incorporated. For more specific studies, of course, the growth of digital archives of manuscript collections is increasingly making it possible to work with greater ease directly from manuscripts, and the increased quality of

5 The recently developed Arabic and Persian OCR by Sakhr Software is perhaps poised to fill this gap.

visual reproduction of digital copies of manuscripts is also a very real boon to researchers.

Digital *archives*, on the other hand, in addition to providing access to data such as texts, also offer new dimensions in multi-media presentation that are exciting for a wide array of fields ranging from history to music, the visual arts, and beyond. Here, digital archives are not just accomplishing more rapidly work that could previously have been done, albeit painstakingly, by hand; they are providing entirely new means of displaying, consuming, and analyzing data through innovative combinations of text, sound, and images.

2. A Brief History of 'Enhanced Texts'

The impulse to enhance the written word with images is nearly as old as the development of writing itself, as can been seen in ancient Egyptian tombs and Babylonian inscriptions, and has never ceased to exist—witness the various Islamic and European traditions of embellishing written texts with miniature images to produce 'illuminated' manuscripts. These texts, however, were in the past each individually produced by hand and were therefore extremely expensive and circulated within a very limited readership. Remarkably soon after Johannes Gutenburg invented movable type, the first printed book with images appeared. It is an edition of a poetic narrative by Johannes von Tepl (c. 1350–c. 1415) composed in 1401 and known either as *Der Ackermann aus Böhmen* (*The Ploughman of Bohemia*) or *Der Ackermann und der Tod* (*The Ploughman and Death*), which was published in 1460 or 61 by Albrecht Pfister (c. 1430–c. 1466) in Bamberg.[6] The illustrations are rather crudely carved woodcuts that then had to be hand colored, but they laid the foundation for the later development of more sophisticated woodcuts, engravings, and copperplate etchings, followed by lithography and the entire tradition of what we now refer to as 'illustrations', derived from the Latin verb for 'to enlighten'.

The first book to be illustrated with photographs was published in 1843 by one of the earliest (perhaps *the* earliest) female photographers, Anna Atkins (1799 – 1871).[7] Using a type of photographic image-making called cyanotype (similar to that used in creating architectural 'blueprints'), which had been invented

6 Marion E.Gibbs, "Der Ackermann aus Böhmen," *The Literary Encyclopedia*, first published 13 July 2004, available at: http://www.litencyc.com/php/sworks.php?rec=true&UID=16326, accessed January 10, 2015.
7 Martin Parr and Gerry Badger, *The Photobook, a History, Volume I* (London: Phaidon, 2004).

only one year earlier, she produced and published volumes with images from her botanical collection of seaweeds, ferns, and other plants. Her efforts were soon imitated by others, and in 1874 Julia Margaret Cameron published the first book in which photographs were used to illustrate a narrative—*Idylls of the King*, by Alfred Lord Tennyson—a retelling of the King Arthur cycle, one of Cameron's favorite photographic themes.[8] From there, of course, increasingly sophisticated combinations of printed texts and images have emerged, including books composed entirely of photographs, comic books, manga, and new cross-media productions.

To this history of various different combinations of images and written texts can also be added the history of recorded sound, beginning with Edison's wax cylinders, through the various formats of the early recording industry, 'long play' vinyl recordings (LPs), cassette and 8-track tapes, CDs, and now digital recordings. Attempts to combine visual texts with audio-recordings, however, have been somewhat more isolated and more haphazard, but began almost as early as the film industry itself. One of the best known and most successful of these efforts was the "Follow the bouncing ball" technique invented by Fleischer Studios (the creators of "Betty Boop") for use in their "Song Car-tune" films. These animated short films allowed audience members in theaters to sing along with the soundtrack by keeping them in rhythm with a "ball" (originally a light on the end of a stick) that "bounced" over the lyrics as they appeared on screen.[9] The first film to feature the "Follow the bouncing ball" technique with a soundtrack was *My Bonnie Lies over the Ocean*, released on September 15, 1925—an early predecessor of the thousands of modern videos that combine audio-recordings and lyrics, now available on YouTube and elsewhere, as well as the antecedent of subtitled films of all sorts that combine image, sound, and text in a variety of manners.

These various impulses to 'enhance' written text with images and sound are now converging with the new capacity of digital and online productions. In what follows, I examine a single digital archive, not at all as an example of 'cutting edge' technology (indeed, quite the opposite), but in order to derive some lessons from mistakes made in the past and to ruminate a bit on how these new presentational modes might enrich our understanding of certain oral traditions that are, in their original form, very much living combinations of language, image, and sound.

---

8 Joanne Lukitsch, *Julia Margaret Cameron* (London: Phaidon, 2001); Julian Cox and Colin Ford, *Julia Margaret Cameron: The Complete Photographs* (Los Angeles: Getty Publications, 2003).
9 See Leslie Cabarga, *The Fleischer Story* (Boston: Da Capo Press, 1988).

3. Digital Archives: One Example

The digital archive project described here is in no manner at the forefront of recent developments in terms of its technology, but it can serve here as a starting point for a discussion about the digital future for archives, databases, textual corpora, and even new forms of data that we can scarcely imagine today. It might also serve as an example of what might—and even must—be done to save massive amounts of audio, visual, and ethnographic materials that are becoming technologically obsolete at a frightening rate.

The Sirat Bani Hilal Digital Archive (www.siratbanihilal.ucsb.edu) at this point exclusively contains materials that I personally collected during fieldwork conducted in Egypt in the 1980s and 1990s (1982–83, 1986–87, 1988, and 1995).[10] The audio recordings were made with a Sony Walkman Professional, a model that was first introduced in 1982, but to which Dolby C noise reduction was added in 1984. That development quickly made the Walkman Professional the most widely accepted substitute for the very large, heavy, and unwieldy Nagra tape recorders that had been the most reliable tool of ethnographic fieldworkers since the 1950s. In particular, the Sony Walkman Professional could be run from AA batteries, which was an extraordinary advantage when conducting fieldwork in areas that did not have reliable sources of electricity, or any electricity at all. The cassettes used during my 1986–87 and 1988 fieldwork trips were top-of-the-line Maxell and BASF Type II High Chromium tapes. In other words, I was fortunate enough to have what was, at that time, the best portable equipment available.

The subject of my research was the Arabic oral epic poem *Sīrat Banī Hilāl,* the epic of the Bani Hilal Bedouin tribe. I was inspired by the examples of Milman Parry and Albert Bates Lord, who conducted fieldwork on Serbo-Croatian oral epic performances in the former Yugoslavia in the 1930s and the 1950s, as well as by a number of scholars who had previously worked on different regional traditions of *Sīrat Banī Hilāl*, including ʻAbd al-Hamid Hawwas, ʻAbd al-Rahman Ayoub, Susan Slyomovics, and others.[11] The fields of folklore and performance

---

10 The materials in the archive were collected, transcribed, and later digitized with the support of grants from Fulbright-Hays, the American Research Center in Egypt, the Harvard Society of Fellows, the National Endowment for the Humanities, the American Council of Learned Societies, and the College of Letters and Sciences of the University of California, Santa Barbara.

11 See Albert B. Lord, *The Singer of Tales* (Cambridge, MA: Harvard University Press, 1960; 2nd ed., 2000); and Susan Slyomovics, *The Merchant of Art: an Egyptian Hilali Oral Epic Poet in Performance* (Berkeley: University of California Press, 1988).

studies had by that time pushed fieldworkers away from the simple collection of texts, a venture that saw the 'text' as being the sole object of study, and had instead moved towards studying oral traditions in context and, more specifically, 'in performance'. This implies not only carefully recording the context of a given performance, but also the exploration of how performers and listeners themselves interpret these events, rather than relying entirely on how the outside researcher understands them. Central to this endeavor, however, is also a recognition that the 'texts' are in fact constantly changing, constantly emerging from a particular interaction between a performer and those present at a specific moment in time, and that the variations from one performance to another are critical to understanding the 'text' itself. This quality has been termed by some scholars the 'emergent' aspect of oral traditions—they emerge in a unique form from a unique social dynamic that cannot later be precisely replicated.[12]

These new concerns led fieldworkers of my generation to record performances not just once, but as many times as possible—from different performers, from the same performers in different settings with different audiences, and so forth. These methods were pioneered by Parry and Lord in their work, and by the 1970s and 80s had become standard practice among folklorists and other ethnographic researchers. The goal had changed from the capturing, editing, and publication of an authoritative version of a 'text' to the study of performances and examining how variations in the 'text' are situated in social contexts.

To put all of this in terms of a different mode of scholarship, folklorists of the nineteenth and early twentieth centuries saw variations in 'texts' much the way we view the manuscript tradition of a single work. The various 'manuscripts' (e.g., folktales, proverbs, ballads, and so forth) were to be compared, a stemma was proposed, and eventually a 'complete' edition was published, using one of several possible modes of annotating the textual variants. This approach understood the transmission of oral traditions as similar to the process of copying manuscripts and viewed variations as the product of 'errors' such as lapses of memory. In the late twentieth century, however, the focus shifted to studying the variations in the texts and posing questions about why that variation had taken place in that particular time and place. In other words, each performance came to be seen as a 'retelling' of traditional materials in which the performer recreates the 'text' according to who the audience is. Let me give a brief example to demonstrate why this process is significant.

---

12 See, for example, Richard Bauman, *Verbal Art as Performance* (Rowley, MA: Newbury House Publishers, 1978).

In the middle of the Bani Hilal epic, there is a famous episode called *'Azīza wa-Yūnus*, in which the beautiful princess 'Aziza attempts to seduce the extraordinarily handsome Yunus, a young warrior of the Bani Hilal tribe, by slowly revealing more and more of herself to him, while he, Galahad-like, struggles to resist her charms. Since both of the protagonists are known for their good looks, this scene allows epic singers to use all of their metaphorical talents in the description of male and female beauty. In a wedding performance with a rather large (and rambunctious) audience that consisted of men, women, and children, one singer began his description of 'Aziza by noting that her head was small and dainty as that of a turtle dove, her neck like a silver chalice in the hand of a sultan, the tresses of her hair as thick as dates ripening on a palm tree, her eyes were like almonds, her cheeks like roses, her lips like cherries, her breasts like pomegranates—a veritable greengrocery of love! All of these metaphors are of course perfectly acceptable for a mixed audience, but the description stopped at her "pomegranates." In a private performance for a group of young men, however, the same poet started at the princess's feet, which were as small and dainty as those of a turtle dove, above which were legs that as were smooth and white as the marble of ancient Roman columns, so pale that one could see her veins like the dark veins in marble, and these two columns supported a "garden" in which there was a "fountain;" her belly had folds as smooth as bolts of silk in a silk merchant's shop, and her navel was like a silver chalice in the hand of a sultan, and so forth, using images that were much more lascivious than his earlier performance, and which (as intended) produced whoops of knowing laughter from his young male listeners. Finally, I have also heard a version of this same scene in which the poet was performing before an audience that included mostly old men, and in which he turned each verse into a joke, along the lines of: "Her eyelashes struck his heart like arrows . . . little did he know that she would soon by striking him on the head with her slippers!" (In Egypt, the ultimate image of the hen-pecked husband is one whose wife beats him with her *shibshib* house-slippers.) The details and the tone of these performances were entirely different, though it is easy to see how some images were transformed from one event to the next; but the scene as a structural unit (i. e., the description of 'Aziza) remained in place. None of these versions is more 'correct' or closer to the 'original'. Instead, folklorists have demonstrated, as did I in my research, that this living, changing quality of oral performance is one of the most important qualities of 'traditional' materials. It is the dynamic nature—the 'emergent' quality—that brings audience members to listen to performances time and again.

This focus on variation, however, posed quite a problem for researchers at a time when the standard mode of publishing their materials was print. Unless the text in question was quite short, it was difficult to imagine publishing multiple versions of texts side by side or even collected into a volume. Since a full performance of the Bani Hilal epic by a master poet can run well over 100 hours, publishing several different versions in print was quite simply impossible. And to publish a single text with extensive footnotes glossing the many different variations (as we do with manuscript variations) would also have produced enormous, unwieldy works that would have been nearly impossible to read as poetry (my few attempts with short passages produced texts that resemble commentaries on the Muʿallaqa of Imruʾ al-Qays, where a single verse of poetry appears at the top of the page followed by an entire page of footnotes and explanations, a format that, as many of us discovered as students, is not at all conducive to introducing the reader to a masterpiece of oral literature!). The only functional solution at that point in time seemed to be to publish one version of the epic as sung by a single poet, with perhaps some limited documentation regarding variations in the footnotes, or with a small number of examples in the introduction.

With that goal in mind, I began the painstaking task of typing up handwritten field transcriptions into an Arabic text in 1988. Being young and brave (and perhaps rather foolhardy), I chose not to type my texts on an Arabic typewriter, but to jump into the very new realm of Arabic 'word-processing'. The choices at that point in time, however, were very limited. Microsoft Word had not yet developed a program that could handle Arabic script, and Nisus Writer, which was developed for Apple Macintosh, was not put on the market until 1989. For users of PCs, the top choice was *Al-Kaatib,* a program developed by Nels Draper of Eastern Language Systems originally for Apple Macintosh and then adapted to Windows as *Al-Kaatib al-duwali.* I remember reading a number of very positive reviews of the program that convinced me that this was indeed the way of the future. Over a period of months, using the *Al-Kaatib* program, I typed out over 50 hours of oral epic performance.

Since approaching these 'texts' as performance put great emphasis on audience interaction, I began by including all audience comments in brackets where they occurred in the text, as in the following example. Here, the young boy, Barakāt, the future Abū Zayd al-Hilālī, is about to fight his first battle against a king of the ʿUqayla tribe, who has wrongfully taken livestock from his mother, Khaḍra al-Sharīfa, as tribute. As is typical for epic battles, the opponents first face off and engage in a battle of words, and in this case, since Barakāt is black and still a child, his opponent mistakes him for a slave and insults him in a variety of ways. The poet is Shaykh Ṭāhā Abū Zayd (d. 1988) of the village of al-Bakātūsh, Egypt:

[Barakāt says] "My greetings to the tribes, my greetings to the Arabs,
    And the best of my greetings is to the King who is with them."

[The King] said to him, "Greetings, my son, two thousand welcomes,
Whose slave are you among the princes?
[Laughter]
Whose slave are you that your master has dandied you up,
And dressed you in such clothing, O so fine!"
"I am ʿAzrāʾīl [the angel] of Death . . .
[Laughter]
. . . for the ʿUqayla tribe,
[Voice: Allah!]
Come to snatch your souls by the will of God!
You, you have [rightful] tribute which you shall take, complete in its reckoning . . .
[Listener offers poet a cigarette]
[Shaykh Ṭāha: May God increase your goodness!
May your prosperity continue!]
You, you have [rightful] tribute which you shall take, complete in its reckoning,
[But] the seizing of this livestock, Our Lord God does not approve."
He said to him, "Boy, go to your mother so she can suckle you!
[Laughter]
I am no *faqīh* that I should teach [a child] the Word of God."
He said to him, "The weight on the steelyard is pretty and small,
But it balances the biggest of loads!"[13]

Since the audience members know full well who is going to come out ahead in the ensuing battle, they take this exchange of taunts as a bit of comic relief, relishing the image of this small black child who will turn the tables and humble the proud and powerful king. And it is not coincidental that it is at this point that a listener leans forward and places a cigarette in front of the singer in appreciation, which the poet acknowledges and then repeats half of a verse to maintain the flow of the performance.

This technique of including all of the interaction with the audience provides some sense of the dynamics of the performance and allows us to get a glimpse of the tone of the moment from the audience's laughter and, in other places, angry outbursts. But it also lengthens the printed text enormously (no matter how it is formatted) and makes it, quite frankly, more difficult to read. I eventually made the decision to keep all of the audience reactions in the text only in the first episode (about five-and-a-half hours of performance), but in the rest of the text to include only the most dramatic interjections.

13 The steelyard is a common form of scale in the Egyptian countryside, used to weigh in crops at harvest time. The long metal arm is mounted such that even heavy loads can be balanced with a small metal counterweight, referred to as a "pomegranate" (*rummāna*).

At this point the American academic system intervened. I was a tenure-track junior professor, and I was given the advice, which many of you also may have been given, *not* to try to publish the edited text and translation until after tenure, since, in the United States, that type of scholarship is not given the same weight as a scholarly monograph. So I set aside the work of transcribing, translating, editing, and formatting, and instead devoted myself to getting a monograph published.[14] That task completed, I applied for and received a National Endowment for the Humanities fellowship (1994–95) and turned back to my texts. One major problem was that the formatting capacity of the first versions of *Al-Kaatib* was quite primitive, and the texts still needed a lot of work to make them visually polished enough to be publishable. At that point, however, I discovered that the *Al-Kaatib* program had been entirely overtaken by Microsoft Word's Arabic editing program. No updates of *Al-Kaatib* were being produced, and eventually Eastern Languages Systems disappeared. There was also no method for converting *Al-Kaatib* files to Word, there was no OCR program for Arabic, and even if these texts were to be produced as a 'camera ready' desktop publication in *Al-Kaatib*, they would forever be frozen in an obsolete format and rendered inaccessible. In order to migrate these texts forward into a format that would survive, there seemed to be no option other than to re-type all of the texts by hand into Word. At least at this stage, since the texts were already typed and no longer in hand-written transcriptions, the work could be handled by anyone with decent Arabic typing skills, but still, several hundred more hours of labor went into the conversion process.

Why is it worth reviewing this bit of 'ancient history' from the Pleistoscene of the digital era? I do so to remind all of us, myself included, that at any one moment, we cannot know whether the program, platform, or format that we are choosing to use is one that will have a long, successful run in the future or, instead, will soon be eclipsed by a newer, better, faster, more compact technology. We can only be sure that that leap forward will indeed happen at some point in the future, sooner or later. When it does occur, we cannot know in advance whether the data we have so painstakingly preserved in one form will be easily or only with great difficulty migrated to the next. It is no longer likely that such a basic function as the production of text will be caught up in the driving forces of obsolescence to such an extent that large bodies of texts become irretrievable, if only because external programs such as OCR will eventually make their conversion possible. But it seems very likely that, of the many different programs we

14 *Heroic Poets, Poetic Heroes: The Ethnography of Performance in an Arabic Oral Epic Tradition* (Ithaca: Cornell University Press, 1995).

are now experimenting with for global positioning, mapping, big data analysis, etc., only a limited number of survivors will still be with us even a few short years from now, let alone a few decades into the future.

One the most significant of the special collections at the University of California, Santa Barbara, the wax cylinder collection of early sound recordings provides a rather remarkable example of this principle.[15] Not only does the collection contain thousands of wax cylinders produced in the Americas and in Europe, but also some of the earliest known recordings from the Middle East. A visit to the physical premises of the collection is also a trip to a museum-like collection of late nineteenth- and early twentieth-century cylinder machines designed to record and play an astonishing number of different sizes and types of cylinders. Not only were various companies competing for markets by creating machines that played only their own specially designed cylinders of a size and shape that would not fit other machines, but even the same company over time produced new models of cylinders and players that rendered older models obsolete. The same dynamic that drives new versions of Word and the incessant upgrades of many different computer programs in our day was already in force over a hundred years ago. But the somewhat chilling lesson of the wax cylinder collection is that it is not enough to have preserved the cylinders themselves; one must also have preserved the 'hardware', the specific model of recorder and/or player that allows those cylinders to be played. For us in modern times, in many cases, it will not be enough to save only our data, but it will also be necessary to preserve a combination of the hardware and software that will allow that data to remain accessible and manipulable in the future. We have only to think of 'floppy discs' to realize how crucial this is.

To return to the construction of the *Sirat Bani Hilal Digital Archive*, the newly edited Arabic texts, now in Arabic script in Word, by the mid-1990s had been produced and were ready to be published in print. This simply did not happen. The project was too large (the combined Arabic texts, notes, and English translations totalled close to 2,000 pages) and the projected readership too small. For a number of years, it seemed like the answer might be to release the texts in CD-ROM format, but in this case, it is probably a good thing that the proposal to do so was never funded. Finally, in the mid-2000s, the new horizons of stable digital archives began to open up and funding sources began to appear. In 2007 I applied for and received an American Council for Learned Societies (ACLS) "Digital Innovation" grant to digitize the audio-recordings and photographs, upload the

15 See http://cylinders.library.ucsb.edu/.

texts in both Arabic script and English translation, and create the *Sirat Bani Hilal Digital Archive.*

The components of the proposal that were perhaps most compelling included the fact that the original cassette tapes, now some twenty years old, were fast reaching the end of their physical functionality. Although 'safe copies' had been deposited both in Cairo, Egypt, and in the Milman Parry Collection of Oral Literature at Harvard University, the original copies were now in peril. The proposal also included, however, a few elements that were, at least back in 2007, rather innovative. One of these was that the Arabic transcriptions and English translations would be constantly amended according to comments by readers. When readers found a mistake in the Arabic transcription or could suggest a more accurate English translation, these ideas could be submitted via the comment function. Ideally, this meant that in a limited sense the continuous correction and improvement of the texts would be 'crowd-sourced'. Another feature was the creation of what we termed a "virtual performance," in which viewers would hear the audio recording and both the Arabic text and the English translation would appear visually, on-screen, synchronized with the recording such that the viewer/listener, in both Arabic and English, would have a sense of the pace of a living performance and could hear and understand both the text and the audience interjections, rather than rapidly skimming through a written text. In addition, the primary materials—the audio-recordings, the Arabic texts, and the English translations—would be supplemented by historical materials—extracts from my fieldnotes as well as photographs of the poets, the village, and performances.

Perhaps the trickiest element of putting together the proposal was obtaining institutional commitment to house and preserve the archive and later to migrate it forward to new technologies as necessary (a requirement for the application). At that time, there were only a handful of other digital projects that were housed within our university library. Although there were other ongoing digital projects at that time—some by notable pioneers in the field, such as Alan Liu, Patricia Fumerton, and Rita Raley—these were still maintained privately by individual researchers or, in some cases, on computers and hard-drives within departmental offices. An archive, in contrast to a database or collection of text, has as one of its primary goals the preservation of materials for the future—that is, beyond the lifetime of the creator(s) of the archive. And even today, it is still sometimes difficult to get an institution to take on the perpetual maintenance of such a collection; I have come across a number of cases of young scholars moving to new institutions and encountering a variety of obstacles when attempting to find institutional homes for digital archives. This, however, will presumably become more common and simpler in the future as the relevant technology becomes more widespread. I should note that the difficulty is more often in getting the host institution to make a commitment to maintain the archive in perpetuity and eventually to migrate it forward to new technologies as required to maintain accessibility. Without such commitments, the digital archives of today are threatened with the possibility of becoming no more accessible than the boxes of 'personal papers' housed in the special collections sections of our libraries.

I was fortunate enough to have the full support of our university library (although even now, eight years later, there are still some issues to be resolved), and so we could begin the actual work of building the archive itself. The current archive was constructed using Drupal, and the video features were created in Quicktime. In hindsight, these might not have been the wisest choices, but these plans were put together in 2007, at least two generations ago in terms of technological advances. The original goal was to have the Arabic texts in HTML, so that changes and corrections could be made simply and directly. However, we were not able to accomplish this, and as a result, and in order to get an acceptable amount of work completed in the one-year period of the grant, we compromised and ended up posting PDFs of the texts. This made updating the texts an unnecessarily complicated process: the original text file had to be located and corrected, then converted into a PDF, and then the old PDF had to be taken down from the website and the new PDF uploaded in its place. Needless to say, keeping up with the suggested changes and corrections sent in by readers turned into a time-consuming task. In addition, the 'comment' feature of the site was soon bombarded with hundreds of spam messages, which eventually we fended off by installing a 'captcha' feature. Our little experiment with 'virtual performance' seems at this point rather crude as a means of creating a form of 'enhanced text', but it was a first step, and there are now remarkable new models for combining text, visuals, and audio-recordings that create very exciting new online 'experiences' for users that we hope to explore in the future.

And then the money ran out! Although a certain amount of maintenance can be done by myself and/or a research assistant, other tasks, such as editing and digitizing the rapidly aging sound recordings or creating additional 'virtual performance' videos, require expertise that must be paid for. So the archive is at the moment no longer being updated. Holding an archive in stasis is a fairly easy task, but updates, renovations, improvements, etc., cost money, and at the moment there are few sources of funding for simply updating a digital archive, as opposed to the comparatively large amounts of funding available for creating one.

I should note that, for all of its technical glitches, this archive is a fully accessible collection—all of the materials are available for download and use at no charge and are copyrighted under a Creative Commons Noncommercial 2.5 Attribution License.[16] We ask only that materials that are published in any way include a citation of their provenance. The most gratifying part of this project, in fact, has been receiving emails from teachers and students at colleges and even high schools who used the archive in classes and, in some cases, referred to these materials in the writing of research papers. In one case, an undergraduate student wrote a Fulbright proposal to travel to Egypt and update my research. He received the grant, conducted the research, and a version of his final report is included in the "Online Resources" section of the archive.[17]

Making materials fully and freely available is, I believe, both a moral and a legal issue, and one that I hope creators of similar archives will address in similar ways. In this specific case, the materials are not 'my' materials. They were the creative production of master artists, all of whom, sadly, are now deceased. The act of making these materials available to their children and grandchildren as well as toother residents of their village, of Egypt, and of the larger world is, and should be, the ultimate goal of such projects.

4. Conclusion

Let me conclude with a few 'lessons learned' and an appeal to scholars in our field. First and foremost, at every step of the way, I learned that we must constantly be planning for obsolescence and technological change. If there is any one approach to this problem, it might simply be to remember that it is not enough to back up our data in multiple copies of the same format or platform, but that we must also copy data into a *variety* of different formats, modes, and platforms, because it will never be clear to us which of those formats will endure and which will not. Second, in the case of digital archives, I cannot stress enough the need to seek a host institution and to obtain commitments to maintain, preserve, and migrate materials forward to new technologies as early as possible. There are dozens and dozens of privately created digital archives, and certainly hundreds of very significant blogs, even just within our field of Islamic and Middle Eastern studies, whose futures are uncertain because they currently exist only under the care of their creator and/or on a privately created website or system. Finally, it seems urgent to rescue ethnographic materials gathered by scholars of my generation and earlier and to make sure that they

16 See http://www.siratbanihilal.ucsb.edu/copyrights-permissions.
17 See Jonathan Hallemeyer, "Beyond Folklore: The Sirat Bani Hilal in Modern Egypt," available at:http://www.siratbanihilal.ucsb.edu/sites/default/files/Beyond%20Folklore.pdf.

are preserved in accessible formats for the future. Many of the traditions documented in these materials are rapidly disappearing, making the need to preserve what documentation does exist all the more critical

My appeal to scholars in our field is to consider making our materials more and more easily available and accessible, and I see digital archives as a relatively easy method of accomplishing this goal. The region of the world we study is, and will probably remain for some time to come, in turmoil. The larger public has a desire to know more about it, but the mass media are focused only on the headlines of the moment and are ill-equipped to provide a more in-depth and broader understanding of this region of the world and its cultures. It is up to us to take the initiative, first of all to make our research interesting and useful, and second, to make it accessible and available. Whether our topics are medieval or modern, narrowly or broadly focused, we should make it our task to secure a place for Islamic and Middle Eastern studies in the sphere of the public humanities, and online is the easiest and most obvious means of doing so.

Bibliography

Bauman, Richard. *Verbal Art as Performance.* Rowley, MA: Newbury House Publishers, 1978.

Cabarga, Leslie. *The Fleischer Story.* Boston: Da Capo Press, 1988.

Cox, Julian, and Colin Ford. *Julia Margaret Cameron: The Complete Photographs.* Los Angeles: Getty Publications, 2003.

Gibbs, Marion E. "Der Ackermann aus Böhmen." *The Literary Encyclopedia.* First published 13 July 2004. Available at: http://www.litencyc.com/php/sworks.php?rec=true&UID=16326. Accessed January 10, 2015.

Hallemeyer, Jonathan. "Beyond Folklore: The Sirat Bani Hilal in Modern Egypt." (Unpublished report). Available at: http://www.siratbanihilal.ucsb.edu/sites/default/files/Beyond%20Folklore.pdf.

Lord, Albert B. *The Singer of Tales.* Cambridge, MA: Harvard University Press, 1960; 2ndedition, 2000.

Lukitsch, Joanne. *Julia Margaret Cameron.* London: Phaidon, 2001.

Parr, Martin, and Gerry Badger. *The Photobook, a History, Volume I.* London: Phaidon, 2004.

Reynolds, Dwight F. *Heroic Poets, Poetic Heroes: The Ethnography of Performance in an Arabic Oral Epic Tradition.* Ithaca: Cornell University Press, 1995.

Sheridan, Cormac. "EPO Neem Patent Revocation Revives Biopiracy Debate." *Nature Biotechnology* 23 (2005): 511–12.

Sirat Bani Hilal Digital Archive. Available at: www.siratbanihilal.ucsb.edu.

Slyomovics, Susan. *The Merchant of Art: An Egyptian Hilali Oral Epic Poet in Performance.* Berkeley: University of California Press, 1988.

Traditional Knowledge Digitial Library (TKDL). Available at: http://www.tkdl.res.in/tkdl/langdefault/common/Home.asp?GL=Eng.

Webber, Sabra J. *Folklore Unbound: A Concise Introduction*. Long Grove, IL: Waveland Press, 2015.

Subject index